ESSAYS ON THE SCIENTIFIC STUDY OF POLITICS

ESSAYS ON
THE SCIENTIFIC
STUDY OF POLITICS

WALTER BERNS – *Cornell University*

HERBERT J. STORING – *The University of Chicago*

LEO WEINSTEIN – *Smith College*

ROBERT HORWITZ – *Michigan State University*

LEO STRAUSS – *The University of Chicago*

Edited by HERBERT J. STORING

HOLT, RINEHART AND WINSTON, INC. NEW YORK

PREFACE

S O DEEP and widespread is the belief, so eminent and able the believers in the value of the contemporary scientific study of politics, that there is not a little impatience with any attempt to question it. This volume makes no claim, of course, on the attention of those who are firmly convinced that the question is settled and the answer clear. But there may be another reason for impatience: a concern lest interminable discussion of *how* to study politics succeeds only in diverting us from the study of it. Sharing this concern, we venture nevertheless to contribute to the discussion. All of us who profess the study of politics are confronted with the prevailing scientific approach, no matter how practical our concern, how slight our interest in methodology, or how keen our desire to get on with the business of direct investigation. These essays articulate our response to that confrontation. They are offered in the hope that they may assist others in similar circumstances.

Our initial procedure was as unsophisticated as that of the student of politics who first seeks, or is offered, guidance to his subject. We did not begin by trying to define "the scientific study of politics," or by considering whether or in what sense it is proper to speak of "the" scientific study of politics. Important as these questions are, they belong properly at the conclusion rather than the beginning of our investigation. Nor did we begin by examining the classics which comprise the heritage of our discipline. While such an examination is certainly necessary to a full exploration of our question, it seemed better to begin nearer home.

We sought, therefore, those political scientists who have made major contributions to the contemporary study of politics, and we took general opinion in the profession as our guide. Thus guided, we selected certain voting studies and the works of Herbert A. Simon, Arthur F. Bentley, and Harold D. Lasswell for thorough examination. No doubt there will be some disagreement, especially with our omissions. It must be conceded that we overlook less popular writers whose contributions to political science may be of more intrinsic significance. We also ignore important contributions made by members of other disciplines, although it is significant that each of our authors is at home in several of the social sciences. Yet our survey of the literature and of the opinions of our colleagues—an unscientific survey, to be sure—suggests that there is general agreement that the men we have selected are among the

v

handful of political scientists responsible for the articulation of the prevailing scientific approach and for the establishment of the most frequently pursued lines of thinking and research. Similar considerations apply to the inclusion of the voting studies, which are widely regarded as the most significant large-scale product of the scientific approach to politics. For this reason they merit the special attention of anyone who questions, or is open to question about, that approach.

Having made our selections, we set about carefully reading and studying our authors' works. We tried to understand in each case what the author sets out to do, why he proceeds as he does, why he thinks that his approach has brought or will bring us closer to an understanding of political matters. This required that the authors be allowed to speak extensively on their own behalf and that their arguments be followed closely, even at the risk of some tedium. It is just to remark that we have often been guided by our authors even in our very criticism, for they have frequently seen and discussed the difficulties which we point out. Our major disagreement with them concerns the implications of these difficulties for the whole scientific enterprise. This fundamental question provides the theme of Professor Strauss' concluding essay.

It should go without saying that we did not begin with minds devoid of ideas on this subject. We entertained, in fact, a serious doubt about the adequacy of the scientific study of politics as now generally conceived and performed. But the biographical fact of our doubt is no more relevant in itself than the fact of our authors' commitment. In neither case was the opinion generated mindlessly; in both cases it is supported by reasons. We have treated our authors as we should wish to be treated. We have not begun with the assumption that they are mere "reflections" of their age or that their work consists of elaborate rationalizations of some prior commitment to science. We have sought to understand as clearly as possible the reasons for their commitment. Where those reasons seem to us deficient, we have said so and tried to show why. Only when this deficiency is established do alternative explanations of the commitment become relevant. Even then they remain subordinate, for we are interested less in the commitment as such than in its worth as the basis of political study. Our concern is that of the student of politics, not the sociologist or historian of political science.

Because of our unfavorable assessment of the prevailing approach to the study of politics, this volume is necessarily largely critical and "negative." The criticisms have positive implications, some of which are discussed in the essays and in the epilogue; but these are, as it were, incidental to the primary intention, which is to subject the central features of contemporary political science to earnest and searching consideration.

These studies were undertaken with the support of the Behavioral Sciences Division of the Ford Foundation, whose financial assistance enabled us to spend the greater part of two summers working together and holding seminar discussions in Chicago. Supplementary grants by the Rockefeller Foundation and the Relm Foundation made it possible to bring the project to completion. Our respective universities provided clerical assistance.

The special character and circumstances of this enterprise make our indebtedness to colleagues heavier than usual. Martin Diamond undertook the initial planning and organization of the project. He and Marvin Zetterbaum participated fully in our summer seminars, and it is an understatement to say that many of their thoughts have found their way into the essays. Some of the men whose work is considered here were asked for and generously provided bibliographical and other specific information. Finally, our debt to other colleagues who read and criticized the essays is particularly great due to the fact that, from a point of view held by many of them, they were contributing to a nuisance. We leave them nameless as an expression of our appreciation of their friendship and their willingness to take a broad view of scholarly cooperation.

H. J. S.

November 1961

CONTENTS

CONTENTS

ESSAYS ON THE SCIENTIFIC STUDY
OF POLITICS

I

VOTING STUDIES

by WALTER BERNS

ACCORDING TO David Truman, it is in the area of voting behavior that modern social or "behavioral" science, especially its research techniques, has had the greatest impact on political science.[1] This impact can be measured both by the amount of work being done in the area and by the extent of the agreement that these techniques have led to a significant advance in our understanding of voting behavior. Leading political scientists have been unstinting in their praise of the several major works to appear in recent years.

There is a large number and somewhat bewildering variety of voting studies, not all of which can—or ought to be—examined here. Instead, our purpose is to identify and then examine what are generally regarded as the most significant of this variety. But even classifying them is not easy. Samuel Eldersveld, for instance, lists six distinct categories according to the "methodological orientation of the research effort." These range from the study that uses election statistics in order to test an hypothesis (such as Stuart Rice's "hunch" that differences in political attitude exist between rural and urban voters) to the "community dynamics" panel study, in which the same respondents are interviewed intensively and repeatedly over a period of, in some cases, several months. In sharp contrast to the simple analysis of election statistics, such studies utilize "the most advanced measurement and survey techniques," [2] and are consequently expected to prove most successful. But success can be measured only in terms of the end sought, whatever it is, and it would therefore seem more appropriate to classify voting studies according to the *intent* of the research effort rather than its methodological orientation. It is appropriate to begin this essay by attempting to understand as precisely as possible the intent of voting-behavior research.

THE INTENT OF THE VOTING STUDIES

The large number of studies based on the interpretation of election statistics begin with questions that indicate an interest in politics. Typical of

[1] David B. Truman, "The Impact on Political Science of the Revolution in the Behavioral Sciences," *Research Frontiers in Politics and Government* (Washington: The Brookings Institution, 1955), p. 213.
[2] Samuel J. Eldersveld, "Theory and Method in Voting Behavior Research," in Heinz Eulau, Samuel Eldersveld, and Morris Janowitz (eds.), *Political Behavior: A Reader in Theory and Research* (New York: The Free Press of Glencoe, Inc., 1956), pp. 269-271.

such studies is Harold Gosnell's *Grass Roots Politics*, published in 1942.[3] Gosnell's method is to examine election statistics, specifically the two-party vote in the counties of six states, and, generally, to relate these statistics to the economic character of the counties. This permits him to draw such conclusions as the following: "A classification of counties showing the highest percentage vote for Democratic nominees for each election from 1924 to 1940 shows that the concentration of Democratic strength shifted from certain rural sections [in Pennsylvania] prior to the New Deal to the industrial and mining areas subsequent to 1934" (p. 37). The book is essentially a study of the relation of political and economic alignments, and the suggestion that the parties are dividing more and more "on the basis of income groupings" (p. 129) leads Gosnell into broad speculation on the future of the American party system.[4]

As Gosnell indicates in an appendix entitled "Methods of Studying Political Behavior," his use of statistics is incidental; that is to say, statistics are tools for the analysis of political behavior, they are "great labor and space-saving devices" (p. 141), and the emphasis remains on what may be learned about politics through their use.[5] Gosnell is not primarily concerned with the development of "scientific laws" of voting or other human behavior. This is also true of V. O. Key's study of *Southern Politics*. Key uses 68 tables and 75 figures to show graphically and dramatically such information as the relation between the number of Negroes and the vote to disfranchise them in southern states. In Alabama, for example, the counties with the highest percentage of Negro residents were the counties with the highest vote for their legal (as opposed to their illegal and extralegal) disfranchisement. Generally, those who were opposed to Negro disfranchisement came from the areas where few Negroes resided.[6]

With the use of such figures, Key is able to show the extent of "friends and neighbors" politics, that is, the extent to which candidates in Democratic primaries in the South draw their principal support from the regions where their homes are located. With the use of scatter diagrams, he is able to de-

[3] *Grass Roots Politics: National Voting Behavior of Typical States* (Washington: American Council on Public Affairs, 1942).
[4] See André Siegfried, *Tableau politique de la France de l'ouest sous la troisième République* (Paris: Librairie Armand Colin, 1913) for a study of social structure and, using election statistics, the political orientation of the west of France, and the effects of this orientation, even after universal suffrage, on a republican and democratic regime. For a somewhat comparable American study, see Arthur N. Holcombe, *The Middle Classes in American Politics* (Cambridge, Mass.: Harvard University Press, 1940).
[5] See François Goguel, "Report on the Present State of the Study of Political Parties, Public Opinion and Elections in France," *Contemporary Political Science: A Survey of Methods, Research and Teaching* (Paris: UNESCO, 1950), pp. 503-514, esp. pp. 510-512.
[6] V. O. Key, Jr., *Southern Politics: In State and Nation* (New York: Alfred A. Knopf, Inc., 1949), p. 544. The vote was on the question of the adoption of the state constitution of 1901. Table 59, p. 545.

termine and to show the extent to which at least some southern politicians can deliver votes to political allies (p. 109, Figure 19). But Key's concern is the politics of the South; he is interested in the "cold, hard fact that the South as a whole has developed no system or practice of political organization and leadership adequate to cope with its problems" (p. 4). Recognizing the "richness and diversity" of the subject, he hopes to sketch "the broad outlines of the structure and character of southern politics. . . ."

It is only hoped that some better understanding of the politics of the South is promoted, for the subject . . . is of the gravest importance. The South is our last frontier. In the development of its resources, human and natural, must be found the next great epoch of our national growth. That development, in turn, must in large measure depend on the contrivance of solutions to the region's political problems [pp. ix-x].

It would seem evident that Key, like Gosnell, uses the research techniques and the language of modern social science not to formulate and test generalizations about electoral behavior, but rather as an aid in political interpretation. He is interested primarily in politics. Others, taking the point of view of social psychology, attach a different significance to these studies. Seymour M. Lipset and his co-authors, in their systematic survey of voting-behavior literature, place studies such as Key's and Gosnell's in the category entitled "The Study of Political Behavior Through Voting Statistics";[7] and what emerges from their discussion is not the extent to which the analysis of voting statistics has assisted us to understand the politics of the South, or of the wheat-growing sections of the West, or of particular regions of France, but rather the extent to which the analysis has established statistical regularities in voting. They then discuss briefly the explanations offered for these regularities. More precisely, they present information concerning voter turnout, the patterns of left and right voting, and "the points at which people are likely to have experiences which affect their political behavior" (p. 1143). In their words: "The present section is a preliminary effort to summarize the statistical regularities that have been found and some of the *chief explanatory factors* that have been proposed in the literature to account for these regularities" (p. 1126, italics supplied). What has developed from the analysis of election statistics, then, is the social scientist's concern with the voting decision as such, as part of his interest in a science of human behavior. "Systematic analysis of the factors affecting [the voting] decision . . . for which a considerable body of empirical data is available, should . . . contribute to the understanding of behavior in many other sectors of modern life" (p. 1125). It is at this point, and for this reason, that the study of voting behavior

[7] Seymour M. Lipset, Paul F. Lazarsfeld, Allen H. Barton, and Juan Linz, "The Psychology of Voting: An Analysis of Political Behavior," in Gardner Lindzey (ed.), *Handbook of Social Psychology*, vol. 2 (Cambridge, Mass.: Addison-Wesley, 1954), pp. 1124-1175.

emerges out of the study of politics; and it is at this point that the political scientist is superseded by the social scientist (the sociologist, the social psychologist, and, eventually, the psychologist), who investigates the voting decision instead of the political situation. His research, unlike Key's and Gosnell's is designed for this purpose.

The social scientists have supplied us with a great body of detailed information concerning electoral behavior.[8] Using election statistics and census data, the earlier students were able to show a correspondence between the Democratic percentage of the vote and the percentage of Catholics in voting districts in a particular state or even in the United States as a whole. With their more sophisticated panel study, Bernard Berelson, Paul Lazarsfeld, and William McPhee can tell us in precise terms that whereas 81 percent of the white, native-born Protestants in Elmira, New York, in 1948, voted Republican, only 35 percent of the Catholics, 33 percent of the Jews, 19 percent of the Negroes, and 18 percent of the Italian-Americans voted Republican (*Voting* p. 62). They are able to demonstrate, moreover, that Catholics tended to vote more Democratic regardless of other factors, such as class status and national origin. They do this by means of multivariate analysis, that is, the introduction of more than two variables. By holding one of the two independent variables constant, class status for instance, it is possible to test interpretations arrived at by simple zero-order analysis between pairs of variables, for instance, religion and vote. From *The Voter Decides*,[9] to mention one more example, we learn that in the opinion of the public sampled, Stevenson suffered in comparison with Eisenhower with respect to the leadership qualities needed for the conduct of foreign relations, but that more people commented favorably on the Democratic party than on the Republican party. Such information, though interesting, does not require us to revise our pre-scientific notions of the way voters behave, nor, for that matter, is its presentation the primary concern of the social scientist.

In fact, the discovery of the demography of the vote, or how demographic groups tend to vote, however interesting as a form of sociological record-keeping, cannot be the primary concern of the social scientist. There is something in the nature of his enterprise that requires him to move beyond these findings to attempt to establish scientific laws of voting behavior. Samuel Eldersveld states this necessity in emphatic terms: "Until researchers in voting behavior escape from paying homage to the marvels of the numerical symbol and concentrate on developing scientific laws with a relatively high

[8] These findings are summarized in the *Handbook of Social Psychology*, and in convenient tabular form in Bernard R. Berelson, Paul F. Lazarsfeld, and William N. McPhee, *Voting: A Study of Opinion Formation in a Presidential Campaign* (Chicago: University of Chicago Press, 1954), pp. 333-347. Copyright 1954 by the University of Chicago.
[9] Angus Campbell, Gerald Gurin, and Warren E. Miller, *The Voter Decides* (Evanston, Ill.: Row, Peterson & Company, 1954).

degree of probability demonstrating causation . . . our discipline can make no progress toward achieving scientific understanding" (*Political Behavior,* p. 273). The social scientist is obliged to move beyond the establishment of simple correlations between demographic characteristics and the vote, for the reason stated by sociologist R. M. MacIver.

Correlation . . . is not a relation between things at all. The relation between quantitative variables is a mathematical relation, a relation of index numbers that may lead us to discover a relation of things. Correlation as such has no dynamic significance, any more than have the resemblances between animals and clouds. We seek out correlations in our search for knowledge of the relations of things. . . . Correlation is simply the correspondence between the fluctuations of our numbers or measurements for the two (or more) groups, taken over a period of time or over an area of their spatial distribution. If the correspondence is close, whether directly or inversely, we want to know why. Does it mean that the correspondent variables are interdependent either on one another or on conditions common to them both? The prospect of an answer to this question alone sustains the scientific quest of correlation. We look for correlations only where we suspect they may be causally significant.[10]

This means, as MacIver stresses throughout his book, that the social scientist must seek the "why" of behavior,[11] and the use of multivariate analysis is thought to be one step in this direction. But it is, at best, only one step. In the words of social psychologist Solomon Asch:

The Republican and Democratic parties are not laws of nature; and the act of voting is a highly specific event embedded in numerous local conditions. Consequently the findings are valid only for a particular point of time. It should be noted that "prediction" in public opinion polling has today a sense quite different from prediction as understood in science. In science prediction grows out of an understanding of functional relations; therefore it is relevant to future events. In public opinion, "prediction" is from a sample to a population. When polls attempt predictions about the future, they must assume that all the unknown factors responsible for decision and action will not significantly change over time.[12]

We are told, for example, that Catholicism is independently related to a Democratic vote; this is a description of how Catholics have tended to vote.

---

[10] R. M. MacIver, *Social Causation* (Boston: Ginn and Co., 1942), pp. 99-100.
[11] There is no necessity to discuss the difficult epistemological question of causation because, beyond doubt, the voting scientists do in fact assume that it is possible to find the causes of votes. Not only do they speak of dependent and independent variables when discussing correlation, but they state their intention in terms of the "determinants" and the "why" of voting behavior. In Herbert Simon's words: "however completely the word 'cause' has been eliminated from epistemology, it is still very much a part of the working vocabulary of most empirical scientists." "On the Definition of the Causal Relation," *The Journal of Philosophy,* July 31, 1952, p. 517. The question is not whether the students of voting behavior seek to provide causal explanations but what kind of causes they look for.
[12] Solomon E. Asch, *Social Psychology* (Englewood Cliffs, N. J.: Prentice-Hall, Inc., 1952), p. 556.

But there is no necessity that the Democractic party continue to support policies and nominate candidates favored by Catholics, or by any other group that has tended to support the Democrats in the past. The identified correlates of the vote are not unrelated to, indeed, may be radically dependent on, political factors that cannot be foreseen.[13] Until the social scientist discovers, in Solomon Asch's terms, the "factors responsible for decision and action," the correlations he finds will be valid only for a particular time and place; the generalizations we have discussed in this section do not involve these factors. These generalizations are still of a "low order," or, as we should prefer to say, they are ephemeral.

For this reason, the social scientist must move beyond the simple description of voting behavior and the generalizations we have discussed in this section. He must try to understand why people vote as they do. The authors of *The Voter Decides* acknowledge this when they say of the simple description of the 1952 election contained in Part One of their study: "the kind of 'social accounting' it presents will have interest in itself for students and practitioners of politics. . . . [But the] second purpose of the presentation in Part One is to provide a background for the analysis carried out in Part Two" (p. 7). The social scientist's search for the *determinants* of voting is not fortuitous.

In summary, the intentions of voting-behavior research vary according to the interest of the researcher. The political scientist uses election statistics as an aid to political interpretation or as statistical support for his findings. The sociological accountant may be content to establish correlations between demographical characteristics and voting. The social psychologist, as such, is interested in voting behavior as a variety of human behavior (voting behavior is not a "type of human behavior that is conceptually distinctive. . . ." [14]), concerning which he hopes to develop scientific laws enabling him to understand so as to predict.

---

[13] When, a few years ago, the Cook County, Illinois, Democrats nominated a man for sheriff who was alleged, not without reason, to be a criminal, they not only lost an office they traditionally controlled, but the entire Democratic ticket suffered, including the United States Senate majority leader, who lost his seat. If at one time, for another example, the few Negroes who voted tended to vote Republican, Chicago's Negro wards going four-to-one for Hoover in 1932, according to Richard M. Scammon ("How Will Negroes Vote?" *The New Republic*, September 16, 1957), by 1951 Samuel Lubell could write confidently that the "Negro's attachment to the Democratic party has been growing stronger," that, in fact, the Negro vote has "virtually solidified in the Democratic party." (*The Future of American Politics* [New York: Harper & Brothers, 1951], p. 95.) Berelson, Lazarsfeld, and McPhee report that in 1948, 81 percent of the Negroes in Elmira voted Democratic (*Voting*, p. 71). But events move swiftly in the twentieth century. Although *The Voter Decides* reports that Negroes were one of only three demographic groups that did not vote more Republican in 1952 than in 1948, when votes are combined with the stated preferences of the non-voters, the Republican share increased from 13 percent in 1948 to 21 percent in 1952 (*The Voter Decides*, Table, p. 71).

[14] Eldersveld, in *Political Behavior*, p. 273.

With studies using statistics as an aid to political interpretation and with the merely record-keeping studies, this essay is not concerned. Our attention is directed to the modern, scientific study of voting behavior, to the study whose goal is the eventual "construction of a theory of political behavior" (*Voting*, p. 329).

THE PEOPLE'S CHOICE

The principal technique utilized by scientific students of voting behavior is the panel survey. It is employed precisely in order to construct "a theory of political behavior," or, to quote Eldersveld again, to develop "scientific laws with a relatively high degree of probability demonstrating causation, particularly by systematic examination of competing hypotheses. . . ." With respect to the determinants of votes, the panel survey type of voting research can do everything the analysis of election statistics can do, and it can also identify the individual voter in order to explore his decision with sociological and psychological questions. Among the voters who can be identified are those who change their political affiliations, and it is thought that in the analysis of their characteristics will be found the clues to the laws of human action. Our analysis of this most sophisticated of voting-research techniques is facilitated by sociologist Peter H. Rossi's essay "Four Landmarks in Voting Research," written from a point of view wholly sympathetic to the intentions of the panel analysts.[15] Rossi acknowledges the achievements and identifies the weaknesses (mostly of a technical nature) of the panel surveys, and indicates the steps to be taken to ensure progress toward the goal of a science of voting behavior. Much progress, he asserts, has already been made. If early studies were too journalistic, being too much concerned with the "topical" rather than the "universal," given over too much to "description" instead of "generalization," *Voting* (1954) and *The Voter Decides* (1954) go beyond these early efforts and attempt to present generalized interpretations of voting behavior. If the early studies, being journalistic, were addressed primarily to "the intelligent layman interested in current politics," *Voting* especially is addressed to "the academic social scientist" (pp. 32-33). Whether, as Rossi assumes, this is a salutary development remains to be discussed later.

Judged by these criteria, *The People's Choice*, a panel study of the 1940 presidential election in Erie County, Ohio, is merely a preliminary work.[16] In Rossi's words, although "the study still stands as a model for the analysis of survey data, the book's style is quite journalistic" being concerned with "particularistic rather than general, topical rather than universal" questions.

[15] Eugene Burdick and Arthur J. Brodbeck (eds.), *American Voting Behavior* (New York: The Free Press of Glencoe, Inc., 1959), pp. 5-54.
[16] Paul F. Lazarsfeld, Bernard Berelson, and Hazel Gaudet, *The People's Choice* (2d ed.; New York: Columbia University Press, 1948).

"A concern for description rather than generalization dominates the treatment of each topic" (pp. 22-23). Nevertheless, the authors do make an effort to find the determinants of voting. Paul Lazarsfeld, Bernard Berelson, and Hazel Gaudet, the authors of *The People's Choice*, select three demographic variables (socioeconomic status [SES], religious affiliation, and rural-or-urban residence) to construct an Index of Political Predisposition (IPP). A separate score is assigned for the various combinations of variables, and the scores are translated into degrees of party predisposition. A wealthy, Protestant farmer, for example, is assigned a scale score of 1, that is, the extreme Republican predisposition; a Catholic on the lowest SES level and living in the city is assigned a scale score of 7, the extreme Democratic predisposition. The correlation between political predisposition and vote intention was sufficiently high [17] to permit the authors to assert confidently that " a person thinks, politically, as he is, socially." Here, the reader might think, is the statement of a law of political behavior, especially when the authors conclude with the flat assertion that "social characteristics determine political preference" (p. 27).

In 1952, Morris Janowitz and Warren Miller, associates of the Survey Research Center of the University of Michigan, published the results of a test to which they had submitted the Index of Political Predisposition, as this had been formulated in *The People's Choice*. They applied the Index to data collected by the Survey Research Center (SRC) during the 1948 election, and achieved results that effectively undermined its efficacy as a predictive tool and, thereby, as a tool of explanation.

In predicting party choice, it was found that when the IPP was applied to the voters in the 1948 SRC national sample, a total of 61 per cent of the voters voted in line with their IPP scores. The votes of the remaining 39 per cent contradicted the IPP-based predictions. . . .

. . . Although the IPP was predictive of a tendency to vote in the expected direction, party-wise, this tendency was of limited statistical significance. The only respondents who followed their IPP scores to a statistically significant degree were the respondents who actually voted Republican.[18]

The Janowitz and Miller article appeared before the publication of *Voting*, thus giving Berelson and Lazarsfeld an opportunity to reply. But instead of defending the Index as an explanation of political preferences, they replied by charging Janowitz and Miller with a "careless reading" of *The People's Choice*, a reading that led to "grievous misunderstandings" (*Voting*, p. 283). They protested that the Index was *not* intended to predict the voting behavior of a total population. It was instead a general finding on implementation.

[17] 74 percent of those with a score of 1 did express an intention of voting Republican, and 85 percent of those with a score of 7 did express an intention of voting Democratic (*The People's Choice*, p. 26).
[18] Morris Janowitz and Warren E. Miller, "The Index of Political Predisposition in the 1948 Election," *The Journal of Politics*, November, 1952, pp. 717-718.

It meant merely that intentions "supported by one's social surroundings are more predictably carried out than are intentions lacking such support." Whereas in *The People's Choice* they had asserted that "a simple combination of three primary personal characteristics goes a long way in 'explaining' political preferences" (p. 27), the new formulation withdraws this claim. But even this drastically narrowed formulation cannot be accepted as a "scientifically-established generalization." In the words of Janowitz and Miller:

even if the IPP is not seen as an index to the political behavior of the total sample, but in the narrow frame of a measure of sociological reinforcement for the tendency of individuals to follow their stated intentions, significant relationships still do not emerge. Of the individuals whose IPP's reinforced their voting intention, 120 voted as intended, 10 voted otherwise. Of the individuals whose IPP's conflicted with their intentions, 68 voted as intended, 11 voted in the direction of their IPP's. The variance is in the correct direction but not to a statistically significant degree.[19]

In conclusion, it is not unfair to say that the construct of an IPP, with its three demographic variables and its supposed value, is symptomatic of a naïve devotion to methodology (in this case a rather crude methodology) unleavened by common sense views of political behavior. Not only Janowitz and Miller, but the unscientific politician, with his practical experience, knows that "social characteristics" do not *determine* "political preference."

THE VOTER DECIDES

The two most acclaimed studies of American voting behavior are *Voting* and *The Voter Decides*. According to V. O. Key, Jr., the latter is the "most impressive analysis yet made of a national election by the survey method." [20] Reviewing the former in *The Journal of Politics* of August, 1955, Avery Leiserson said:

It is impossible to overestimate the import of the present volume for the scientific understanding of voting behavior. Here we have the beginning for politics of the kind of systematic, cumulative research which is so important in the natural sciences, and which makes possible the verification and qualification of our propositions about voting behavior that formerly were founded on such speculative evidence [p. 485].

With respect to voting as such, these two studies are not only much more ambitious than the work of the political scientists who analyzed voting statistics, but they are acknowledged to be more advanced than *The People's Choice*.

Both are panel surveys resting on repeated interviews with the same re-

[19] *The Journal of Politics*, November, 1952, p. 718.
[20] Foreword to *The Voter Decides*, p. ix.

spondents. The authors of *Voting*, continuing in the manner of *The People's Choice*, carried on four interviews with a panel consisting of about 1000 residents of Elmira, New York, before and after the 1948 presidential election. *The Voter Decides* is based on two interviews, one before and one after the 1952 presidential election, with respondents representing a nation-wide sample. The panels were selected according to probability samples, the details of which need not concern us.

If the authors of *The People's Choice* are sociologically oriented—that is, if the variables they introduce into their questionnaires and then correlate with the vote are sociological in character—Angus Campbell, Gerald Gurin, and Warren Miller, the authors of *The Voter Decides*, are psychologically oriented. They look for the "attitudes, perceptions, and group loyalties which mediate between the external environmental facts and the individual response" (*The Voter Decides*, p. 8), or the "psychological variables which intervene between the external events of the voter's world and his ultimate behavior [because] successful identification and analysis of these 'intervening variables' should provide insights into the problem of voter motivation beyond anything we can hope to achieve through attempting to relate specific campaign events to the vote, or by classifying the votes of the major demographic classes" (pp. 85-86). They argue, in effect, that a causal relationship between socioeconomic status and vote cannot be demonstrated, that the statistical correlations in this sphere take on secondary significance once the proper psychological variables are identified and held constant. The search for psychological variables is the search for the motivational factors, and the intention of *The Voter Decides*, it should be understood, is to explain the motivations of the voters. Its second and major part is entitled "The Motivation of Voting Behavior." Specifically, the authors seek to discover *why*, compared with 1948, there was such a "great increase in the vote" in 1952, and *why* this vote went so heavily to the Republicans. "These are the two questions with which this book is mainly concerned" (p. 11).

Campbell, Gurin, and Miller, propose six psychological variables for study (p. 86). Three of these—identification with one of the political parties ("party identification"), concern with national governmental policy issues ("issue orientation"), and attraction to the presidential candidates ("candidate orientation")—are selected for intensive analysis, while the others are discussed in appendixes. There is no need to describe the manner in which each of these three concepts is related to voter participation and to presidential preference, or to detail the specific findings regarding these relationships. It is sufficient for our purpose to quote their conclusion at some length:

Participation in the 1952 presidential election has been found to relate with various degrees of significance to each of the three variables which have been the main concern of this study. Those people who were motivated by all three of these factors, with no partisan conflict among them, nearly all participated in the election, at least to the extent of voting. The fewer of these factors present for an individual, the less likely he was to vote or to engage otherwise in the election process. In other words, we have shown a direct relationship between the number of political factors motivating a person and the likelihood of his taking political action.

Similarly, we expected that a combination of congruent forces favoring a candidate would be more likely to result in preference for that candidate than would a smaller number of such forces. We have found that those people who felt themselves strongly identified with one of the major parties, held strongly partisan views on issues which were consistent with those of their party, and were strongly attracted by the personal attributes of their party's candidate expressed preference in nearly every case for the candidate their party put forward. In contrast, among those people for whom none of these factors was active, equal numbers preferred each of the two candidates [pp. 182-183].

We learn that the Republican success in 1952 was due in large part to the "switching of a large number of former Democratic supporters to Eisenhower." And why did one of every four Truman supporters of 1948 vote for Eisenhower in 1952? ". . . a strong positive orientation toward Eisenhower is left as clearly related to the switch" (pp. 165, 170).

Rossi says of this conclusion:

How useful explanations in terms of variables all on the same "level" are is open to question. It helps us little to know that voters tend to select candidates of whom they have high opinions. Voting for a candidate and holding a favorable opinion of him may be regarded as alternative definitions of the same variable [*American Voting Behavior*, p. 41].

This criticism, while applicable to most cases, is not altogether fair to *The Voter Decides*. Surely the Republican party slogan in 1952 was correct in assuming that those who "liked Ike" liked him as President and would, therefore, vote for him; but it is possible to like a candidate and not to vote for him, or to hold favorable opinions of both candidates and to vote for one of them (and, perhaps reluctantly, against his opponent) on other grounds. Nevertheless, it is true that *The Voter Decides* goes to elaborate lengths to establish the obvious. Who ever doubted that if a person liked Eisenhower as a man, agreed with Eisenhower on the issues in the campaign, and, in addition, was a life-long Republican voter, he would be likely to vote Republican in the 1952 election? Yet this study, unlike others that have been made, does recognize the saliency of political factors to voting behavior; it does recognize, what students and practitioners of politics have always assumed, that the candidates and the issues in the election affect the way people vote. Though it is singularly naïve, it does make an attempt to explain voting, as *The People's Choice*, with its use of crude sociological variables, could never do. While it does not probe, it at least identifies the voters' opinions on political things, out of which, until shown to be erroneous, we can assume comes their political behavior.

Rossi's concluding remarks indicate the direction to be taken if the panel analyst is to move beyond journalistic descriptions of voting behavior and discover the determinants of voting. "The more interesting problems," he writes, "start where the author's [sic] analysis ends. Why does a voter develop a favorable opinion of a candidate? What are the conditions under which his opinion and his vote do or do not coincide?" (p. 41) The potentialities of the panel survey are not fully utilized by Campbell, Gurin, and Miller; the search for the "why" of the vote is not carried far enough. "By contrast," he continues, "the model of explanation employed in Voting transcends several levels of data. The voter's opinions on issues are considered a determinant of his vote, but, in turn, his opinions are considered as dependent variables. The individual is located in the social structure of Elmira and within primary groups—conditions of experience which transform attitudes." It is to Voting, then, that we must direct our principal attention.

VOTING: SOCIAL POLITICS

Voting, according to Rossi, "represents the most thorough-going attempt to present a generalized interpretation of voting behavior." Gone are the "traces of topical, journalistic concerns" that characterize The People's Choice. Voting is a book that sets out to provide the " 'total' picture of the central decision in voting—how and why people come to favor this candidate rather than that one" (Voting, p. xii). The authors speak later of seeking the determinants of voting (p. 277), and still later of developing a "theory of political behavior" (p. 329). Yet it is extremely difficult, if not impossible, to say precisely what the authors' intention is. At times they suggest a much narrower aim, asking not why but "how people come to vote as they do," specifically how "social" and "political" factors affect already formed dispositions. Sometimes the book is said to be, in the authors' own language, a study of the "formation of preferences," and sometimes a study of the "implementation" of preferences already formed. Finally, it is not entirely clear whether the book is mainly about the political phenomenon of voting or the more general phenomenon of human choice. These are not merely verbal difficulties, nor are they adequately resolved by saying that sometimes the authors study one question and sometimes another. They are expressions of a fundamental ambiguity. In the Introduction, the organization of the book is described as follows:

The book develops two major themes—loosely called the "social" and the "political." With reference to the first, it is a study of the formation of preferences. The book contains a social and psychological analysis of the ways individuals and groups make a "choice" in a matter not of immediate personal knowledge or, often, of directly appreciated effects. With reference to the second theme, this is a study of the behavior of the electorate in a free democratic society. The theory and values of democracy make certain assumptions about, or state certain requirements for, the democratic voter—his political interest, participation, principles, information, discussion, rationality. This study reports on the actual behavior of one sample of democratic citizens in a major election. Thus, confrontation of democratic theory with democratic practice is the second implied theme that runs throughout the book [p. x].

These two themes do not, however, simply run parallel to one another. They are in fact competing claimants, and the tension between them is evident in almost every chapter as well as in the confrontation of the "social" and "political" sections of the book. The "social" theme predominates (even in the "political" chapters), as is indicated by the authors' opinion that questions of the "formation of preferences," or "the ways individuals and groups make a 'choice' " are part of the "social" theme.[21] The political discussions proper have something of the character of random asides or afterthoughts; yet the book culminates (necessarily, we shall argue) in a political theory. To understand Voting it is necessary to consider these two themes, their different implications, and the authors' attempt to reconcile them; and we begin, in this section, with the "social" theme.

At the beginning of Chapter 6 of Voting, the authors, after referring to the findings in the preceding chapters, to which we have referred briefly, write: "We dealt, so to speak, with the social *what*; now we deal with the *how* and *why*." The principal findings of the study have to do not with the social correlates of a vote, but with the influence of primary groups on voting—especially the role of political discussion taking place within such groups—and, secondly, with the role of issues. The second part of Chapter 6 ("Social Process: Small Groups and Political Discussion") is entitled "The Nature of Political Discussion," and here we learn that political discussion takes place in the family, among fellow workers and, generally, "among people of like characteristics"—that is to say, among those who are likely to be in a position to talk with each other. We learn also that this discussion is made up primarily of the "exchange of mutually agreeable remarks"—in fact, during the campaign "mutual agreement between the discussants outnumbers disagreement ten to one . . . and only 6 per cent [of the cases] involve some degree of argument between the discussants" (pp. 116, 106).

Chapter 7, entitled "Social Effects of the Campaign: Personal Influence and Political Polarization," is given over completely to an analysis of "voting

---

[21] This is stated again at the beginning of Chapter 13 where they write: "In this chapter we deal with some conditions that *determine* the way a man votes and hence with some ideas coming from social psychology and sociology" (p. 277).

changes." [22] To begin with, voting changes are said to be proportionate to the type of discussion reported by the respondents. "The results are important to repeat: those who talk with compatible persons remain most firm in their prior convictions; those who cannot recall any discussion of politics in their groups are unstable generally, often receding into nonvoting or neutrality; and those in contact with opposition preferences show it by their heavy rate of defection to that opposition" (p. 120).

It is important to be clear about the character of these explanations and the data upon which they rest. In Chart LVII, on page 119, we are informed that (1) 88 percent of those who discussed politics with persons of the same party as themselves did not change their party preferences from August to October—that is, 12 percent of those who talked with compatible persons *did* change; (2) 76 percent of those who recalled no discussion did not change; and (3) 78 percent of those whose discussions were with members of the opposite party did not change. One fact above all seems to emerge from these statistics: at least 76 percent of each category of voters did not change their party preferences no matter whom they talked with. It is perfectly legitimate to say on the basis of these data that those "who discuss politics with the opposition are *more likely* than others subsequently to take on that opposite preference in their own voting . . ." (p. 119, italics supplied). It goes much too far, however, to say of those who did not recall any political discussions that they are "unstable generally," considering the fact that 76 percent of this group did *not* change.

The authors go on to show that voting changes are correlated with the political preferences of family members, that people "under cross-pressures (e.g., between class and religion) change their vote during the campaign more than people in homogeneous circumstances" (p. 148), and so on. In short, although the authors suggest that "political discussion is central to voting changes" (p. 138), they prove at most that political discussion is one factor explaining change and that political discussion might have contributed to nonchange. Furthermore, they explain voting stability and change in terms not of arguments advanced in political discussion, not in terms of opinions about public questions, but in terms of the "social support" or lack of it provided by politically compatible associates. Political change is a function of political discussion, but that discussion is a function of the individual's immediate social environment. [23] This is not unreasonable as a rough rule of thumb, but the possibility that men might vote as they do as a result of

---

[22] "The main purpose of a panel study is to characterize changers . . ." (*Handbook of Social Psychology*, p. 1153). What changes is not, of course, "votes," but expressions of intentions, even though Berelson, Lazarsfeld, and McPhee use the former expression throughout the book.

[23] The same explanation is offered in the case of voting changes by time units. For example: "Shifts in voting between generations, then, are dependent upon and consequences of social location, social support, and social control" (p. 138).

a thoughtful consideration of the political situation is only rarely and reluctantly admitted by Berelson, Lazarsfeld, and McPhee.

Thus the stability of a voting preference "varies with the chances of social support for it." The more likely an individual voter is to encounter others with similar preferences within his group, the more likely he is to maintain that preference. Hence: "Paradoxical as it may seem, the minority preference in a given group is influenced to stay a minority partly because it *is* a minority. The circumstances that produce an unequal distribution of political preferences within a group also produce an unintended means of maintaining the inequality—namely, unequal chances for social support of unpopular versus popular views in the group" (p. 126). And: "One-sided distributions of social attitudes can develop *sui generis* powers of maintaining themselves over and beyond any good 'reason' for that persistence arising external to the group."

With no *external disturbance*, exchanges of preferences can easily fall into this stability-maintaining type. Our results document a process whose consequences can be aggregate persistence (despite individual turnover) of *one-sided* distributions of social attitudes, prejudices, tastes, and habits. It is a process that can lead to individual changes that, in the aggregate, do not modify group distributions. The latter must come from *external* influences. "Social politics" is, in pure or undisturbed form, conservative politics [p. 127, first italics supplied].

The voting changes discussed here add up to zero! One party always wins, even though individual turnover (inexplicably) continues. "Equilibrium points are reached such that the greater *rate* of loss from the minority equals in *amount* the numbers needed to replace small rates of erosion from the majority, pending an outside influence (e.g., wars, depressions)." In the absence of political factors, which the authors refer to as outside influences— as if voting had nothing to do with politics—what they have described could stand as an accurate picture of voting behavior. "What would happen if the processes we have outlined went on *undisturbed* for long periods of time?" (p. 134, italics supplied) The question suggests their difficulty, for it is to ask what would happen if the social processes affecting the political act of voting were undisturbed by politics. What would happen if voting were not a political act?

But their "social politics" did not take place in the absence of "political politics," to coin a term that the authors of *Voting* force upon us. They observed the scene during a presidential campaign, and this is of decisive importance to the sociological analysis itself. A campaign gives rise to a relatively high frequency of political discussion, and this discussion is the instrument of social pressure. Between campaigns, on the other hand, there is relatively little political discussion and during "the no-discussion period . . . one expects relaxation of social controls and thus of the one-sidedness of preferences within social groups" (p. 139). Between campaigns people are exposed to much the same political news and comment from the newspapers, radio, television. "Thus there is continued influence from outside stimuli equal across all groups," leading to "much the same secular trend between campaigns on the part of all types of voters, without regard to majority/minority social influences." Consequently, during such periods, "if the holders of unpopular views in the group keep quiet—provided that there are external forces working for both sides—they should find their ranks mysteriously growing" (p. 142, italics supplied). "That is, in stable times, social majorities in self-contained communities should recede in off-year elections . . ." (p. 146 n., italics supplied). "The proviso hardly needs to be added that all this might happen if 'other things are equal' " (p. 147 n.). Thus, while purporting to exclude political factors as somehow external to the social processes that issue in the voting act, that "social" explanation proves to depend for its basic categories on the presence or absence of a political campaign.

In Chapter 13, "The Social Psychology of the Voting Decision," the authors formulate the principal result of their discoveries as follows: "We can say that the proper vote intention is stronger and more durable than the deviant one, or we can say that the vote intention which has a smaller probability of finding social support in the environment is more likely to be unstable" (p. 282).[24] "Social support," a finding to which the authors attach great significance, means that a person is more likely to carry out an intention already formed if it is supported by his environment. The reader might be tempted to protest that this tells us very little about "the formation of preferences," but in their summary in Chapter 13, the authors illustrate their enterprise with a diagram (p. 278) that indicates that their intention is limited to studying preferences already formed.

The authors' concern in Voting, they say, is with the process labeled "Implementation" in the diagram. "Our efforts are directed toward finding out 'how they make up their minds,' or 'carry through their intentions,' or, to

[24] They then add: "The interesting point to note is that this finding has great generality and turns up in various areas of action." Of the three examples they cite, one, John Clausen's study of soldiers' postwar vocational plans, has nothing to do with social support, which is obvious even from their comments on it. The second, Peter Rossi's "Residential Mobility in Philadelphia," (published by the Free Press of Glencoe in 1955 under the title Why Families Move) provides no evidence that residential mobility is affected in any way by "social support." The third is a study in which S. M. Lipset "found that Jews were more likely than non-Jews to say that they would refuse to sign the [California loyalty] oath"; on checking their subsequent action, Lipset is supposed to have discovered, consistently with the "social support" theory, that "those with the 'proper' social characteristics (in this case, the Jews) were more likely to have carried out this intention than were those whose social characteristics were indicative of less support from their social environment." The article cited, Lipset's "Opinion Formation in a Crisis Situation," The Public Opinion Quarterly, Spring 1953, pp. 20-46, is the source of the finding that Jewish students were more likely than non-Jewish students to say that they would refuse to sign the oath; but Lipset does not present, here or elsewhere, any findings relating to the implementation of these intentions, by students or faculty, and he has in fact made no such study.

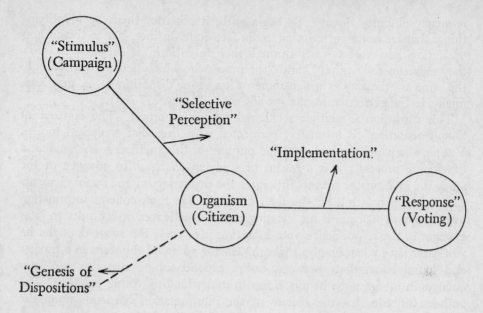

Fig. 1. A psychologist's view of the vote.

put it in terms of the general scheme of the psychologist, how dispositions in May are finally crystalized or realized or—as we choose to say—'implemented' into a response to the demands of society for a vote in November." They have no concern with the process labeled "Genesis of dispositions," but devote themselves wholly to learning how dispositions already formed are implemented—and this despite their stated intention to study "the formation of preferences." Instead of attempting a general statement on voter motivation, they are content here with a detailed account of the evidence for the "discovery" that intentions "supported by one's social surroundings are more predictably carried out than are intentions lacking such support" (pp. 280, 283).

No one will quarrel with this innocuous and narrow conclusion,[25] but it is impossible to rest content with it. No doubt there are difficulties in understanding the process of the "genesis of dispositions," or "why people come to favor this candidate" rather than another, but the notion of "implementation," however ingenious and "operational," does not avoid these difficulties;

[25] But as Morton Grodzins has said of another study with which Professor Lazarsfeld was associated: "It must be said that this is a pretentious and awkward way to state the obvious. . . . How large a foundation grant, how many runs on the IBM countersorter were needed to come to this conclusion?" Review of Paul F. Lazarsfeld and Wagner Thielens, Jr., *The Academic Mind, Ethics*, April 1959, p. 200.

it merely obscures them.[26] To begin with, it obscures them by identifying things that are not identical, that are in fact quite distinct. Yet to the authors of *Voting*, how voters "carry through their intentions" is the same as "how they make up their minds," and "the process by which acts are carried out" the same as "the way in which more or less vague dispositions . . . may lead, finally, to the performance of a specific act . . ." (pp. 277-280).

This confusion is neither accidental nor unimportant. The concept of "implementation" is intimately connected with the chief analytical tool of *Voting*, the panel method, and the purpose of this method is to "analyze a developing process"; it is a means of studying *change*. "In advance of the study the investigator tries to anticipate the psychological and social elements that might play a role in the final decision." He then collects information over time and analyzes it by "relating earlier experiences or attitudes to later changes in the respondent's vote intention" (p. viii). But what does the investigator have when he gets through? Having recorded the steps in a process and found correlations between earlier experiences or attitudes and later changes in intention, is he any closer to understanding voting behavior? The authors concede that the success of the interpretation "depends upon the variety and the subtlety of the questions that are asked prior to any actual change" (p. viii); that is, it is necessary to have in advance "the right psychological variables" (p. 290).[27] Though there is little or no attempt to show that they *have* the right psychological variables, the authors do attempt to demonstrate that, contrary to the allegations of some critics, the panel method enables the investigator not merely to record the steps in a process but to catch the "psychological mechanisms" that sustain it. They illustrate this contention with a specific case of change in intention on the part of many voters:

the psychologically most interesting (and, at the same time, the politically most relevant) phenomenon [in 1948] was the last-minute return of many voters to an earlier disposition. These were persons who had voted for Roosevelt in 1944 and often had many demographic characteristics or past political allegiances which would predispose them to a Democratic vote. In June, 1948, however, they expressed little confidence in Truman and intended to vote for Dewey. Yet just before election day they changed in their intentions. Their final Democratic vote was thus the reactivation of a previous tendency.

26 The authors admit that implementation, like any new term, is not "entirely satisfactory"; but they think it will suffice, "provided the reader gives up his personal associations with the word and thinks only of the purpose for which the scheme is introduced here" (p. 280). That purpose, we are told in a footnote on the same page, is to "locate, relative to each other, the points which various students select out of a broad problem-complex of concern." This is not especially helpful, since we know only that the point that "implementation" is meant to locate lies somewhere between the genesis of a disposition and the performance of an act.
27 Surprisingly, in view of this, some variables were included for no better reason than "because they are traditional to all social research . . ." (p. 286).

Thus what appears to be a *change* in intention, the generation of a new disposition, is explained, via the "psychological mechanism" of "reactivation," as a special case of *implementation* of intention. Broadly, the explanation is that as the election approaches the "deviant" turns to his social environment for guidance and that environment tends to support the party that is "right" for him. Thus "these people turn back in the direction of the party that is *natural* for their type of person" (pp. 291-293).

Although the authors call this "reactivation," the data are not themselves sufficient to support the conclusion that the *same* tendency or predisposition that led these voters to vote for Roosevelt in 1944 reasserted itself in 1948 and led them to vote for Truman. It is conceivable that their 1948 vote was based on quite different grounds. Although the authors do not, curiously, concern themselves here with the initial deviation,[28] it is clear that *that* must be explained in terms other than "social support." But if the initial deviation was due to something other than "social support," may not the return be also? Perhaps the changing political situation had something to do with both the initial deviation and the return.[29] We do not know on the basis of the "social" facts presented here whether the process is to be understood as the reactivation of predispositions or the generation of new dispositions, and so long as we confine ourselves to the point called "implementation," we cannot know it.

More broadly, while the panel method may have enabled the authors of *Voting* to go beyond the establishment of static correlations and to draw "a composite picture of the typical 'reactivation' sequence," it remains subject to Solomon Asch's criticism that "the study of sociological uniformities fails to supply . . . the functional relations between conditions and consequences." Of course, as he points out, and as the practice of the authors of *Voting* confirms, students of social regularities "never fail to introduce psychological assumptions." It is on such assumptions, not on the correlations provided by the panel method, that the "psychological mechanism" of "reactivation" rests. But Asch's moderate criticism is precisely applicable: "Usually, however, these [psychological assumptions] are quite general; they represent little more than common sense ideas, which themselves need study and revision" (*Social Psychology*, pp. 532, 533). Conceivably this will be remedied *ex post facto* in an as yet unpublished essay by Lazarsfeld dealing with the psychological assumptions underlying *Voting* and *The People's Choice*.[30] This will not, however, dispose of the basic argument of the psychologists, which is that what intervenes between social characteristics and the voting act is in-

---

[28] But see below, p. 32.
[29] See below, pp. 32-33, 41-43.
[30] See A. J. Brodbeck, "The Problem of Irrationality and Neuroticism Underlying Political Choice," *American Voting Behavior*, pp. 122 ff.

dividual psychological processes and that these must be investigated directly if voting is to be understood.[31]

PSYCHOLOGICAL POLITICS

While the voting studies considered here rely mainly on the establishment of social regularities, they involve or imply some kind of psychology, however inadequately articulated it is. In The Voter Decides the three so-called psychological variables prove on inspection to be nothing more than common sense political categories, yielding the most commonplace conclusions. The other three psychological factors on which data were collected [32] are discussed in the appendixes, where we learn, for example, that "the higher one's sense of political efficacy, the higher the level of his participation in the 1952 election" (p. 190). As mechanisms intervening "between the external events of the voter's world and his ultimate behavior" these three factors seem no more psychological than the ones discussed in the body of the book. Nevertheless, both The Voter Decides and Voting, even in their very defects, point to direct psychological investigation as a means of understanding voting.

Fortunately, several essays by psychiatrists in the Burdick and Brodbeck volume on American Voting Behavior enable us to examine a more forthright and more sophisticated psychological approach. In considering them, several qualifications need to be borne in mind: (1) the application of the principles and insights of psychiatry to voting behavior is still in a primitive stage, as these authors emphasize, and specific findings and interpretations are speculative and tentative to a degree unusual even in the social sciences; (2) the authors do not always agree with one another, and a broader representation from the different schools of psychology and psychiatry would reveal more disagreements, some of a fundamental kind; (3) Voting shares much common ground with these essays, but because of the extent to which its psychological assumptions are not articulated it would be exceedingly difficult to say in detail how far this agreement extends.

Like Voting, however, these essays seek out the non-rational, non-political answers to the question of why people vote as they do. The psychiatrist brings his understanding of the individual psyche to bear on this question, which the panel method as such proves unable to answer. The basic arguments, as presented by C. W. Wahl, are that "the great unconscious depths of man's personality play a significant, if not crucial, role in initiating his social behavior and group formations," and that "intensive psychotherapy constitutes the most searching and the most thorough of all methods of individual human study yet devised," offering "an insight into human character and

[31] The "missing link" between "conditions and consequences" is analyzed below. See pp. 40 ff.

[32] "Conformity to the group standards of one's associates," "A sense of personal efficacy in the area of politics," and "A sense of civic obligation to vote" (The Voter Decides, p. 86).

motivation which no other method can equal." [33] Wahl contends that "identifications, such as our choice of political party . . . are *primarily* expressions of individual needs to secure gratification of repressed wishes for a certain type of parental image; a type that will vary depending on the nature and circumstance of the past parental relationship" (pp. 263-264, italics supplied). He goes on: "Hence, much of our political behavior and candidate choice are, in my view, largely unconscious, subrogative attempts to recapitulate the primary and parental identifications or to form new secondary identifications antithetical to the parental ones." The vote, he argues, "is more than an individual or legislative act; it is a powerful form of affirmation or of protest."

The possibilities of this kind of explanation of voting behavior are explored in more detail by Richard E. Renneker, an associate director of psychosomatic research in a Los Angeles hospital. Reviewing the clinical record of 42 patients in psychoanalytic therapy or psychoanalysis, he found that there "was *always* some sort of meaningful relationship between the voting history of the patient and of the *dominant* parent." [34] He shows how different forms of voting behavior may be traced to parental relationships. Thus we learn that "*the presidential candidate is commonly regarded by the unconscious as a father substitute* (e.g., Washington as the 'father' of his country)." Roosevelt "was mourned as a father, and his passing reactivated unresolved oedipals all over the country." Even Truman (a most unlikely father figure, one might have thought) is made to fit into this scheme. At first, it is true, Truman suffered by comparison with his predecessor.

The feeling was like that of a family which loses the respected, loved father—no one can take his place. A new man starts coming around regularly but no one takes him seriously for awhile because "he isn't daddy." New events may gradually bring him into positive focus and so blur the memory of father. Truman imperceptibly emerged as the cocky, confident fighter who wouldn't back down for anyone. There was much critical press comment over his violent attacks upon the critics of his daughter, but more people felt vaguely reassured and pleased by them than otherwise. He was like a living demonstration of the Americanism: "My father can lick any father on the block." His courageous, jut-jawed campaign against the personally unconvincing Dewey pulled in the legions of those who would rather have a strong father figure in their corner just in case [pp. 404-406].[35]

[33] "The Relation Between Primary and Secondary Identifications: Psychiatry and the Group Sciences," *American Voting Behavior*, pp. 262, 265. As a method of studying human beings psychotherapy does suffer two disadvantages, according to Wahl: the psychotherapist really is obliged (by "medical ethics") to devote himself primarily to the welfare of his patients rather than to use them for research purposes; and there are not enough patients to be statistically significant at the present time.
[34] "Some Psychodynamic Aspects of Voting Behavior," *American Voting Behavior*, p. 399.
[35] This should be compared with the data in *Voting* (pp. 262-270) which, so far as they are reliable, indicate that what was decisive in Truman's victory was not an improved picture of Truman but an increased concern with economic issues and a decreased concern with the character of the candidate.

It is difficult to escape the uneasy feeling that this is less an explanation than a clever exercise. It would be equally plausible to say that those who voted for Dewey saw him as a great father figure too—Tom Dewey, the strong and confident fighter of evil, who had applied the "razor strap" to many a gangster in the "woodshed," the good family man and devoted father, the potential unifier of the great American family. Hence, who is elected would not depend on the "father" quality, but on something else. This mode of analysis is infinitely flexible. Both the lines it takes and the number of layers of irrationality it professes to uncover are determined more by the ingenuity of the analyst than by anything demonstrably present in the subject under investigation.[36] Franz Alexander, for example, reports the case of a patient, "suffering from a serious neurotic condition, a strong liberal," who decided not to vote for a certain candidate because he felt that he and the candidate suffered from the same kind of emotional problem.

It turned out that he strongly identified himself with this presidential candidate and felt that he should not become President just as he himself should not become President. His ambitions were connected with a great deal of guilt, and therefore he expected failure and humiliation. Because of his close identification with the candidate he did not want him to run, then be defeated and humiliated.[37]

But if the patient had voted for the candidate, would an explanation in almost these same terms be any less plausible? We might, for example, explain a favorable vote by saying that the patient hoped thus to help the candidate (and through the candidate to help himself) succeed, avoid humiliation, and overcome his feelings of guilt. Or, deferring to what would probably be a more common taste among the *aficionados* of psychotherapy, we might say that his favorable vote would have been an expression of a neurotic desire to harm himself through the candidate by abetting his inevitable defeat and humiliation. But, on the basis of the evidence presented by Alexander at least, a much better explanation has been ignored: this patient came to the reasonable conclusion that a neurotic would probably make a poor President.

What we have here is a case in which the patient, though neurotic, may have been acting in a reasonable manner. The tendency (to put it no more strongly) of the psychological, like the sociological, mode of analysis is to overlook that possibility. Consider a case that strikes closer to home. Discussing the voting behavior of sons whose fathers frustrated their needs for love, dependence, and a masculine frame of reference, Renneker found that these individuals "did not really speak *for* a candidate but always *against* one" (p.

[36] See Wahl, in *American Voting Behavior*, p. 276. Cf. *Voting*, p. 241, and *American Voting Behavior*, pp. 278-279, 401.
[37] Franz Alexander, "Emotional Factors in Voting Behavior," *American Voting Behavior*, p. 305.

408). This was—of course—an expression of strong unconscious hostility towards their fathers.

A political scientist, who was a superpurist, reached the ultimate in this type of voting behavior. He set himself the professional task of identifying the negative qualities of both candidates. In order to do this he had decided not to vote and thus to avoid emotional blindness in the service of defending his choice against himself. This was a neat maneuver which freed him from the necessity of going through the motions of being for something. It also allowed free rein to his critical, hostile feelings unconsciously directed toward father figures. He was ostensibly operating in the interests of science, in fact, people admired him for greater purity of investigative method, therefore people—including himself—didn't dream that his real satisfaction came from the exercise of his hostility [p. 410].

This is not without some plausibility; many social scientists are concerned lest an immersion in value-free science serve as a way of avoiding political responsibility. But if the psychotherapist explains the behavior of a political scientist in this way, must we not do the same with that very explanatory behavior of the psychotherapist, and of his analyst, and so on in infinite regression? [38] And what does the explanation explain? Must we not first look to the scientific study that this political scientist pursued? Perhaps if we find it unintelligible or radically defective, and therefore inexplicable on its own ground, we may have to resort to an examination of his unconscious frustrations in order to understand why he wrote nonsense. But that would require that we know first whether he has produced nonsense or a work of genuine scientific interest. If he has accomplished the latter, or even if he has made a genuine attempt at it, that is surely indispensable for understanding his behavior, whereas his unconscious response to a "negative father" must be of secondary concern, and might well be irrelevant.

Alexander provides an interesting confirmation of this point, although he does not consider its implications. Discussing the case of an upper class voter who strongly identified himself with "intellectuals" as a class, he makes a distinction between a "genuine" identification with the intellectual role and a "pseudo intellectualism" which is "utilized as a protest against the family." He points out that both can be present in the same person. "In this observed case, the patient turned toward intellectual pursuits first as a rebellion against his family's attitude but as time went on his interest became more and more genuine; it became an integral part of his ego, and the original rebellious motivation *lost significance*" (p. 303, italics supplied). It lost, that is to say, the power to explain why this individual voted as he did. An explanation in terms of "the original rebellious motivation" would miss the

[38] Renneker has indeed turned this mode of analysis on himself, though he has not yet (so far as is known) attempted a psychological explanation of his psychological explanation of his own behavior as a researcher in the area of psychotherapy. See "Countertransference Reactions to Cancer," *Psychosomatic Medicine*, September-October, 1957, pp. 409-418.

most important aspect of his voting behavior, which was a genuine concern with intellectual questions and therefore a "genuine feeling of belonging to persons of the same interest and occupation. . . ."

This suggests a much broader question. Supposing the usefulness of this kind of analysis in treating seriously disturbed patients, is it not severely strained when applied to voters at large? The psychotherapist seems to answer in the negative. According to Wahl, pathological states are "bold, magnified canvases on which can be seen more clearly the processes less evidently operative in other individuals . . ." (p. 268).[39] One of Wahl's specific suggestions is that we need to study the psychological antecedents of the "revolutionary personality." "Not because such persons constitute a sizeable proportion of the voting population in this country, but because they show, in magnified form, the manifestation of drives and needs which, in attenuated or altered forms, are just as apt to find expression in the Democratic and Republican parties." But does it not make all the difference whether these subconscious drives and needs issue in revolutionary activity or in a vote for the Democratic or Republican party? Wahl implicitly concedes this in what follows:

And we must also learn to distinguish the dissenter and the individualist from the revolutionary. The former are often execrated today as though they were the latter. The dissenter, however annoying he may be to some, manifests a quality which is of great good to mankind; our political and social life must be organized in such a way as always to give him a forum. The revolutionary wishes to force his dissenting views on the social fabric and the lives of others. This is hardly to be condoned even though it is ostensibly all for the eventual good of mankind [pp. 277-278].[40]

There is a vital distinction to be made between the ordinary dissenter and the revolutionary, a distinction that is not psychological but political. What is decisive is not the psychological underpinning they share, but the different political significance of their behaviors. The dissenter does "great good to mankind" and must be given a forum; the revolutionary is harmful, his activities are only "ostensibly" for the good of mankind and are "hardly to be condoned." On the psychotherapist's own ground then, and granting that there is some of the neurotic in all of us, the further we move from neurotic behavior to more "mature" or "rational" behavior, the less relevant are the lessons drawn from a study of extreme cases of mental sickness and the more

[39] He concedes that later "maturational experiences may largely bind up . . . early wounds to the psyche, and no subsequent neurosis need eventuate"; but maturation is always uneven and imperfect and "in all persons there is a latent core of irrationality which impels us to pursue and attempt to gratify latent frustrated needs."

[40] Are all revolutionary activities only "ostensibly all for the eventual good of mankind," and are all revolutionaries (Washington, Cromwell, Jefferson, and Milton) neurotic and harmful to society? If not, must we not conclude that Wahl's "science" is limited to the present situation in the United States?

necessary is a clear understanding of mental health. Political behavior requires an understanding of political health, for it is on the basis of this understanding that we make the distinction, no less relevant psychologically than politically, between, for example, the sick revolutionary and the healthy dissenter.

Each of the writers we have been considering is driven in this direction, but only one deliberately confronts the issue. In the concluding essay of *American Voting Behavior*, Arthur J. Brodbeck seeks to do more than to use psychotherapeutic experience to unearth the unconscious, nonrational determinants of voting behavior. Discussing "The Principles of Permanence and Change: Electioneering and Psychotherapy Compared," he suggests that both the science of psychotherapy and what he calls the "science of electioneering" are "social engineering sciences." He argues that both may be viewed in very much the same way and that consequently the latter may utilize materials coming out of the former (which is "of course" the "most highly developed social engineering science"). (p. 420)

Brodbeck's first task is to establish the "political" or "democratic" (the distinction is never clear) character of psychotherapy. He says that the usual view among psychotherapists is that, unlike the case in electioneering, the therapist does not advocate any policy; but even if that is true, there is a real power struggle going on within the patient.[41] Moreover there "is perhaps more of a 'myth' about the 'value-free' psychoanalyst than a reality" (p. 421). Even if he refrains from suggesting any policy, "he still helps the patient exposed to the campaign to face the problem *in special ways* which he judges will help the patient solve the problem in a reasonably 'rational' manner." Indeed, Brodbeck says that one can schematize the diverse views of psychotherapy in political terms, according to the therapist's conception of his role; and this is not a mere academic exercise. "For the psychotherapist can be quite reasonably seen as having the goal of *trying to exercise power for the recognition and examination of unconscious impulses which have been kept political prisoners without adequate trial by jury.*" There is a kind of political education in psychotherapy, "for much of it consists in trying to make the patient become a more effective person socially in getting what he wants from life" (p. 434).

Brodbeck's political psychotherapy is intended chiefly to lay the basis for his psychotherapeutic politics. The main example he gives of the application to politics of psychotherapeutic principles has to do with the phenomenon that Harry Stack Sullivan called "selective inattention"—a learned but unconscious failure to notice certain aspects of the environment or to profit from experience. This may result in "a partial or complete failure to gratify

[41] For example: "The marital mate who does *not* want a divorce and the 'third person' who *wants* the divorce so as to marry the patient are contenders for power, for a vote" (*American Voting Behavior*, p. 420).

the motives and reach outcomes important to the person" (p. 425). The individual who behaves in this fashion behaves irrationally and therefore, according to Brodbeck, undemocratically.

I have, in other context [sic], defined "irrationality" as an inability to continue to learn how to actualize one's values in better and better ways. By better, I mean, of course, more *skillful*, but in addition, there is the factor of doing so *without damaging others or the self for the continuing growth and development of all* [p. 428].

The person who "selectively inattends" behaves irrationally in both senses; in particular, his behavior may harm other persons who come in contact with him. "In a sense, then, irrationality is bound to be incompatible with democratic conditions, since *autocratic contempt* for some of the factors involved in an interpersonal situation are part and parcel of the maintenance of it."

Unfortunately Brodbeck does not elaborate the definition of irrationality here or refer us to any other discussion of his. What is decisive, however, is that although up to this point the end of human behavior seemed to be self-gratification simply, Brodbeck now contends that rationality also requires some concern for the good of others, and this implies some common good. He does not, it is true, say much about this common good except that it consists of the "continuing growth and development of all"; he does not consider how it is apprehended or what its psychological bases are; but it is clear from his political discussion that it is a substantive and not merely a procedural good. It is not to be arrived at by a mere counting of hands:

when people ballot without thinking about issues and the records of candidates first, we are reminded of the spectacle of hand-raising in totalitarian countries that make hollow mockeries of balloting practices. . . . [A] high regard for democracy depends upon the use of campaigns for (a) educating this public and (b) the handling of "resistances" which appear as selective inattention patterns among the voters [p. 430].

Brodbeck sharply criticizes political leaders for their failure in these respects. Whether and to what extent the skilled psychotherapist might teach political leaders "techniques for the science of electioneering which will reduce patterns of inattention" among the voters is a question we need not consider, since Brodbeck does little more than assert the possibility. Presumably one important technique would be to talk about the real issues facing the country which, according to the authors of Voting at least, Truman did in 1948 and Dewey did not (*Voting*, p. 237).

What is more important is the alleged basic compatibility between the principles of psychotherapy and those of democratic politics that enables such transfers of techniques to be made.

Psychoanalysis rests upon the idea of giving the censored, the weak, the contemptible aspects of the personality greater respect and a just hearing. It, thus, in its way, embodies the idea of "a free forum" in which the self-images of the participants are challenged and tested against one another. Ideally, psychoanalytic practices thus are fully consonant with democratic principles [*American Voting Behavior*, p. 435].

The therapist does not permit the patient to submit to his government. Rather he helps the patient to understand himself and thus to free himself from his unconscious and irrational self—or at least to reduce the extent of his servitude—and to govern himself by reason. The course of psychotherapy is "democratic" then, in the sense that all claims to govern the patient's behavior—even the contemptible ones—are given a fair hearing. But these claims are not all equal. The contemptible aspects of the personality are given some respect and are heard; but they do not rule. Personal self-government is not a matter of yielding to the strongest passions of the moment, any more than political self-government is merely a matter of counting heads. Whether it is ever possible in principle to say of an individual that he is sufficiently in command of himself to require no further psychotherapeutic assistance, we need not inquire; but it is clear (certainly Brodbeck takes for granted) that the body politic is never free of the need for leadership. Even in a government by the people there is necessarily a distinction between governors and governed. And, Brodbeck emphasizes, the quality, the health of democratic government depends decisively upon the quality of its leadership.

Obviously this raises age-old questions about the nature of political leadership and its compatibility with self-government, questions to which political thinkers of all times have given their best thought. More than that, it brings into question Brodbeck's implicit identification of "political" and "democratic." Brodbeck is aware of these questions at a certain level. He recognizes that in the eyes of many the perennial tension between leadership and democracy will be magnified by the transformation of the political leader into the psychotherapist. Many today fear "the full application of psychoanalytic principles to the analysis and operation of institutions," because of a growing fear of the "manipulators." Brodbeck seeks to allay such fears by pointing out that psychotherapy itself is gravely concerned with this problem. "There is [sic], thus, within psychoanalysis, some principles governing processes of 'manipulation' or 'counter-transference' which themselves can be applied to the study of political campaigns and which serve to check and balance the exploitation of psychoanalytic principles regarding permanence and change for non-democratic purposes" (p. 436). Brodbeck does not tell us what these principles are, nor do the articles to which he refers us.[42] We are left with nothing but the most primitive statement of the political problem.

[42] Indeed, these articles demonstrate, if anything, the utter inadequacy of psychoanalytic theory to deal with this problem. One author seems to rely on the psychoanalyst's posses-

Brodbeck attempts, then, to draw a fundamental parallel between the science of psychotherapy and the science of electioneering with a view to laying the foundation for an exchange of insight, technique, and principle between them, and especially from the former to the latter. His specific and frankly tentative suggestions are less important than the foundation on which they rest. Unfortunately, that foundation is extremely nebulous, and no amount of refinement in the sphere of technique can remedy that. Brodbeck's conception of a healthy democracy is so vague as to be almost entirely without meaning. And although there are random suggestions about improving political leadership, there is nothing like a coherent account of the responsibilities of political leadership in a democracy or of provisions to be taken against its corruption. Consequently, there can be no coherent account of the uses to which the principles and techniques of psychotherapy might be put in a democracy. Brodbeck fails to find in psychotherapeutic theory an adequate basis for a theory of democracy,[43] but his article is as significant for

sion of solid, everyday virtues, "intelligence and creative ability," "courage, tenacity, and integrity"; and he attempts to resolve the problem with a burst of poetry: "Living out their years in a climate of hatred and dependence and torment, they [the psychoanalysts] nevertheless maintain that the life of man has meaning, can be understood, and that his suffering is in part remediable. . . . They stand by. Hatred they endure, and do not turn away. Love comes their way, and they are not seduced. They are the listeners, but they listen with unwavering intent, and their silence is not cold." Allen Wheelis, "The Vocational Hazards of Psychoanalysis," *The International Journal of Psycho-analysis,* vol. XXXVII, parts II-III, 1956, pp. 180, 184. Another author, considering how the psychotherapist can protect himself against unrealistic feelings of superiority, makes some "suggestions [that] come to mind." These consist mostly of prudential advice such as might have been given to men in high places at any time: have adequate training; do not be unwilling to admit that you may be wrong; do not associate only with a very narrow circle of professional acquaintances. Finally, he suggests as an "essential safeguard" "a constant cherishing of, and working toward, a democratic kind of interpersonal relationship with all people. . . ." The psychotherapist ought to do this, because "authoritarianism is psychologically unhealthy for those who dominate as well as for those who are dominated. Only in an atmosphere of democratic interrelationships can both the psychotherapist and his patients achieve their fullest development." Judd Marmor, "The Feeling of Superiority: An Occupational Hazard in the Practice of Psychotherapy," *American Journal of Psychiatry,* November 1953, p. 376. Even if we grant (as we can scarcely do on the basis of the discussion here) the meaningfulness of this proposition, it amounts to nothing more than a restatement of the problem. There is nothing in any of the articles cited remotely resembling psychoanalytic principles which serve as checks against the use of "manipulation" for "non-democratic" purposes.

43 On the contrary, it is evident, by the end of the article at least, that the ground of the analogy between psychotherapy (however democratic its trappings and benevolent its intentions) and democracy is profoundly problematic. Initially the intrapersonal struggle was likened to a "campaign" with different "candidates" (for example, the wife and the "third person") contending for the patient's "vote." The psychotherapist was outside this campaign, helping the patient to see the issue in true perspective and to decide how to "vote." But when Brodbeck moves to the political scene the candidate is told that, in addition to his direct advocacy, he must take on a responsibility for educating the public and reducing its selective inattention. He must take on the character of psychotherapist as well as candidate. Of course it is true, as Brodbeck says, that all candidates have an interest in maintaining democracy; but so do all "candidates" in the psychological sense have an interest in maintaining the integrity of the individual, yet that does not stop them from tearing

what it attempts to do as for its failure. It amounts to a recognition that a psychological examination of voting behavior, if it is to be more than an irrelevant exercise in ingenuity, must rest on some conception of political health and that that concept, in turn, requires an inquiry into the relations between those who rule and those who are ruled. However superficial his political understanding, it is remarkable that, beginning with the most radically non-political approach to voting behavior, Brodbeck is led to attempt to establish its political foundation.

VOTING: "POLITICAL" POLITICS

Like *American Voting Behavior*, *Voting* culminates in a theory of democracy. Just as Brodbeck attempts to build a theory of democracy on his psychotherapeutic principles, so Berelson, Lazarsfeld, and McPhee attempt to build one on their sociological or social psychological principles. Before examining this latter venture, however, it is necessary to consider the second, "political," theme of *Voting*; for the authors do purport to study the "political processes," and in two chapters of Part III they deal extensively, in fact almost exclusively, with the issues in the 1948 campaign. On the basis of their previous discussion, it is somewhat surprising to see in Chapter 9 the extent to which they assume that issues play an important role in determining how people vote.

The voters, in 1948 at least, tended to disagree most on what the authors designate as "Position" issues. "The major issues of direct cleavage between Republicans and Democrats in 1948 Elmira were Position issues reflecting differences in material interests . . ." (p. 194). But not all the cleavages were on such issues; there was also some disagreement on "Style" issues.[44] There were also some cases in which an individual voter was placed under cross-pressures, agreeing with one party's stand on one issue, but with the other party's stand on another issue. "How are such inconsistencies overridden?" ". . . voters with an attitudinal foot in each camp, so to speak, tend to choose the party that corresponds to their own position on those issues to which they assign particular weight." "A voter may assess the political situation from several standpoints; from one, the Democrats appear better to him and, from an-

---

him apart to such an extent that he requires the assistance of the psychotherapist who is above this destructive dispute. Whether on the political side the analogy carries so far, Brodbeck does not consider. See below, pp. 292 ff.

44 Position issues are: "taxation, labor-management, tariffs, farm prices, freight rates, monopoly, price control, etc." Style issues are: "prohibition, religious education, civil liberties, UNESCO, immigration, intergroup relations, blue laws, candidates' personalities, governmental corruption, etc." (p. 184) Position issues are regarded as " 'more real' " (p. 185), which is interesting (among other reasons) because international affairs are referred to as Style issues (see pp. 189, 197, 213). One might have thought that international problems are as "real" as monopoly, for example.

other, the Republicans do. His decision is likely to follow the aspect given greater weight by him . . ." (pp. 200-202).[45] There is no mention of peer group influence here; the voter is seen as voting according to the importance he attaches to the issues in the campaign.

In Chapter 12, the authors are concerned with the political effect of the campaign and specifically with the trend to Truman made up primarily of former Democrats who had temporarily defected to the Republicans. In striking contrast to their discussion of the same question in Chapter 13, which has already been considered, they begin by speculating why these individuals defected in the first place.

The potential for change is always present in a two-party democratic system. It is there simply because new events bring new problems and new leaders to deal with them. And these were the central conditions explaining the "defection" to the Republicans of potential Democrats at the beginning of the 1948 campaign. First, the Democratic leader was in disfavor (even within his own party) and, second, new issues attracted (the Democrats would say "distracted") the voters [p. 257].

New problems, new leaders—a new political situation within which the voters had to exercise their political responsibility. But many of these defectors returned. Why? Not, according to the discussion here, simply because of the "social support" or pressure of primary groups; but because Truman emphasized the familiar "economic labor-consumer 'class' issues," and these voters with Democratic predispositions became convinced that these issues were sufficiently important to outweigh any reservations they might still have about Truman himself. "There was a sharp increase in the saliency of class issues among potential Democrats from June to October" (p. 273). True, "an improving appreciation of Truman was partly involved in the process," but the "rally was due more to a change in standard than to a change in evaluation" (p. 270).

It is significant that here, in the context of a political explanation, the authors take the voters' own explanations of their behavior seriously (at least up to a point). "In their own reasons for change to Truman the respondents reveal a marked shift in the standard by which they were judging the campaign" (p. 269). We are not told here, as we are when the analysis is social psychological, that change in opinion followed the socially-induced decision to " 'return to the fold' " (p. 294). Indeed, the reader of this chapter would have no idea of the enormous importance earlier attributed to the conforming pressures of primary groups. Here, it would seem, Truman's campaign and its effect on these voters individually was the decisive factor.

[45] This seems rather sensible on the part of the voter. The parties, too, seem rather sensible. We learn, for example, that they tend to disagree more on unsettled issues than they do on "settled" issues, or issues not yet at the "Gateway"—that is, those not yet politically important (see pp. 209 ff).

Obviously the influence of primary groups may be consistent with and relevant to a political explanation of the kind presented here, although the authors make little or no attempt to show the connection between their two explanations of the 1948 election. According to the earlier "social" analysis, the fundamental point was not the (admittedly) political genesis of social groups and thus of political opinion, but the transformation of political interest into enduring social groups.

The solid foundations of American political parties are in distinctive social groups that not only have "interests" involved but have sufficient social differentiation from other groups, sufficient continuity between generations, and sufficient closed or in-group contact in successive generations to transform these initial *political* interests into persistent and durable *social* traditions. It is the re-emergence of these traditions, as much as fresh political developments, that characterizes a modern presidential election campaign [p. 147].

This, it would seem on the basis of what we are told in *Voting* itself, depends on the election. In 1948, we learn in Chapter 12, not only did political factors (new problems, new leaders) threaten to break the Democratic party, but a political factor (Truman's campaign) was responsible for keeping it patched together. But the patching was only temporary, because the "persistent and durable" social tradition that supported the Democratic majority eroded or is in the course of eroding—and not for any "social" reasons, but because by 1952 "the old concerns [by which the authors mean political concerns] appeared to have run their life-history, so to speak, and new Style issues (e.g., communism in government) established themselves" (p. 272). Since new problems bring new issues, activating "new sets of dispositions," since, in fact, a "modern presidential campaign is won or lost on the basis of a multitude of appeals" (p. 270), we can expect some campaigns to be fought over style issues and others over the characteristics of the candidates. The loss of a "magnetic leader" and his replacement by a "less impressive man" may also result in voting changes. Why do "people come to favor this candidate rather than that one"? *Because they agree with his stand on the issues or because they are attracted by his personal qualities or both.* As one of the Elmira respondents put it: "We have had better Presidents than Truman, but he is the best man running now because he is for labor."

The authors of *Voting* recognize (at least some of the time) that however detailed and concrete their data about the voting behavior of the citizens of Elmira in 1948 and however intricate the correlations they establish, the results remain ephemeral unless they can transcend the particular situation and reveal the "factors responsible for decision and action," to use Solomon Asch's phrase. But in seeking to provide a political explanation of voting they, like the authors of *The Voter Decides*, resort to ludicrously vague generalities. Political understanding is not advanced by the conclusion that an individual votes according to his judgment of the issues and the candidates, and that a conflict between these will be resolved in favor of the one that the voter thinks is more important. Nor is it a significant discovery to find that a Catholic labor unionist with a Democratic predisposition and whose associates have Democratic predispositions will be more likely to vote Democratic than a wealthy Protestant stock broker who associates with wealthy Protestant stock brokers. Like Brodbeck (but with far less justification, considering the relative scope of the two enterprises), the authors of *Voting* end where political analysis begins.

There are times, however, when the authors of *Voting* seem to think that political institutions and political leadership should be central to any study of political behavior. They remark in their chapter on small groups and political discussion that to view friends and co-workers as "groups" of which the voter is a "member" is "customary but not entirely appropriate," because these immediate associates actually "serve less as closed cliques than as *contact points* through whom the individual is connected to whole networks of social relations that affect political behavior. The networks are organized in major socioeconomic and ethnic blocs, and at their center are the main institutions of the community and its ultimate leadership" (p. 94). This suggests that a study of voting behavior, unless it is content to nibble at the edges of its subject, ought to focus on political institutions and leadership. *Voting* does contain two chapters on the "institutions of the community" (mainly labor unions and the political parties), but "at only a few points is it possible really to show the links between the efforts of the various institutions and the decisions of the voters themselves" (p. ix).[46] "Organizations like the political parties have been described qualitatively, but . . . they are seldom linked systematically with our data" (p. 301).[47] Chapter 8 in *Voting* is, then, almost unique, because it promises to provide this link.

In the discussion of political parties in Chapter 8, an attempt is made to confront democratic theory with democratic practice, one of the promised themes of the "political" section. And practice, again and again, is found to fall short.

What function is a local political organization supposed to perform in a national election? Presumably it is supposed to interpret the national party line within the community; to influence people to vote the right way, by reinforcing

---

[46] "Here," the authors suggest, "a new task looms for the next study." But how can it have happened that at this late stage in this vast cumulative enterprise the analysis of voting can still be a stranger to political parties? This is scarcely less surprising than the suggestion also made here that *The People's Choice* made a substantial contribution by pointing up "the unresolved problem of the role of political issues in the campaign."

[47] The tenuousness of the link is indicated by the fact that the chapters on social and political institutions were written by John P. Dean and Edward Suchman rather than Berelson, Lazarsfeld, and McPhee.

the faithful, converting the opposition, and activating the indifferent; and to mobilize the vote on election day.

In the ordinary community of Elmira—not unlike towns where millions of "typical" Americans live and vote—the party is not particularly successful at any one of these [p. 177].

However capable the party leaders were in their day-to-day activities, "they did not provide firsthand policy-making or direct responsibility for articulate debate on the political issues that most deeply concerned the principal interests in the community, nor did they see such tasks as their affair. Measured against such criteria for adequate leadership, the Elmira parties fail to provide the community with the kind of local guidance that might be expected in a decision process that brought nearly three-quarters of its citizens to the polls" (p. 163). "What the local parties did not do was to guide the political hands of the community—theoretically its central task" (p. 178). According to this chapter, then, there was a serious breakdown in party leadership in Elmira. This would seem to lead to the conclusion either that this community is politically sick or that "adequate leadership" was to be found elsewhere. In the end, the senior authors accept neither of these conclusions but, instead, revise downward their standard of political health (without, however, re-examining Elmira's political parties from this new point of view).

As for the central question of leadership in a democracy, the only analysis made of it (significantly in the "social" section of the book) illustrates the transformation that political questions are made to undergo in order to fit them for the authors' sociological mode of analysis. They begin with a quotation from James Bryce: " 'Opinion does not merely grow; it is also made. There is not merely the passive class of persons; there is the active class, who occupy themselves primarily with public affairs, who aspire to create and lead opinion' " (p. 109). Apparently accepting both Bryce's definition of this class and the importance he attributes to it, the authors continue: "Given such specialists, the political genius of the citizenry may reside less in how well they can judge public policy than in how well they can judge the people who advise them how to judge policy." But instead of pursuing the questions thus suggested, the authors very quickly retreat to questions more easily handled with their analytical tools.

They point out that the "banker and mayor and union officer may be 'opinion leaders' in a distant sense, but ordinary voters listen to near-by influencers." Therefore, "one might properly speak less of leaders than of a complex web of opinion-leading relationships." This transformation of opinion leadership into "opinion-leading relationships" provides the basis for the authors' definition of "opinion leader": an individual who is at the center of several such relationships. Specifically, they define as opinion leaders the 23 percent of their panel who said that they were consulted about politics as much as or more than other people they knew and who also said that they had recently talked about politics. The size and definition of this group indicate already how far the authors have moved from Bryce, and from the realm of political leadership. Indeed, as the discussion continues, the notion of leadership slips away entirely. The authors found that "opinion leaders" also seek advice more than other people,[48] and this reminds them that "in practice there must be unending circuits of leadership relationships running through the community, like a nerve system through the body." The so-called leaders become "junction points" in a nerve system that turns back on itself endlessly, and that apparently has no brain. Thus what is important is the network of relationships and the number of contacts between junction points rather than what goes on within that system or what governs it. The authors care very little, as we have seen, about what is said in political discussion, except as it can be interpreted as evidence of some sociological or psychological force pushing the voter one way or the other. But the result is that they have no grounds for judging what they here concede to be a central question, how well can the citizenry judge the people who advise it on public policy? Nor are the grounds of the opinions of the "opinion leaders" investigated, an inquiry that might well lead to the finding that, while "the banker and mayor and union officer" are distant opinion leaders they are also the critical ones—if it is to them that the 23 percent who constitute the junction points look for guidance. Bryce's characterization of opinion leaders is not without difficulties, but at least it provides the basis for a more than merely record-keeping study of public opinion.

By the end of this discussion, however, the authors have abandoned Bryce altogether. Opinion leaders are distinctive but not too distinctive, above the socioeconomic class of their followers but just a little above, "traveling the same road as their followers but . . . a little ahead" (p. 113). They are not leaders at all but embodiers of relationships—junction points, statistics.

MODERN SOCIAL SCIENCE AND THE STUDY OF VOTING

In the introduction to their collection of essays on *American Voting Behavior*, Burdick and Brodbeck advise the reader to study the first essay in the collection, the one by sociologist Peter Rossi, "so as to comprehend the 'scientific culture' which sought to remove the study of voting behavior from the armchair speculators and place it with the hardworking empiricists." Writing out of this "scientific culture," Rossi is critical mainly of the technical shortcoming in the studies conducted by the hard-working empiricists. Our concern is not with these, nor with the misrepresentations that arise out of

[48] The difference is not large—52 percent as against 43 percent (see p. 110).

sheer carelessness—except as these may throw light on the nature of the whole enterprise. In some cases, it is true, Berelson, Lazarsfeld, and McPhee appear to have spent so little time in the armchair examining their data that they commit errors due to carelessness, and this despite the fact that we have been led to believe that "rigorous analysis" and "empirical analysis" are synonymous terms. On page 55, for example, they write: "Socioeconomic status . . . is directly related to the final vote decision (Chart XX)." But the chart shows that whereas the Republican proportion of the vote decreases with the decline in socioeconomic status from upper to lower-middle class, it increases slightly among the lower class. On page 70, they say that "the younger Catholics vote more Republican" than the older Catholics; but the chart shows that whereas the middle-aged Catholics vote more Republican than the older group (41 percent as opposed to 18 percent), the younger Catholics vote Republican in about the same proportion as those who are middle-aged (38 percent as opposed to 41 percent), and the slight difference, if one were to attach significance to it, undermines their generalization.

More frequently, the authors report their findings in such gross form as to lead to conclusions that either miss their real significance or restate the most threadbare commonplaces. On pages 207-209, they write that while more people approved of labor unions than disapproved of them, "the warmth of their acceptance diminishes from left to right on the spectrum." The chart on page 209 bears this out in general, but the authors do not comment on the surprising fact that there is more extreme hostility toward the unions among the strong Democrats in Elmira than among the strong Republicans (11 percent as opposed to 6 percent of each group believing that the country would be "better off without them"). They also write that whereas 34 percent of the skilled workers look to professional and managerial persons for political advice, "only 8 per cent" of the latter look to the skilled workers (p. 104, italics supplied). But would it not be more reasonable to regard it as significant that *as many as* 8 percent of the professional and managerial class seek the advice of the skilled workers? As for the commonplaces, what armchair speculator would be surprised to learn that "youth seems to have much more respect for their elders' [political] opinions than the elders do for youth's" (p. 104)? What armchair speculator would write the following: "This is an important consideration: the more reading and listening people do on campaign matters, the more likely they are to come to recognize the positions the candidates take on major issues" (p. 229)? And what armchair speculator needs to be told that interest in the election increases "from August to October," that is, as election day approaches (p. 246)?

The hardworking empiricist is handicapped, in a way the armchair speculator is not, when it comes to interpreting the statistics he collects—"facts" do not speak for themselves, and especially "facts" that at one stage are merely holes in punch cards.[49] His scientific techniques are of no assistance when it comes to interpretation; whether one should write *only* 8 percent of professional and managerial persons seek the political advice of skilled workers, or, *as many as* 8 percent of professional and managerial persons seek the political advice of skilled workers, is not an empirical question in their sense of "empirical." Interpretation here depends on the significance one attaches to the findings, and significance cannot be determined merely by comparing the value of the numbers. If the "scientist" deprives himself of the benefit of common sense because of his preoccupation with empirically-established "facts," he will end up reporting the predominant relation, frequently stressing what to the man of common sense is a platitude or even misleading. He will be naïve.

Connected with their political naïveté is the authors' habit of attributing fallacious opinions to unidentified armchair speculators and then demonstrating the fallaciousness of the opinion. After showing that Catholicism is strongly related to a Democratic vote, they conclude:

Here, then, we find a condition not anticipated nor endorsed by classical political theorists: a *nonpolitical,* associative factor with strong influence upon the electoral decision. Regardless of other demographic characteristics—and despite democratic claims, protestations, or theories to the contrary—there is a strong "religious vote" in this country [p. 66, italics supplied].

When one considers that from the time of Plato and Aristotle through at least the time of Rousseau, there have been political philosophers who taught the necessity of religious homogeneity within civil society; when one remembers the religious issues that brought about such events as the civil wars in England, the landing at Plymouth Rock, and the early struggles over disestablishment in the American states; when one remembers such historical phenomena in the United States as the Know-Nothing party, "Rum, Romanism, and Rebellion," the unsuccessful presidential-election effort of Al Smith, and the controversies over sending representatives to the Vatican; and—to cut short what is an almost endless list—when one remembers the traditional argument about birth-control laws in this country, one wonders what "classical political theorists" and what history books the authors have read. No doubt it is not easy to interpret the data collected—to extract, as V. O. Key says, "the more or less hidden meaning from the data"[50]—but it would be easier for the hardworking empiricists were they not to deprive themselves of the benefits of common sense and the political knowledge extant before the advent of modern social science. Our concern, however, is not with

---

[49] Indeed, Rossi's main criticism of *Voting* is what he regards as a "discrepancy between data and interpretation" and a "superstructure of interpretation only shakily supported by its empirical base" (*American Voting Behavior,* pp. 36, 34).
[50] Foreword to *The Voter Decides,* p. xii.

their naïveté and carelessness; it is with their basic approach to the study of voting.

According to Rossi, the first landmark in scientific voting research is Stuart Rice's *Quantitative Methods in Politics*.[51] Despite the revolutionary character of this work, however, Rice continues to be much influenced by "historians" and "journalists," and his interpretations, therefore, "incline . . . to historical particulars rather than to general statements."

To the extent that he does depart from this predominant style, he seems to be led to do so by his techniques. For example, he starts out with the problem of how the enfranchisement of women affected the balance of support for political parties. His analysis leads him to classify issues into a more general framework of "moral" versus "economic" issues, which differ in their ability to generate differences between the sexes [*Amercan Voting Behavior*, p. 13].[52]

Rice's preoccupation with the "journalistic" and "topical" is attributed by Rossi to the fact that Rice did his research at a time "when social psychology was just beginning to turn to empirical research." He was pulled one way by his desire to address himself to the political problems of the day and another way by his commitment to certain techniques, with the result that, while *Quantitative Methods in Politics* is more "topical" or political, it is also far more self-conscious about its methodological foundations than is, for example, *Voting*. Rossi finds it "interesting to note that more recent monographs employing the same approach no longer require such an extensive argument for the utility of an empirical political science" (p. 437 n.).[53] The presumption is, apparently, that both the meaning and the utility of "empirical political science" can now be taken for granted. But that presumption requires some investigation.

Rice contends that the phenomena of politics are functions of group life and that the study of groups is the province of the sociologist (*Quantitative Methods*, p. vii). Although some of Rice's successors would disagree with this jurisdictional claim, they usually agree that the phenomena of politics are functions of something else, and they therefore agree in the attempt to reduce the political to the sub-political. We had occasion earlier to mention Solomon Asch's criticism that "the study of sociological uniformities fails to supply . . . the functional relations between conditions and consequences," [54] and we have seen that the same criticism applies to the study of psychological

---

[51] New York: Alfred A. Knopf, Inc., 1928.

[52] Rice's distinction between the "moral" and the "economic" is the equivalent of Berelson, Lazarsfeld, and McPhee's distinction between "Style" and "Position." The latter distinction is merely given a "scientific" cover. See above, p. 31.

[53] It is also interesting to note that of the 27 authors of essays in *American Voting Behavior*, only six are political scientists, most of the others being sociologists, social psychologists and psychiatrists.

[54] See above, p. 21.

uniformities. Conditions and consequences are not joined immediately, but by some mediating agency that is missing in descriptions of voting that are confined to sociological and psychological uniformities. This missing agent is opinion. Opinion mediates between sub-political sociological and psychological conditions and political consequences. The central place of opinion seems to be recognized in the subtitle of Voting: "A Study of Opinion Formation in a Presidential Campaign." Yet one of the most striking features of the book is the absence of any discussion of the question, what is opinion?

If we ask a man why he made a certain choice, either he replies that he does not know or he gives a reason (and if he does not know, he is likely to give a reason for that). Whatever its substance, that reason will consist of or reflect some opinion of what is at stake, some desired end or good; and it will also consist of an opinion on which of the available alternatives is more likely to conduce to that end or good. If a market researcher asks a respondent why he bought a particular brand of soap, the reason is likely to be that he thinks or has heard that the soap is an effective cleansing agent, which implies that it is good to be clean, or that all soaps are equally good cleansing agents but that this one is less expensive, which implies that it is good to save money.

One way of ascertaining why people vote as they do would be to ask them directly and to pay attention, at least initially, to their answers, which, once again, consist of reasons, in this case, political reasons. For instance, from the few explanations reported in Voting, we learn that the voter does not say that his choice was governed by his socioeconomic status or by his ability to find social support for it or by his class interest; [55] he says that Truman "is the best man running now," or that Dewey is " 'the best man,' " or that the " 'Democrats as a whole are more for the middle class and poor,' " or that his "party is good for the whole community" (pp. 270, 293-294, 80). These answers imply that the best man should be President or that it is good for the country that a party favor the middle class and poor as opposed to the rich, or, that a party ought to present a program that is good for the whole community rather than one that favors only a part of the community. When he changes his vote intention, he does not speak of cross-pressures or of reactivation; he says, for example, that he began by regarding Dewey as the best man and with the idea that "maybe changing the government would help," but that he concluded that the Taft-Hartley Act was wrong.

Each of the opinions reproduced in Voting, however naïve or uninformed, is a political opinion, precisely because it expresses a view of the common good. Just as choice in general is governed by an opinion of some end or good, so most voters know that the choice they are asked to make in an election involves the common good. If a man actually votes with a view only to

[55] "Thus the class basis for vote, which clearly exists, is not overtly admitted. To a large extent, this is probably due to the requirements of the 'American Creed' that rejects the notion of serving class interests through political action" (Voting, p. 80).

his own good, he is not likely to admit it; instead, he will, as the authors of *Voting* assert, "rationalize": "rather than acknowledge that they support their own party because it is to their own interest to do so (i.e., because it is the party of their class), the respondents tend to believe or to rationalize that their party is good for the whole community" (pp. 79-80). Rare is the man who will admit publicly that he voted only with his own interests in mind.[56] Whether true or not, the voters ordinarily give political reasons for their votes, not private reasons. Since the authors of *Voting* do not bother to raise the question of what is opinion, it is not surprising that they ignore the opinions involved in voting.

According to the description in *Voting*,[57] the "organism" (the voter) is subjected to the "stimulus" of the campaign and his "response" is a vote, almost as if he (or it) had no choice in the matter. But a human being is not an inert object that moves only by being moved. Certainly a voter usually brings to the election campaign a voting "disposition" (that is, an opinion) that was generated earlier, and if this disposition were all he brought to the campaign, it would be sufficient to study merely how that disposition is "implemented" during the campaign. That, however, would not be a "study of opinion formation." But it is not all he brings. Being a creature able to form opinions, the voter brings along with the opinion the very faculty that enabled him to form it in the first place. To describe the vote as an "implementation" of a "disposition" generated before the campaign gets underway, is to ignore the possibility of opinion-generation during the campaign, by ignoring the possibility that the opinion-forming faculty can be active during the campaign. But if this faculty was active once, we cannot assume without investigation that it will not be active again, and if it is active, the earlier disposition might not only *not* be implemented, or "reactivated," it might be replaced by an entirely new disposition.[58] What is ignored by the authors of *Voting*, to speak more precisely now, is the uniquely human faculty to form opinions, in this case, political opinions.

We do not contend that the respondents must be taken at their word, or that votes are always or even usually the immediate result of a thoughtful consideration of the political situation; but we do contend that a human being is endowed with a unique faculty that makes it possible for him to form opinions, and that, as the subtitle of *Voting* itself suggests, the study of voting must concern itself primarily with that faculty. No doubt much voting is habitual, and conceivably a dog might be trained to follow the ex-

[56] The men who dye the oranges they put on the market with a toxic coal-tar color do not say it is all right for people to be poisoned, but rather that the amount of the toxic color will have no deleterious effect. See *Flemming* v. *Florida Citrus Exchange*, 358 U.S. 153 (1958).

[57] See Figure 1 reproduced above, p. 19.

[58] See above, p. 21.

ample of its master and to pull a lever marked Republican every time it sees a band waving the "bloody flag" and playing "The Battle Hymn of the Republic." But the similarity in the results of the two acts (two "votes" for the Republican ticket) does not mean that the acts issue from the same cause. Even if the man votes in thoughtless response to those symbols, his act rests (as the dog's does not) on some opinion about what the symbols stand for; he can give a reason for his response to them.[59] In fact, the condition of their "visibility" to him is an opinion of what they represent. Without the opinion, either his or someone's whose example he follows (and whether he follows someone's example depends on his opinion of that person or of the example), the "stimuli" of the campaign could not affect him one way or the other; or, to state this another way, the sociological or psychological "conditions" cannot possibly produce "consequences" except by way of the agency of opinion. This faculty to form opinion is involved both in the opinion that leads one man to vote in defiance of the position for which there is social support in his primary groups and in the opinion that leads another man to vote in line with the group position.

Man alone of all the animals has this faculty to form opinion, which is why man alone is a political animal. The reduction of such political acts as voting to sub-political conditions is equivalent to the denial of the significance of this uniquely human faculty. Perhaps this is what V. O. Key and Frank Munger had in mind when they said that the "style set in the Erie County study of voting, *The People's Choice*, threatens to take the politics out of electoral behavior." [60] Ordinarily when the social scientist considers political opinion at all, it is only to assert that opinion is a function of some sociological factor such as "cross-pressures" or "social support," or some psychological factor, such as the attempt "to recapitulate the primary and parental identifications" (*American Voting Behavior*, p. 264). In the example already referred to, Berelson, Lazarsfeld, and McPhee report part of a voter's explanation of his change to Truman:

I thought Dewey was the best man. I thought maybe changing the government would help. *I vote for the man.* . . . *I thought Truman wasn't qualified to do* what he stood for, but now I wonder. . . . Now I don't know. . . . [But] *I'm more for unions.* I don't believe in the Taft-Hartley Law. The Democrats as a whole are more for the middle class and poor . . . [*Voting*, pp. 293-294].

Even on the basis of this fragment, something of this individual's conception of voting reveals itself. He "thought" and "thought" and "thought"; he "wondered"; he doesn't "know." He is trying, or at least claims to be trying,

[59] It need not, of course, be a good or adequate reason; the point is that he can give some reason, and the dog cannot.
[60] V. O. Key Jr. and Frank Munger, "Social Determinism and Electoral Choice: The Case of Indiana," *American Voting Behavior*, p. 281.

to reason out how he ought to vote; but the authors of V*oting*, because of their opinion that political opinions are in no important degree functions of the reasoning faculty this voter claims to be using, do not take the explanation seriously. Consequently, they assert dogmatically that when "he is about to 'return to the fold,' he begins to advance the argument which could reunite him with his occupational fellows in a common loyalty." They might be right, but their failure even to consider the voter's explanation deprives their explanation of the probative value they claim for it. How can they know without investigation that this voter's political opinions did not arise out of a thoughtful consideration of the political situation?

Other responses are dealt with in the same summary fashion. When voters assert that "their party is good for the whole community," the authors of V*oting* promptly accuse them of rationalizing (pp. 79-80), and the possibility that the voters might be right is not even given the status of what the social scientist calls a researchable hypothesis. But again, how can they be so certain of this when they do not even ask the voters to defend such assertions?

As choice in general is governed by an opinion that is a view of some end or good, what is at stake in the voting choice is the public or common good—or so the voters themselves believe. One justification of the social scientist's refusal to pursue the analysis in political terms is the assertion that there is no such thing as the common good (and, therefore, no such thing as the political). In the words of Robert A. Dahl: "rigorous analysis in a positivistic spirit can leave nothing more to the 'common good' than simply the set of subjective preferences that happen to be those of the observer who invokes the phrase." [61] Certainly the authors of V*oting* deny the existence of an objective common good. They do this by resorting, as Dahl does, to the customary social science practice of putting quotation marks around the term (or its various equivalents), indicating thereby that it cannot be used seriously in a scientific vocabulary (pp. 54, 84, 219, etc.). They do this, as we mentioned above, by accusing respondents, who claim to be guided by the common good when casting their ballots, of rationalizing. They do this by denying implicitly that there is a community capable of having a common good: "Towns like Elmira are *not* one community but many divergent ones . . ." (p. 131). They do this implicitly by asserting that voters are not guided by the common good when they cast their ballots.

If the "community interest" were in actuality the basis for political decision in our society, that would not necessarily mean that all men would have to agree: some could be right and others wrong, or some logical and others illogical, or some perceptive and other [sic] unperceptive. However, in that case, we could assume that political differences would distribute themselves at random through-

[61] "Political Theory: Truth and Consequences," *World Politics*, October 1958, p. 91.

out the society, that is, that they would not be correlated with basic social groupings. But they are [p. 54].[62]

Under these circumstances it would be decidedly "unscientific" for them to follow the examples of Tocqueville, Bryce, and Ostrogorski, three famous students of American politics who did their work before the advent of modern social science. These earlier observers would not have hesitated to ask a respondent why he thought Truman was "the best man running," or why he was for unions, or why he was "for the middle class and poor," or why his party was "good for the whole community." If the respondent mentioned political discussions that influenced his decision, these earlier investigators would have inquired into the nature of the discussion to discover the appeals made and arguments used, whether the voter was swayed by class interests or concern for the common good, whether his view of the common good was unduly influenced by his personal interest, and whether his understanding of the political situation was based on knowledge or ignorance. If voting behavior turned out to be habitual for most people, they would have wondered why the habit was created in the first place and why allegiance to a party is maintained in the face of, perhaps, changed circumstances. Such an analysis, if carried on intelligently, would have led to politically relevant results. But the modern social scientist rejects the criteria needed for such an analysis. His science does not permit evaluation, although, as we shall see, this does not prevent Berelson, Lazarsfeld, and McPhee from slipping in an occasional evaluation when necessary or convenient.

The authors of *Voting*, however, do not limit their defense of their methodology to a display of its scientific credentials and the consequent rejection of the idea of the common good. They are in fact led to attempt to provide a political defense of their methodological concern with the sub-political. The last chapter of *Voting* is given over to this attempt. Here the authors present a political theory of sorts aimed at providing, as Berelson says elsewhere, "a systematic statement in terms of which public opinion studies can be meaningfully organized." [63] This theory is thought to be superior to the older, "normative" theory because "political theory written with reference to practice has the advantage that its categories are the categories in which political

[62] This seems to be a gratuitous assumption. Why must we draw that conclusion? Can we not agree that of course the average voter's understanding of the common good is influenced by his place in society, and being thus influenced by the horizons imposed by his limited experience and associations, he tends to take a partial view, a view that is merely a reflection of the true interest of the whole? Whether every argument made by modern social science "in a positivistic spirit" to prove that there is no such thing as the common good or public interest is not equally destructive (but not more so) of the idea of a class or group (and ultimately an individual) interest, need not be discussed here. See below, pp. 202-203.

[63] Bernard Berelson, "Democratic Theory and Public Opinion," *The Public Opinion Quarterly*, Fall 1952, p. 330.

life really occurs" (*Voting*, p. 306).[64] Thus, they do not actually reject political theory as such, they merely reject an older kind of political theory in favor of a new and superior political theory. This means that the sharp distinction they sometimes speak of between the social theme and the political theme, and the sphere of empirical research and the sphere of exploring "the relevance, the implications, and the meaning of empirical facts" (p. 306),[65] cannot be maintained. Facts, as we said above, do not speak for themselves. The selection and interpretation of facts about voting behavior imply a political theory. The last chapter is an explicit defense of their political theory, which is, at the same time, a defense of their methodology.

The classical theorists of democracy, according to Berelson, Lazarsfeld, and McPhee, set down certain requirements of citizenship in a democratic regime: interest and participation in political affairs; a "capacity for and . . . practice of discussion"; and a knowledge of the issues, "what their history is, what the relevant facts are, what alternatives are proposed, what the party stands for, what the likely consequences are." The democratic citizen, futhermore, is "supposed to cast his vote on the basis of principle . . . with reference to standards not only of his own interest but of the common good as well." He "is expected to exercise rational judgment in coming to his voting decision." Finally, the population is supposed to be socially and politically homogeneous (pp. 307-309).

But Elmirans gave no evidence of sustained interest, many voted "without real involvement in the election," even party workers were not "typically motivated by . . . civic duty." There was "little true discussion between the candidates, little in the newspaper commentary, little between the voters and the official party representatives, some within the electorate." The citizen was not well informed on the issues in the campaign; he misperceived the political situation; his perception was "colored by emotional feeling." Many voted out of habit or for their groups, unthinkingly. In short, the authors of *Voting* conclude, people's decisions as consumers are more carefully calculated than their decisions as voting citizens (pp. 307-311).

One cannot be certain whether these conclusions (although they may be true) are meant to be taken seriously here. It is impossible to say that the voters are uninformed without some conception of what a voter ought to be informed about, just as it is impossible to say that there is little "true discussion" without knowing what a political discussion ought to be. (As we

[64] One of the most common prejudices among modern social scientists is that the political theorists of the past wrote without "reference to practice." It would be interesting to know who in their opinion belongs in this category. Moreover, it is a fact that a very large part (and that the scientifically "purest" part) of such studies as *Voting* are *not* written in terms of the "categories in which political life really occurs," but in terms of sub-political categories that are remote from, if not alien to, the practice of politics.

[65] Cf. Lasswell's distinction between "scientific political theory" and "political philosophy," below, pp. 228 ff.

pointed out above, the authors seldom bother to tell the reader what was actually said in the discussions that took place.) These assertions show again that the authors of *Voting*, despite their methodological commitment, are not altogether successful in suppressing the question of the common good; on some occasions they permit their common sense to break through the crust of their methodology.[66]

Nevertheless, a pre-"scientific" observer of politics would have counseled severe remedial measures or might even have despaired if his study revealed a situation similar to the one here described by the authors of *Voting*. They do neither. They do neither because if the "democratic system depended solely on the qualifications of the individual voter, then it seems remarkable that democracies have survived through the centuries." [67] They neither despair nor counsel severe remedial measures because the American democracy, despite the character of the American citizen whose decisions in front of the soap counter are said to be more carefully calculated than his decisions in the voting booth, is a healthy system, one that "survives and grows" (pp. 311, 312). It does not require the qualities prescribed by "traditional normative theory," and what it does require America possesses in abundance.

Berelson, writing in *The Public Opinion Quarterly*, tells us what he means by political health.

Does community interest refer to agreement on procedures, or to an outside criterion (and if so, what), or to the residual decision after the various self-interests have balanced themselves out, or to genuine concern for other groups, or to restraint upon self-interest, or to deviation from the predominant vote of one's group? The more one looks into the matter, the more it appears that one man's self-interest is another man's community interest, and that many people sincerely identify the one with the other. . . .

In a current study of opinion formation (the Elmira study), we concluded that it is more satisfactory to analyze this question in terms of the forces making for political cleavage and political consensus within the community. The health of a democratic order depends on achieving a nice balance between them: enough cleavage to stimulate debate and action, enough consensus to hold the society together even under strain.[68]

[66] Thus, they also refer to "the obvious political importance of elections" (p. vii); but their social science does not permit them to make this statement. The importance of neither voting nor the study of voting can be established by the scientific method—as this is understood in modern social science. The scientific method merely assures them that the answer to a question will be scientifically correct given certain conditions; it does not guarantee that the right questions will be asked or the important subjects studied. What is it that gives elections their "obvious political importance"? To answer this question, these social scientists would be required to engage in *political* discourse. See below, pp. 48 ff, 142 ff, 317 ff.

[67] Anyone with even a cursory acquaintance with history is forced to wonder what democracies they have in mind in this statement. Democracies have come into being for centuries, but how many of them have survived for centuries?

[68] Fall 1952, p. 328.

In *Voting* the point is made as follows:

Similarly there are required *social* consensus and cleavage—in effect, pluralism
—in politics. Such pluralism makes for enough consensus to hold the system together and enough cleavage to make it move. Too much consensus would be
deadening and restrictive of liberty; too much cleavage would be destructive of
the society as a whole [p. 318].[69]

With this as a background the authors go on to assert that classical democratic theory is in error in demanding too many qualities from the individual citizen; it overlooks that certain qualities, if present in the electorate
as a whole, will conduce to the public interest even if individual citizens are
unintelligent, disinterested, and unwilling to participate in politics. What is
decisive to political health is neither political institutions nor the individual
citizen, the chief objects of concern to former theorists, but certain "social"
characteristics that "form the atmosphere or the environment in which both
operate" (p. 313). Whereas the classical democratic theorists might have despaired at the picture of the democratic voter drawn by modern social science,
the authors of *Voting* find nothing incompatible between the American
electorate and a revised and reasonable understanding of the qualities needed
to constitute a healthy democracy. Disinterestedness, even apathy, are valuable if not carried to extremes; heterogeneity permits a balance between progress (defined merely as movement or change) and conservatism; neglect of
politics is not without value: "Change may come best from relaxation" (pp.
86, 318). It is interesting to note that there is nothing "scientific" or "empirical" about the way they arrive at this changed (and lowered) conception
of political health, yet it is on the basis of it that they draw this *decisive*
conclusion.

What is implicit throughout the book suddenly becomes explicit here in
the last chapter. It is unnecessary to consider the question, what is opinion?
It is unnecessary to evaluate the voters' explanations of their behavior. It is
unnecessary to pay attention to that human faculty that makes the generation
of dispositions possible. It is, in short, unnecessary and wrong to study voting
from the point of view of the common good as understood by classical democratic theory. Despite its incapacity to deal with such matters as these, indeed, precisely because of its avoidance of them, the methodology of *Voting*
cuts through to the conditions of a healthy democracy, truly and newly defined. This methodology permits them to describe voting behavior from the
point of view of the elements that really produce a healthy democracy, which
is defined as a balance between the "forces making for political cleavage and
political consensus." The healthy democracy, they say, is the consequence of
sociological (and irrational) forces, and consists in pluralism, because plural-

[69] For a critique of this "social" conception of pluralism see Burdick, "Political Theory
and the Voting Studies," *American Voting Behavior*, pp. 141-144.

ism makes "for enough consensus to hold the system together and enough cleavage to make it move." The classical theorists of democracy from "Mill to Locke" (!) (p. 323), to whom we might otherwise have looked for guidance in our study of politics, are refuted.

Unfortunately, it is difficult to be certain whom the authors of Voting regard as a theorist of democracy, because, except in the awkward fashion indicated above, they fail to specify the men whose teachings they claim to have refuted. This is to be regretted especially because the democratic credentials of some of these theorists are much disputed, for example, in the case of Rousseau. But we know that the question to which Rousseau directs his attention is one that all classical democratic theorists deal with; and if Rousseau teaches that democracy requires racial, economic, and religious homogeneity,[70] it is not sufficient merely to assert that a healthy democracy, even of the "moving cohesiveness" type, does not require racial, economic, and religious homogeneity. Before we would be justified in discarding Rousseau's teachings, it would be—or one might think it would be—necessary to show that this understanding of political health is superior to Rousseau's, or that we have reached the state where homogeneity is no longer so important to a healthy democracy.

No discussion of this question is to be found in Voting, yet the question concerns the very possibility of a profoundly heterogeneous but healthy democracy. Have the problems of heterogeneity been solved only at the price of the conformism and uniformity of a mass technological society? How important is religion in the United States? What will be the effect of the potentially explosive racial differences, which will probably remain important for some time? To what extent is the wealth that is the product of our technological society responsible for the apathy that mitigates the dangers of heterogeneities? If the apathy we need is the result of the wealth, what, if anything, had to be sacrificed in order to attain the wealth and what is the relation of the sacrificed element to a healthy democracy?[71] In the light of the evidence of a lack of public spirit in the United States, was Rousseau writing utter nonsense when he wrote:

It is through the hustle of commerce and the arts, through the greedy self-interest of profit, and through softness and love of amenities that personal services are replaced by money payments [and] as soon as public service ceases to be the chief business of the citizens and they would rather serve with their money than with their persons, the State is not far from its fall.[72]

[70] Rousseau, The Social Contract, iii, 4; iv, 8.
[71] See Joseph Cropsey, Polity and Economy: An Interpretation of the Principles of Adam Smith (The Hague: Martinus Nijhoff, 1957), esp. pp. 88 ff.
[72] The Social Contract, iii, 15. Cf. "A Reporter at Large," The New Yorker, October 26, 1957, pp. 114-169.

And what is the effect of the wealth (needed for the apathy needed to mitigate the heterogeneities) on religion, and what is the relation of religion to a healthy democracy? [73] None of these questions is even raised in the last chapter in *Voting*. Yet we are assured that the American democracy is healthy. No doubt instability and stagnation are to be avoided if possible, and perhaps pluralism is superior to the unity advocated by such men as Rousseau, but this too requires an argument it does not get in *Voting*.

To refute the teachings of John Stuart Mill, to continue, is it really sufficient to argue that what Mill and others had to say "is defective . . . in its concentration on the *individual citizen* [while ignoring] certain collective properties that reside in the electorate as a whole . . ."? Berelson, Lazarsfeld, and McPhee assert that the actual political system, even without the traditionally prescribed qualities—or perhaps because of the lack of these qualities —not only continues to work, but does so "perhaps even more vigorously and effectively than ever" (p. 312). But is it not essential before dismissing the old teaching, to wonder why someone like Mill would disagree? Consider what Mill had to say about voting:

But the exercise of any political function, either as an elector or as a representative, is power over others. Those who say that the suffrage is not a trust but a right will scarcely accept the conclusions to which their doctrine leads. If it is a right, if it belongs to the voter for his own sake, on what ground can we blame him for selling it, or using it to recommend himself to any one whom it is his interest to please? . . . His vote is not a thing in which he has an option; it has no more to do with his personal wishes than the verdict of a juryman. It is strictly a matter of duty; he is bound to give it according to his best and most conscientious opinion of the public good. Whoever has any other idea of it is unfit to have the suffrage; its effect on him is to pervert, not to elevate his mind. Instead of opening his heart to an exalted patriotism and the obligation of public duty, it awakens and nourishes in him the disposition to use a public function for his own interest, pleasure, or caprice; the same feelings and purposes, on a humbler scale, which actuate a despot and oppressor. [74]

What is the understanding of political health implicit in these remarks on voting? Consider whether, on the basis of the following excerpts, Mill would

---

[73] *The Social Contract*, iv, 8. See also Washington's Farewell Address: "Of all the dispositions and habits which lead to political prosperity, religion and morality are indispensable supports. In vain would that man claim the tribute of patriotism who should labor to subvert these great pillars of human happiness, these firmest props of the duties of men and citizens. The mere politician, equally with the pious man, ought to respect and to cherish them. A volume could not trace all their connections with private and public felicity. . . . And let us with caution indulge the supposition that morality can be maintained without religion. Whatever may be conceded to the influence of refined education on minds of peculiar structure, reason and experience both forbid us to expect that national morality can prevail in exclusion of religious principle."

[74] J. S. Mill, *Considerations on Representative Government* (*On Liberty and Considerations on Representative Government*), (Oxford: Basil Blackwell, 1948), pp. 231-232.

agree to the understanding of a healthy democracy as a moving cohesiveness.

[Except under representative government] the public at large remain without information and without interest on all the greater matters of practice; or, if they have any knowledge of them, it is but a *dilettante* knowledge, like that which people have of the mechanical arts who have never handled a tool. Nor is it only in their intelligence that they suffer. Their moral capacities are equally stunted. . . . Let a person have nothing to do for his country, and he will not care for it. . . . Religion remains: and here at least, it may be thought, is an agency that may be relied on for lifting men's eyes and minds above the dust at their feet. But religion, even supposing it to escape perversion for the purposes of despotism, ceases in these circumstances to be a social concern, and narrows into a personal affair between an individual and his Maker, in which the issue at stake is but his private salvation. Religion in this shape is quite consistent with the most selfish and contracted egoism, and identifies the votary as little in feeling with the rest of his kind as sensuality itself.[75]

Mill argues that the active character is superior to the passive, because it is the active character that promotes the "three varieties of mental excellence, intellectual, practical, and moral"; and, because of "the influence of the form of government upon character," this becomes an argument in favor of representative government. Had they read Mill with even a modicum of care, the authors of *Voting* would have learned that the emphasis of his argument is not on these excellences as prerequisites of representative government, but rather on representative government as a means of promoting these excellences! In addition, they might then have seen the distance separating a "moving cohesiveness" from Mill's "Ideally Best Polity."

It is of course possible, even likely, that our modern problems are not satisfactorily solved by such classical democratic theorists as Rousseau and Mill, and no one would argue that they merit close study merely on antiquarian grounds. But even the few examples given here are sufficient to show that they raised questions that are relevant, indeed crucial, to the discussion in the last chapter of *Voting*, and therefore to the whole enterprise. The authors' failure to take classical democratic theory seriously in their haste to suggest its "revision . . . by empirical sociology" (p. 322) is only an aspect of their failure even to begin a penetrating consideration of the problems of modern democracy. Ignoring these older thinkers and the questions they raise, the authors of *Voting* confine their discussion to trivialities and present conclusions that might very well be wholly false.[76]

---

[75] *Considerations on Representative Government*, pp. 137-138.
[76] Indeed, they do not seem to take seriously any writing on political theory. Their chapter begins with a reference to, and purports to take its bearings from, an article by Alfred Cobban entitled, "The Decline of Political Theory" (*Political Science Quarterly*, September 1953, pp. 321-337). They are only partly correct in saying that Cobban attributes this decline to the fact that modern theorists, unlike the theorists of the past, do not write with a practical purpose in mind, because they are not concerned with the "aims" of political

In an earlier chapter the authors flirt with another explanation of cleavage and consensus, and something of the mood (for it is impossible to put it more exactly) of that earlier discussion seems to have carried over into the last chapter. Addressing themselves to the question of "how the political system as a whole handles the resolution of issues," the authors suggest in Chapter 9 that issues have a characteristic "life history," moving from their introduction by a small vanguard through the "political gateway" where they hang in the balance, to their near-unanimous acceptance. Political cleavage turns on the issues at the "political gateway." The authors conclude that "to understand the process of cleavage on the issues, one must understand the broader historical trends on which the cleavage is based and of which the campaign issues are topical manifestations" (pp. 210-211). Yet in the final chapter we are instructed that political health is "enough consensus to hold the system together and enough cleavage to make it move," with no reference at all to these historical trends.

In the earlier discussion, in Chapter 9, the authors argued that as "events and the needs of society push such [specific] proposals into, through, and beyond the political gateway of decision, party dispositions facilitate or inhibit not so much the final decision as the speed of acceptance" (pp. 211-212). This suggests that the political theory of Voting depends upon a notion—a largely implicit and wholly unexplored notion—of "historical trends." However it may appear to the actors, political activity does not really affect the question of what is to be done, but only the question of when? The decisions themselves are determined by some historical process. As public housing and social security have passed through the gateway, so compulsory health insurance, new (Brannan-type) farm plans, and new controls on corporations (the authors' examples of issues not yet at the gateway) will do so, and political activity will determine only whether this is sooner or later.

If we examine the last chapter of Voting with this notion of "historical trends" in mind, the authors might be understood as arguing that a political system should (and that the American system does) adopt a posture that invites history to act upon it, not so suddenly as to do violence to the system and not so slowly as to fail to "adapt" altogether, but steadily following its determined course. Two points must be emphasized. First, it is impossible

---

society. Cobban also says: "If political theory has become generally disengaged from practice, and if this is one cause of its decline, it will be worth while asking why this has happened" (p. 332). And what does account for this disengagement, this theory filled with artificialities, dealing with "arbitrarily" chosen issues, and written in "various esoteric jargons"? Cobban says: "What I want to do is to suggest that modern political theory has largely ceased to be discussed in terms of what ought to be; and the reason, I believe, is that it has fallen under the influence of two modes of thought which have had a fatal effect on its ethical content. These, and they have come to dominate the modern mind, are history and science" (p. 333). Had they read Cobban with, again, even a modicum of care, they would have seen the inappropriateness of using him as they do.

to examine this theory, or even to say with any confidence that it is the one on which the authors rest, because we are provided with nothing but the barest, formal outline of what the theory is, in spite of the absolutely crucial character of the questions it raises for the whole study of voting.[77] Second, whether the basis of the authors' "revision" of classical democratic theory is some notion of historical trends or whether they finally rest (as they seem to do in Chapter 14) on nothing more than a moving cohesiveness, the revision is not made by "empirical political sociology," but by another political theory or theory of history. Either one of these theories serves the authors' purpose in this last chapter, because either justifies their approach to the study of voting. The significance of this chapter is missed if it is regarded as nothing more than an incidental essay in political theory, unconnected with the rest of the book. It is, on the contrary, the essential political ground on which is built their whole social psychological enterprise. Only if this ground is tenable can they argue, as they must, that our criticism (that their approach ignores the political in voting) is based on an outmoded notion of political health.

However, their own notion of "the health of a democratic order" would be more convincing if it were supported by reasonable argument—which they make no effort to supply—and if, when speaking of the "forces making for enough consensus to hold the system together and enough cleavage to make it move," they were to pay some attention to the character of the system cohering and the direction in which it is moving. It would also be more convincing if, when assuring us that the apathy, unintelligence, and heterogeneity in Elmira are actually conducive to political health, they were to do more than hint that the ability to deal with its political problems might have some relation to the health of a political system. The un-"scientific" student of politics would say that one way to measure American voting behavior today is by the requirements of survival in the face of the Soviet Union, the most urgent political fact of our time, and that a democracy is not healthy if incapable of adopting measures reasonably calculated to provide for the common defense.[78] He would argue that it makes a difference whether, when the United States is faced with the decision of whether to spend billions of dollars for missile development, the voter thinks only of

---

[77] Cf. below, Bentley (pp. 176, 183-184); Lasswell (pp. 242 ff).

[78] The authors are not entirely successful in suppressing questions of this kind, in spite of their conclusion that a discussion confining itself to political cleavage and consensus is "more satisfactory." When they wonder "how a democracy ever solves its political problems," they suggest that there are problems to be solved more or less well. When they assert that "somehow the system not only works on the most difficult and complex questions but often works with distinction" (p. 312), they suggest a standard of distinction beyond stability and change. When they assert that "too much consensus would be deadening and restrictive of liberty" (p. 318), they suggest that a healthy democracy has the substantive aim of protecting individual liberty.

the taxes he would have to pay to support such a program without regard to the requirements of defense. Not only do the authors of *Voting* deny this implicitly, and explicitly too when they say that to insist "at all strongly" that a citizen vote with reference to the common good is to make "an impossible demand" (p. 309), they assert such behavior to be unnecessary for a healthy democracy. Without it our democracy is better than ever. Still, the question is of critical importance. Can a healthy democracy be the consequence of merely sociological forces, depending in no way on citizens capable of rational thought and action? They assure us it can be and is. But this assurance is not supported with an argument. Instead, they introduce into their analysis at this point (and not by chance) what it does not require an Arthur Bentley to call a "spook." [79] "Where the rational citizen seems to abdicate," they conclude, "nevertheless angels seem to tread" (p. 311). Their healthy democracy cannot be preserved in any other way.

Suppose there was a voter—one of the authors of *Voting*, for example—who appreciated the virtues of this democracy and decided to vote with a view to its preservation, perhaps out of the fear that the angels, following the example of the rational citizen, might decide to abdicate too. How would such a voter proceed? His problem would be to vote in such a way as to maintain the balance between cleavage and consensus. This, of course, would depend on how others intend to vote. If the others think only of their selfish interests, and he knows the strength of these interests, he might be able to calculate how they are going to vote, then act accordingly; but this one vote would have very little effect in maintaining the pluralistic balance. On the other hand, to the extent that others think and act as he does, with a view to preserving the balance, it becomes difficult to know how they will (and therefore how he should) vote; in fact, the more citizens there are who try to vote with a view to the public interest (that is, with a view to preserving the balance), the more difficult such a vote becomes. The way out of this dilemma is a pre-election meeting (or meeting of *minds*) of all those who, whatever their substantive political ideas—left or right, labor or capital, farm or city—and whatever their positions on the issues—civil rights or anti-civil rights, a small and balanced budget or greater defense spending, federal aid to education or state independence of federal subventions—agree nevertheless to cast their ballots with a view only to maintaining the pluralistic balance.

Such a thing is not impossible in the real world, but it depends on factors that are not present in the world of Berelson, Lazarsfeld, and McPhee. It depends on a community of interest brought into being not by a similarity of social characteristics or psychological drives, but by the willingness of some members of the community to forego their narrow selfish interests in order to protect the broader community interest. Now even if one were to say that

[79] See below, p. 157.

such voters would be foregoing merely a short-range selfish interest in order to protect a long-range selfish interest, the decisive thing is that they would have to *think* about this, they would have to calculate, they would have to act on the basis of a rational consideration of the whole political (or, as the authors of *Voting* would say, social) situation. In the absence of the angels, the preservation of the healthy democracy would depend on a community of rational citizens, willing to forego voting on the basis of the substantive political issues in order to preserve the balance between cleavage and consensus. Since, according to the authors of *Voting*, the rational citizen seems to have abdicated and, therefore, plays no part in keeping the democracy healthy; since the authors implicitly deny the existence of citizens, or perhaps one should say persons, capable of voting on any basis other than that of their selfish class interest; since in fact one premise of this kind of research is the impossibility of rational action, they are driven to the suggestion of the band of angels. The democracy is maintained in health by some inexplicable ghostly agency, providentially guarding the selfish, blind citizenry from any harm. Readers of *The Governmental Process* will recall that David Truman solves the same problem with a spook labelled "potential groups." [80]

According to *Voting*, it does not matter whether the political campaign is characterized by "true discussion." It does not matter whether the party workers are motivated by civic duty. It does not matter whether social groups are inactive in the campaign. It does not matter whether citizens have any interest in the election or whether they are ignorant of the issues. It does not matter whether there are political leaders or merely junction points in a brainless system. No part of the system is critical (except perhaps the angels?); no part is any closer to the *reason* for the system than any other part; no part is governing. Our institutions do not do what they are supposed to do according to the older understanding of politics, our citizens lack the qualities they are supposed to have, but we have a healthy democracy nevertheless: we move and we cohere.[81]

Indeed, despite their reference to "the obvious political importance of elections" (which must be seen as one of their common-sensible asides), if it does not make any difference how people vote, are we entitled to conclude that for Berelson, Lazarsfeld, and McPhee voting itself is not important? Rossi tells us that Lazarsfeld began studying voting not because he thought it was important, but because he could not get the money for a panel study of consumer preferences. "Despairing of obtaining financial support for a panel study of consumer preferences, Lazarsfeld hit upon the idea of studying the impact of a presidential campaign upon a panel of voters. . . . With this less commercial focus, financial support was obtained from the Rockefeller

[80] David B. Truman, *The Governmental Process: Political Interests and Public Opinion* (New York: Alfred A. Knopf, Inc., 1951), ch. 16.
[81] Cf. the assumption of order underlying Bentley's group analysis, below, pp. 217-224.

Foundation for a panel study of the 1940 presidential campaign" (*American Voting Behavior*, pp. 15-16).[82] It would be of interest to learn whether the authors of *Voting* reject the implications of this revealing, but not surprising, disclosure.

CONCLUSION

Democratic elections are one way of deciding the political question of who should rule and of what should be the character of that rule. One test of an electoral system is the extent to which it is democratic, that is, the extent to which everyone is permitted to participate in the choice. Another test, and perhaps the decisive one, is the quality of the men elected to office, for the primary purpose of elections is to choose these men; and the quality of the men chosen depends, in part, on the individual voters who choose them. The study of voting behavior is altogether proper, provided the purpose of voting is not forgotten in the formulation of the questions asked in the study.

Why people vote as they do, or what motivates the voters, is a question related to the purpose of voting. Asking it might enable the political scientist to determine the extent to which voters act with a view to the common good and the extent to which they act intelligently. The simplest way of determining why people vote as they do would be to ask them directly, but to do this, and to pursue the question to the point where it would be possible to distinguish a genuine from a spurious concern for the common good, would pose problems the modern social scientist feels he must avoid. His response is to ask questions the respondents can, and perhaps do, answer accurately (such as their age, sex, education, religion, and voting choice) and to report their answers with statistical exactitude. The result is the sacrifice of political relevance on the altar of methodology. The questions asked and pursued are determined by the limits of the scientific method rather than by the subject matter, which is voting or, more specifically, the purpose of voting. They prefer exact, statistical answers to less exact, politically relevant answers. As Morton Grodzins has said, "The scientist who defines his technique first and his problem second has placed second things first." [83]

Are voters intelligent, do they act wisely, do they make a genuine effort to evaluate candidates and their stands on issues in terms of what is required by the political situation? Intelligent observers of the political scene, here and elsewhere, have despaired at the lack of intelligence and the extent of selfish-

[82] See also Brodbeck, *American Voting Behavior*, p. 123: "It is an 'accident' that Professor Lazarsfeld chose to study these questions in terms of voting decisions. They could have been answered in many other areas of applied social science."

[83] *Ethics*, April 1959, p. 200. The self-imposed restraints of the psychologically oriented social scientist are of a different kind, but the effect is the same. He may ask his subject why he votes as he does, but he does not take the reply seriously, using it instead as a vehicle into the subject's unconscious motivations.

ness; the authors of Voting claim to confirm this by showing, for example, the extent of ignorance on issues, but they do not despair because of their peculiar notion of political health. Now, it may be true that the average voter is even ignorant of how the presidential candidates stand on the issues, but before we can draw conclusions from this information we have to know from their own lips why they voted as they did, for they may have voted for reasons remote from the particular issues discussed by the candidates. Before we could condemn this, we should have to decide whether the issues on which the voters were misinformed were the important issues in the election, whatever their status in the campaign. For example, it is doubtful that price control and the Taft-Hartley Act were as important in the 1948 election as the authors of Voting claim they were. Union officials described the latter as a "slave-labor act," but perhaps the mass membership of the unions recognized this for the gross exaggeration it was. This is suggested by Senator Taft's huge plurality in his re-election to the Senate in 1950. Moreover, as the authors themselves say at one point, "the political genius of the citizenry may reside less in how well they can judge public policy than in how well they can judge the people who advise them how to judge policy" (p. 109). Even a relatively high degree of ignorance regarding the particular policy questions facing the country may be offset if the citizens show good sense in choosing whom to trust, both in their primary groups and in the national government.[84]

Are we told in defense of these voting studies that whereas previously our knowledge of the determinants of voting was based at best on the shrewd guesses of intelligent observers, we now have, or will have, scientific knowledge of these determinants? We have no such thing. The Voter Decides tells us that Eisenhower was elected in 1952 because a large number of former Democrats voted for him, and they voted for him because they were attracted by him, or oriented "toward" him. Voting tells us that "intentions supported by . . . social surroundings are more predictably carried out than are intentions lacking such support." But the determinants of voting are by no means identified precisely; what is known is that a host of factors are related to vote. In the words of Avery Leiserson: "there are any number of indices of group affiliation in the sense of interpersonal association and contact, as well as subjective identification and class consciousness, that are correlated with political attitudes." [85]

Are we told that science is a slow incremental process, and that slowly

---

[84] "Deciding who should constitute the government in power is a consideration distinct from determining what should be the appropriate policy on the many major issues that public opinion and legislative judgment must decide during any one party's tenure of office." Avery Leiserson, Parties and Politics: An Institutional and Behavioral Approach (New York: Alfred A. Knopf, Inc., 1958), p. 163.

[85] Parties and Politics, p. 153.

there will emerge from study after study the real regularities underlying voting behavior? In a review of what had been discovered about voting behavior, four social scientists, including Professor Lazarsfeld, wrote a few years ago:

the success of a panel study depends largely upon the ingenuity the investigator uses in introducing relevant variables into his time series. It cannot be said that we have at the present time a general theory from which the most relevant variables can be deduced.[86]

Since that statement was written, a group of researchers at the Michigan Survey Research Center has succeeded in developing a general theory, based on the rediscovery (by empirical political science, at least) of the fact that political behavior is a function of political opinion, and that political opinion is a function of political events and problems.[87] Whether empirical political science generally will proceed further along these lines to deduce the "relevant variables" from this "general theory," remains to be seen.

There is a shocking contrast between the importance, and today, the urgency of political problems and the modern social scientists' interest in voting behavior. What in these studies could possibly justify the time, energy, and enormous sums of money consumed in their making? Even assuming their findings to be accurate, of what political interest are they? Are we told that because of these studies we now have knowledge of the gap between older democratic theory and practice? As we have seen, Voting does not present an adequate description of practice—it does not demonstrate, for example, that there was an absence of "true discussion." But assuming that we do have some knowledge of the gap between theory and practice that was formerly hidden, what follows from this discovery? Do we, following Berelson, Lazarsfeld, and McPhee, revise our goals downward by ignoring requirements of a safe and sound political order? Or, are we not still required to try to discover the goals and requirements of political life and then to recommend those measures that can be said reasonably to conduce to these goals and fulfill these requirements?

Lazarsfeld's interest in voting behavior was the result of an accident—his inability to get funds for a study of consumer preference. The political scientist can only hope that the time has not yet come when there is no significant difference between voting and the purchase of goods to be consumed by the purchaser alone and when Madison Avenue can sell votes as it sells cosmetics. But he is obliged to wonder about the factors that might contribute to such a catastrophe.

[86] *Handbook of Social Psychology*, vol. 2, p. 1163.
[87] See appendix to this chapter, pp. 58 ff.

APPENDIX: The American Voter

THE FOREGOING analysis of voting studies was written before the appearance of a new work from the Michigan Survey Research Center, *The American Voter*.[88] The intent of this work and its general approach are similar to those of *The Voter Decides*, and its merit consists in the extent to which it is informed by political considerations and to which it carries the search for causative factors.

Instead of being content to identify "psychological" attitudes, similar to those in *The Voter Decides*—and which Rossi criticized as being largely tautological—the authors of *The American Voter* look upon the six "psychological" attitudes [89] or "attitude forces" as "intervening variables linking behavior with a host of antecedent factors" (p. 120). That is, they recognize that voting choice is governed by what we have called political opinion, and they seek to discover the antecedent causes of this opinion, which they hope to state in the form of deep-seated laws of social behavior. Though their purpose is the same as that of Berelson, Lazarsfeld, and McPhee, they are critical of the "social approach" to the study of voting behavior because of the ephemeral character of its findings, among other reasons.

A correlation between the fact of being a Negro and the casting of a Democratic ballot gives us interesting information, yet information pitched at a low level of abstraction. Generalizations of this sort tend to fall by the wayside with the passage of sufficient time, if not reformulated in more general terms. In the case of Negroes, for example, there is evidence to indicate that not more than a decade or two ago the relationship was reversed, with Negroes tending to favor the Republican Party. And it seems entirely plausible that the relationship might become reversed again in the fairly near future, without upsetting any very deep-seated "laws" of social behavior.

Such laws we presume to exist, and with proper phrasing they should not only outlast reversals of voting pattern but should predict them [pp. 36-37].

The question concerns the character of these laws and whether they will

[88] Angus Campbell, Philip E. Converse, Warren E. Miller, and Donald E. Stokes, *The American Voter* (New York: John Wiley and Sons, Inc., 1960).
[89] "In the elections of 1952 and 1956 the elements of politics that seemed most clearly to be objects of popular attitude were these: the personal attributes of Stevenson; the personal attributes of Eisenhower; the groups involved in politics and the questions of group interest affecting them; the issues of domestic policy; the issues of foreign policy; and the comparative record of the two parties in managing the affairs of government. We have conceived evaluative orientations toward these classes of things as six dimensions of partisan attitude" (p. 67).

provide an understanding of voting behavior in any way superior to the understanding possessed by any intelligent observer.

The authors of *The American Voter* use the figure of a funnel to illustrate the pattern of the factors influencing the vote decision. The axis of the funnel represents the time dimension, with the narrow stem being the election itself.

Events are conceived to follow each other in a converging sequence of causal chains, moving from the mouth to the stem of the funnel. The funnel shape is a logical product of the explanatory task chosen. Most of the complex events in the funnel occur as a result of multiple prior causes. Each such event is, in its turn, responsible for multiple effects as well, but our focus of interests narrows as we approach the dependent behavior. We progressively eliminate those effects that do not continue to have relevance for the political act. Since we are forced to take all partial causes as relevant at any juncture, relevant effects are therefore many fewer in number than relevant causes. The result is a convergence effect [p. 24].

The "field" of the six "psychological forces" is looked upon as existing in a plane drawn at right angles to the axis and intersecting it just prior to the point at the stem representing the election. The factors responsible for these psychological forces are found in the "political core" that runs back along the axis, as well as in the "non-political" conditions forming a "shell around this political core." This is partially summarized in a statement at the end of the book: "Taking the individual's voting act as a starting point, we have moved backward in time and outward from political influences to trace the intricate pattern of causality leading to behavior at the polls" (p. 521).

The non-political conditions that form a shell around the political core, or "the social and economic elements in the causal nexus," are investigated directly in the seven chapters constituting the fourth section of the book. Chapter 15, entitled, "Agrarian Political Behavior," to cite one example chosen more or less at random, demonstrates that farmers are less involved than urban workers in group activities and have, therefore, fewer contacts with political groups, with the result that they are psychologically freer to respond directly to economic conditions and to " 'vote the rascals out.' " [90] Whatever the influence of the non-political elements on initial party choice, or however much a knowledge of social processes may add to an understanding of political behavior, "in building [their] metaphor of the causal funnel," the authors stress the importance, not of the conditions found in the "shell" around the core, but "of [the] 'political core' running backward in time, which more often than not provides the clearest explanation of current behavior" (p. 292). It is to their discussion of this political core that we shall direct our attention.

[90] Another result of this investigation is the discovery of evidence to support the hypothesis that "*the higher the identification of the individual with the group, the higher the probability that he will think and behave in ways which distinguish members of his group from non-members*" (p. 307). On "identification," see below, pp. 93-95; 130-132.

The strongest of the antecedent factors to be found in the political core of the funnel, and one highly correlated with each of the six attitudes constituting the "field of psychological forces," is partisan loyalty: "Few factors are of greater importance for our national elections than the lasting attachment of tens of millions of Americans to one of the parties" (p. 121). In fact, "prior party attachments form the great watershed for public reaction to current political events."

With the examination of this phenomenon in Section III it was natural to ask what conditions lead to the formation of partisan allegiances *initially*. The instrumental character of the political system would suggest that if we trace a party commitment deep enough into the past, we must sooner or later encounter recognizeable "beginnings," and that these beginnings are likely to involve pressures arising outside the political order as narrowly defined [p. 292].

They then probe the causal funnel for the beginnings of partisan allegiances, and these beginnings, they suggest, are unpolitical, at least as this is narrowly defined.

But the authors' understanding of political is so narrow that one wonders whether politics exists at all for them. They say, for instance, that the "act of voting is not an end in itself; rather, it is a choice of means toward other ends [and more] often than not, these ends concern facets of human experience that are at core non-political, involving problems of economic security, the disruptions of war, rights of minorities, the distribution of social status, and the like" (p. 118). But if these are not political problems, what are? Certainly the events they identify as the "beginnings" of partisan loyalties have always been thought of as political. For example, we find here that it was the "passage of the Kansas-Nebraska Act in 1854" that led to the "violent reaction in the East and Midwest" and to "the creation of the Republican Party"; then the "Free Soil movement . . . and the Homestead Act of 1862 created a resource of rural Republican strength throughout the Northern and Western areas. Within a short period the political contours of the nation had been drastically reshaped [and the] distribution of partisan attachments in the nation today, a century after the Civil War, follows the same regional lines laid down at that time" (p. 152).

Similarly, "the greatest economic catastrophe in American history" gave rise to some persistent party loyalties: "Judging from what we know about party identification in the 1950's and from such insights as we can derive from the election returns of the earlier period, we can hardly doubt that the decade of the Great Depression saw a profound reorientation of political partisanship." As for the party attachments of various minority groups, we are told that the strongly Democratic character of the Jewish vote "appears to be largely a consequence of the Depression and subsequent events during the Roosevelt period [such as] the rise of the Nazi dictatorship in Germany and the opposition of the Roosevelt Administration to it. . . ." The former attachment of Negroes to the Republican party was "a consequence, of course, of the Civil War [but it] is impossible to know whether the shift of Negro allegiances to the Democratic standard . . . occurred as the reactions of individual Negroes to the personalities and events of the times or as a mass movement resulting largely from the mobilization of Negro sentiment by an articulate leadership" (pp. 156-160).

Surely, these beginnings of partisan loyalty do *not* lie "outside the political order" as properly and popularly and customarily defined. Indeed, the authors may not mean to be understood as regarding them as non-political, despite their reference to such things as civil rights and the disruptions of war as "at core non-political." When they write that the beginnings of partisan loyalty "are likely to involve pressures arising outside the political order as narrowly defined," they may mean that they can be traced to these great political events but that they also "involve" other pressures. At any rate, the reader cannot help being struck by the familiarity of their explanation.

Like *Voting, The American Voter* shifts its attention in its last chapter from the causes of voting behavior to its consequences. The superficiality of the electorate's understanding of "concrete policy alternatives" accounts for the difficulty in interpreting a national election "in terms of a policy mandate." This means that public officials are given great freedom in framing the policies of government, limited by the pressures exerted by politically active groups, not by the electorate as a whole as such. (Still, one would suppose that the extent and direction of this limitation depend on the character of the President chosen by the electorate as a whole.) What the electorate does express in an election is broad mandate, such as the one to Eisenhower in 1952 "to produce a solution" to the Korean War (pp. 544, 546).[91] And "why is it that the party vote oscillates about an equal division over time rather than developing a persistent, and perhaps increasing, margin for a majority party?" Various factors are said to be at work here, but the authors discuss one that arises out of their study: "the party division of the vote is most likely to be *changed* by a negative public reaction to the record of the party in power." Thus, the majority party, "once it is in office, will not continue to accrue electoral strength; it may preserve for a time its electoral majority, but the next marked *change* in the party vote will issue from a negative response of the electorate to some aspect of the party's conduct in office, a response that tends to return the minority party to power" (p. 554). As the authors recognize, this answer is not sufficient, but it is surely superior to the explanations in *Voting*, precisely because it is a political explanation.[92]

Thus, if the Michigan Survey Research Center continues its work along

[91] See also Aristotle, *Politics*, 1282 a8-24.
[92] See above, pp. 17-18.

the lines of *The American Voter*, we can expect the "deep-seated 'laws' of social behavior" that are finally discovered to involve factors that, essentially, are political and, however they might be designated by associates of the Center, have always been considered to be political. So much is almost conceded by our authors: "As we have pushed behind the initial attitudes supporting the vote decision we have become impressed by the importance of antecedents that must be conceived in political terms" (p. 291).[93] The importance of this rediscovery of the political by empirical political science should not be minimized, for it provides the opportunity for a new beginning, a beginning that could lead to valuable studies of the politics of mid-twentieth-century America.

[93] "Even here, however, the primary antecedent remains political. For the most potent factor differentiating responses [to a presidential candidate] is not economic status, social milieu, or variation in deep-seated temperament, but quite simply the political party, which more often than not has been espoused years before the candidate takes up a position as an object in the psychological field" (p. 292).

II

THE SCIENCE OF ADMINISTRATION

Herbert A. Simon

by HERBERT J. STORING

THE MOST significant recent contributions to the study of administration have undoubtedly been made by Herbert A. Simon. He was one of the first to popularize the vocabulary of decision-making which, it is scarcely an exaggeration to say, is the native tongue of a growing body of students. If the approach to administrative problems which this vocabulary is intended to facilitate has not yet replaced the traditional one, it seems likely to dominate the field for many years. One of Simon's earliest books, *Administrative Behavior*, will provide the chief focus of this essay.[1] Besides being his most widely read and influential book, it is still the best comprehensive presentation of his theory; and it contains, at least in germinal form, almost every one of the problems to which his later writings are devoted. It has recently been reconsidered by its author and found to be essentially sound. It is, however, skeletal or tentative in some important respects, and it will be necessary to make frequent reference to other works in what is by now an immense body of writing.

THE VOCABULARY OF DECISION-MAKING

Simon's early work exhibits the concern of an intelligent citizen with good government, particularly municipal government. In 1938, for example, he and Clarence Ridley argued that somehow, "whether by reason or by chance," the amount of municipal government expenditure and its allocation must be determined; and they aimed to show how it could be done reasonably.[2] The cry of the previous generation of reformers had been for honesty, but it was time to develop another criterion, namely, efficiency. Ridley and Simon defined this as "the ratio of the effects actually obtained with the available resources to the maximum effects possible with the available resources." "In its broadest terms, [the concept of efficiency] is scientific method applied to government." The method was fairly easy to apply to private business (whence it was taken), but its application to government required some substitute for the profit-loss criterion. Simon and Ridley thought that this could be found by stating the goals of public organizations in such a way that degrees of

[1] *Administrative Behavior, A Study of Decision-Making Processes in Administrative Organization*, 2d ed. (New York: The Macmillan Company, 1957). The second edition, which will be cited here, is identical with the first (published in 1947) except for the addition of a new introduction (pp. ix-xxxix).
[2] "The Criterion of Efficiency," *The Annals of the American Academy of Political and Social Science*, September 1938, pp. 20-25.

achievement could be measured accurately and objectively. It was emphasized that these new standards of measurement were intended to be not merely "theoretical concepts devised by academicians" or "playthings for statisticians," but "practical tools by means of which practical legislators and administrators can meet the practical need of choosing between alternative courses of action." This practical political goal was, however, an extremely difficult one to achieve, even in dealing with such relatively simple questions as the most efficient case loads for welfare workers,[3] and Simon was led into deeper theoretical considerations.

Simon has recently described how his and Ridley's original goal, "to substitute rational decisions for . . . snap judgments" in municipal government, led him to search for theoretical guidance.

When I attempted twenty years ago to find answers to some questions of municipal organization—e.g., whether a recreation department should be administered by the school board or the city government, or how the city planning function should be organized . . . —I discovered that no theory existed that could provide the answers, and I was forced into an analysis of the ways in which organization affects human choice. Finding no better answers to this new stratum of questions, I thought it necessary to reexamine the theory of rational decision-making. The latter task required me, in turn, to settle in my own mind some basic problems of logic [*Administrative Behavior*, pp. xiii-xiv].

There was a body of administrative theory available, and there were purportedly scientific principles of administration which were regarded by many as useful if not yet definitive. But Simon found that these "principles" were essentially useless as they stood (*Administrative Behavior*, ch. 2).[4] Each of them confronted another which was of equal status but incompatible with it, and there was nothing in the theory to indicate which was applicable. For example, efficiency was supposed to be increased by limiting an administrator's "span of control"; on the other hand, efficiency was supposed to be increased by keeping the number of hierarchical levels to a minimum. There was no way of knowing which of these suppositions was to prevail in any particular situation. The principles turned out to be merely proverbs, the theory nothing but a more or less systematic summary of crude homely wisdom.

Although the analysis to which Simon subjects his forebears is not beyond criticism, there can be no doubt that he is right in his main conclusion that

[3] See Clarence E. Ridley and Herbert A. Simon, *Measuring Municipal Activities* (Chicago: The International City Managers' Association, 1938); Herbert A. Simon, *et al.*, *Determining Work Loads for Professional Staff in a Public Welfare Agency* (Berkeley: University of California, Bureau of Public Administration, 1941).
[4] For an exposition of these "principles" Simon refers the reader to Luther Gulick and L. Urwick (eds.), *Papers on the Science of Administration* (New York: Institute of Public Administration, Columbia University, 1937), and L. Urwick, *The Elements of Administration* (New York: Harper & Brothers, 1945).

these "principles" of administration were proverbial and unscientific.[5] There was no conceptual framework within which these proverbs might find their measure, and that is what Simon sought to provide in *Administrative Behavior*. This book grew out of its author's "conviction that we do not yet have, in this field, adequate linguistic and conceptual tools for realistically and significantly describing even a simple administrative organization—describing it, that is, in a way that will provide the basis for scientific analysis of the effectiveness of its structure and operation" (p. xlv). Every major question arising out of Simon's writings is implicit in this remark. Note especially that the notion of "effectiveness" is basic to the whole enterprise as here described: we need conceptual tools in order to describe administration "realistically and significantly"; description is realistic and significant if it can provide the basis for *scientific* analysis, and particularly scientific analysis of *effectiveness*. Simon's intention is not to provide "principles" of administration or even a "theory of administration," but a set of concepts or tools for describing "in words, exactly how an administrative organization looks and exactly how it works." "If any 'theory' is involved, it is that decision-making is the heart of administration, and that the vocabulary of administrative theory must be derived from the logic and psychology of human choice" (pp. xlv-xlvi).[6]

"Administration," we are told, "is ordinarily discussed as the art of 'getting things done.'" Simon directs our attention, instead, to decisions about doing. How do organizations decide what is to be done? More particularly, how is the behavior of the operative employee influenced within and by the organization? The central word in the new vocabulary is "decision" or "choice" or "selection" (the words are used synonymously), and Simon is interested in whole series of decisions culminating in the decision of the operative employee to behave in a certain way. Though this decision-making theory is to be the basis for the scientific reconstruction of our everyday vocabulary, it makes use of concepts which are, at first, quite familiar. We can see im-

[5] In criticizing the concept of "unity of command" as held by Luther Gulick, for example, Simon gives a definition of authority which is then used to demolish Gulick's ideas (*Administrative Behavior*, pp. 22-26). Whatever the merits of Simon's definition (see below, pp. 132-142.) and however guilty Gulick may be for not providing one of his own, that definition does not convey what *Gulick* means by authority. Again, Simon says: "Administrative efficiency is supposed to increase with an increase in specialization. But is this intended to mean that *any* increase in specialization will increase efficiency?" (p. 21) There is no reference, but the guilty party again appears to be Gulick who, however, does not unqualifiedly assert the former and explicitly warns that he does not mean the latter. See his "Notes on the Theory of Organization," *Papers on the Science of Administration*, pp. 4-5.

[6] Due perhaps to an extreme modesty, Simon is not altogether clear about whether or not *Administrative Behavior* presents a "theory of administration." (Cf., for example, pp. 61, 66, 240.) He is right in disclaiming theory as his predecessors conceived it— *Administrative Behavior* does not purport to solve administrative problems but to provide a way of talking about them—but the definition of words and discussion of how to use them involves the most profound theoretical questions.

mediately the sense of talking about administration in terms of decisions, though in common language we might distinguish between selection, choice, and decision; and we have no difficulty accepting the proposition that administrative study involves the description of how organizations decide what is to be done. Nor are we startled by the proposition that "a general theory of administration must include principles of organization that will insure correct decision-making, just as it must include principles that will insure effective action" (p. 1). Naturally we want to be able to describe decisions in such a way that we can distinguish between better and worse ones, though we may doubt that any theory can insure correct decision-making and effective action. The decision is not yet the basic unit, according to Simon, for it is but the consequence of certain premises.[7] These premises behind choice are of two kinds, value premises and factual premises; and here the language of common sense and the language of science begin to diverge. Simon takes pains to point out that the fact-value distinction is not the same as the traditional distinction between policy and administration, though there is a connection. Every decision, no matter how low it occurs in the administrative hierarchy, has its value premises, and every decision has its factual premises. These components of decision can rarely be separated in practice, but the distinction is crucial for purposes of analysis.

We are possessed now of the primary vocabulary needed to describe human behavior in organizations. We see a complex system of decisions, each of which may provide premises for decisions taken elsewhere in the organization, until they issue in the behavior of the operative employee. We observe that there are various ways of translating decisions taken at one place in the organization into premises for choice elsewhere—such as the exercise of authority, or the giving of advice, or the provision of training. We also see that not all premises of decision come from the formal hierarchy; informal groups, for example, are likely to provide many of the premises for decisions taken within organizations. Indeed some of the most important premises of decisions, such as notions of honesty and fair play, professional standards of performance, and commitments to broad social objectives, do not originate in the organization at all but in a much wider context. Thinking about organization in this way leads us to an appreciation of the intricacy of the

[7] There is some disagreement about whether the basic unit of analysis in *Administrative Behavior* is the "decision" (as Banfield contends and as Waldo assumed) or the "premise of decision" (as Simon now emphatically asserts). The prevailing use in *Administrative Behavior* supports Simon; but there is unquestionably confusion of language. The fact that two scholars of stature could have been misled on such a fundamental matter in a book which has as its chief purpose the construction of a clear and precise vocabulary is not without significance. See Dwight Waldo, "Development of Theory of Democratic Administration" and "Replies and Comments," *American Political Science Review*, March 1952, p. 97, and June 1952, pp. 494-495, 503; Edward C. Banfield, 'The Decision-Making Schema," and Herbert A. Simon, " 'The Decision-Making Schema': A Reply," *Public Administration Review*, Autumn, 1957, p. 284, n. 5, and Winter 1958, p. 62.

background of any decision and to an understanding of how better decisions might be made. We may, for example, identify obstacles in the way of communicating decisions from one place to another and consider more effective means of communication. By thus analyzing the decision-making process into its elements, students may better understand administration, legislators may choose among alternatives more wisely, and administrators may achieve correct decisions.

THE LOGIC OF HUMAN CHOICE: CORRECT DECISION-MAKING

MEANS AND ENDS

The crucial question around which most of Simon's work turns is, what is "correct decision-making"? "Correctness," Simon asserts, is not a term that can be applied (except "subjectively") to ends or values themselves.

"Correctness" as applied to imperatives has meaning only in terms of subjective human values. "Correctness" as applied to factual propositions means objective, empirical truth. If two persons give different answers to a factual problem, both cannot be right. Not so with ethical questions [*Administrative Behavior*, p. 53].

Simon takes as a "fundamental premise of this study that ethical terms are not completely reducible to factual terms." He does not try to "demonstrate conclusively the correctness of this view," but he refers his readers to some of the literature on logical positivism and briefly reproduces the familiar argument. The conclusion is that "there is no way in which the correctness of ethical propositions can be empirically or rationally tested"(p. 46).

The position to which the methodological assumptions of the present study lead us is this: The process of validating a factual proposition is quite distinct from the process of validating a value judgment. The former is validated by its agreement with the facts, the latter by human fiat [p. 56].

Simon is so wholeheartedly committed to this doctrine that he is inclined to be impatient with any inquiry into its foundations. Thus he has complained that the chapter on "Facts and Values" in *Administrative Behavior* "has aroused comment . . . all out of proportion to its importance in the book as a whole . . ." (p. xxxiv). He can justly claim that any criticism of his work ought to be guided by the intention of that work rather than by some external standard. He does not purport to provide a philosophical foundation for his "methodological assumptions" but to put them to work in the construction of a vocabulary for "realistically and significantly" describing administration; and it is with the latter that any criticism must be primarily concerned. That is not to say, of course, that the basic assumptions must be treated as sacred inviolable territory. Among Simon's many merits is his willingness to raise the question, what constitutes an adequate vocabulary? His determination to raise this and other fundamental *questions* about administrative study is what distinguishes his work from the administrative handbooks which constitute such a large part of the literature. These questions carry him far beyond mere administration, and some of his most influential studies deal with social science as a whole.

Since it will be necessary to follow Simon's discussion of correct decision-making, or rationality, through many twists and turns, a prefatory sketch may be helpful. The discussion moves between two poles, which are directly connected with the fact-value distinction: on the one hand is an omniscient calculational capacity; on the other hand, an omnipotent personal preference. Simon begins with the proposition that correct decision-making, or rationality, is taking appropriate means to reach designated ends. But he discovers that the language of means and ends suffers from serious difficulties, arising from the tendency of this language to blur the distinction between facts and values. He attempts, therefore, to construct a model of rationality, the "behavior alternative model," which is based squarely on the fact-value distinction. Instead of beginning with ends, the decision-maker in this new model begins by considering all alternative courses of action and their consequences before deciding which of them will maximize the achievement of his values. Though analysis is complicated by the fact that Simon is constantly driven back to the language of means and ends, the "maximizing" behavior alternative model best expresses his understanding of rationality. He freely admits, however, that this model suffers from a number of disadvantages so severe that no one could possibly act rationally in this sense. If anyone tried to act according to the strict "logic" of human choice he would be led into limitless calculation, and he would never choose.

Simon finds the solution to this problem in the psychological side of human choice, which provides both the "limits" on rationality and the basis for it. The argument follows two main lines. In *Administrative Behavior*, Simon attempts to show that organizations limit the environment of decision, thus reducing the members' decision-making problems to manageable proportions and also enabling them to share in a higher or broader rationality than they could hope to achieve as mere individuals. This part of Simon's argument depends on a shift in the grounds of analysis from individual values or preferences to organizational ends, but that shift is questionable on his own premises, as will be seen. In recent years, Simon has been more concerned with a different way of dealing with the limitlessness of the maximizing behavior alternative model. He has reformulated the model of rationality so that the actor is allowed to seek not for the best course of action (the one that will maximize the achievement of his values) but for a course of action that he regards as "good enough." This greatly simplifies decision-making, since the actor defines by his fiat what is "good enough." However, it also reveals with startling clarity what was always implicit in Simon's conception of rationality—the absolute subservience of "rationality" to nonrational preferences.

Let us turn to a more detailed examination of Simon's argument. "Correct decision-making" is defined initially as taking "appropriate means to reach designated ends. The rational administrator is concerned with the selection of these effective means." This requires us "to achieve perfect clarity as to what is meant by 'the selection of effective means' " (*Administrative Behavior*, p. 61).[8] Once the ends are given (in a suitable form), the correctness of any decision can in principle be tested scientifically.

Decisions can always be evaluated in this relative sense—it can be determined whether they are correct, given the objective at which they are aimed—but a change in objectives implies a change in evaluation. Strictly speaking, it is not the decision itself which is evaluated, but the purely factual relationship that is asserted between the decision and its aims [p. 49].

To the extent that "ends" are only means to further ends—as putting out fires is a means to the broader end of reducing fire losses—they can be evaluated as factual questions.

Since most imperatives are not ends-in-themselves but intermediate ends, the question of their appropriateness to the more final ends at which they are aimed remains a factual question. Whether it is ever possible to trace the chain of implementation far enough to isolate a "pure" value—an end that is desired purely for itself—is a question that need not be settled here [p. 50].

However reasonable it may be for most practical purposes, and especially in administration, to subordinate the problem of final ends or "pure" values, it cannot be ignored when our objective is theoretical or linguistic clarity. Nor do quotation marks dispose of the problem, as Simon knows perfectly well. These "pure" values provide the platform on which rational behavior must rest; yet on examination they seem necessarily to be so broadly conceived as to provide no ground at all. He goes on:

A municipal department may take as its objective the providing of recreation to the city's inhabitants. This aim may then be further analyzed as a means toward "building healthier bodies," "using leisure time constructively," "preventing juvenile delinquency," and a host of others, until the chain of means and ends is traced into a vague realm labeled "the good life." At this point the means-ends connections become so conjectural (e.g. the relation between recreation and character), and the content of the values so ill defined (e.g. "happiness"), that the analysis becomes valueless for administrative purposes.

One way in which Simon attempts to deal with the vagueness of ultimate ends is to hinge the analysis on intermediate ends which, if they suffer the

---

[8] Note that Simon here appears to use "appropriate" and "effective" synonymously.

theoretical disadvantage of lack of finality, at least have the merit of concreteness.

Most objectives and activities derive their value from the means-ends relationships which connect them with objectives or activities that are valued in themselves. By a process of anticipation, the value inhering in the desired end is transferred to the means. . . .

. . . Since the results of administrative activity can be considered as ends only in an intermediate sense, the values that will be attached to these results depend on the empirical connections that are believed to exist between them and the more final goals [pp. 52-53].

Simon seems to suggest that we can talk about "more final goals" and yet "more final goals" indefinitely, without ever reaching the question of final goals. As Dwight Waldo complains, "In reply to any question concerning [values], the logical positivist points to an escalator that ascends and ascends but never arrives anywhere." [9] Sometimes Simon replies, in effect, that to ask anything more is to make impossible demands of human rationality.

At best it might be hoped that the process of decision could be subdivided into two major segments. The first would involve the development of a system of intermediate values, and an appraisal of their relative weights. The second would consist in a comparison of the possible lines of action in terms of this value system. The first segment would obviously involve both ethical and factual considerations; the second segment could be pretty well restricted to factual problems [p. 53].

The difficulty still is that the intermediate values need to be given weights, but there is no way to assign such weights except by measuring them in terms of the final values. (It is true that weights might be assigned arbitrarily, by "fiat," but then the values would no longer be "intermediate.") As Simon says later, it is "through the hierarchical structure of ends [that] behavior attains integration and consistency, for each member of a set of behavior alternatives is then weighed in terms of a comprehensive scale of values—the 'ultimate' ends." He notes that a high degree of conscious integration is seldom achieved in actual behavior, but "what remains of rationality" in the behavior of men and organizations "is precisely the incomplete, and sometimes inconsistent, hierarchy [of ends] that has just been described" (pp. 63-64). As this statement implies, the language of means and ends points to the conclusion that rationality is fundamentally an ordering of ends.[10] Simon's "methodological assumptions" lead, on the contrary, to the conclusion that rationality does not extend to the sphere of ends. This difficulty suggests that there is something wrong with either Simon's basic assumptions or the

[9] *American Political Science Review*, June 1952, p. 503, n. 5.
[10] See below, pp. 77 ff.

language of means and ends. Drawing the latter conclusion, Simon seeks to approach rationality with a new terminology.

The shift in Simon's discussion of rationality is not immediately evident, for it is introduced with no more than a mild warning that "this analysis of rational behavior in terms of a means-end hierarchy may lead to inaccurate conclusions unless certain cautions are observed" (pp. 64-66). There are three dangers: (1) "the ends to be attained by the choice of a particular behavior alternative are often incompletely or incorrectly stated through failure to consider the alternative ends that could be reached by selection of another behavior"—by concentrating on certain ends we may overlook others that we would have wanted more if they had occurred to us; (2) "in actual situations a complete separation of means from ends is usually impossible, for the alternative means are not usually valuationally neutral"—therefore means-end terminology may not successfully separate the factual and the value elements of decisions; (3) "the means-end terminology tends to obscure the role of the time element in decision-making"—it may be forgotten that the realization of a particular end at a given time limits the ends that can be realized at that and other times. By the end of this discussion, these warnings have become "objections" to the means-end terminology, but it is not easy to say how deeply Simon thinks the objections cut. They do not mean, he says here, that the language of means and ends is "unusable," only that it must be used "with considerable care and sophistication."

The trouble with means-end language, according to Simon, is its failure to make a complete separation of factual and value questions, which is "the only valid distinction" (p. 184). But is this failure intrinsic to means-end language, in Simon's view? It might seem that if the decision-maker were to begin with a clear and comprehensive view of his ends, or values, he could proceed to consider the means best calculated to promote them as purely factual questions, and thus avoid the difficulties to which Simon says means-end language may lead. It is not clear from Simon's discussion whether he would accept this or not, whether he regards means-end language as inherently unsound or merely inconvenient, and if the former, what exactly is the reason. In a review of *The Theory of Games* by von Neumann and Morgenstern, Simon indicated much more drastic objections to means-end language than those that he was writing at about the same time in *Administrative Behavior*.

Sociology has been forced to treat of human behavior (at least in its rational aspects) in terms of "ends" and "means"; for example, these are fundamental categories in [Talcott Parsons'] *The Structure of Social Action*. It could easily be shown that these two terms complicate rather than simplify the analysis of human rationality, and it is to be hoped that they will now be discarded, both in sociology and in ethics, in favor of the schema of "alternatives," "consequences," and "values" attached to "consequences." . . . This schema quite obviously owes its origins to the utility calculus of economics, but in its generality it can be applied, at least descriptively, to all behavior, whether rational or not.[11]

When Simon writes in *Administrative Behavior* that "rationality has to do with the construction of means-ends chains," he also notes that "Talcott Parsons analyzes social action systems with the help of these same terms in *The Structure of Social Action*" (p. 62; n. 3); but he does not say that they should be "discarded" because they "complicate rather than simplify." Indeed, according to *Administrative Behavior*, the language of means and ends is usable, given due care and sophistication, though "under some [unspecified] circumstances another terminology may be clearer," and that is a theory of decision based on alternative behavior possibilities and their consequences. This new terminology is said to meet all the objections that have been made to means-end language.

The most striking and in a sense the most significant aspect of the behavior alternative model of rationality is its beginning point. Instead of beginning (as does means-end language) with what the decision-maker wants to achieve, or with values, the new terminology begins with the fact that he is at any moment faced with a large number of behavior alternatives. Decision or choice is the selection of one of these alternatives for each moment's behavior. A series of such decisions is called a "strategy." "The task of rational decision is to select that one of the strategies which is followed by the preferred set of consequences" (p. 67). Rational decision, therefore, involves three steps: (1) listing all alternative strategies, (2) determining all consequences following from each strategy, and (3) evaluating these sets of consequences.

The practical advantage of the behavior alternative model is that, instead of beginning with vague questions of values, the decision-maker begins with hard questions of fact which are amenable to scientific analysis: what are the alternative strategies and what are their consequences? What Simon understands this to imply theoretically is not clear from his extremely loose discussion; but he seems to have something like the following in mind. Decision, when conceived in terms of means and ends, is governed by the ends in view, which guide and limit the decision-maker's consideration of means. This guidance appears to be a great advantage, to say the least, since it means that the decision-maker does not have to consider everything. However the appearance is deceiving, for when we subject the ends to scrutiny we are led to "final ends" (or, in fact-value language, "pure values") which seem to have no content at all. It is from such nonentities as that "vague realm labeled 'the good life' " that decision, according to the means-end conception,

[11] *The American Journal of Sociology*, May 1945, pp. 559-560.

takes its bearings. But if the "final ends" are empty and meaningless, they can provide no guide to rational choice, and anything built on this foundation must share the original defect. Thus while means-end language implies that the ends of behavior, or values, are primary, the behavior alternative model implies that the conditions of behavior, or facts, are primary.[12] The behavior alternative model not only separates the factual and value spheres—that in itself would not solve the problem arising from the emptiness of general statements of values; it also attempts to provide a kind of autonomy for the factual sphere, an autonomy which is not possible so long as that sphere is conceived as consisting of "means," with their inherent dependence on "ends." Obviously, values or preferences cannot be ignored altogether, but the behavior alternative model seeks to provide a way of ordering facts that is not dependent upon values. It describes a method of rational choice which, as method, is not dependent upon the preferences of the chooser. It seeks to free the "logic" from the "psychology" of human choice.

It is important to note that propositions about human behavior, *in so far as it is rational,* do not ordinarily involve propositions about the psychology of the person who is behaving. Let us explain this rather paradoxical statement. In a given situation, and with a given system of values, there is only one course of action which an individual can rationally pursue. It is that course which under the given circumstances maximizes the attainment of value. Hence, psychological propositions, other than descriptions of an individual's value system, are needed only to explain why his behavior, in any given instance, *departs* from the norm of rationality [p. 149].

Rationality is problem solving, and a perfectly rational being would be a perfect problem solver capable of arriving at the one best solution. Psychological propositions enter a discussion of rationality for two reasons: (1) human beings are not perfect problem solvers; (2) an individual's value system sets his problems—a purely rational being would be a problem-solving machine with no problems. These are the " 'limits' to rationality" or the limits that "bound the area of rationality" (pp. 40-41) which later come to occupy a much more prominent place in Simon's work.

Let us examine first the ways in which the human being is a defective problem-solver. Regarding the first step in rational decision, Simon says:

Imagination falls down . . . in conceiving all the possible patterns of behavior that the individual might undertake. The number of things that a man, restricted

---

12 Simon's fundamental argument, which is neither clearly stated nor consistently adhered to, seems to be that general statements of ends or values are necessarily empty and meaningless, and that values are only meaningful as expressions of preference between concrete alternatives. In that case, the concrete alternatives must obviously be prior to an expression of preference between them. For a characteristically ambiguous allusion to this problem see Simon's comments in "Research in Comparative Politics," *American Political Science Review,* September 1953, p. 666. And see below, p. 78.

only by physical and biological limitations, could do in even so short an interval as a minute is inconceivable. He has two legs, two arms, a head, two eyes, a neck, a trunk, ten fingers, ten toes, and many sets of voluntary muscles governing each. Each of these members is capable of complex movements individually or in coordination.

Of all these possible movements, only a very few come to mind at any moment as possible behavior alternatives. Since each alternative has distinct consequences, it follows that many sets of possible consequences never reach the stage of valuation, since it is not recognized that they are possible consequents of available behavior alternatives [p. 84].

To the extent that an actor does not consider every behavior alternative open to him, however irrelevant some may seem to common sense, he is not acting rationally according to Simon. He cannot know whether to give serious consideration to a particular behavior alternative until he has identified it, predicted its consequences, and compared the values attached to it with the values attached to all other behavior alternatives. He cannot, that is to say, know which alternatives are relevant until he has considered them all, and failure to recognize this is one of the objections to means-end language. On the other hand, if ever a man tried to fulfill this requirement of rationality he would be a candidate for the psychiatrist's couch. Simon attempts to come to grips with this problem in his later work, but in *Administrative Behavior* it is avoided only by the use of common sense examples which imply a limited range of alternatives. When he cites the example of an engineer about to build a bridge, he does not suggest that the engineer ought to consider whether to pick up his pencil, scratch his ear, smoke a cigarette, ask for a raise, or quit his job—to say nothing of even more absurd behavior possibilities. In such cases Simon invariably refers to the alternatives relevant to the purpose at hand. This procedure is open to no criticism in itself, but it involves a return to the scientifically untenable, common sense conception of means and ends.

The second requirement of rationality is no less difficult:

the subject, in order to perform with perfect rationality in this scheme, would have to have a complete description of the consequences following from each alternative strategy and would have to compare these consequences. He would have to know *in every single respect* how the world would be changed by his behaving one way instead of another, and he would have to follow the consequences of behavior through *unlimited stretches of time, unlimited reaches of space,* and *unlimited sets of values.* Under such conditions even an approach to rationality in real behavior would be inconceivable [p. 69, italics supplied].

How is it, then, that such an approach is not inconceivable? "Fortunately, the problem of choice is usually greatly simplified by the tendency of the empirical laws that describe the regularities of nature to arrange themselves in relatively isolated subsets." [13] How we know these regularities of nature is explained in several ways, not all of them consistent with the logical positivist assumptions. At one point Simon notes the slight insight a human being has into "the regularities and laws that would permit him to induce future consequences from a knowledge of present circumstances," but he says that the human being has developed some "working procedures" that partially overcome the difficulty. "These procedures consist in *assuming* that he can isolate from the rest of the world a closed system containing only a limited number of variables and a limited range of consequences." But apparently this is not a mere assumption or working procedure, for on the next page we are told: "Rational choice will be feasible to the extent that the limited set of factors upon which decision is based corresponds, *in nature*, to a closed system of variables—that is, to the extent that significant indirect effects are absent" (pp. 81-83, italics supplied).[14] Finally we read: "It is very fortunate that the consequences of human activities are so strictly segregated; if they were not, the problem of reaching rational decisions would be impossible" (p. 185, italics supplied).

That the significant consequences of our actions are limited is one of the assumptions of means-end language. Whether this assumption can be raised to the level of knowledge of nature is obviously an extremely difficult question which cannot be answered by common sense alone. But for the present what is important is that Simon's behavior alternative model depends upon precisely the same kind of assumption. Moreover, in spite of the positivistic foundations of Simon's thought, he does not say—more precisely, he does not always say—that we merely hypothesize closed systems in the real world. He has some knowledge of the nature of the real world. Without the possibility of such knowledge, rational choice would not, according to Simon's own explanation, be "possible" or "feasible"; it would in fact be inconceivable.

A crucial assumption of the common sense language of means and ends is that a decision-maker's responsibility is limited to the courses of action that would have been considered and the consequences that could have been foreseen by a reasonable man at the time of decision. Simon imposes, on the other hand, an unlimited responsibility, an imposition which leads in principle to paralysis and in practice to utter irresponsibility. He avoids these results only to the extent that he resorts, again, to the common sense assumption.

Having listed all behavior possibilities and determined all of the consequences following from each, the decision-maker has to determine which is to be preferred. Here problem-solving meets problem. How the rational decision-maker determines preferences is a matter of some obscurity, but Simon's usual explanation is suggested in his summarizing remark that "roughly speak-

---

[13] What Simon means by a *"relatively* isolated" subset is not made clear.
[14] When Simon speaks, as he does here, of "significant" indirect effects, another problem arises, since significance is not a question of fact but of value. See below, pp. 142 ff.

ing, rationality is concerned with the selection of preferred behavior alternatives in terms of some system of values whereby the consequences of behavior
can be evaluated" (p. 75). The various alternatives must be measured in
terms of some prior "system of values" in the actor's mind. The perfectly
rational decision would culminate in a determination of preference in the
light of a comprehensive hierarchy of values.

A different explanation is suggested, however, by Simon's remark that
"rational behavior involves a listing of the consequences in their order of
preference, and the choice of that strategy which corresponds to the alternative highest on the list" (p. 73). This seems to imply that, having considered
the alternatives and predicted their consequences, the actor has only to imagine himself to be *in* each of the future states of affairs thus revealed. He
will then immediately know (or, more precisely, feel) which of them he
prefers, and he can behave accordingly. He need not know why he prefers
one rather than another, and he is not troubled with weighing alternatives
in terms of a system of values or ends; he simply calculates the possibilities
and then exercises his raw, unarticulated preference. Simon does not adopt
this explanation, even though it seems to follow naturally from the behavior
alternative model, perhaps because he is concerned with organizations, and
an organization cannot exercise a preference.[15] However that may be, the
explanation that Simon does adopt represents yet another return to the language of means and ends, for the "system of values" in terms of which alternatives are selected is none other than a "hierarchy of ends." The chapter
on rationality in *Administrative Behavior* ends precisely where it began.

Where, then, has the behavior alternative model led us in our attempt to
achieve "perfect clarity" about the meaning of "the selection of effective
means" and thus of rationality? Formally this model meets, as Simon said
it would, all of the objections to means-end language. If an actor were to
proceed according to the strict requirements of the behavior alternative model,
he would not fail to consider all the alternatives, he would not fail to make
a clear distinction between facts and values, and he would not overlook the
time variable. If that were all, then Simon could say (as he did in his review of *The Theory of Games*) that the language of means and ends should
be "discarded" altogether. But the actor cannot possibly proceed in this way.
He cannot conceive of all the alternatives, he cannot predict all of the

[15] See below, pp. 90 ff. A more fundamental investigation would require an inquiry into the
difference, if any, between an "end," a "value," and a "preference," but Simon does not
consider this question. (For the beginnings of such a consideration, from a point of view
with which Simon is sympathetic, see Chester Barnard, *The Functions of the Executive*
[Cambridge, Mass.: Harvard University Press, 1938], pp. 18-19.) "Preference" expresses his
meaning most precisely and consistently with his philosophical predispositions, but he uses
the terms as if they were interchangeable. It is not accidental that he uses them all, however, for in practice they are allowed to carry the different connotations ordinarily associated
with them. See below, pp. 325-326.

consequences, and the question of the integrating ends or preferences remains as unsettled as ever. These difficulties force Simon to return again and again to the language of means and ends. He does not, however, draw what might seem to be the natural conclusion: that the behavior alternative model is doubtful even as a guide or standard because what it guides the actor to is insanity.

One further point remains to be considered before turning to Simon's discussion of efficiency, and that is the notion of a "higher" rationality that runs throughout *Administrative Behavior*. It will be helpful first to take a common sense view of the matter. Rationality, as ordinarily understood, admits of degrees. It is recognized, in the first place, that individuals may exhibit more or less rationality in the way they pursue any given ends, even irrational ends. But it is ordinarily thought that only a man who exhibits rationality with respect to ends, as well as means, deserves to be called truly rational, or rational in the highest sense. Implicit in this common sense view is the idea that rationality with respect to means is fundamentally subordinate to rationality with respect to ends. Of course Simon recognizes different degrees of rationality in the first or purely instrumental sense. What is interesting is that he is led to imply, if not to recognize, degrees of rationality with respect to ends as well.

Through the hierarchical structure of ends, behavior attains integration and consistency, for each member of a set of behavior alternatives is then weighed in terms of a comprehensive scale of values—the "ultimate" ends. . . .

Both organizations and individuals . . . fail to attain a complete integration of their behavior through consideration of these means-end relationships. Nevertheless, what remains of rationality in their behavior is precisely the incomplete, and sometimes inconsistent, hierarchy that has just been described [pp. 63-64].[16]

What is rational in behavior is "the hierarchical structure of ends." But how can Simon say that rationality has to do with the hierarchical structure of ends when rationality is supposed to be confined exclusively to the selection of appropriate means? He does not answer, but two ways of dealing with this question may perhaps be inferred. Both would involve an argument that this "hierarchical structure of ends" is only a means to something else, and therefore not beyond the reach of rationality. Both would fail, as will be shown, because they only shift the question to the status of the "something else."

First, it might be argued that this "hierarchical structure of ends" is a means to integrated and consistent behavior. Rationality has nothing to say about the preferences or values by which behavior is governed except that they

---

[16] It might be objected that since this quotation occurs before the behavior alternative model is introduced, it is unfair to tax Simon with it at this point. But the chief significance of the introduction of a "system of values" into the third stage of the behavior alternative model is precisely to reintroduce the argument here under consideration.

be ordered in such a way as to permit integrated and consistent behavior. More or less rational behavior would then be more or less integrated behavior, and Simon's identification of "rationality" and "integrated behavior" is one of the grounds of his distinction between different degrees of rationality. However, this identification is seldom explicit, because it leads to the unacceptable conclusion that the choice of rational means depends ultimately on the choice of the rational end, namely, integration.[17]

A second way of attempting to reconcile the assertion that rationality has to do with a hierarchy of ends with the assertion that rationality is nothing but the selection of appropriate means would be to argue that even a purely instrumental rationality requires an ordering of preferences. Preferences must be brought to the level of consciousness and given order and stability over time if they are to serve as the basis of calculation and choice. While it cannot be said that the pursuit of one value is more rational than the pursuit of any other value—this being a matter of personal preference or fiat—rationality does require a consciously articulated, stable system of values. The possibility of rational behavior would be seriously limited if an individual were to remain unconscious of his preferences, or to change his mind frequently about what he wants, or to want inconsistent things. The more consciousness and order and stability of preference—the more raw preference is transformed into a hierarchy of ends—the more room there will be for that calculation which is the essence of rationality. The highest degree of calculation, or problem-solving, would be possible when every particular problem was part of one comprehensive problem. The paradoxical conclusion is that the end of rational behavior is not getting what one wants but calculating how to get what one wants.[18]

Though fragments of these arguments may be found here and there in the intricate convolutions of Simon's descriptions of rationality, it must be repeated that he does not make them directly, for he does not even articulate the question that his own remarks suggest. That failure is not accidental, for such an articulation leads into forbidden territory. Simon sets out to understand what rationality is so that he can judge degrees of rationality—more or less, higher or lower, broader or narrower. However, when these judgments are subjected to even moderately close scrutiny, they are seen to imply a knowledge of the end of rational behavior, whether "integration," or the problem solving process itself, or something else. Simon's own enterprise points to the conclusion that fundamentally rationality has to do with ends. This conclusion is of course inconsistent with the basic premises of his

[17] It is true that "integration" appears to be a formal rather than a substantive end, one "integration" being as rational as another; but it is impossible to say exactly what Simon has in mind, since he finds no occasion to provide even a rudimentary discussion of what "integrated behavior" means. See pp. 79, 80-81; and below, pp. 99 ff. Cf. Barnard, *The Functions of the Executive*, p. 294.
[18] See below, pp. 115-119.

science, which deny that ends or preferences are amenable to rational evaluation. The inconsistency could be surmounted either by reconsidering the
scientific premises or by abandoning the intention to make judgments about
degrees of rationality. In his later work Simon goes far in the latter direction;
but in *Administrative Behavior* (the scientific premises being unquestionable)
he lives as well as he can with the inconsistency.[19]

EFFICIENCY

Simon ordinarily uses the term "rationality" when he speaks of the abstract principle, while he ordinarily uses the term "efficiency" when he speaks
of the application of the principle, particularly its application in organizations.
However, the ground of the distinction between the two terms, which is implicit in their separate treatment, is obscure. Often Simon allows the two
words to carry into his science the different connotations they have in common language. Efficiency, as ordinarily understood, seems to be a narrower
conception; it is partial, instrumental. Rationality, on the other hand, seems
to be broader; it is somehow comprehensive, and it has to do with ends as
well as means, with values as well as facts. This common sense distinction is
implicit, for example, in Simon's remark that efficiency is "a principle that is
implied in all rational behavior. . . ." He immediately goes on to say, "In its
broadest sense, to be efficient simply means to take the shortest path, the
cheapest means, toward the attainment of the desired goals" (p. 14).[20] But,
for Simon, efficiency "in its broadest sense" is rationality, and it would make
as much sense to say that "rationality" is a principle that is implied in all
"efficient" behavior. The common sense distinction between the two conceptions is alien to Simon's basic assumptions, which require a narrowing of
rationality by denying it entry into the sphere of ends [21] and a broadening of
efficiency by making it comprehensive in the sphere of means. Strictly speaking, rationality and efficiency are identical. They express the same formal

[19] At the end of the chapter on rationality in *Administrative Behavior* (pp. 76-77), Simon
defines different kinds of rationality—"objective," "subjective," "conscious," "deliberate,"
"personal," and "organizational." There are a number of interesting features of this discussion. For example, Simon does not consider the complications arising out of the fact that
his definitions overlap. (Cf. his discussion of "personal-organizational" and "subjective-
objective" rationalities on p. 243.) Also there is no definition of "unconscious" rationality,
although the discussion suggests that there is such a thing. The important point, however,
is that this set of definitions represents an attempt to avoid the question of how to judge
degrees or levels of rationality by shifting to a discussion of *kinds* of rationality, which are
apparently all at the same level. In practice Simon makes little use of these definitions,
because he is not ready to abandon his intention to talk about degrees of rationality.
[20] See p. 223: "Given a complete set of value and factual premises, there is only one
decision which is consistent with rationality."
[21] As was indicated in the previous section, Simon is not altogether consistent in this
denial; and, in fact, the basis of the distinction in *Administrative Behavior* between rationality and efficiency, so far as there is any basis, is the tacit admission of rationality into the
sphere of ends.

principle: act so as to maximize the attainment of whatever it is you want.

Simon's discussion of efficiency begins in much the same way as his earlier discussion of rationality, and it turns on the same set of problems. The differences, which are mainly differences of emphasis, arise out of the greater practical concern in the discussion of efficiency. According to Simon, the criterion of efficiency as applied to administrative decisions is strictly analogous to the concept of the maximization of utility in economics (p. 182).[22] "The 'administrative man' takes his place alongside the classical 'economic man' " (p. 39). But administrative man (or more precisely, public administrative man) does not have a profit and loss sheet to guide him. "Hence, some substitute must be found in public administration for money value of output as a measure of value" (p. 175).[23] Simon suggests, as he did in his earlier work, the substitution of "a statement of the objectives of the activity, and . . . the construction of indices that measure the degree of attainment of these objectives." And: "it is desirable to state the objectives so far as possible in terms of values"; only if they are expressions of "relatively final ends" are they suitable value indices. On the other hand, the values of public service can seldom be expressed in the "tangible and objective" terms necessary for the measurement of results.

A serious dilemma is posed here. The values toward which these services should be directed do not provide sufficiently concrete criteria to be applied to specific decisional problems. However, if value-indices are employed as criteria in lieu of the values themselves, the "ends" are likely to be sacrificed for the more tangible means—the substance for the form [pp. 175-176].[24]

Here Simon bravely grasps one horn of this now familiar dilemma. While the lack of a common measure of value is a great difficulty, it must be overcome. Efficiency can be applied only after the relative weights of different values have been fixed. This will not be easy; but somewhere, sometime in

22 Simon says that he does not assert that this criterion always does dominate administrators but that if they were rational it would. There is, however, much inconsistency of language on this point. For example, "efficiency comes forth again as a basic criterion of decision in the public organization, since the controlling group will attempt to attain a maximum of organization objectives . . . with the resources at its disposal" (p. 121, italics supplied; see also p. 186).

23 Simon seems to think that "input" can "usually" be measured in terms of money costs. Unfortunately, it is impossible to say precisely what his views are, for the whole discussion has a distressingly loose quality (see p. 174).

24 Cf. Herbert A. Simon, Donald W. Smithburg, Victor A. Thompson, Public Administration (Copyright 1950 by Alfred A. Knopf, Inc.), pp. 504-505: "This task of defining objectives is perhaps the most difficult step in the evaluation of efficiency. . . . When we come to the U.S. State Department, or a public school system, specification of the objectives in meaningful and measurable terms becomes almost impossible." (In Public Administration, as in the collaborations referred to later in this essay, Simon's appears to be the predominant influence and the book may be taken to represent his views; see Administrative Behavior, pp. xxxvii.)

the administrative process, weights are actually assigned. The problem cannot be avoided by hiding it among the unexpressed premises of choice.

Simon points out that organizations often try to avoid the problem of comparing values by concentrating on certain *policies* (desired ends or objectives) and regarding *administration* (alternative means of reaching those ends) as valuationally neutral. This procedure, he argues, leads "inevitably" to an indefensibly narrow and " 'mechanical' " understanding of efficiency (p. 184). The policy immediately in view is not the only value that needs to be considered; or, to put the same point differently, administration is not always valuationally neutral. This is another statement of the objections to means-end language which led Simon to the behavior alternative model. The criterion of efficiency demands that a comprehensive view be taken of both facts and values. "The criterion of efficiency dictates that choice of alternatives which produces the largest result for the given application of resources" (p. 179, in italics).[25] It dictates, as the form of this proposition suggests, the maximizing behavior alternative model. But to attempt the comprehensive view provided by the behavior alternative model is to attempt to see the infinite. Moreover, this model does not solve but only postpones the basic problem of measuring "results," comparing "values," stating "final ends." What might have been sufficient in an abstract discussion of rationality will certainly not suffice when rationality is to be put to use. The discussion of efficiency in *Administrative Behavior* reflects Simon's perplexity in the face of, on the one side, a narrow notion of efficiency which is untenable and, on the other side, a comprehensive notion of efficiency which is incapable of application.

In practice, Simon assumes that the decision-maker begins with certain goals, or values, or ends.[26] Sometimes he admits the validity of the companion notions of desired ends and neutral means even in principle, provided they are not carried too far. Thus he suggests that "to consider the administrative activity itself as valuationally neutral is an abstraction from reality which is permissible within broad limits but which, if carried to extremes,

---

[25] It was the failure to take such a comprehensive view that led Luther Gulick to think that the value, "efficiency," may come into conflict with other values, such as "democracy." Thus "we are in the end compelled," Gulick says, "to mitigate the pure concept of efficiency in the light of the value scale of politics and the social order." "Science, Values and Public Administration," *Papers on the Science of Administration*, pp. 192-193. For Simon there can be, strictly speaking, no question of "mitigating" efficiency in the light of other values: properly understood, efficiency serves *all* values. He does not, however, always speak strictly; see *Public Administration*, p. 21; "A Comment on 'The Science of Public Administration,' " *Public Administration Review*, Summer 1947, p. 201, n. 4.

[26] "We have seen that the criterion which the administrator applies to factual problems is one of efficiency. . . . It is his function to maximize the attainment of the governmental objectives (assuming they have been agreed upon), by the efficient employment of the limited resources that are available to him" (*Administrative Behavior*, pp. 186-187).

ignores very important human values" (p. 184).[27] Apparently, then, the notion of neutral means is legitimate within limits.[28] Yet he immediately goes on to condemn as a "fallacy" the evaluation of alternatives in terms of "only those values which have been previously selected as the *objectives* of the particular administrative activity under consideration"—which is only the other side of the "neutral means" coin. He continues:

The effects of some administrative activities are confined to a rather limited area, and indirect results do not then cause much difficulty. The activities of the fire department usually have an effect on fire losses, but very little relation to the recreation problem in the community (unless ardent fire fans form a large part of the community). Hence the fire chief does not have to take recreation values into consideration in reaching his decisions. . . . But the mere fact that activities do not *usually* have valuationally significant indirect effects does not justify us in ignoring such effects if they are, *in fact*, present.[29] That is, the fire chief cannot, merely because he is a fire chief, ignore the possibility of accidents in determining the speed at which his equipment should respond to alarms.

This all seems commonplace, yet . . . in actuality, administrators in reaching decisions commonly disclaim responsibility for the indirect results of administrative activities. To this point of view we oppose the contrary opinion that the administrator, serving a public agency in a democratic state, must give a proper weight to *all* community values that are relevant to his activity, and that are reasonably ascertainable in relation thereto, and cannot restrict himself to values that happen to be his particular responsibility. Only under these conditions can a criterion of efficiency be validly postulated as a determinant of action [pp. 185-186].[30]

Simon concedes that the extent to which administrators can give attention to indirect effects is severely limited in practice by "psychological considerations," but it is important to observe what enormous demands the criterion of efficiency, strictly conceived, places on the actor. It is true that Simon only requires the fire chief to weigh values that are "relevant to his activity" and

[27] He goes on to list some of these very important human values in five sentences. For example, "Wage policies, promotional policies, and the like need to be considered not only from the viewpoint of incentives and result-efficiency, but also from that of distributive justice to the members of the group." It is scarcely necessary to point out that there is no basis in Simon's science for "important human values" or for "distributive justice," though these phrases do indicate that *Administrative Behavior* is still guided partly by the political orientation which we have noted in his early work. Cf. *Public Administration*, p. 542.

[28] Simon does not give any account of those limits except to say that "when a choice between alternatives involves any valuationally significant difference in the work activity this difference must be included among the values to be weighed in reaching a decision" (p. 185). This implies that we know in advance whether there is any "valuationally significant difference" between alternative means, but according to Simon's analysis, that is precisely what we do not know until all of the alternatives have been considered and their consequences predicted and weighed. See above, p. 76.

[29] Again it should be noted that whether there are "significant" indirect effects is not, on Simon's premises, a question of "fact."

[30] Five pages later Simon says that "a fire prevention division need consider only the impact of its activities upon the number of fires that will occur."

that are "reasonably ascertainable in relation thereto," but are there, according to this approach, any values that are not relevant? His examples are commonsensical: the fire chief needs to give some consideration to traffic safety but little or none to the recreation program. But the appearance is deceiving, as may be seen quickly by considering the elementary fact that the money spent to run the fire department might be spent on something else, the recreation program for example. Indeed, elsewhere in *Administrative Behavior*, Simon uses this very example. He says that a fire chief is likely to think that a city with low fire losses is a good thing and that new fire-fighting equipment would promote this end. "The demands of rationality would require, of course, that before deciding whether a new piece of equipment is needed he consider the other purposes for which the money could be spent: street repairs, an addition to the municipal hospital, and so on" (p. 92).[31] Thus if it is the responsibility of the fire chief to give proper weight "to *all* community values that are relevant to his activity," he must give a proper weight to all community values simply. They are all relevant, because he is spending money that might instead be spent to pursue them. The qualification disappears. Of course this is ridiculous. "If the fire chief [by now a rather confused fire chief] were permitted to roam over the whole field of human values—to decide that parks were more important than fire trucks . . .—chaos would displace organization, and responsibility would disappear" (p. 13).[32] Unquestionably Simon is grappling here with a serous problem of public administration, though a fire chief might reasonably argue that it is less his problem than the mayor's. It is also unquestionable that the common sense approach to this problem lacks scientific precision and certainty and that the proverbial solutions are often extremely vague. But the behavior alternative model radically distorts the problem as it arises out of "the real warp and woof of administration" (p. xlvi), without putting us any closer to a solution. Simon avoids the chaos to which the behavior alternative model leads only by resorting to common sense, "proverbial" qualifications such as "proper weight," "relevant," "reasonably ascertainable," and "significant."

To the extent that there is a prevailing theoretical direction in *Administrative Behavior*, it is towards the rigorous model of rationality, towards an analysis, that is to say, based on the scientific distinction between facts and values rather than the common sense distinction between means and ends. It is only by means of the behavior alternative model that the actor can sort out all the factual and value elements, and thus it is only by this means that he can maximize the achievement of his values. The whole discussion is

---

[31] See also James G. March and Herbert A. Simon, *Organizations* (New York: John Wiley & Sons, Inc., 1958), p. 176.

[32] Strictly speaking, in Simonian terms, "responsibility" would not disappear, but one *kind* of responsibility would be replaced by another kind. Simon's remark contains an implicit "value judgment." See below, pp. 103 ff., esp. p. 107, n. 56.

characterized, however, by a profound uncertainty of the utility of this model, a continual turning back to the ambiguous means-end language, and an almost complete failure to use the behavior alternative model when administration is actually described. Again and again the strict version of rationality is softened by resorting to common sense language, common sense qualifications, and common sense examples. Simon's argument in *Administrative Behavior* is: Be rational—but be reasonable about it.

In *Public Administration*, Simon's next major book, an attempt is made to provide a more systematic and defensible accommodation of the hard and soft versions of rationality-efficiency. The discussion here provides an especially clear illustration of the internal tension in Simon's thought, and it constitutes one important step in the transition from the concept of rationality of *Administrative Behavior* to that of his later work. In *Public Administration* Simon and his co-authors hold the definition of rationality the same, while narrowing that of efficiency (pp. 490 ff). Efficiency is now presented as a simplified method of choice, an approximation to rationality. The hard, indeed impossible, requirements of full rationality are avoided by (1) concentrating on those consequences to be sought or avoided rather than looking at all possible consequences, (2) ignoring the problem of unanticipated consequences, (3) giving a "relatively" neutral value to other consequences, and (4) considering the alternative consequences that have to be given up by carrying out one plan rather than another—that is, calculating opportunity costs. Simon presents here the same conception of efficiency criticized so heartily, if not always consistently, in *Administrative Behavior*. What is presented in *Public Administration* as a "simplified method of choice" wherein the actor "focusses on certain desired and undesired results," was described in *Administrative Behavior* as the "fallacy" of including "in the evaluation of alternatives only those values which have been previously selected as the *objective* of the particular administrative activity under consideration" (*Administrative Behavior*, p. 185). Unfortunately we cannot dispose of the matter simply by recording a change of mind on Simon's part, for the earlier objections to this simplified notion of efficiency have not been disposed of. Simon does suggest how these objections might be met.

> Of course . . . if our decision-maker is not neutral as to means . . . he can always patch up his criterion of efficiency by broadening the concept of "results." He can include in "results," for example, the effect of an administrative plan upon the health and satisfactions of his employees or upon the wages of contractors' employees, if this is something with which he is concerned. But in so doing, he gradually merges the criterion of efficiency with the broader criterion of rationality, and the two terms again become synonymous [*Public Administration*, p. 494].

If they do again become synonymous the problem of the decision-maker is of course not simplified. Simon's recently expressed preference for the efficiency of *Public Administration* over that of *Administrative Behavior* is not difficult to sympathize with. It is unquestionably true that the strict version of efficiency is "applicable largely to rather low-level decisions" (*Administrative Behavior*, p. xxxv), if even there. Any possibility of a kind of efficiency that does not make the extreme demands of the earlier model will be eagerly received by anyone who is interested in more than empty formalism. But is there, on Simon's premises, any such possibility? Are not efficiency and rationality synonymous in principle? [33] They are indeed, as descriptions of the logic of human choice. But the new concept of efficiency is produced by introducing psychological considerations into the pure logic of rationality. Immediately following the section of *Public Administration* quoted above, Simon says: "The efficiency criterion simplifies the process of decision for him only if there is actually a large area of consequences that he is *willing* to regard (at least approximately) as neutral, scarce means" (italics supplied).[34] Here is the key to the simplification, though its implications are not explored. The distinction between those consequences which are sought and those towards which the actor is neutral—between what is to be regarded as "end" and what as "means"—is "not *logical* but *psychological*" (*Public Administration*, p. 492). There is, come to think of it, no reason at all why the actor cannot concentrate on certain consequences and take an indifferent view of other consequences to any extent he likes. He is perfectly free, for example, to ignore even those "very important human values" mentioned in *Administrative Behavior*. He can consider "the effect of an administrative plan upon the health and satisfactions of his employees . . . if this is something with which he is concerned"; but he need not do so, if this is something with which he is not concerned. He generates his values by his fiat, and he can value anything he likes in any way he likes. The way is thus opened for a reconstruction of the notion of rationality, and to this reconstruction a major part of Simon's recent writing has been devoted.

THE PSYCHOLOGY OF HUMAN CHOICE: THE INDIVIDUAL AND ORGANIZATION

Before turning to Simon's new rationality, we must consider the psychological side of human decision-making, where we shall find the foundations of Simon's organizational and political theory. The beginning point of his psychology, and of his politics, is "a single, isolated individual" wholly un-

---

[33] Introducing this discussion in *Public Administration* (p. 490), Simon and his co-authors say that efficiency "in its broadest sense . . . is often used as a virtual synonym for 'rationality.'" They continue in a footnote: "This is the meaning to which 'apologists' for efficiency—i.e. those who believe that efficiency is the proper criterion for administrative evaluation—are *inevitably* driven" (italics supplied). The "apologist" for efficiency referred to is Simon himself, in chapter 9 of *Administrative Behavior*.

[34] Cf. p. 277: "the means organizations adopt to achieve their goals are never neutral."

touched by any civilizing influences. It is impossible, Simon says with remarkable understatement, for such an individual "to reach any high degree of
rationality" (*Administrative Behavior*, p. 79). Beset by an infinite quantity
of disordered urges within himself, he confronts a world infinitely complex.
Yet however vast and uncharted the sea of possibilities and however dark the
forest of ignorance, this trembling beast must somehow act. He may of course
simply respond to whatever stimuli present themselves to his attention.
Simon distinguishes this "stimulus-response" pattern of behavior from the
more sophisticated and more human "hesitation-choice" pattern. "If rationality is to be achieved, a period of hesitation must precede choice, during
which the behavior alternatives, knowledge bearing on environmental conditions and consequences, and the anticipated values must be brought into
the focus of attention." Man thinks before he acts. The trouble with the
"hesitation-choice" pattern is, as we have seen, that it seems to lead to an
indefinite period of hesitation, or, as Simon says, to vacillation and calculation "until the time for action [is] past" (p. 89).[35] This difficulty may be
partly overcome by the limited range of stimuli that present themselves and
the even smaller range that reach the individual's span of attention. "A
stimulus, external or internal, directs attention to selected aspects of the situation to the exclusion of competing aspects that might turn choice in another
direction" (p. 90). But while this psychological mechanism frees the individual from the grip of what would otherwise be an infinite inertia, it can do so
only by subjecting him to the "stimulus-response" behavior pattern, which is
inconsistent with rationality. Put quite simply, the basic problem is this: to
the extent that the individual merely responds to the stimuli that present
themselves to him, he does not act rationally; to the extent that he tries to act
rationally, he cannot act at all.

Simon finds the solution of this problem in organization: "the behavior of
the individual acquires a wider context of rationality through the environment
of choice social organization provides for him" (p. 93, n. 14). But individual
behavior does not acquire this "wider context of rationality" by the mere fact
of social organization; for the conventional environment provided by the organization is no less accidental and arbitrary than the natural environment
of the primeval forest, so long as it is viewed from the point of view of the
individual. Even in an organization, the individual acts mainly in response to
stimuli that present themselves to him, and he is far from rational in making
his decisions.

In so far, then, as choice is initiated by impingement upon the individual of
accidental and arbitrary stimuli, it would seem that the integrated busyness of the
adult is simply a more patterned busyness than the random movements and shift-

35 The "time for action" depends. of course, altogether upon subjective individual preference.

ing attentions of the child. The organized wholes of which it is composed are larger and more complex but, as wholes, no more closely related to any over-all system of values than those of the child. The study of administrative behavior as a rational activity would hardly seem useful unless this difficulty can be removed by showing that the stimuli that initiate choice are not, or at least need not be, arbitrary, when viewed from the standpoint of the organization as a whole rather than from that of an individual member [pp. 92-93].

Rational behavior, or the highest form of rational behavior, is behavior guided by some "over-all system of values"; such behavior can be found only in organizations, and *only when viewed from the standpoint of "the organization as a whole."* "The organization," according to Simon, "takes from the individual some of his decisional autonomy, and substitutes for it an organization decision-making process" (p. 8). It is perhaps not so important whether there ever were individuals who had "decisional autonomy," but it is of crucial importance that Simon regards the individual as decisionally autonomous in nature.

The behavior patterns which we call organizations are fundamental, then, to the achievement of human rationality in any broad sense. The rational individual is, and must be, an organized and institutionalized individual. If the severe limits imposed by human psychology upon deliberation are to be relaxed, the individual must in his decisions be subject to the influence of the organized group in which he participates. His decisions must not only be the product of his own mental processes, but also reflect the broader considerations to which it is the function of the organized group to give effect [p. 102].[36]

Organization limits the natural autonomy of the individual by placing him in an environment that will adapt his decisions to the organizational objectives and by providing him with the information needed to make these decisions correctly. "By limiting the range within which an individual's decisions and activities are to lie, the organization reduces his decisional problems to manageable proportions" (p. 199). Thus the great "limit" on the deliberations of the autonomous individual is the absolute lack of limitation. And the "relaxation" of this limit is accomplished precisely by an organizational limitation of the individual's decision problem. We perceive this paradoxical freeing of the individual from the slavery of his autonomy by viewing his decisions in the light of "the broader considerations to which it is the function of the organization to give effect"—in the light, that is to say, of the organizational ends or goals. However, it does not follow, according to Simon, that there are social goals that are natural to man; this is subject only to the qualification that no pattern of social behavior could survive that did not

[36] Cf. Barnard, *The Functions of the Executive*, p. 2. See also "Comments on the Theory of Organizations," *American Political Science Review*, December 1952, p. 1134.

anticipate and provide in some manner for the satiation of the stimuli of hunger, sexual desire, and fatigue. Beyond this, institutional arrangements [and, presumably, goals] are subject to infinite variation, and can hardly be said to follow from any innate characteristics of man. Since these institutions largely determine the mental sets of the participants, they set the conditions for the exercise of docility, and hence of rationality in human society [p. 101].[37]

In spite of the arbitrariness of any particular pattern of institutional arrangements and goals, some such pattern provides the foundation of the higher rationality and of the science of administration. "The task of administration is so to design this [organizational] environment that the individual will approach as close as practicable to rationality (judged in terms of the organization's goals) in his decisions." And administrative theory "must be a critique of the effect (judged from the point of view of the whole organization) of the organizational structure upon the decisions of its component parts and its individual members" (p. 241).

This is the point of view adopted by Simon whenever he turns from vocabulary-making to administrative analysis. It is analysis of a kind long familiar to students of administration, and it takes its bearings from a belief in the reality of some common purpose as the reason for administrative action. The individual is seen as subject to numerous kinds of influence, some tending to adapt his behavior to organizational goals, some interfering with that adaptation. Using the Simonian analysis, the administrator or the student of administration can evaluate the effectiveness of formal and informal organization in achieving the organizational goals. But why, from Simon's point of view, is it the task of administration to design the organizational environment so that individuals will act rationally, "judged in terms of the organization's goals"? Why should we look at what goes on in an organization "from the point of view of the whole organization"? Is there, according to Simon's theory of organization, any whole from whose point of view we can look? Let us apply a Simonian analysis to one of Simon's examples.

When two men cooperate to roll a stone that neither could have moved alone, the rudiments of administration have appeared. This simple act has the two basic characteristics of what has come to be called administration. There is a *purpose*— moving the stone—and there is *cooperative action*—several persons using combined strength to accomplish something that could not have been done without such a combination. In its broadest sense, *administration* can be defined as the activities of groups cooperating to accomplish common goals [*Public Administration*, p. 3].

Why did these men cooperate? Each of them was full of wants, and the satisfaction of these wants could be accomplished only by means of a series of

[37] It is difficult to know what the first sentence here is supposed to mean. Leaving aside the question of whether a stimulus can be satiated, it is manifest that institutions or organizations do survive without providing for the *satiation* of these desires of their members.

cooperative acts. These wants may have come together in a number of ways: by threats of physical violence by one partner on the other (in which case the "want" of the second partner was to remain unharmed), by paid employment of one partner by the other, by a contract based on a perception by both partners of some more or less stable conjunction of interests. The point of importance is that, however the cooperation came about, it is misleading, or at least radically insufficient, to say that its goal or purpose or end was to move the stone. This group task was only instrumental, and there were as many ends as there were individual wants being satisfied. For example, one member (or both) of this incipient organization might well have decided to cooperate with the intention of letting the stone roll back and crush his partner to death, thus allowing him to acquire the partner's food or his wife. Even if they both in fact desired the stone to be moved, the true situation is obscured if we say that they desired the same end; the end is always the satisfaction of some individual desire.

The point may be stated more broadly. According to Simon, men's wants are insatiable. Resources are limited. To the extent that a man acts rationally, he will seek to use all the resources available to him to maximize his gratifications. Other men are resources, and I may combine with them in order to harness them to the gratification of my own wants. Of course I cannot have it all my own way (although I should like to), so I must give up some gratifications to gain more gratifications—much as I have to feed my horse to get any work out of him. This giving up is expressed in the statement of the objectives of the organization in which I participate; these objectives are a short-hand statement of the terms of my association with other men: "the organization objective is, indirectly, a personal objective of *all* the participants. It is the means whereby their organizational activity is bound together to achieve a satisfaction of their own diverse personal motives" (*Administrative Behavior*, p. 17). The organizational objective is always a *means* to the satisfaction of personal wants, and it is on those individual wants rather than some common goal or end that the organization rests.

Let us see how this affects the kinds of decisions a rational individual in an organization has to make.

When choice takes place in a group situation, the consequences of a course of action become dependent not only upon the individual's selection of a particular alternative, but upon the selections of the other members of the group as well. . . .

Hence, the set of alternatives available to the *group* must be carefully distinguished from the set of alternatives available to the *individual*. . . . The alternative that the individual actually selects for his own behavior may be quite distinct from the alternative that he would select if he could determine the behaviors of all the other group members.

If the individual's expectations of the behaviors of his colleagues are accurate they will usually be rather different from the way he wishes his colleagues would behave. Since his own decision, to be rational, must be related to his expectations rather than his wishes, he must aim not at that alternative *among all those possible for the group* which he prefers, but at that alternative *among all those possible for him* which he prefers [*Administrative Behavior*, p .105].

It is not insignificant that the first example following this summary is that of a military campaign. According to Simon's scheme, everyone is my enemy, either active, in the sense that he will try to use me, or passive, in the sense that he will try to avoid being used by me. An obvious requisite to success in this struggle is to avoid allowing one's wishes about what others will do to cloud realistic expectations of what they will do. The fundamental situation is only obscured by Simon's second example.

Now a very special situation arises when all the members of the group exhibit a preference for the same values and for the same outcomes out of all those possible of realization by the group. All the firemen fighting a fire are agreed on the aim of their joint behavior—to extinguish the fire as quickly as possible. In such a case there is one set of behaviors for the members of the group which, on entirely objective empirical grounds, is the most expeditious for the accomplishment of this aim. The members of the group may disagree as to what this best solution is, but any such disagreement is on a factual level—a question of judgment, not of values.

Simon is suggesting that the common aim is agreed upon and that no one questions it, at least while the fire-fighting is going on. However, that is certainly not necessary, and to the extent that the individuals are acting rationally in Simon's terms, it is not correct. If the individual acts rationally he will always evaluate the organizational aims as means to the satisfaction of his own personal desires. Every interesting decision-making situation is sure to raise questions about the terms of his participation in the joint enterprise. To give only the most obvious example, if the fireman is ordered to do something that will very probably cost him his life, he may well decide that refusing the order and taking the punishment is "that alternative *among all those possible for him* which he prefers." [38]

Fundamentally organization is constituted by a series of individual calculations through which all members of an organization "agree in finding one plan preferable to any alternative that would be open to them *as individuals* if there were no cooperation" (*Administrative Behavior*, p. 107). But of course individuals do not always enter organizations or govern their behavior

---

[38] In *Public Administration* (pp. 296-297), Simon says: "In our discussion, we will perhaps pay more attention to the causes of disharmony in intergroup relations than to the conditions of harmony. We do not intend to imply by this that disharmony is the rule, and harmony the exception. . . . Especially when an external danger threatens a whole organization does one find all groups within it pulling together to ward off the danger, even as conflict within a nation diminishes during time of war." These comments only reinforce our conclusion that, according to Simon, harmony is (or rather, may be) a by-product of disharmony. Cf. below pp. 197 ff.

within them with such a clear-headed pursuit of their own wants. Indeed, if they always tried to keep their wits about them in this way their participation in organization would not have the limiting character that frees them from the infinity of choice which is their natural condition. Nor, in this case, would there be any basis for a science of administration based (as Simon says it must be based) on organizational ends. Both of these difficulties may be overcome, in Simon's opinion, once it is recognized that individuals may take the ends of the organization as their own ends; they may "identify" with the organization or its ends.

The values and objectives that guide individual decisions in organization are largely the organizational objectives. . . . Initially, these are usually imposed on the individual by the exercise of authority over him; but to a large extent the values gradually become "internalized" and are incorporated into the psychology and attitudes of the individual participant. He acquires an attachment or loyalty to the organization that automatically—i.e. without the necessity for external stimuli—guarantees that his decisions will be consistent with the organization objectives [p. 198].

It is precisely the uncalculated and nonrational commitment to the organization that saves the individual from his awful autonomy, and on this commitment his human rationality rests. But why, Simon asks, does an individual employ "one particular organizational value scale as his criterion of choice, rather than one or more of all the innumerable other scales he might use" (p. 204)? It is in the context of this question that he introduces the concept of identification, which he defines as follows: "a person identifies himself with a group when, in making a decision, he evaluates the several alternatives of choice in terms of their consequences for the specified group" (p. 205, in italics). Or, as he says later, "identification is the process whereby the individual substitutes organizational objectives . . . for his own aims as the value-indices which determine his organizational decisions" (p. 218). He suggests three "contributory factors" to the "phenomenon of identification": (1) personal interest in organizational success, (2) transfer of private-management psychology to public administration, and (3) focus of attention (pp. 208-210).[39] Regarding the first, Simon says:

The decision which is made in terms of organizational values is, to that extent, impersonal; but attachment to the organization derives from personal motives. The individual is willing to make impersonal organizational decisions because a variety of factors, or incentives, tie him to the organization—his salary, prestige, friendship, and many others.

If these are the factors that tie him to the organization, then the sense in

[39] Note that there is an unexplained change in terminology in this discussion. What begins as a discussion of the "contributory factors" helping to explain identification becomes a discussion of "element[s] in the process of identification."

which his decisions are "impersonal" is not at all clear. There are two possibilities: either the individual makes his decision in terms of a calculation of personal advantage, or he does not. In the former case there is no "identification" and the decision is not "impersonal"; but in the latter case his personal motives do not explain his behavior, although they may explain his initial entry into the organization. The second contributory factor suggested is the transfer to public business of private-management psychology. Attitudes about "my business" and "my profit" may be carried over to the public sector of the economy "through lack of recognition of the fundamental differences in the assumptions that underlie these two segments." This suggestion is perhaps better passed over. It is frankly tentative; it applies only to the "public segment of the economy"; it rests on the assumption that there is a fundamental difference between the public and the private segments, which runs counter to the main thrust of Simon's argument; and Simon grants that it is "extremely difficult . . . to separate this factor from the elements of personal motivation which would continue to bind the individual to the organization even in a nationalized economy."

These two factors may "contribute" to identification, but it is in the third factor, if anywhere, that we must find what identification is.

A third element in the process of identification is the focusing of the administrator's attention upon those values and those groups which are most immediately affected by the administrative program. When an administrator is entrusted with the task of *educating* Berkeley's children, he is likely to be more clearly aware of the effect of any particular proposal upon their learning, than of its possible indirect effects upon their health—and vice versa. He identifies himself, then, with the organization objective.

It is clear that attention may narrow the range of vision by selecting particular values, particular items of empirical knowledge, and particular behavior alternatives for consideration, to the exclusion of other values, other knowledge, and other possibilities. Identification, then, has a firm basis in the limitations of human psychology in coping with the problem of rational choice.

The question, why an individual selects one organization rather than another remains unanswered. Either he chooses on the basis of a calculation of self-interest or he does not. In the latter case he is said to "identify" with the organization that he happens to choose, or that chance throws his way. Perhaps we can say that an individual often goes into an organization because he sees more gain for himself than is offered by any alternative that comes to his attention; he stays in it partly from a continued perception of gain but mainly because the restricted organizational environment does not often present him with stimuli demanding a reconsideration of his participation.[40]

[40] See Simon's somewhat different and fuller account of the psychological bases of identification in *Public Administration*, pp. 101 ff. Simon's use of the concept of identification is as gross a case of the dressing out of proverbial wisdom in scientific language as anything

Identification is explained finally (to the extent that it is explained at all) by the psychological limits on the span of attention. That is to say, the surrender of decisional autonomy to the organization, via identification, is no more rational than any other kind of surrender and no less arbitrary than the random adaptation to stimuli that characterizes the child or the pre-organization man. It is in fact nothing more than a return to the childish or brutish "stimulus-response" pattern of behavior. "Social institutions may be viewed as regularizations of the behavior of individuals through subjection of their behavior to stimulus-patterns socially imposed on them" (p. 109). The behavior of organization man rests on precisely the same ground as the behavior of pre-organization man. It remains the case, within organizations as without, that, from the individual's point of view, "choice is initiated by impingement upon the individual of accidental and arbitrary stimuli . . ." (p. 92).

It is, moreover, the individual's point of view that we must concern ourselves with if we are to remain within the bounds set by Simon's basic assumptions, his own assertions to the contrary notwithstanding. His leap from individual preferences to "the organization as a whole," essential as that is to the higher rationality and to the administrative science, is accomplished only at the cost of violence to his theory of human behavior. Orientation in terms of organization goals is, on the basis of Simon's own theory, false and misleading, because there is no "organization as a whole." There are no "broader considerations to which it is the function of the organized group to give effect." There is nothing but the interaction of subjective individual wants. When an individual "identifies" with an organization or its goals, he is in fact submitting to the service of those individuals in the organization whose wants are most closely connected with the ostensible objectives or the survival of the organization. And when the scientist prescribes for "the whole organization," he is in fact prescribing for those same individuals. The scientist commits himself, perhaps unwittingly, as a partisan in the struggle of men against men.[41]

---

that can be found in the older administrative science. The term is used as if it explains something about human behavior, but it is at least as imprecise as the most ordinary common sense observations. In *Public Administration* (p. 107), for example, Simon describes this situation. A police sergeant is warned that his patrolmen are spending too much time eating pie and too little time on patrol. "He may recognize the force of the complaint and yet feel that some allowance should be made for the men, who are generally doing (he believes) a good job. The sergeant's reaction to the competing demands of his superiors and his working group will depend on the relative strengths of his loyalties. In such situations it is hardly possible to generalize about the result, except to say that in some cases one loyalty, in some cases the other, wins out." Simon's own description of the case suggests that the sergeant's reaction would be at least as likely to depend on his judgment of the merits of the criticism as on the *ex post facto* attribution of loyalty mentioned here. Simon's frequent use of the older term, loyalty, as the equivalent of "identification" is another case of the retention of pre-scientific notions in his allegedly scientific vocabulary.
41 Cf. the case of Bentley, below p. 178.

This partisanship does not immediately appear from Simon's practical discussions of organization, which ordinarily have a familiar and commonsensical character. But the serene good sense on the surface cannot entirely conceal the churning of contradiction below. Some examples will help to make this clear. Like all writers on administration, Simon lays great emphasis on coordination. The assumption throughout is that the achievement of organizational goals is what organization is for, and therefore the members must work together. "The sum total of the activities of the members of an organization must be coordinated or meshed together if the organization is to accomplish its purposes" (Public Administration, pp. 130-131). Twice in Administrative Behavior Simon uses the activity of building a boat to illustrate the importance of coordination (pp. 9-10, 139). On a common sense level his argument is reasonable. If people band together to build a boat, they ought to work according to some single plan. It is, however, insufficient from Simon's point of view to say that people band together "to build a boat"; they band together to satisfy certain personal desires. One man may want to have a boat, another to make a monetary profit, another to enjoy the physical proximity of other individuals. Taking the latter point of view (which has equal status with the others), the goal is not the boat at all but certain satisfactions inhering in the joint activity. Such satisfactions might be decreased by a coordinated plan for completing the boat and increased by a considerable amount of disorganization and delay in finishing the ostensible task.[42]

Again in his treatment of communications, a subject that bulks large in the science of administration, Simon argues that effective communication is necessary if the organization is to accomplish what it sets out to do. "The communications system in an organization appears . . . no less vital than the nervous system in a human body—and the consequences of its imperfections no less disorganizing" (Public Administration, p. 243). But why does it matter in any fundamental way if an organization is "disorganized"? Disorganization is likely to be an advantage to some participants, a disadvantage to others, and a matter of indifference to still others. Why prescribe for the bosses rather than, say, for the workers?

The point is especially well illustrated, curious as it may seem, in what presents itself as one of Simon's most scientific and value-free books, Organizations. Here Simon, together with James March, considers various approaches to the study of organization and attempts to state empirically verifiable propositions growing out of these approaches. But the effect is to show how the behavior of the employees may be manipulated so that they will do what the bosses want them to do. Discussing, for example, the unanticipated consequences that may arise from certain stimuli, Simon says, "We shall be interested particularly in how these unanticipated consequences restrict the

[42] See Public Administration, p. 64.

adaptiveness of the organization to the goals of the top administrative hierarchy." At another place he points out that "integration into the community gives rise to nonorganizational identifications that may be dysfunctional" (*Organizations*, pp. 36, 72).[43] What is meant is "dysfunctional" from the point of view of those in control of the organization; the question is not even raised whether such identifications would be "dysfunctional" from the point of view of the employees or of the broader community itself.[44] One more example from *Organizations* will suffice. Simon is concerned with how the individual employee is influenced to produce, or to conform to the demands of the organizational hierarchy. One of the influences, he suggests, is the character of the evoked set of alternatives, that is, the possible courses of action that an individual thinks of. The old-fashioned management theory was that "direct orders from supervisors would preclude the evocation of other alternatives, whereas participation would considerably increase evocation." In fact the opposite is often the case, and Simon suggests that this may be explained in terms of two different mechanisms.

Certainly most studies suggest that the more the *felt participation in decisions* . . . , the less the visibility of power differences in the organization . . . , and that the latter, in turn, lessens the evocation of organizationally disapproved alternatives. . . . Moreover, most students of the subject argue that *(provided the deception is successful)* the perception of individual participation in goal-setting is equivalent in many respects to actual participation. Thus, actual influence over the specific decision being made is of less importance to the individual than acknowledgement of his influential position.

At the same time, the second mechanism is also plausible. The greater the amount of felt participation, the greater the *control of the organization* over the evocation of alternatives . . . ; and therefore, the less the evocation of alternatives undesired by the organization . . . [p. 54, second italics supplied].[45]

It is perhaps not surprising that many workers' representatives remain intensely suspicious of a science of organization that takes upon itself to teach

[43] Simon distinguishes three "aspects" of human behavior that need to be taken into account by an adequate theory of human behavior: "the instrumental aspects of human behavior, . . . the motivational and attitudinal, and . . . the rational" (p. 6). The remarks cited here fall in the section dealing with the second of these, but the "instrumental" view of human behavior in organization governs the entire discussion.

[44] Such questions are raised and discussed, on the other hand, by Frederick W. Taylor, whose greater breadth may be seen in his emphatic but (as it has happened) vain argument that the mere "mechanisms" of scientific management, such as time and motion study, must not be separated from the "broad general principles" or the "underlying philosophy" of scientific management. See *The Principles of Scientific Management* (New York: Harper & Brothers, 1911), pp. 28-29, 128-130. Simon and March ignore Taylor's warning and evaluate his contribution in precisely the way Taylor argued against (*Organizations*, pp. 19-20).

[45] The numerical expressions have been omitted. Cf. *Public Administration*, p. 122: "Consultation of the group, rather than the attempted imposition of arbitrary authority upon it, shows respect for the dignity of the group and of the individual."

employers lessons like this. It would not take much ingenuity to show the workers how to play this game too, but Simon does not do so. What is more important, however, is not this particular (and probably unintentional) bias but the contradiction in Simon's thought, of which this bias is only one symptom. The importance of "identification" in the Simonian vocabulary is that it is supposed to provide the link between individual preferences and organizational objectives or ends. It seems to succeed only because of its fundamental ambiguity. Strictly speaking, as we have said, identification with an organization or with organizational goals is a non-rational commitment which serves those individuals who have most to gain by the preservation of the organization or the accomplishment of its goals. It cannot under any circumstances serve "society" or "the organization as a whole" or "the common good," because these are only appearances which mask the reality of individual desires. Yet Simon refers to such well-known phenomena as bureau chiefs overestimating the importance of their programs as examples of "faulty" identification; he suggests that broadening the basis of identifications "clearly, is the end to be aimed at"; and he gives advice about how to encourage "loyalty to the larger group" (*Administrative Behavior*, pp. 211, 216-217). Again and again Simon implies that there are narrow identifications which tend to obstruct the pursuit of common purpose, and broad identifications which tend to promote it. Indeed, he does more than imply it.

In the chapter on "identification" in *Administrative Behavior*, he argues that the "correctness" of any decision may be judged from two different standpoints. "In the broader sense it is 'correct' if it is consistent with the general social value scale—if its consequences are socially desirable. In the narrower sense, it is 'correct' if it is consistent with the frame of reference that has been organizationally assigned to the decider" (p. 199). Simon concedes that "the phrase 'social value' is not entirely a happy one, particularly in view of the insistence upon ethical relativism," and he uses it only "for lack of a more descriptive and accurate term. . . ." The puzzle is what it is descriptive of. It is significant that Simon identifies "social value" with what is "socially desirable" rather than "socially desired," even though the latter would seem to be more consistent with the ethical relativism insisted upon. In the end, the phrase "social value" is defined in purely formal terms: "What is meant by 'social value' here is the objectives of some larger organization or social structure in relation to the 'organizational values' of its components" (p. 200). This is a statement, in organizational terms, of the means-end chains already discussed. The "socially desirable" is elbowed off the stage, as "ultimate ends" were, by restating the matter in terms of a formal relation. But an unacknowledged substantive notion of "the socially desirable" continues to exert its influence from the wings.

SIMON'S POLITICAL THEORY

While Simon argues that "the rational individual is, and must be, an organized and institutionalized individual," he does sometimes find room for a higher form of thought.

The highest level of integration that man achieves consists in taking an existing set of institutions as one alternative and comparing it with other sets. That is, when man turns his attention to the institutional setting which, in turn, provides the framework within which his own mental processes operate, he is truly considering the consequences of behavior alternatives at the very highest level of integration. Thought at this comprehensive level has not been common to all cultures. In our Western civilization it has perhaps been confined to (1) the writings of utopian political theorists and (2) the thought and writings surrounding modern legislative processes [*Administrative Behavior*, p. 101].

Whether this "highest level of integration" results from an exercise of rationality is a question that Simon leaves unexplored. When he says that a man who considers the institutional setting of his own mental processes "is truly considering the consequences of behavior alternatives at the very highest level of integration," he is using the vocabulary of the behavior alternative model of rationality. And it is difficult to understand what is being described in the paragraph quoted if not rationality; certainly it is something more than the exercise of preference. It would not seem unfair to conclude that what Simon identifies as "the highest level of integration that man achieves," or political "thought," is the highest form of rationality. Yet if we were to draw that conclusion the implications would be astounding, and they would require a fundamental revision of what we had understood to be Simon's theory of human behavior and human rationality. For if what Simon is describing in the paragraph quoted is rationality, then an individual's rationality is not necessarily dependent upon and confined by some non-rational commitment to or "identification" with an organization. An individual can reason his way to an "integration" beyond existing organizational boundaries—which we had thought provided the limits as well as the indispensable basis of rationality—and apparently some utopian political theorists and students of the legislative process have done so. That implies, in turn, that there is some basis for such an integration beyond that provided by the existing organizational environment. It implies, that is to say, an objective basis for integration that is accessible to reason; and, since integration of behavior depends upon ends or values (p. 4), it implies objective ends or values that are accessible to reason.

Simon attempts to avoid these difficulties by calling this highest integration not rationality, but "thought" at a "comprehensive" level.[46] But difficulties remain even in this looser formulation. The argument now runs as follows: in spite of the absolute dependence of human "rationality" on some given organizational environment and goals, it is possible for some men to engage in a kind of political "thought" that transcends the existing organizational setting. While this political "thought" is like science in going radically beyond the mental processes of the ordinary organization-bound individual, it is not scientific thought. Whereas the first principle of social science is the *distinction* between facts and values, the first principle of this political "thought" appears to be an *integration* of facts and values. By making a place for political thought, ill defined as it is, Simon seems to open the way for a challenge to the supremacy of science.

That Simon is not willing to follow his argument so far as to say that this political thought is "rational" is perhaps less surprising than that he should make the argument at all. Of what use is it? The answer appears in some remarks made in the course of Simon's discussion of identification, from which it appears that some kind of transorganizational "thought" is not only possible but the necessary or desirable basis of organizations themselves. He says that, while identification is useful

in depersonalizing choice within an organization and enforcing social responsibility, it may be equally harmful if it colors and distorts the decisions that precede the establishment of the organizational structure itself. The construction of socially useful organizations requires an unprejudiced assessment of all the values involved. Prejudice is bound to enter if the assessor's judgment is warped by his identifications. Hence, the personal loyalty to organizational values which is generally so useful an aspect of behavior in an organization may be correspondingly harmful when encountered in the fields of invention and promotion, that is, in the tastes of the administrator at the higher levels of the hierarchy [p. 219].[47]

The proper functioning and, especially, the founding of organizations depend upon a "taste" that rises above "personal loyalty to organizational values." The exercise of this "taste" implies at least the possibility of political "thought" as described above. The health or "social usefulness" of organizations depends upon the ability of some men to transcend their own organizational context and to compare, coolly and with unwarped judgment, "the institutional setting[s] within which . . . their own mental processes operate" with other possible settings. Well-made and well-managed organizations depend upon men who are capable of "an unprejudiced assessment of all the

[46] Evidence that this "thought" is not supposed by Simon to be "rationality" is provided by the sentence following the paragraph quoted above. "Human rationality, then, gets its higher goals and integrations from the institutional setting in which it operates and by which it is molded." Thus an existing institutional setting is where human *rationality* gets its "higher goals and integrations," but it is not (according to the preceding remarks) necessarily where comprehensive human *"thought"* gets them.

[47] Cf. Alexander Hamilton, James Madison, and John Jay, *The Federalist*, No. 37.

values involved"—capable, that is to say, of "truly considering the consequences of behavior alternatives at the very highest level of integration."

These remarks, if taken seriously, point to the need for an inquiry into the
transorganizational "thought" on which organizations depend,[48] and for a
view of human rationality that can comprehend the possibility of political
"thought." But there is, as we have suggested, a tension between the demands
of this needful political thought and the demands of science. Political thought,
as understood here, concerns itself with "the highest level of integration."
That must mean that political thinkers try to make true statements about
the ends of human behavior, about values—if only the end or value of integration. But Simon knows in advance that such an attempt is futile, because
it is unscientific. He knows that only factual propositions can be called "true"
or "false" and that value judgments are "validated" by nothing more than
"human fiat." Given this knowledge, he quite sensibly prefers to study solid
questions of fact rather than to record the fiats of others or to proclaim
counterfiats of his own. Nevertheless, just as every factual statement rests
upon value assumptions (if only the assumption that the factual statement
is worth making), so a science of administration rests upon some political
assumptions.[49] Simon recognizes this dependence, and that is why he makes
the remarks we have been considering. But he does not go so far as to engage
in political thought himself, perhaps fearful that any move in that direction
would immediately lead to questions about the foundations of his science.[50]

Thus far we have suggested that Simon's science of administration requires
political thought (systematic thinking about the integration of human behavior and therefore about the ends of human behavior) at the same time
that it denies any place for it. But is it possible that the difficulty can be
resolved by finding the elements of a political theory in the science itself?
Simon says at one point that "if the distinction of factual from ethical questions is a valid one," certain conclusions seem to follow. One of these is that
"responsibility to democratic institutions for value determination can be
strengthened by the invention of procedural devices permitting a more effec-

[48] The superiority of Simon's mentor, Chester Barnard, lies mainly in his attempt to make
such an inquiry, though he can do so only by allowing his science to become thoroughly
infected with non-scientific assumptions. See The Functions of the Executive, Part IV.
See also Philip Selznick, Leadership in Administration (Evanston: Row, Peterson & Company, 1957). Cf. Public Administration, pp. 102 ff.
[49] This is not to assert, of course, that the validity of a factual statement depends upon
value assumptions but that the decision to make that particular factual statement has, like
every decision, its value premises. In the same way, every decision to make a scientific
proposition with respect to administration has its political premises.
[50] As does Selznick's powerful attempt to deal with this range of questions. Consider, for
example, the implications of Selznick's discussion of the organizational "self," of the "true
commitments" of the organization, of "institutional integrity," and of "truly felt needs
and aspirations of the institution." Leadership in Administration, pp. 21, 62, 72-73, 119-
122, 154.

tive separation of the factual and ethical elements in decisions" (pp. 57-58). Here we seem to have deduced a fundamental political proposition from the scientific fact-value distinction itself, namely, that the distinction between facts and values ought to be reflected in governmental arrangements. The appearance is deceiving, however, for the proposition depends upon a wholly unarticulated assumption about the kind of responsibility that "democratic institutions" require. That is a value question and the only way to answer it, according to the Simonian method, is to find out what the people want. If the people's fiat includes a demand to decide the so-called factual questions, there is no reason why they should not do so; and in such a case this "more effective separation" would only get in their way.[51] What is certain, however, is that the science of administration requires such a separation. Something like the traditional "rule of law" is absolutely necessary to the application of the science of administration on any considerable scale, for it is only thus that the "value" elements of political decisions can be articulated and held constant long enough for the science of administration to be brought to bear on the "factual" elements. Neither the oriental despot nor the tumultous democracy of the marketplace has room for the science of administration, and the scientist has a natural preference for a political order where he can ply his trade. Whether this preference is as arbitrary as any other is a question Simon has not troubled to examine.

Is there, however, a more fundamental political implication to be drawn out of the scientific distinction between facts and values? Does the distinction in fact provide the basis for a democratic political theory? At first glance the answer seems to be no. According to science, as Simon understands it, one political system, one set of political values, is as good (or as arbitrary) as another.

To make practical recommendations for organization action one must assume either that he possesses values that are generally shared or that his values are "right" in some absolute sense. Plato, in his *Republic*, tried to realize the second alternative: to devise a society in which "philosopher kings," because of training and wisdom, would establish the correct value system for the community. In the constitutional governments of the Western world, we have tended to operate on the contrary theory: the community should decide—by the political processes we call democracy—what values are to be sought, and the administrator should be bound by those values [*Public Administration*, p. 22].

[51] The civil service reformers of a previous generation encountered a similar difficulty; they argued that the function of government was to give effect to the will of the people, but they did not allow that the people might will to have a spoils system. See for example, Frank Goodnow, *Politics and Administration* (New York: The Macmillan Company, 1900), chs. 1, 2; and L. Gulick, "Notes on the Theory of Organization," *Papers on the Science of Administration*, p. 11. As the question arises in Simon's work, the basic theoretical problem is whether a commitment to rationality or efficiency is merely a value judgment like any other. See below, pp. 142 ff.

That would seem to be conclusive; Plato did it his way, we do it ours. Yet it is clear that Plato was wrong and that in a very fundamental way we are right. What Simon calls the "democratic belief" receives some support from the fact-value distinction. The contrary view, on the other hand, is refuted by it, for it must make the false claim to the possession of values which are "'right' in some absolute sense." When Simon says that "democratic institutions find their principal justification as a procedure for the validation of value judgments," he probably means to say that democratic institutions have more of a justification than other kinds of institutions. This is confirmed by the remarks that follow: "There is no 'scientific' or 'expert' way of making such [value] judgments, hence expertise of whatever kind is no qualification for the performance of this function" (Administrative Behavior, pp. 56-57).[52] The distinction between facts and values and the arbitrariness of everything in the value sphere seem to lead to the conclusion that liberal democracy, where something like this distinction and the equal status of everyone's values are recognized, is the best or even the only legitimate form of government. Simon does not explicitly draw that conclusion or even push on to a further exploration of the problem, perhaps because even the scattered remarks that he does make come perilously close to the heretical deduction of an "ought" from an "is." Further probing might bring into question even this cardinal doctrine of the logical positivist's faith.[53]

Simon does have a kind of political theory, but it is fragmentary and most of its crucial assumptions are unexamined. It is based neither upon science nor upon comprehensive political "thought." Simon is content, whenever the science of administration cries out for political foundation, to adopt the political opinions nearest at hand, and his political theory consists mainly of a thoughtless universalization of the liberal democratic institutions and values of the United States. Freedom of speech and association and standards of decency and fair play, as understood in the United States, are often taken for granted as, apparently, in the nature of things. It is frequently impossible to know whether what is being said is supposed to refer to the United States, or to Western liberal democracies, or to all political communities. We are told, for example, that "in public administration final responsibility for determining objectives rests with a legislative body" (Administrative Behavior, p. 52), a proposition that is simply not true in many countries and that is not simply true even in the United States. Questions of scientific method seem to have occupied so large a share of Simon's span of attention as to give him a severe case of political myopia. This helps to explain the fact that his administrative science takes its bearings from the goals of top management.

[52] Cf. p. 219 and Ridley and Simon, The Annals of the American Academy of Political and Social Science, September 1938, p. 22.
[53] See below, pp. 142 ff.

We now can see why the term "efficiency" is most commonly used in connection with the values and opportunity costs of activity as viewed by the managerial group in an organization, rather than the values and opportunity costs as assessed by employees or some other group. The political mores of our society place upon the managerial group the task of maximizing the achievement of democratically defined values with the use of resources that are to be regarded largely as neutral means [*Public Administration*, p. 502].

Scientist though he is, Simon absorbs into his own theory the "political mores of our society."

This universalization of American democratic values is of the utmost importance when considering Simon's concept of equilibrium within and between organizations, for the "political mores of our society" provide the implicit substance of what is explicitly a purely formal theory. The equilibrium concept is Simon's substitute for a political theory: an explanation of social behavior that is universal, nonnormative, and yet consistent with the unexplored and largely unarticulated liberal democratic faith which constitutes part of his pre-scientific baggage. The elements of the theory of equilibrium are already before us. "Individuals are willing to accept organization membership when their activity in the organization contributes, directly or indirectly, to their own personal goals" (*Administrative Behavior*, p. 110).[54] The organization is a constantly renegotiated contract among its members. Its managers, in the course of seeking the most advantageous terms for themselves, mediate between the various elements of the organization and thus keep the organization in being. This does not mean that there is some natural harmony among the members of an organization. In *Public Administration*, Simon explicitly warns against the notion "that there is a preordained identity of interests among the various participants in administrative organization, by virtue of which the 'enlightened self-interest' of the managerial group corresponds to the long-run self-interest of employees" (p. 502). Each individual will try to get all he can, but no one, Simon thinks, will be able to get too much.

Whatever group exercises the power of determining the basic value criteria [of an organization] will attempt to secure through the organization its own personal values. . . . But their power of control does not in any sense imply that the control group exercises an unlimited option to direct the organization in any path it desires, for the power will continue to exist only so long as the controlling group is able to offer sufficient incentives to retain the contributions of the other participants to the organization. No matter what the personal objectives of the control group, their decisions will be heavily influenced by the fact that they can attain their objectives through the organization only if they can maintain a positive

[54] Simon's chapter on the equilibrium of the organization is largely a restatement of Chester Barnard's fuller discussion in *The Functions of the Executive*, pp. 56-59, chs. 11, 15.

balance of contributions over inducements, or at least an equilibrium between the two [*Administrative Behavior*, p. 119].

In this necessity for each member of the organization to consider the probable behaviors of each other member of the organization, Simon seeks to bring back into his theory something like a common purpose. The argument is that the strategically placed managers cannot go too far in exploiting the other members of the organization because of their own desire to maintain the organization. Similar restraints follow from the requirements of the intergroup equilibrium. All organizations are surrounded by enemies or potential enemies, and they must seek allies in order to survive. To gain the adherence of allies an organization must to some degree adjust its program to their interests. "Hence, organizations are in a continual process of adjustment to the political environment that surrounds them—an adjustment that seeks to keep a favorable balance of political support over political opposition" (*Public Administration*, p. 389). From this follows a theory of organization in which an equilibrium, engineered by the opportunism of organizational leaders, arises out of a conflict of interests. If an organization fails to adjust to its political environment—that is, if it seeks to take too much and give too little—it fails to survive, thus automatically reaping the just punishment for antisocial behavior.

Before we can rest content with the comforting promise of this unseen hand, it is necessary to be sure that we do not, following Simon, confuse what we see in American political life today with what is intrinsic to the theory of equilibrium. In particular we are likely to overestimate the substantiality of the restraints placed upon the manager of an organization by his need to retain the cooperation of others unless we are perfectly clear about the kinds of "inducements" he may offer them. Of course the boss wants his profit, the worker his wage, the customer his shoes; but although the model is economic, the inducements are not necessarily material: " 'World peace' or 'aid to the starving Chinese' may be just as much a personal goal for a particular individual as another dollar in his pay envelope. . . . Nor should intangible egoistic values, such as status, prestige, or enjoyment of organization associations, be forgotten" (*Administrative Behavior*, p. 111). Shrewd employers (and politicians) have long seen the possibilities implicit in these observations. Aiming himself, say, at the accumulation of money and the things it will buy, an employer may pay his employees partly in some intangible "egoistic" or "idealistic" values which cost little more than the salary of a "human relations" expert or two. He may, for example, induce them to produce at a high rate by deceiving them into thinking that they are really participating in making company policy. Or by holding a threat of sanctions in the background, he may induce his employees to contribute services in return for a promise to withhold the sanction. The chapters on planning in *Public Admin-*

istration suggest the possibilities clearly enough, in spite of their overlay of liberal democratic values.

In very general terms, the problem of inducement is to make the person to whom the plan is directed feel that conformance is preferable to nonconformance. The individual to whom the plan is directed must be induced to *choose* the new behavior of the plan in preference to the old behavior. He is not "forced" to behave according to the plan in any literal sense. Literally to force a person is to apply physical force to his body as by dragging him. Inducement does not use physical force except occasionally in some aspects of the apprehension and punishment process. Instead, it operates on the individual's motivations so that he directs himself to behave as planned [pp. 452-453].

Of course it is true that even the most powerful manager does not have "an unlimited option to direct the organization in any path [he] desires." But the manager's desire to keep the organization in equilibrium may be fulfilled in such a large variety of ways—ways in which Simon offers him valuable instruction—that any substantial restraints may fade away. Even fewer are the restraints when the manager does not expect to gain by continued association with the organization; he may harvest the virgin timber in one organization and move on to the next. It goes without saying that Simon does not impose on the manager any ethical restraints; he does not seriously exhort the manager to do his duty. "Knowledge of administration is amoral . . . , for it is knowledge of how to manipulate other human beings— how to get them to do the things you want done" (p. 22). Simon teaches fundamentally that the manager is free to engineer any kind of equilibrium, to use any kind of inducements, and to demand any kind of contributions that he can get away with—and to do this with the aim of gratifying whatever desires he chooses. That the manager will not be permitted to get away with anything too raw, that the equilibrium of the organization will not be the equilibrium of terror and brain washing of *1984*, is part of Simon's unexamined political faith.

Identical considerations apply to the equilibrium between organizations. Indeed the shift from the interindividual equilibrium to the interorganizational equilibrium raises the same difficulties already encountered in the shift of attention from the individual to the organization. Here, it is true, Simon's analysis takes its bearings from organizational survival rather than organizational ends, but on examination the survival of an organization proves to have the same lack of objective value as its goals. Organizational survival is merely the point at which a large number of want-gratification lines of different individuals meet. Survival of the organization is a good only to the extent that it serves those individual wants (pp. 388-389), and this means, strictly speaking, that there is no way to look at organizations but from the point of view of the individual. Moreover, Simon grants that survival of the organization is not a sufficient standard of evaluation in any case. Most organizations provide an excess of satisfactions over contributions, and there is always the question of who is to get the surplus? [55] The unadorned answer is, "whoever can," but in the concluding paragraphs of *Public Administration* (pp. 560-561) Simon seeks to present this conclusion in a more respectable form.

Is American public administration responsible? One way of answering the question is to say that if organizations survive in a democracy, they are being responsive to the goals and values promoted by the democratic political processes.

Simon correctly anticipates that there will be objections to this answer.

This is not the same as saying: "What is, is right." The procedures of accountability we have today are not the only possible procedures. We have suggested some of the alternatives . . . and have raised some of the questions of fact and of value that will have to be settled before we can make an intelligent choice among them. . . . Really fundamental changes in responsibility involve equally fundamental changes in the whole political structure.

Obviously this does not meet the objection. To say that existing procedures and an existing political structure are not the only possible ones says nothing about whether or not they are right. Simon's conclusion might be reformulated to read: "What is, is as right as anything else." [56] But he is unwilling to leave his readers with that.

But even if we accept the present accountability procedures as given, we still have an opportunity as individuals to participate in these procedures. As individuals in a democratic society we can criticize surviving, and even flourishing, administrative organizations. Our criticism, if it becomes widespread enough, enters into the survival picture, becomes a part of the political process, and forces changes in administration.

Does this depend upon the fact that we happen to be "individuals in a democratic society," upon such things as our right to criticize the government

[55] Unlike the physical equilibrium, the social equilibrium can, according to Simon, show an output greater than input (see *Administrative Behavior*, p. 181). This is understandable when it is recalled that the "output" (in the form of inducements to participants) may include such diverse things as money, a feeling of prestige, and a sense of serving world peace. The absolutely subjective, and therefore immeasurable, character of the "inducements" in this scheme appears even more clearly in Barnard's fuller discussion, *The Functions of the Executive:* "it is *impossible* to balance output and input [of organizations] in detail" (p. 252, see also ch. 11).

[56] Simon seeks to convey the impression that it is possible to speak of degrees of responsibility, as it is possible to speak of degrees of rationality. However, on his premises there is no question of "more or less" responsibility but only "*whose* values underlie the program. That is, we may ask where an agency got the particular values it seeks to attain, to what groups or influences it is responsive. Why is the ECA seeking to promote European recovery and international trade? Is this because of Congressional direction, a mandate from the Executive, or the influence of pressure groups, or do the program values originate in some other source? When the question is stated in this way, we are dealing with the problem of *responsibility*" (*Public Administration*, p. 489).

and our possession of the franchise? Apparently so. Simon's formal equilibrium theory is sufficiently flexible to enable us to find an equilibrium under the most absolute tyrant, but the *kind* of equilibrium he has in mind clearly depends on the general acceptance of certain liberal democratic values.[57] What presents itself as a substitute for the traditional kind of normative political theory turns out on examination to depend wholly upon crucial value assumptions. The substitute amounts to no more than a refusal to examine the most important part of the problem.

Not only does Simon fail to explore the political values on which his theory of equilibrium rests, but his teaching tends to undermine them. To complete the peroration of *Public Administration:*

We have pointed out that the administrator still has many alternative ways of doing things within the limits imposed by the requirements of survival. He still has the power to bring us satisfaction or irritation and frustration. If we do not like what the administrator does within his residual area of freedom—if we do not like the policeman's lack of manners—we can do something about it. We may not be able to do anything alone, but we can try to find others who feel as we do, and with whom we may combine forces. Then, what was previously a matter of discretion to the administrator may be moved into the area of the political process—the administrator may have to change his ways to survive.

If people are lethargic, the administrator may have a wide area of freedom of choice. If they are alert and willing to give some effort to their government, they may bring more of the administrator's decisions within the controls of the political process. If survival is the test of responsibility, an alert citizenry can change the conditions of survival. Today, as always, eternal vigilance is the price of freedom.

If an alert citizenry can change the conditions of survival so, and perhaps more easily, can an alert potential tyrant. The "alert citizenry" of which Simon speaks is nothing but an aggregation of individuals who, to the extent that they act rationally, cooperate with each other strictly with a view to getting as much and giving as little as conditions allow. In *Administrative Behavior* Simon points to Hobbes' political philosophy for an "extreme form" of the proposition that an organizational plan may come into being provided that the potential participants "agree in finding one plan preferable to any alternative that would be open to them *as individuals* if there were no cooperation" (p. 107 and note). But compared even with Hobbes, it is Simon who is the extremist. The democratic overlay, the undefended assumption of unstated rules of the game, the vapid call for vigilant citizens—however sincerely meant—will not deceive the careful reader. The tendency of Simon's hard teaching is not liberal democracy—or even a Leviathan that, though absolute, is protective of the natural rights of each individual—but a tyranny

[57] See, for example, *Public Administration*, pp. 483-486.

in which government becomes the means of harnessing all but one man to the gratification of that one. That such an outcome is unlikely is due to moral restraints of which Simon's teaching gives no account and which, indeed, it tends to weaken. So-called common ends are, according to Simon, never anything but means to the satisfaction of numerous arbitrary individual wants; they do not therefore provide, for those who appreciate their true character, the basis for any such restraints as a sense of fair play or of community responsibility. The only restraint for those students whom Simon has enlightened is his warning not to attempt to give less than conditions demand or to take more than they allow. But conditions can be changed; Simon teaches his students, and especially those presently in positions of power, how to increase the effectiveness of organization as an instrument for their own self-gratification.

THE NEW RATIONALITY: "SATISFICING"

Much of Simon's recent work has been concerned with reconstructing the model of rationality presented in *Administrative Behavior* or (what amounts to the same thing) attempting to bridge the gap between the rational and the psychological parts of human behavior. A radical doubt of the description of rationality that was developed by the economists and statisticians (and that is basic to *Administrative Behavior*) is out in the open. "We have become so accustomed to this general description of the process of rational choice that its preposterousness only becomes evident when we try to use it to describe in detail how real human beings go about making real choices in a real world." [58]

The social sciences suffer from a case of acute schizophrenia in their treatment of rationality. At one extreme we have the economists, who attribute to economic man a preposterously omniscient rationality. Economic man has a complete and consistent system of preferences that allows him always to choose among the alternatives open to him; he is always completely aware of what these alternatives are; there are no limits on the complexity of the computations he can perform in order to determine which alternatives are best; probability calculations are neither frightening nor mysterious to him. Within the past decade, in its extension to competitive game situations, and to decision-making under uncertainty, this body of theory has reached a state of Thomistic refinement that possesses considerable normative interest, but little discernible relation to the actual or possible behavior of flesh-and-blood human beings.

At the other extreme, we have those tendencies in social psychology traceable to Freud that try to reduce all cognition to affect. . . . The past generation of behavioral scientists has been busy, following Freud, showing that people aren't

[58] Herbert A. Simon, "Recent Advances in Organization Theory," *Research Frontiers in Politics and Government* (Washington: Brookings Institution, 1955), p. 33.

nearly as rational as they thought themselves to be. Perhaps the next generation is going to have to show that they are far more rational than we now describe them as being—but with a rationality less grandiose than that proclaimed by economics [*Administrative Behavior*, p. xxiii].

Administrative theory, as Simon sees it, finds its place between these extreme views: "it is precisely in the realm where human behavior is *intendedly* rational, but only *limitedly* so, that there is room for a genuine theory of organization and administration."

The central concern of administrative theory is with the boundary between the rational and the non-rational aspects of human social behavior. Administrative theory is peculiarly the theory of intended and bounded rationality—of the behavior of human beings who satisfice because they have not the wits to maximize [p. xxiv].

The new approach has to do with what Simon calls the principle of "bounded rationality."

The capacity of the human mind for formulating and solving complex problems is very small compared with the size of the problems whose solution is required for objectively rational behavior in the real world—or even for a reasonable approximation to such objective rationality.[59]

Like the treatment of efficiency in *Public Administration*, the new definition of rationality is an attempt to simplify decision-making problems in order to bring them within the powers of human computation. This simplification involves two "crucial amendments" to the global rationality of economic man on which *Administrative Behavior* rests so heavily. First, the economic man's goal of maximizing is replaced by the goal of satisficing; the administrative man looks not for the best alternative open to him but for a course of action that is " 'good enough.' " Thus he can make his choices "without first examining all possible behavior alternatives and without ascertaining that these are in fact all the alternatives." Second, instead of dealing with the "real world" in all its complexity, as the economic man is supposed to do, "administrative man recognizes that the world he perceives is a drastically simplified model of the buzzing, blooming confusion that constitutes the real world." Since "he treats the world as rather 'empty,' and ignores the 'interrelatedness of all things' (so stupefying to thought and action), administrative man is able to make his decisions with relatively simple rules of thumb that do not make impossible demands upon his capacity for thought" (*Administrative Behavior*, pp. xxv-xxvi).[60] By postulating limited goals, limited alternatives, and

---

[59] Herbert A. Simon, *Models of Man, Social and Rational* (New York: John Wiley & Sons, Inc., 1957), p. 198. (Simon puts this sentence in italics.) Presumably the reader is expected to supply his own definition of "reasonable."

[60] On the satisficing model, see *Organizations*, chs. 6 and 7; this model is foreshadowed in *Administrative Behavior*, pp. 96-100. Although Simon frequently writes as if he were

limited consequences, the problems to be solved are reduced to manageable, one might say human, proportions.

Regarding the second of these simplifications, Simon says that

the intended rationality of an actor requires him to construct a simplified model of the real situation in order to deal with it. He behaves rationally with respect to this model, and such behavior is not even approximately optimal with respect to the real world. To predict his behavior, we must understand the way in which this simplified model is constructed, and its construction will certainly be related to his psychological properties as a perceiving, thinking, and learning animal [*Models of Man*, p. 199].

Clearly if a man acts according to some simplified model of the real world, then to predict his behavior "we must understand the way in which this simplified model is constructed," and that will no doubt lead us into psychological considerations. But even if our only objective is to predict his behavior (and all the more if we are to judge the degree of rationality he exhibits), we must also know how adequately his model represents the real world. To take the most obvious example, if we are to predict his behavior we must know not merely his expectations of the consequences attached to various behavior alternatives but what the consequences really are. Simon constantly admits this. For example, when he hypothesizes that a decrease in satisfaction will generally lead to increased search for alternative programs, he says that this search behavior "depends on an underlying belief on the part of the organism that the environment is benign and *on the fact* that search is usually reasonably effective." Again, "the most important single factor evoking the alternative of leaving [an organization] appears to be the *objective existence of serious work alternatives* . . ." (*Organizations*, pp. 50, 53; italics supplied).

By his actions, the individual tests his model, and his future behavior will be affected by how well the model holds up when confronted with the real world. "The basic reason why the actor's definition of the situation differs greatly from the objective situation is that the latter is far too complex to be handled in all its detail." Thus "rational behavior calls for simplified models that capture the *main features* of a problem without capturing all its complexities" (*Organizations*, pp. 151, 169; italics supplied). This implies that the model, while a simplification, is a simplification of some objective reality. It also suggests that that reality may in principle be perceived as a whole, otherwise there would be no possibility of saying that a particular simplification captures the "main features" of a problem. However, Simon is uncomfortable with the implications of this common sense position; and he

really distinguishing the situation of administrative man from that of economic man, it is clear that fundamentally he is presenting a description of human behavior, not just of administrative behavior. The economists' model, as presented by Simon, is just as preposterous when applied to a businessman as when applied to a public administrator.

sometimes suggests that "the situation as it 'really' is" is "more precisely" expressed as the situation "as it appears to an outside observer" (p. 151). That is, on the contrary, much less precise. We are not interested in the opinion of some outside observer about, for example, the existence of serious work alternatives, but in their "objective existence."

This is of course a manifestation of the question of the constitution of the real world and of the kind of knowledge men can have of the real world which, as we have seen, Simon never squarely confronts in *Administrative Behavior*.[61] His main argument there was that rationality is possible because of the existence of closed systems in nature, of which men can, at least in principle, have knowledge. Further reflection appears to have led him to a less sanguine view. Contrast the "regularities of nature" of 1947 and the "fixed and unchangeable rules that nature insists upon" of 1950 with the "buzzing, blooming confusion that constitutes the real world" for Simon in 1957 (*Administrative Behavior*, pp. xxv, 69; *Public Administration*, p. 438).[62] If this last view of the world is correct, Simon's emphasis on the actor's simplified model of it is understandable, since that model is the only coherent world that there is. In that case, however, it is difficult to see how there is any possibility of rational behavior at all, since any attempt to behave rationally (no matter how well conceived relative to the imaginary model) must be subdued by the buzzing, blooming confusion that the behavior must confront.

Due to his inability to deal satisfactorily with the problem of the relation between the real world and men's (including scientists') models of it, Simon has devoted his main attention to the other simplification of rationality: the substitution of "satisficing" for "maximizing." The simplification in the realm of facts proves to be of no use, for the facts are intractable; their confusion is not affected by the order of an imaginary model. In the realm of values, on the other hand, the actor can make his simplification stick, for there he can do what he likes. "It will be seen," Simon says, "that an organism that satisfices has no need of estimates of joint probability distributions, or of complete and consistent preference orderings of all possible alternatives of action" (*Models of Man*, p. 205). We shall begin by examining two quasi-mathematical papers in which the model is described.

In "A Behavioral Model of Rational Choice," the crucial simplification is the assumption that instead of a completely ordered specification of the value of each outcome, the actor uses a much rougher method of evaluation, such as "satisfactory or unsatisfactory" or "win, draw or lose." Given this simplification, it is possible to define "rational decision-process" thus:

61 See above, pp. 76-77
62 In 1958, on the other hand, we are given "at least the small consolation that the world appears to be so constructed that the means-ends relations are not nearly as complicated and intertwined as they might be" (*Organizations*, p. 32).

(i) Search for a set of possible outcomes . . . such that the pay-off is satisfactory . . . for all these possible outcomes. . . .

(ii) Search for a behavior alternative . . . whose possible outcomes all are in [that set of outcomes above] [*Models of Man*, p. 248].[63]

Given this method, the actor has to gather a relatively small amount of information. Instead of predicting the outcome of all possible behavior possibilities, he has only to consider that range of behavior possibilities which, on the basis of his crude preliminary information, seem likely to have consequences that are satisfactory. His information-seeking activities are limited, that is to say, by his willingness to search for a *satisfactory* course of action rather than the best one. How much it is simplified depends of course on what he is willing to regard as satisfactory. This model receives further elaboration both here and elsewhere, but its character is sufficiently clear. For the present we need note only that it provides no answer to the objection which the Simon of *Administrative Behavior* would raise:

somewhere, sometime in the administrative process [and the same applies to any choice] weights actually are assigned to values. If this is not done consciously and deliberately, then it is achieved by implication in the decisions which are actually reached. It is not possible to avoid the problem by hiding it among the unexpressed premises of choice [p. 177].

That is just what the satisficing model seeks to do.

In the second essay, "Rational Choice and the Structure of the Environment," the focus is said to be on the environment of decision rather than on the characteristics of the decision-maker, and the aim is to "discover, by a careful examination of some of the fundamental structural characteristics of the environment, some further clues as to the nature of the approximating mechanisms used in decision making" (*Models of Man*, p. 262).[64] Curiously, in view of this intention, "the environment we shall discuss initially is perhaps a more appropriate one for a rat than for a human." The rat is presumed to have but a single need—food (say, cheese). It is capable of resting, exploring, and food getting; it has a given range of vision, rate of metabolism, and storage capacity. Its environment consists of a surface (or maze of paths), bare except for widely scattered "little heaps of food, each adequate for a meal." "It has the capacity, once it sees a food heap, to proceed toward it at the maximum rate of locomotion." Its problem is not to starve.

[63] The mathematical expressions have been omitted. This essay was originally published in *The Quarterly Journal of Economics*, February 1955.
[64] This essay was originally published in *The Psychological Review*, March 1956. Simon points out that "environment" is ambiguous and that he refers not to the totality of the physically objective world but to those aspects of the totality that are relevant to the organism's needs and perceptual apparatus. The most significant modification here of the maximizing model has to do not with the environment but with the organism: the assumption of limited ends or a fixed aspiration level.

Now I submit that a rational way for the organism to behave is the following: (a) it explores the surface at random, watching for a food heap; (b) when it sees one, it proceeds to it and eats (food getting); (c) if the total consumption of energy during the average time required, per meal, for exploration and food getting is less than the energy of the food consumed in the meal, it can spend the remainder of its time in resting (p. 263).[65]

Simon concedes that "there is nothing particularly remarkable about this description of rational choice, except that it differs so sharply from the more sophisticated models of human rationality that have been proposed by economists and others." Even that is not so remarkable when it is remembered that the description here is admittedly closer to the rationality of a rat than of a human being. Simon goes on to prove, with the same labored prolixity and with an elaborate mathematical overlay, that the rat's chances of survival will depend upon the extent of its storage capacity and its range of vision and on the richness of the environment in cheese and in paths along which it can move. Moreover he shows that even if the organism has more than one goal (say, water as well as cheese), there need not be any "utility" problem if the organism is given sufficient storage capacity, since its postulated needs are not insatiable. There may be a "more efficient" procedure, and some possible ways of increasing efficiency are suggested; "but the point is that these complications are not essential to the survival of the organism" (p. 271).

Characteristically, Simon spends little time discussing the relevance of studying the rationality of this rat to understanding the rationality of human beings. He does say:

The principal positive implication of the model is that we should be skeptical in postulating for humans, or other organisms, elaborate mechanisms for choosing among diverse needs. Common denominators among needs may simply not exist, or may exist only in very rudimentary form; and the nature of the organism's needs in relation to the environment may make their nonexistence entirely tolerable [p. 272].

Three comments are in order. (1) It is not immediately evident that a course of action that is "tolerable" is therefore "rational." (2) The skepticism of which Simon speaks is in no sense the outcome of the model. As Simon clearly indicates, the skepticism preceded the model and was what led to its construction; the model did not generate any hypotheses. (3) The model itself carries no implications one way or another with respect to whether we should postulate for humans, or other organisms, elaborate mechanisms for making choices. Simon has made certain assumptions, shown how an or-

---

[65] Indeed, it had better spend the remainder of its time resting or doing exercises to expend the extra energy. If it immediately proceeds with further exploration and consumption (food getting) and if it continues to build up surpluses of energy, it runs a grave risk of eating itself to death.

ganism might make choices given these assumptions, and found that under certain conditions a very simple "satisficing" choice mechanism would enable it to survive. Having done that, he knows no more or less than before about the relevance of this model to "humans or other organisms." In *Administrative Behavior* he asserts that human wants are insatiable (p. 213), and nowhere in the later writings is that retracted. In this essay he assumes limited wants or needs. That is the crucial assumption, and the model itself says nothing about whether it is a reasonable one to make in the case of "humans or other organisms."

The most important conclusion we have reached is that blocks of the organism's time can be allocated to activities related to individual needs (separate means-end chains) without creating any problem of over-all allocation or coordination or the need for any general "utility function." The only scarce resource in the situation is time, and its scarcity, measured by the proportion of the total time that the organism will need to be engaged in *some* activity, can be reduced by the provision of generous storage capacity [*Models of Man*, p. 271].

As Simon here implies, the "satisficing" models, stripped of their mathematical elaborations, involve a return to an extremely crude version of means-end language.[66] It is for this reason that when the new version of rationality is presented without these elaborations, it often has a sensible and familiar ring. "Examples of satisficing criteria that are familiar enough to businessmen, if unfamiliar to most economists, are 'share of market,' 'adequate profit,' 'fair price'" (*Administrative Behavior*, p. xxv).[67] A favorite example of the difference between the "maximizing" and the "satisficing" models is

---

[66] It is not contended that the mathematical description and manipulation are irrelevant, only that they are, so far as the main argument is concerned, unnecessary. Without in any way denying the value of mathematical reasoning and notation in the exploration of certain technical problems in the social sciences, the proof of the pudding is (if we may venture a proverb) in the eating; and the "eating" in the case of a mathematical model in the social sciences is not the manipulations but the results. Of course Simon would not dispute this, at least in principle. The results in "Rational Choice and the Structure of the Environment" are summarized by Simon as follows (pp. 272-273): (1) "In this paper I have attempted to identify some of the structural characteristics that are typical of the 'psychological' environments of organisms." We are not told here what kind of "organisms" these characteristics are supposed to be relevant to, but there is virtually no evidence presented here that they are typical even of rats, to say nothing of human beings. (2) This organism can get along with simple perceptual and choice mechanisms. "In particular, no 'utility function' needs to be postulated for the organism, nor does it require any elaborate procedure for calculating marginal rates of substitution among different wants." This amounts to saying that if an organism has no need to weigh diverse needs it has no need of any elaborate mechanism for weighing diverse needs—which is undeniable. (3) "The analysis set forth here casts serious doubt on the usefulness of current economic and statistical theories of rational behavior" and "suggests an alternative approach" "more closely related to psychological theories" and "in closer agreement with the facts of behavior as observed in laboratory and field." As we have suggested above, the analysis set forth here does no such thing. That doubt and that suggestion preceded the model, they were what gave rise to it, and they are in no way affected by the mathematical explication and manipulation.
[67] See also *Models of Man*, pp. 196-206; *Organizations*, pp. 190-191.

the difference between looking for the sharpest needle in a haystack and looking for a needle sharp enough to sew with (*Organizations,* p. 141). "Satisficing" is a new name for an old idea. It is sensible to say that a rational man seeks a course of action that is good enough; and that is surely preferable to saying that he seeks the unique best way. But Simon gives scarcely any systematic consideration to what would seem obviously to be the next question, the one that points to the basis on which we distinguish more or less rational behavior in ordinary life: good enough *for what?* Is the standard of "good enough" to be sought in the survival of the organism? In what the organism says is good enough? In what it "feels" is good enough? Sometimes Simon expresses his idea by saying that humans engage in "intendedly rational behavior," which he shrewdly defines as "the kind of adjustment of behavior to goals of which humans are capable—a very incomplete and imperfect adjustment, to be sure, but one which nevertheless does accomplish purposes and does carry out programs" (*Research Frontiers in Politics and Government,* pp. 30-31). This raises precisely the same kind of question: what is it that intendedly rational behavior intends? On this vital question, the importance of which Simon does not deny, the scientific precision on which he prides himself evaporates into confusion, contradiction, and vagueness.

The standard of survival was sometimes used by Simon in his early writings, and we have considered some of its difficulties. In "Rational Choice and the Structure of the Environment," the survival of the choosing organism is the primary test. This makes sense in a rough way, especially if you are dealing with rats (though rats also reproduce). Elsewhere Simon has suggested that while the economists' theory of the firm has been concerned with finding the "optimal" behavior, theories of organization have also been concerned "with the whole set of *viable* solutions—that is, solutions that permit the survival of the organization. . . ." Organization theory is generally concerned "with the conditions necessary for organizational survival, that is, the conditions under which the participants will continue to participate." [68] But obviously the survival of an organization does not depend upon the continued participation of every one of the participants. A new organization is not necessarily called into play when one employee quits and is replaced by another. Yet no other criterion of survival is presented. Does a city government survive when it is taken over by a gang of thieves? Will the public school system of the deep South have survived if integration of the races is accomplished? If the schools are turned over to private hands? There is no suggestion of how questions such as these are to be approached. Simon can never say whether an organization survives because he never provides an adequate definition of what an organization is.[69]

[68] "A Comparison of Organization Theories," *Models of Man,* pp. 170, 173. This essay was originally published in the *Review of Economic Studies,* vol. 20, no. 1, 1952-1953.
[69] See below, pp. 129-130. See also *Models of Man,* p. 254, n. 7.

Moreover, as Simon himself often points out, mere survival is rarely the question. There are almost always numerous courses of action consistent with survival, and some choice has to be made among them. "In general, the survival criterion will not yield a unique solution to the values of inducements and contributions." Simon attempts to deal with this problem by suggesting that:

To restrict further the set of viable solutions, a weak optimality condition can be imposed that does not involve any assumption of interpersonal comparison of satisfactions or utilities. A viable solution is regarded as optimal if no further increase could be made in the net satisfaction of any one participant without decreasing the satisfaction of at least one other participant [*Models of Man*, p. 173].

This is weak in more ways than one. Even if we could measure "satisfaction," we are still left without a unique solution, as Simon concedes. More interesting is the fact that this version of the greatest happiness of the greatest number is simply plucked out of the air without the least attempt to ground it in anything. Simon goes on to say that we may obtain a unique solution by selecting the solution in which "the employee" captures the whole of the surplus, or "the entrepreneur," or, presumably, the customer. We may indeed build our model on any basis we like. What Simon actually does, as we have seen, is to take the point of view of the employer or those at the top of the administrative hierarchy.

It is necessary then to judge the rationality of behavior in terms of what the individual or organization *regards* as good—or good enough. Throughout his writings, particularly in his examples, Simon takes what people say they want as the values in terms of which rationality is to be judged in their case. On the other hand, he points out that "much human behavior has its roots very deep in the subconscious and non-rational parts of the mind," and he warns that we cannot be satisfied "with an individual's own reasons or rationalizations for what he has done" (*Public Administration*, p. 73). For the same reason we presumably cannot be satisfied with his "reasons or rationalizations" for what he wants to do. How then do we identify in any particular case what intendedly rational behavior *really* intends? By no other means finally than behavior itself. "The clearest way to determine which ends are sought for their own sake, and which for their usefulness as means to more distant ends, is to place the subject in situations where he must choose between conflicting ends" (*Administrative Behavior*, p. 63). This must also be the way to test the extent to which avowed preferences are real preferences. Can we ever say, then, that a decision is not rational? What would that mean? It would mean that a man (or an organism or an organization) had not dealt with his environment in such a way as to maximize the achievement of his values or—and here there is no fundamental difference—in such a way as to "satisfice." But the values, the goals, are settled by his often unconsciously determined preferences. Shall we not find that he acted perfectly rationally every time, *given his value premises or preferences*, many of which are entirely unknown and unknowable to him? Even if an individual does not take some simple and obvious action necessary to the achievement of his stated goal, is not the reason always that in the depths of his unconscious he is giving preference to some other "value"? [70]

Another manifestation of this same difficulty arises out of the "commonplace of experience that an anticipated pleasure may be a very different sort of thing from a realized pleasure." "Even when the consequences of a choice have been rather completely described, the anticipation of them can hardly act with the same force upon the emotions as the experiencing of them" (*Administrative Behavior*, p. 83). Or, as Simon says in one of the "satisficing" essays, "The consequences that the organism experiences may change the payoff function—it doesn't know how well it likes cheese until it has eaten cheese" (*Models of Man*, p. 255). There is no reason to expect that what I now think that I shall like tomorrow I shall in fact like tomorrow. But then the basis for the exercise of rationality crumbles beneath my feet. I may as well confine myself to getting whatever pleasure I can out of today's cheese because, however well I predict what the morrow will bring, I cannot know how I will react to it. [71] Yet yesterday's decisions do somehow guide those of today, and Simon has always laid great stress on this tendency.

There is nothing which prevents the subject, or the organization, having chosen one strategy on Monday, from selecting a different one on Tuesday. But the Monday decision, in so far as it has been partly acted out before its reconsideration, has already narrowed down the strategies available on Tuesday. . . . Hence, the individual or organization can be committed to a particular line of action from the fact that, having once initiated it, *it appears preferable* to continue with it rather than to relinquish completely the portion which has already been carried out.

This time-binding character of strategies deserves the greatest emphasis, for it makes possible at least a modicum of rationality in behavior, where, without it, this would be inconceivable [*Administrative Behavior*, pp. 67-68, italics supplied].

Indeed this narrowing of alternatives is "a necessary, though not a sufficient, condition of rationality." "It is the existence of these long-term, irrevocable decisions that *more than anything else* accounts for the relative consistency of both personal and organizational behavior over periods of time" (pp. 68, 66; italics supplied). This last statement is at best very care-

[70] See *Public Administration*, p. 73: "Many of the behaviors that appear to an observer irrational and inexplicable are simply reflections of the struggle going on within the human personality." Simon goes on to distinguish the behavior of the neurotic (which is "ill-adapted to the situation") and the behavior of the "objective" person, a normative distinction that has its roots in psychological speculations which do not sit comfortably with Simon's logical positivism.

[71] See Harry V. Jaffa, "Comment on Oppenheim," *American Political Science Review*, March 1957, p. 55, n. 3.

lessly put. It is clear that yesterday's decisions limit choice today. Past decisions are "irrevocable" in the sense that they irrevocably close certain alternatives and open others. But they are not irrevocable in the sense of committing present behavior to the pursuit of previously decided values. On Simon's premises it is never a past decision but always a present one (whether or not conscious) that accounts for consistency of behavior over time. There is consistency to the extent that "it appears preferable" *now* to stick to the old strategy and the old values. It is, in fact, a preference for consistency that accounts for the so-called "long-term irrevocable decisions," rather than the other way around. The "long-termness" of yesterday's decision is revocable at will. It is no doubt true that most people do stick to fairly consistent values and lines of behavior over time, but on Simon's premises there is no more reason in such behavior than there would be in the most fickle kind of behavior imaginable. Thus while recognizing that consistency in behavior (and in preference) over time is necessary to even "a modicum of rationality in behavior," Simon must at the same time admit that inconsistency is every bit as rational as consistency. The non-rational preferences on which rationality rests not only determine the goals to be pursued, they also determine whether or to what extent choice will be made according to the method of "rationality." The Simon of *Administrative Behavior* sometimes refers to a "higher" or "broader" rationality. He might say that this fickle individual really ought to stick to wanting something, for unless he settles on some rather consistent set of wants, he is going to have very little sustained opportunity for problem-solving and therefore for fulfilling his nature as a rational human being. With the satisficing notion and its frank admission that rational behavior need seek not for the maximization of previously defined values but for any solution regarded by the actor as "good enough" for the time being, Simon gives up whatever hold he may have had upon even this prescription. The actor can refute utterly any proposition the scientist may make about the requirements of rational behavior by replying simply, "That isn't my idea of a good time."

Simon is not unaware of the difficulty stemming from the mutability of preferences, but he attempts to convert it into an advantage. This is done by means of the "aspiration level" concept. Simon suggests that in the case of some organisms under some circumstances the aspiration level may rise and fall in some ascertainable relation to the ease or difficulty of getting what is valued. The "vague principle" here is that

as the individual, in his exploration of alternatives, finds it easy to discover satisfactory alternatives, his aspiration level rises; as he finds it difficult to discover satisfactory alternatives, his aspiration level falls. . . .

Such changes in aspiration level would tend to bring about a "near-uniqueness" of the satisfactory solutions and would also tend to guarantee the existence of satisfactory solutions. For the failure to discover a solution would depress the aspiration level and bring satisfactory solutions into existence [*Models of Man*, p. 253].

One could say either that we always want slightly more than we can get and therefore remain always just unsatisfied or, as Simon chooses to put it, that we are always about satisficed—or about to be satisficed.

There is, however, another way of meeting a failure to discover a satisfactory solution, and that is to look around some more—to search for behavior alternatives previously ignored. Simon continues:

> In one organism, dynamic adjustment over a sequence of choices may depend primarily upon adjustments of the aspiration level. In another organism, the adjustments may be primarily in the set [of alternatives considered]: if satisfactory alternatives are discovered easily, [the set of alternatives considered] narrows; if it becomes difficult to find satisfactory alternatives [the set considered] broadens. The more *persistent* the organism, the greater the role played by the adjustment of [the set of alternatives considered], relative to the role played by the adjustment of the aspiration level [p. 254].

One way of solving a problem arising out of the absence of any obvious way to get what you want is to persist in looking for some such way; another "solution" is to reduce your wants to something that is easily attainable. Thus the possibility of instability of preferences over time is transformed, by a sleight of hand, from a fundamental limit on rational behavior into an explanation of how the problems of rational beings are often solved—and rationally! [72] The trouble is that there is no reason why the intellectual problems of rational behavior cannot be reduced indefinitely by this process. Thus the absurd inhabitant of the maximizing model—a being that achieves perfect rationality in the pursuit of inexplicably stable preferences by means of an inconceivable information-gathering and calculational capacity—is replaced by that of the "aspiration level" model—a being whose wants are absurdly flexible and who might solve all of its problems by wholly eliminating its wants.

The "satisficing" model is, to begin with, a rather crude version of means-end language, in which the notion of "good enough" is made to serve the function of a prior end, guiding and limiting calculations with respect to means. So far, Simon only makes explicit the common sense assumptions to which he again and again resorts in his earlier work. The theoretical difficulty arises when he attempts to address the question, what is "good enough"? Finally, Simon's answer seems to be that an actor's definition of "good enough" is to be explained in terms of the aspiration level concept: "over time, the aspiration level tends to adjust to the level of achievement. That is to say, the level of satisfactory performance is likely to be very close to the

[72] "the aspiration level itself may be subject to an adjustment process that is rational in some dynamic sense" (*Models of Man*, p. 254).

actually achieved level of recent performance" (*Organizations*, pp. 182-183). This explanation amounts, in psychological terms, to a return to the "stimulus-response" pattern of behavior; only Simon now chooses to call it "rational in some dynamic sense" (*Models of Man*, p. 254). The aspiration level concept is the psychological knot that ties up the loose ends of the satisficing model, but unless we are willing (with Simon) to close our eyes to its most important implications, we must see that it ends by strangling rationality altogether.

In his review of the second edition of *Administrative Behavior*, Edward Banfield contends that Simon has "kicked the props out from under the decision-making schema by discovering that administrative man, instead of seeking a maximum, seeks only what is 'good enough.'" [73] Simon, on the other hand, asserts that he has "few, if any, major changes to propose in the basic conceptual framework," and he regards his later writings as a series of elaborations and rather minor modifications of the thesis (or theses) of *Administrative Behavior* (*Administrative Behavior*, p. x). Banfield points out that the maximizing model never purported to describe actual behavior, and speculates that Simon "may now feel that the concepts efficiency and rationality are too unrealistic to be useful even as guides to a 'practical' science of administration. He does not, however, say this in so many words." Indeed of the standard of good administration under the satisficing model, "Simon in the Introduction to the new edition says nothing." He says very little about it anywhere in his recent work. Nevertheless, while Simon seems to have "kicked the props out" from under the maximizing model, he does, rather uncomfortably and very quietly, retain just that model as the background of his discussion of satisficing. We reach this conclusion even in the face of what seems to be an explicit denial:

It may be said in defense of the theory of games and statistical decision theory that they are to be regarded not as descriptions of human choice but as normative theories for the guidance of rational decision. Even this defense seems to me untenable, but I shall not pursue the issue here. We are interested here in the prediction and description of human behavior, rather than in normative rules of conduct [*Models of Man*, p. 203].[74]

Unfortunately, Simon does not pursue the question anywhere except casually and unclearly, as for example when he concedes that the maximizing models do have "considerable normative interest" (*Administrative Behavior*, p. xxiii). There is no hint in his later work of a different notion of rationality from that of the maximizing model. Quite the contrary, he often refers in his later writings to the satisficing models as approximations. Approximations to

---

[73] "The Decision-Making Schema," *Public Administration Review*, Autumn 1957, p. 285.
[74] It seems clear from the context that Simon intends his remarks to apply also to classical economic theory and to the "maximizing" model of *Administrative Behavior*.

what? To nothing but the maximizing model which now stands in such ill favor:

in many situations we may be interested in the precise question of whether one decision-making procedure is more rational than another, and to answer this question we will usually have to construct a broader criterion of rationality that encompasses both procedures as *approximations*. Our whole point is that it is important to make explicit what level we are considering in such a hierarchy of models, and that for many purposes we are interested in models of "limited" rationality rather than models of relatively "global" rationality [*Models of Man*, pp. 254-255, italics supplied].[75]

There is a hint again of that endless escalator—but it must have an end, and that can be nothing, on Simon's premises, but the maximizing principle. Sometimes this is all but admitted. "One can hardly take exception to these requirements [of the maximizing model] in a normative model—a model that tells people how they *ought* to choose" (*Organizations*, p. 138).[76] Simon's rebuttal to Banfield suggests the level at which this question is now dealt with.

My argument is that men satisfice because they have not the wits to maximize. I think this is a verifiable empirical proposition. It can be turned around, if anyone prefers: If you have the wits to maximize, it is silly to satisfice.[77]

The "satisficing" notion was always implicit in the maximizing model, because the actor could will or prefer anything he liked, not excluding rationality itself. At the same time, the global "maximizing" standard of rationality is implicit in the satisficing model, because it remains the only available ideal, to which any sort of satisficing rationality whatever is an approximation. It is precisely this ambiguity that characterizes Simon's conception of human choice. Rationality, strictly speaking, is both impossible and empty, and Simon tries to bring it within the range of possibility and to give it some content in two ways. First, he tries to view individual behavior within the context of an organization wherein the individual's choice problem is both limited and related to some "over-all system of values." This attempt fails because it depends on looking at individual behavior "from the standpoint of the organization as a whole rather than from that of an individual member" (*Administrative Behavior*, p. 93), and there is no way consistently with Simon's theory to adopt such a standpoint. Second, Simon tries to reconstruct the concept of rationality itself. The claim is "not to substitute the irrational for the rational in the explanation of human behavior but to recon-

[75] "Relatively 'global' rationality" as distinguished from "'limited' rationality" comes under the same section of the Simonian dictionary as "reasonable approximation to . . . objective rationality" and "rational in some dynamic sense" (pp. 198, 254).
[76] On the contrary, one can (on Simon's assumptions) easily take exception to these requirements if he pleases, just because they are in a normative model. See below, pp. 147-149.
[77] *Public Administration Review*, Winter 1958, p. 62.

struct the theory of the rational" (*Models of Man*, p. 200), but there is less reconstruction than watering down. This recent attempt to prevent real behavior from disappearing altogether into the emptiness of "perfect rationality" has only caused the rational element of decision-making to collapse into its psychological base. Simon bridges the gap between what he understands to be the psychological and the rational aspects of human behavior only by jumping, with considerable agility, from one to the other. The great synthesis for which he seeks would require the discovery in human nature of something more than a bundle of urges served by a "complex information-processing system" (*Organizations*, p. 9).

THE LANGUAGE OF SCIENCE

THE CASE AGAINST COMMON SENSE

Throughout his work, Simon has been primarily concerned with the preparation of linguistic tools by means of which administration can be approached scientifically. He finds ordinary language radically defective for two reasons. First, its terms are not "operational" and, therefore, not solidly founded on empirical observation. Second, it does not sufficiently distinguish between facts and values, and it fails to recognize the subjectivity and non-rationality of values.[78] In reply to some of the broader criticisms of his work, Simon might well argue that precision in the statement of even rather little things is preferable to vagueness about everything. It is for this reason that it has been necessary to refer to the looseness, vagueness, and frequent resort to common sense in Simon's own vocabulary. Whether an enormous lack of precision is characteristic of today's scientific approach to the study of politics the reader must judge for himself. That it is not peculiar to Simon is evident from other essays in the present volume. Part of the absence of a consistently scientific concern with precision and accuracy of expression may be due to mere carelessness on Simon's part, arising perhaps from the great frequency with which he goes to press,[79] and is therefore of only secondary interest or importance. But the dullness of his linguistic tools also has a deeper lying cause.

Simon begins, as we have seen, with an attack on the proverbial character of the traditional principles of administration.

It is a fatal defect of the current principles of administration that, like proverbs, they occur in pairs. For almost every principle one can find an equally plausible and acceptable contradictory principle. Although the two principles of the pair will

78 While these two defects of ordinary language are closely connected, this section will deal mainly with the former and the next section, pp. 142 ff, mainly with the latter. Also see below, pp. 321-322.
79 Those with a taste for the empirical may like to know that the rate over the past twenty years has been approximately one article, or review, or comment every two months, and a book every two years. Many of these were of course written in collaboration with others.

lead to exactly opposite organizational recommendations, there is nothing in the theory to indicate which is the proper one to apply [*Administrative Behavior*, p. 20].

Simon's argument is not merely against the masking of proverbs in pseudo-scientific language—to that extent, his criticisms of men like Gulick are justi-fied—but against the value of proverbs themselves.

It may be objected that administration cannot aspire to be a "science," that by the nature of its subject it cannot be more than an "art." Whether true or false, this objection is irrelevant to the present discussion. The question of how "exact" the principles of administration can be made is one that only experience can an-swer. But as to whether they should be logical or illogical there can be no debate. Even an "art" cannot be founded on proverbs [p. 44].[80]

Or can it? Certainly Simon finds the proverbs difficult to keep down. He gives as one example of the trouble with proverbs, "the customary discus-sions of 'centralization' *vs.* 'decentralization,' which usually conclude, in effect, that 'on the one hand, centralization of decision-making function is desirable; on the other hand, there are definite advantages in decentraliza-tion.'" Two hundred pages later he presents his own conclusion on this sub-ject: "some measure of centralization is indispensable to secure the advan-tages of organization: coordination, expertise, and responsibility. On the other hand, the costs of centralization must not be forgotten" (pp. 35, 239). Proverbs are legion throughout Simon's own administrative analysis, and they are often the very proverbs against which he inveighs so vigorously and so often.[81]

Simon's attack on the proverbs of administration has not always been so emphatic as the one he makes in *Administrative Behavior*. In 1945 he criti-cized L. Urwick's *The Elements of Administration* for being unscientific and proverbial; but he went on to admit that it contains "some very homely, and on the whole very sound, advice on how to administer." He urged that "it is time for administration to have done with homely wisdom, . . . par-ticularly when it seeks for 'principles' rather than mere practical counsel. . . ." Apparently homely wisdom does not need to be thrown out in the latter case, at least for the present.

[80] See also, Herbert A. Simon, "The Proverbs of Administration," *Public Administration Review*, Winter 1946. That proverbial wisdom is not in itself conclusive in any particular situation goes without saying, but it is not therefore "illogical." The proverb does not claim to be sufficient to decide a particular case. It purports to do no more than to alert us to a problem, to sharpen our sense of timing, and to remind us of what we and others have learned in the past. It does not claim to free us of the burden of judging the reasonableness of alternative courses of action. The proverb assumes that its addressee has both some ex-perience in action and some understanding of the ends of action.
[81] See for example his discussion of "Functionalization in Relation to Efficiency," *Ad-ministrative Behavior*, pp. 190-192, and his discussion of span of control and specialization, *Public Administration*, pp. 131-132, 147.

This reviewer would be the last one to cast stones at the author in protest against his use of the venerable proverbs of administration. The proverbs have been culled from the experience and thought of successful administrators, and represent almost the sum and substance of our written knowledge of administration at the present time. It will be time enough to throw them out when we can substitute for them a logical, realistic, and workable theory of administration.[82]

The argument in this review is that the art of administration *is* founded on proverbs, which provide the basis for "very sound" practical advice, but that it would be better to replace the art by a science.

In a reply to Edward Banfield's review of the second edition of *Administrative Behavior*, Simon accuses his critic of a lack of candor in failing to present the case against "wisdom" or "common sense" with the same fervor with which he presents the case against "science." Simon therefore undertakes to do so.

1. We have applied "wisdom" to administration for 2,000 years. It has allowed us to carry out many administrative tasks reasonably well. However, I don't detect much progress from the "wisdom" literature in administrative theory during the past fifty years. Aristotle and the Hoover Commission sound much alike, except that the former was a good deal more sophisticated than the latter about the relation of politics to administration.
2. Many other areas of human knowledge began to progress—in both their theoretical and applied aspects—when scientific method was applied to them. I refer not primarily to the physical sciences, but to the much closer parallel of biology and medicine. You can find the same kinds of impassioned pleas for "wisdom" in medicine a century ago as we find in administration today. Meanwhile, the sale of Lydia Pinkham's Vegetable Compound has fallen off; the sale of thyroid extract has increased.[83]

Simon concedes that "wisdom" has allowed us to carry out many administrative tasks "reasonably well" (though it is not, apparently, "good enough" when measured against the scale of Simon's preferences). "Reasonably well" is a common sense notion. We know the value of this old fashioned "wisdom" by an exercise of just that kind of wisdom; yet strictly speaking we are supposed to know nothing except what we know scientifically. But Simon discerns no progress. He does not say why the lack of progress is an argument against "wisdom," and that would seem to be necessary since we have been getting along "reasonably well" with what wisdom we have. Indeed on the basis of Simon's own account of the relative value of Aristotle and the Hoover Commission, it seems possible that we have actually fallen back in our understanding of administration. When we remember that serious attempts to apply science to administration began in this country just about fifty years ago and that there has been very little "wisdom" literature in the field during

[82] *Public Personnel Review*, April 1945, pp. 121-122.
[83] *Public Administration Review*, Winter 1958, p. 63.

that time (though there has been much scientific literature more or less diluted with "wisdom," as in the Hoover Commission reports), we may wonder whether our lack of progress or our regression, whichever it is, is due to too little science or too much.

Turning to the second paragraph of the indictment, scientific activities in other areas do indeed raise a serious question about traditional wisdom in the area of human affairs, though whether success in the marketplace is the best test is perhaps open to question. It is important, however, to be clear about what the question is. It is not "common sense" versus "science." Virtually no one claims that common sense, or proverbial wisdom, is sufficient either as a guide to action or as a means of understanding human behavior. The question is whether the admittedly necessary transcendence of common sense is to be achieved by science, as understood by Simon, or by an exploration of human ends, to which common sense points but which it alone is not competent to undertake. It is interesting that Simon should think that biology and medicine provide the "closer parallel" to administration, for scientific method in these fields is still guided to a great extent by old common sense ideas. Biologists are still able to talk about needs (by which they do not mean wants), and the vocabulary of medicine is full of words, like illness, defect, recovery, and health, which Simon would have to label value judgments and therefore out of place in any science. If ever a vocabulary was in need of scientific reconstruction it is that of the physicians.[84]

SCIENCE AND COMMON SENSE

It is important to understand the radical break from common sense language which Simon proposes. The language of science is to be no mere refinement of common sense but a different language altogether. Simon argues that

commonsense, far from providing the basis for social science, is not even expressed in the same language as social science. Rather, it is a part of the data with which social science must deal. Systematic ambiguity between these two languages—the common practice of using for social science the same vocabulary and rules of grammar as are used in the society we are studying—should never conceal from us the fact that two distinct languages really are involved.[85]

This "systematic ambiguity" may give rise to dangerous confusion, "unless

[84] Nor is it sufficient to say, as Simon does in *Public Administration* (p. 19), that while the "values" of the medical researcher "provide a motive for his work, . . . they have nothing to do with the content of his discoveries." It is perfectly true that both the discoveries and the techniques of medical research may have wide applicability; but research in medical science as such is not merely motivated but is fundamentally guided by the "values" implied in "health": "Soundness of body; that condition in which its functions are duly discharged." *Shorter Oxford English Dictionary.*
[85] Charner Perry, et al., "The Semantics of Political Science," *American Political Science Review*, June 1950, p. 408.

we assume that our social scientist is a man from Mars (or from a flying saucer), who does not communicate with the people whose behavior he is observing and predicting, or alternatively, that he is a man to whose predictions other people do not pay any particular attention." If we do make one of these assumptions "we may exclude statements in the language of social science from the system of behavior to which these statements refer." Indeed, "this is an exclusion we cannot avoid. . . ."

Simon is chiefly concerned with the well-known difficulty that what the scientist says about behavior may affect future behavior and thus interfere with his predictions.[86] This is, however, only a superficial aspect of the fundamental difficulty which is indicated by the proposition that we "cannot avoid" excluding statements in the language of social science from the system of behavior to which these statements refer. Simon tries to avoid the paradox of excluding the sayings of human scientists from the system of human behavior by resorting to outer space.

Let us, for simplicity, adopt the Martian alternative. Then we must distinguish statements in Martian from statements in English. The former are propositions of social science that refer to social phenomena, including English language phenomena. Our Martian, being incurably addicted to the methodology of the natural sciences, wishes to make generalizations and predictions about the behavior of the curious people who speak English.[87]

Simon then goes on to argue that this Martian might make precisely the same kind of investigations about his phenomena that the natural scientist makes about his. Even though the social scientist expresses his propositions in English, he is to be understood, a la Martian, as using an entirely different language from the English language used by those he is observing. The relation between the Martian-scientist and the human beings he studies is identical to the relation between the geologist and his rocks and the rat psychologist and his rats. Any "generalizations and predictions" that the Martian-scientist may make about human behavior are as irrelevant to his own behavior as generalizations about rat behavior are irrelevant to the behavior of the rat psychologist as such. The analogy is imperfect because rats cannot study the behavior of rats, at least not as rat psychologists do, but Simon does not consider the significance of this discrepancy.

What about the "closer parallel" of biology and medicine? Biologists and physicians deliberately confine themselves to the study of certain aspects of man, and thus their sciences do not have to account for their own behavior as biologists or physicians. Simon, on the other hand, has no such limited aim. He seeks to lay "foundations for a science of man that will accommodate

[86] See "Bandwagon and Underdog Effects of Election Predictions," *Models of Man*, pp. 79 ff. This essay was originally published in *Public Opinion Quarterly*, Fall 1954.
[87] *American Political Science Review*, June 1950, p. 408.

comfortably his dual nature as a social and as a rational animal" (*Models of Man*, p. vii).[88] As part of this endeavor, he speaks about speech and reasons about reason; and he is therefore obliged to account for his own speech and reasoning, as well as that of the other human "organisms" under his microscope. This is an obligation that he cannot fulfill. The behavior of the scientist as such—the activity, that is to say, of the search for truth—is beyond the science of human behavior. What purports to be a vocabulary for the description of human behavior cannot describe the highest form of it.

The inability of Simon's science of man to account for the behavior of scientists is only one face of the difficulty inherent in the contention that the language of the science of man is (or should be) altogether divorced from the language of man. The other face is Simon's complete inability to keep the two languages separate. In practice, he forgets that "two distinct languages are involved." The language of the science of man proves to depend fundamentally on what are on its own grounds illicit borrowings from the language of man. Contrary to Simon's assertion, common sense *does* provide the basis for his social science. The effect of his approach is only to ensure that the basis is unexamined.[89]

Simon states the first task of administrative science as follows:

Before a science can develop principles, it must possess concepts. . . . The first task of administrative theory is to develop a set of concepts that will permit the description, in terms relevant to the theory, of administrative situations. These concepts, to be scientifically useful, must be operational; that is, their meanings must correspond to empirically observable facts or situations [*Administrative Behavior*, p. 37].[90]

We can best judge the performance of this task by considering parts of Simon and March's recent book, *Organizations*, and then examining at

---

88 To the extent that medical science concerns itself with psychological rather than merely physical health, it does indeed require a comprehensive view of human beings and therefore of psychologists as such. See above, pp. 24-25.

89 This is even more emphatically the case in Simon's mathematical essays where he goes to the greatest lengths to free himself from dependence upon the language of ordinary life. Simon admits at one point in *Models of Man* (p. 90) that mathematics cannot solve all the problems thrown up in analysis; but he asserts that verbal reasoning cannot do so either— "except by a legerdemain that consists in introducing a host of implicit and unacknowledged assumptions at each step of the verbal argument. The poverty of mathematics is an honest poverty that does not parade imaginary riches before the world." What is under discussion, however, is not mathematics but mathematical *social science*. Simon's intention is not to present "mathematics for mathematics' sake," but to lay "foundations for a science of man" and to provide "a useful framework for deepening our understanding of the nature of man" (pp. vii-ix). There is of course no question about the honesty with which he pursues this intention, but it is certainly questionable whether he says anything important about "man, social and rational" that does not involve resort to "implicit and unacknowledged assumptions at each step of the . . . argument."

90 Simon does not explain how, since the concepts must precede the theory, it can be known whether they are "relevant to the theory." This is an aspect of the broader problem of relevance, discussed below, pp. 142 ff.

somewhat greater length Simon's definition and use of the concept of authority. In *Organizations*, Simon sets out to "review in a systematic way some of the important things that have been said about organizations by those who have studied them and written about them." There is, however, a difficulty.

Much of what we know or believe about organizations is distilled from common sense and from the practical experience of executives. The great bulk of this wisdom and lore has never been subjected to the rigorous scrutiny of scientific method. The literature contains many assertions, but little evidence to determine —by the usual scientific standards of public testability and reproducibility— whether these assertions really hold up in the world of fact.

It is, therefore, necessary to "restate some existing hypotheses in a form that makes them amenable to testing, giving considerable attention to the operational definition of variables . . ." (pp. 4-6).[91]
A prime characteristic of this book, and, one may say, of this procedure is the refusal to take anything for granted until it has been tested in the "usual scientific" way. One example is sufficient.

The role of unambiguous technical terms in permitting coordination by feedback is shown by the Christie-Luce-Macy experiments (Macy, Christie, and Luce, 1953) with "noisy marbles" in the Bavelas network. Participants in the experiment were given some colored marbles, and they were required to discover what color was held by all of them. Control groups were given marbles that had solid colors like "red," "yellow," etc. Experimental groups were given streaked marbles whose colorings did not correspond in any simple way to color designations in common language. Comparison of the performance of the control with the experimental groups showed (a) that the latter were much hindered by the lack of adequate technical vocabulary, and (b) that their performance became comparable to that of the control groups only when they succeeded in inventing such a vocabulary and securing its acceptance throughout the group [pp. 162-163].[92]

Yet absolute skepticism in some cases goes along with an absolute reliance on common sense in other cases. Many of the basic concepts in *Organizations* are not defined, operationally or any other way, the most striking example being the word "organization" itself.

This book is about the theory of formal organizations. It is easier, and probably more useful, to give examples of formal organizations than to define the term. . . . [F]or present purposes we need not trouble ourselves about the precise boundaries to be drawn around an organization or the exact distinction between an "organization" and a "nonorganization." We are dealing with empirical phenomena, and

[91] The variables are numbered so that their relations may be expressed symbolically. "Thus, if a proposition states that the value of dependent variable 3.7 varies with the values of independent variables 3.3, 3.4, and 3.6, we will number the proposition '[3.7: 3.3, 3.4, 3.6]' " (pp. 8-9).
[92] See also p. 59, where it is reported to be "fairly well established" that "an individual's family places constraints on his behavior in the organization (Hoppock, 1935)."

the world has an uncomfortable way of not permitting itself to be fitted into clean classifications [p. 1].[93]

No doubt it does and no doubt we all know pretty well what an organization is, just as we know what a man is. What is surprising is that this pre-scientific, common sense knowledge should be allowed to stand as the foundation of the whole scientific superstructure of variables and hypotheses and propositions of *Organizations*. The fact that Simon sometimes takes special pains to broaden the common sense notion of organization only emphasizes his ultimate reliance on pre-scientific understanding.

> The distinction between units in a production-distribution process that are "in" the organization and those that are "out" of the organization typically follows the legal definition of the boundaries of a particular firm. We find it fruitful to use a more functional criterion that includes both the suppliers and the distributors of the manufacturing core of the organization (or its analogue where the core of the organization is not manufacturing). . . .
> Taken too literally, this conception of organizations incorporates almost any knowledge about human behavior as a part of organization theory [pp. 89-90].

The traditional understanding of organization is too narrow, but Simon's conception (based on an unspecified "more functional" criterion) is too broad—if "taken too literally." Apparently we are to take both with the proverbial grain of salt.

Even the superstructure of variables and propositions proves to be much less scientific than might appear on the surface. In *Organizations*, as in *Administrative Behavior*, the concept of identification plays a central role. The "basic proposition" in *Organizations* is that "the stronger the individual's identification with a group, the more likely that his goals will conform to his perception of group norms" (p. 65).[94] For this to be a genuine scientific proposition, we would need some way of observing and measuring the two variables independently so that we could test it. Leaving aside any difficulties that might arise with reference to the second one (the conformity of the individual's goals to his perception of group norms), it is impossible to measure the first (the individual's identification with the group), because we are never

---

[93] Neither is organization defined in the body of *Administrative Behavior*. In the introduction to the second edition Simon says: "In the pages of this book, the term *organization* refers to the complex pattern of communications and other relations in a group of human beings" (p. xvi). This scarcely needs comment; it would include, for example, the relations in a group of human beings walking on a crowded sidewalk. Simon avoids this in the definition of "*formal organization*" given on p. 147 of *Administrative Behavior*: "a set of abstract, more or less permanent relations that govern the behavior of each participant." The difficulties here are obvious enough, including the meaning of "more or less permanent," the question whether "relations" can "govern," and the fact that an organization governs only some part of the behavior of the individual. See C. Barnard's deeper, if not ultimately more satisfactory, consideration of this problem, *The Functions of the Executive*, pp. 73-81.

[94] The rest of the quotations in this subsection are taken from *Organizations*, pp. 65-68.

told what identification is. Nowhere is it suggested how identification might be established empirically or its strength tested. As far as one can tell from *Organizations*, identification is precisely the conformity of an individual's goals to his perception of group norms. The so-called proposition is (if anything) a concealed and, be it noted, nonoperational definition.

Simon then goes on the suggest five "basic hypotheses" (later called "propositions") about the "factors" (later called "basic variables") affecting the strength of identification. Having done that, he describes "some important factors that affect these five variables." Can we perhaps proceed by taking the "basic proposition" discussed above as a rough (and nonoperational) definition of identification and regard what follows as a discussion of the variables that affect identification so defined? Unfortunately the same problem crops up again and again. Let us take the first of the "basic hypotheses" about the factors affecting the strength of identification: "The greater the *perceived prestige of the group* (3.65), the stronger the propensity of an individual to identify with it [3.53: 3.65]; and vice versa [3.65: 3.53]." The "perceived prestige of a group," in turn, "is a function of the *position of the group in the society* (3.68) and the character of *individual standards* (3.69) [3.65: 3.68, 3.69]." Whether this is supposed to be a testable hypothesis and if so how we can identify "perceived prestige" except as a combination of "position of the group in society" and "individual standards" are questions that are unanswered. Simon does, however, go on to take up each of these variables. "The position of a group in society is determined by its possession of symbols of success in the culture," three of which are given attention here.

First, the greater the *success in achieving group goals* (3.70), the higher the position of the group in the society [3.68: 3.70]. Second, the higher the average *status level* (3.71) of group members, the higher the position of the group in the society [3.68: 3.71]. Third, the greater the *visibility of the group* (3.72), the higher the position of the group in the society [3.68: 3.72].

Again there is no way suggested of independently establishing or measuring the dependent variable. We may have here the elements of a definition of "the position of the group in the society," but we do not have a set of hypotheses about the factors affecting it because it is never independently defined.[95] Simon then goes on:

Visibility, in turn, results from characteristics of the group that either distinguish it from other groups or increase the probability that it will be observed. Thus, the greater the *distinctiveness of the group* (3.73) (whether with respect to goals, membership, or practices), the greater its visibility [3.72: 3.73]; the greater the *size of the group* (3.74), the greater its visibility [3.72: 3.74]; the

[95] If we did have testable hypotheses we could perhaps measure the extent to which the high degree of 3.72 possessed by such a group as American Negroes results in a high degree of 3.68.

greater the *rate of growth of the group* (3.75), the greater its visibility [3.72: 3.75].

Once again, if we had some way of establishing "visibility" we might be able to conduct experiments to see whether in fact it "results from" these characteristics; but no such way is provided.

Obviously this procedure could be carried on indefinitely, and just as obviously no amount of such regression brings us any closer to meaningful (as Simon understands meaningful) propositions about the variables that affect identification—or about the factors that affect the variables that affect identification. *Organizations* is systematic, and it is unnecessary here to raise any questions about its internal consistency. The major difficulties arise when an attempt is made to connect the system with the real world. This connection has to be made, according to Simon, by means of the operational definition. The failure to provide such definitions of crucial terms means either that no connection between the verbal (or numerical) system and the real world is established or that such a connection is established only covertly by means of the very nonoperational, pre-scientific, common sense notions whose inadequacy initiated the scientific enterprise.[96]

AUTHORITY

No less important than identification in the Simonian vocabulary is the word "authority," and the definition of this word in *Administrative Behavior* is specifically pointed to as an example of an operational definition. The definition merits close attention, both to understand a basic concept in the science of administration and to see how Simon goes about replacing the vagueness of common language and common sense with scientific precision. In the new introduction to *Administrative Behavior*, written in 1957, Simon observes:

> There is no consensus today in the management literature as to how the term "authority" should be used. This is a matter of some regret to me, since I had hoped that the definition employed here, and derived from Barnard, would gain currency because of its obvious convenience and utility [p. xxxiv].[97]

One reason for the failure of others to recognize this "obvious convenience and utility" may lie in the fact that Simon seems to have a distaste for defin-

[96] The reader may wish to examine Simon's discussion of his theory of equilibrium, where the problem discussed here is taken up, and his discussion of the behavior of the "satisficing" individual or organization, with a view to satisfying himself that the difficulties suggested here are not confined to the concept of identification. See *Organizations*, pp. 84 ff., 140 ff.

[97] In 1951 Simon set out a symbolic formulation of his definition of authority and asserted that "this is the definition of authority that is most generally employed in modern administrative theory," citing Simon, *Administrative Behavior*, and Barnard, *The Functions of the Executive*. "A Formal Theory of the Employment Relation," *Models of Man*, p. 184. This essay was first published in *Econometrica*, July 1951.

ing the same word twice in the same way. It will be convenient to collect the main definitions to be found in *Administrative Behavior*.

[1] A subordinate is said to accept authority whenever he permits his behavior to be guided by the decision of a superior, without independently examining the merits of that decision [p. 11].

[2] A subordinate may be said to accept authority whenever he permits his behavior to be guided by a decision reached by another, irrespective of his own judgment as to the merits of that decision [p. 22].[98]

[3] "Authority" may be defined as the power to make decisions which guide the actions of another. It is a relationship between two individuals, one "superior," the other "subordinate." The superior frames and transmits decisions with the expectation that they will be accepted by the subordinate. The subordinate expects such decisions, and his conduct is determined by them [p. 125].

[4] At the expense of a possible abuse of the term, we shall use "authority" broadly, and comprehend under it all situations where suggestions are accepted without any critical review or consideration [p. 128].

[5] Authority is exercised over an individual whenever that individual, relaxing his own critical faculties, permits the communicated decision of another person to guide his own choice [p. 151].

According to Definitions 1 and 4, an individual permits his behavior to be guided by the decision of another "without independently examining the merits of that decision" or "without any critical review or consideration." Authority can operate "upward" and "sidewise" as well as "downward" in an organization. "If an executive delegates to his secretary a decision about file cabinets and accepts her recommendation without reexamination of its merits, he is accepting her authority" (p. 12). This leaves us with the curious conclusion that if, in another case, the secretary receives an order from her boss, examines the merits, disagrees with the order, but nevertheless accepts it, she is *not* accepting authority as defined here. Definition 2 avoids this difficulty. Here the crucial circumstance is that the subordinate accepts the decision, not necessarily without examining the merits, but "irrespective of his own judgment as to the merits of that decision," which is of course a different matter. In Definition 5 the issue is completely blurred, since Simon says only that the individual permits the decision of another to guide his own choice, "relaxing his own critical faculties." What kind of "relaxation" or how much is left entirely vague. The ambiguity between Definitions 1 and 4 and Definition 2 is somewhat clarified in *Public Administration*. Here we are told of two "instances of the acceptance of authority."

[A person] may carry out the proposal [of another] without being fully, or even partially, convinced of its merits. In fact he may not examine the merits of the proposal at all.

[98] This is the definition specifically pointed to as an example of an operational definition. See p. 37.

He may carry out the proposal even though he is convinced it is wrong—wrong either in terms of personal values or of organizational values or both [p. 182].

What Simon intends to exclude from his notion of authority is the situation where an individual examines the merits of the proposal and on the basis of this examination becomes convinced that he should carry it out. But now a new difficulty arises. Let us consider the subordinate who customarily gives independent examination to the "proposals" or orders given by his superior but who accepts them whether he agrees or not. It would appear, on the basis of the examples given here, that those cases where he agrees with the proposals are not instances of authority, even though he would carry out the proposal in any event. The definition might have been patched up by using the phrase of Definition 2 in *Administrative Behavior*, "irrespective of his own judgment as to the merits of that decision." That is probably the least unsatisfactory expression and its consistent use would have saved some unnecessary confusion; but it would not have settled more basic difficulties.

Definition 3, which is the main definition in the chapter on authority, has a different form. Here, it seems, we are told not merely when authority is exercised or accepted, but what it is. Authority is a kind of power, "the power to make decisions which guide the actions of another." But Simon does not go on to define power. Instead he returns to an explanation in terms of behavior.

The relationship of authority can be defined, therefore, in purely objective and behavioristic terms. It involves behaviors on the part of both superior and subordinate. When, and only when, these behaviors occur does a relation of authority exist between the two persons involved. When the behaviors do not occur there is no authority, whatever may be the "paper" theory of organization.

The behavior pattern of the superior involves a command—an imperative statement concerning the choice of a behavior alternative by the other—and an expectation that the command will be accepted by the other as a criterion of choice.

The behavior pattern of the subordinate is governed by a single indeterminate decision, or criterion for decision, to "follow that behavior alternative which is selected for me by the superior." That is, he holds in abeyance his own critical faculties for choosing between alternatives and uses the formal criterion of the receipt of a command or signal as his basis for choice [pp. 125-126].

All of the basic questions concerning Simon's definition and use of the concept of authority are embodied in this definition and explication. Significantly, Simon reverts here to the traditional language of command-obedience, but that causes some difficulty. He argues, for example, that "in so far as the recommendations of a staff agency are accepted without reexamination on their merits, the agency is really exercising authority, as we have defined that term" (p. 135); but these recommendations are not commands. And what of the secretary whose boss accepted her recommendations for a filing system, an example that is repeated here? She issued no command, no "imperative statement." She need not have "expected" her boss to accept the recommendation without examination. It may have been a complete surprise to her; but it is, according to Simon, no less an instance of authority for that. Again and again Simon falls into confusion regarding this matter. He asserts, for example, that

unity of command does not actually exist and cannot be established in real organizations. . . . To impose unity of command, we would have to prevent employees from accepting the proposals of specialists in whom they had confidence or whose authority seemed legitimate to them by reason of their functional status [*Public Administration*, p. 214].

We should have to do no such thing. We should have to prevent employees from accepting such proposals only when that would conflict with the orders of their hierarchical superiors. To say that an employee is obliged to obey only his immediate line superior is not to say that he can never accept the advice of, say, the accounting department. Simon is trying to make the point that members of organizations sometimes allow their behavior to be guided by others than their formal superiors. Of course that was always known, but it was thought important to make a distinction between the advice-acceptance relation and the command-obedience relation. Simon destroys that distinction, but finds it necessary constantly to revert to it *sub rosa*.[99] For example:

It is certainly undesirable for the organization that the subordinate who receives conflicting commands relating to the *same* decisional premise should be either punished for not carrying out both commands, or placed in a position where he may carry out either command that he prefers. In the . . . second case he will retain his original discretion, hence will not be subject to any real authority [*Administrative Behavior*, pp. 140-141].

Yet five pages later Simon repeats that authority, as used here, "refers to the *acceptance* by the subordinate of the decisions of the superior. . . ." Strictly speaking, whether the subordinate is subject to any "real" authority in the second case above depends entirely on how he uses the discretion left with him. If he uses it to accept the decision of someone—whether one of his commanders, or his wife, or anyone else—he subjects himself to authority that is as "real" as authority can be.

In fact, Simon constantly resorts to the "systematic ambiguity" between the language of common sense and the language of science, using either his behavioristic conception of authority or the common sense command-obedience

[99] In *Public Administration* (pp. 180-181), Simon makes an attempt to give this distinction some theoretical basis by distinguishing between the legal and the psychological aspects of authority. The distinction breaks down because the "legal" has for Simon no other basis than the psychological. The issue is not sufficiently developed by Simon to permit any useful analysis.

conception as it suits his convenience. It is the common sense conception that he has in mind when he describes the opposition of most persons "in our society" to "the use of authority in an arbitrary manner." And again when he says that "it is authority that gives an organization its formal structure. . . ." And again when he explains that authority "secures coordinated behavior in a group by subordinating the decisions of the individual to the communicated decisions of others" (*Public Administration*, pp. 70-71; *Administrative Behavior*, pp. 124, 134). "Authority," as defined behavioristically does not give the organization its formal structure. According to the formal structure, bosses have authority over secretaries, not the other way around. Neither does "authority" as thus defined necessarily "secure coordinated behavior in a group." It may have quite the opposite effect, depending on whose decisions the members of the group decide to accept.

Simon does sometimes make a distinction between formal authority and authority in fact, or as he expresses it at one point, between specific instances of authority and superior-subordinate "roles." "It is necessary to distinguish . . . between specific behaviors which are momentary instances of the exercise of authority, and the roles played by two persons over a period of time which involve an *expectation of obedience* by the one and a *willingness to obey* by the other" (*Administrative Behavior*, p. 126). Yet this distinction is constantly ignored or blurred. Sometimes he says that this relationship between roles is an "authority relationship." For example, the scheme of formal organization is said to establish "authority relationships," and in military organizations it is said to be "absolutely necessary to provide a continuity of authority, and a certainty in authority relations at all times" (*Administrative Behavior*, pp. 148, 145). Yet authority is defined in terms of discontinuous instances of behavior. "When, and only when, these behaviors occur does a relation of authority exist between the two persons involved." Simon is willing to say both that there is a continuing authority relation between the captain and private and that whenever the private is not obeying a command of the captain (or *vice versa!*) "there is no authority, whatever may be the 'paper' theory of organization."

Even if we ignore this difficulty, there is another which is especially important from Simon's point of view. Simon claims to define the relation of authority in "purely objective and behavioristic terms," but how far does he make this claim good in the case of the crucial circumstances of each of the definitions? Is an "independent examination of the merits" of a decision empirically observable behavior? Or an exercise of "judgment"? Or "critical review or consideration"? Or "relaxation of critical faculties"? And what of the "expectations" that, according to Definition 3, are part of the relation of authority? There is not the slightest attempt by Simon to demonstrate that any of these are empirically observable or deducible from what is empirically observable, leaving us with the suspicion that they are examples of that "soul stuff" which, according to a stricter behaviorist, "gives us absolutely no help in interpreting the doings of social men." [100] In the introduction to the second edition of *Administrative Behavior*, Simon provides still another formulation of his definition: "Authority, we say, exists when the behavior premises of another are accepted as bases for decision" (p. xxxv). The trouble again is that what is crucial in this definition is not behavior, but whether the behavior was determined by the acceptance of the premises of another or in some other way (such as a conviction about the merits of the case), and we cannot observe that empirically.

"Expectations" is the source of another difficulty which this time Simon does consider.

If authority were evidenced entirely in the acceptance of explicit commands, or in the resolution of disagreements, its presence or absence in any relationship could be sought in the presence or absence of these tangible concomitants. But it is equally possible for obedience to anticipate commands. The subordinate may, and is expected to, ask himself "How would my superior wish me to behave under these circumstances?" Under such circumstances, authority is implemented by a subsequent review of completed actions, rather than a prior command. Further, the more obedient the subordinate, the less tangible will be the evidences of authority. For authority will need to be exercised only to reverse an incorrect decision.

This phenomenon. . . . affords a striking example of the manner in which expectations and anticipations govern human behavior, and the difficulties which result from this for the analysis of human institutions. . . .

Any study of power relations which confines itself to instances where the sanctions of power were invoked misses the essential fact of the situation. To avoid this fallacy, authority has been defined in this study not in terms of the sanctions of the superior, but in terms of the behaviors of the subordinate [*Administrative Behavior*, pp. 129-130].

To avoid this fallacy, however, Simon falls into another. He suggests that authority is present where obedience anticipates as well as where it follows command. Then the mere behavior of the subordinate is not sufficient to tell us whether there was an authority relationship or not. Where there was no explicit command, we have to know whether the subordinate acted as he did because of an anticipation of what the superior would have commanded had he issued a command or for some other reason. But these expectations or anticipations "govern" behavior; they are not behavior, and they are not logically deducible from behavior. Returning to the example of the secretary, we do not know by looking at her behavior whether she was exercising authority over her boss or he was exercising authority (by anticipation on her part) over her.

[100] Arthur F. Bentley, *The Process of Government* (San Antonio, Tex.: The Principia Press of Trinity University [Tex.], 1949), p. 110.

In spite of his disappointment at the failure of his definitions of authority to sweep the field, Simon is not entirely satisfied with the way the underlying problems are dealt with in his early writings. "After putting these problems aside for some years, I returned in about 1950 to the task of defining political power, only to find myself as unable as ever to arrive at a satisfactory solution" (*Models of Man*, p. 5). He attacked this "central problem of political science" in an article, "Notes on the Observation and Measurement of Political Power," first published in 1953.[101] We can comment only on those aspects of the discussion that bear most directly on our two major concerns: What is authority, or influence, or power? How does the scientist go about replacing the vagueness of common sense and common language with the exactness and precision of science?

Rejecting definitions of power in terms of "value position" (for reasons which we shall examine later), Simon adopts Lasswell and Kaplan's definition of "influence process": " 'The exercise of influence (influence process) consists in affecting policies of others than the self' " (*Models of Man*, p. 65). He then goes on to discuss several difficulties in the direct observation of influence, especially those arising out of the "rule of anticipated reactions." If everyone's predictions about everyone else's behavior were perfectly correct it would be impossible to say who was influencing whom.

Fortunately for political scientists—who would otherwise be largely debarred from observation of the central phenomenon of their science—the members of the body politic are often far from accurate in their predictions. . . . The unpredicted and the unexpected provide a break in the usual chain of intended connections and, serving as something of a substitute for controlled experimentation, permit us to observe the construction of the separate links [p. 68].

Granting that under these conditions we can identify which was the independent and which the dependent variable, a difficulty remains which Simon does not consider. We can never know how deeply such an "experiment" allows us to see into the real power relations, because we can never know the *extent* of the miscalculation that allows us to see anything at all.

Passing over Simon's discussion of many interesting but long-noted aspects of the problem of power (for example that the strength of a regime depends partly on how strong people think it is), we can turn to his concluding discussion of the units of observation. He points out that quantities may be measured in various ways, such as by the use of cardinal numbers, ordinal numbers, and vectors; and it is necessary to inquire what "kind" of quantity best represents influence and power. Simon examines a "particular class of power relations," namely, that denoted by the term "authority." The definition is still different from those we have observed. "We will say that an

[101] *Models of Man*, pp. 62-78. This essay was first published in *Journal of Politics*, November 1953.

individual accepts *authority* when his choice among alternative behaviors is determined by the communicated decision of another" (p. 75). It will be observed that all the difficulties previously encountered in stating the conditions under which an acceptance of another's decision is an instance of authority are here swept aside by saying simply that the choice is "determined" by the communicated decision of another. How does this affect the problem of observing and measuring authority?

Simon points out here, as he does in all his discussions of authority, that

authority is never unlimited—the range of alternative behaviors from which the superior may select the particular choice he desires of the subordinate is a finite range. The limits within which authority will be accepted we will call the *zone of acceptance*.[102]

He then suggests how authority might be measured.

Let us regard each possible behavior that B can perform as an element in a set, and let us designate the set of all such possible behaviors by V. The set of behaviors that B will perform at A's command (the subset of V corresponding to B's zone of acceptance) we will designate by S. Then we can use the size of the set S as a measure of A's authority over B.

But what kind of a quantity is the size of S? Suppose that at one time B will accept any order in the set S, but at some later time he will only accept orders in S', which is a part of S. Then we are surely justified in saying that A's authority has decreased. Under such circumstances, comparisons of "greater" and "less" are possible. But it may happen that the zone of acceptance changes from S' to S" where these are intersecting (overlapping) sets neither of which entirely includes the other. In this case we cannot say that A's authority has increased or that it has decreased—our sets are not completely ordered. The kind of quantity that appears most suitable for measuring the degree of authority of A over B is what the mathematician would call a "partial ordering" [pp. 75-76].

This may be disappointing, but Simon very wisely points out that "if power relations are only partially ordered, then we shall certainly end up by talking nonsense about them if we insist that they should be represented by cardinal numbers, or that we should always be able to predict 'greater' or 'less' of them. If we feel disappointment, it should be directed at the phenomena with which we are confronted rather than at the kind of quantity that appears to represent them."

The first thing to note is that Simon makes no use at all in the model

[102] This notion was taken from Barnard (see *Administrative Behavior*, pp. 11-12), and it is implicit in the equilibrium concept already discussed. It has not been thought necessary to examine it in any detail here, but the reader may wish to sample Simon's rigorous reasonings: "Psychological propositions are important for determining the area within which authority will be respected, and the degree to which the intent of the order-giver will actually be carried out; but in so far as the authority is actually accepted they have no significance for determining what the subordinate's behaviors will be" (*Administrative Behavior*, p. 150).

presented here of "V," the set of all possible behaviors that B (the influenced) can perform. He does not measure the size of S in terms of V. He does not, that is to say, suggest that the authority of A can be measured by calculating what proportion of the behaviors that B might possibly perform is contained in the set that B will perform at A's command. This would have had the advantage of being a completely ordered system, but obviously we cannot count the number of behavior possibilities in V. In spite of the way the model is constructed (to be explained, perhaps, by habit), V really has nothing to do with the measurement of authority, as Simon sees the problem here.[103] It is S (the set of behaviors that B will perform at A's command) that we are interested in. But how do we observe that?

The procedure is relatively straightforward; we observe what kinds of decisions are accepted and what kinds are not. If His Majesty's first minister decides that several hundred additional lords shall be created to establish the supremacy of the House of Commons, will His Majesty accede to the request? The observation falls within our general definition of influence: how does the behavior of the influencee vary with the behavior (in this case the decision) of the influencer? [p. 77]

He points out that the difficulties arising from the rule of anticipated reactions are present here too. In particular, "because of the effect of expectations, the zone of acceptance may be suddenly narrowed when the influencee judges that he will be joined in resistance to authority by others." Simon closes the discussion by saying that "to pursue these matters further would carry us rapidly into some rather difficult mathematical questions." But have we not skipped very rapidly over some rather difficult nonmathematical questions?

Is the observation procedure so straightforward as Simon says? What we have to measure is the influencee's zone of acceptance ("the set of behaviors that B will perform at A's command"), but we can never observe that; at best all we can observe are discrete instances of the acceptance of the decisions of A by B. (Strictly speaking, as we have seen, we cannot observe even that.) Since, as Simon points out, "the zone of acceptance may be suddenly narrowed" or, presumably, broadened, we cannot simply construct today's zone of acceptance out of the history of accepted decisions. The king might refuse to create new peers at the behest of a tyrannical House of Commons if he

---

[103] One wonders what V is doing in the model at all, because it raises a serious question about Simon's argument. Is it necessarily true, as he asserts, that a decrease in B's zone of acceptance from S to S' (a part of S) necessarily justifies our saying that A's authority has decreased? Might not V also decrease, even drastically (say, to V')? And if that is a possibility then we have no reason to expect that $\frac{S'}{V'}$ will be smaller than $\frac{S}{V}$. It is therefore questionable whether A's authority has decreased. More generally, the model here raises many of the difficulties that have already been considered in connection with the behavior alternative model of rationality.

thought the country would support him. In the comment quoted above, Simon obscures the issue by saying first that "we observe what kinds of decisions are accepted and what kinds are not," and then by asking "will His Majesty accede to the request?" We cannot answer this question on the basis of these observations. Finally, is every element in the set of behaviors that B will perform at A's command equally important and therefore to be given equal weight? Simon implies the affirmative; yet it is perhaps not accidental that he gives an example of great political, not to say constitutional, importance. It would seem elementary that the amount of authority (or influence or power) depends not merely on the number of the influencee's acts that the influencer can determine but also on the kind. This is not a criticism of Simon's determination to quantify authority but of his failure to give a satisfactory answer to the question, what is it that is being quantified?

Like Humpty Dumpty, we will insist that a word means what we want it to mean. But if our aim is to construct a body of science, and if we already have in view the general range of phenomena to be explained, our definitions may be willful, but they must not be arbitrary. If we were to say that we would measure a man's power by his height, this would be an internally consistent definition, but one hardly useful in exploring the phenomena referred to in common speech as the phenomena of power [p. 63].

Note that "we already have in view the general range of phenomena to be explained" *before* we attempt to construct a body of science.[104] Simon proceeds to defend his distinction between values and power on the grounds that he is "conforming to common usage." "If we list specific values—wealth, wisdom, or what not—then the statement that 'A possesses certain of these values' is not what we *mean* when we say 'A has power' " (pp. 63-64).[105] But why does Simon use an argument based on common sense in one case and not in another? For it can surely be said of any of his definitions of authority that this is not what we *mean* when we speak of authority. Why should we accept a definition of authority that leads, for example, to the virtual obliteration of the distinction between authority and influence, a distinction we had thought vital to the study of politics? Simon replies to this query in *Public Administration* with the following intriguing remark:

[104] Apparently if we did *not* have the general range of phenomena to be explained already in view, our definitions could be both willful and arbitrary, though it is not clear why we would be making any definitions in that case. See above, p. 128, where Simon's formula for dealing with this problem is to say that "the first task of administrative theory is to develop a set of concepts that will permit the description, *in terms relevant to the theory*, of administrative situations" (italics supplied).

[105] Simon goes on to give what he says is a "second defect" of definitions that equate power and values, but it too depends entirely on the "common usage" argument. For other examples of Simon's defense of his concepts on the grounds that they conform to common sense, see *Administrative Behavior*, p. xxvi; *Models of Man*, pp. 11-13, 50-51; *Organizations*, p. 138.

In the last analysis this is just a question of definition—of how one wishes to use words—and we will exercise an author's prerogative of defining the word in our own way and then using it as we have defined it. Nevertheless, the usage proposed here has good precedent in the writings of Chester I. Barnard and others. It has been adopted because it seems more useful to us than do other definitions in describing the realities of administration [p. 183].[106]

Thus Simon gives three reasons for the definition he has chosen: (1) he "wishes" to define the word in his own way, that being his prerogative as an author; (2) there is good precedent for defining the word this way (Barnard is the only author cited); (3) it seems "more useful to us" than other definitions in "describing the realities of administration." Preference, precedent, usefulness. In the end, Simon apparently relies on the last. "Without any expectation that the reader will accept the *authority* of this proposal, the material in this chapter may help *convince* him of the convenience of the usage." Simon had some knowledge of the realities of administration before he made his "operational" definition of authority, and it is in the light of this knowledge that the "usefulness" of the scientific definition is to be judged. Even in this case, then, where the definition seems to run contrary to common sense, its defense, so far as it has one, rests finally on common sense.

THE VALUE OF SCIENCE

Closely connected with the nonoperational character of common language is its evaluative character. The common sense way of knowing is not neutral with respect to values; frequently it does not even distinguish between "facts" and "values." Common sense knowledge of what an organization is, for example, is part of the same knowledge by which better and worse organizations are distinguished. Simon's official doctrine is that common sense language, and therefore the values inherent in common sense language, are data with which social science must deal, but that they do not enter into the science itself. He argues that the idea that "values" are the source of a fundamental difference between the social and the natural sciences is a mistake that arises out of failure to understand the distinction between theoretical and practical sciences.[107] The propositions of the former, he says, take the form, "if X then Y," while the propositions of the latter take the form, "do X to achieve Y." The propositions of the practical science have an imperative or ethical element and thus cannot be said to be true or false except as the im-

---

106 Cf. *Public Administration*, p. viii: "We take definitions seriously. We urge the reader to do likewise."
107 See *Administrative Behavior*, Appendix; "A Comment on 'The Science of Public Administration,'" *Public Administration Review*, Summer 1947; Perry, et al., *American Political Science Review*, June 1950, pp. 407-411. Cf. Luther Gulick's discussion of this question in *Papers on the Science of Administration*, pp. 191-192; and see below, pp. 309-310.

perative element is ignored—that is, except as they are translated into the purely factual propositions of theoretical science. So long as this is remembered, it does not matter very much whether the scientist speaks descriptively or imperatively. We know in the latter case that it is only the factual aspects of his proposition that are subject to verification, and that what he is saying is, *if* you want X then you must do Y. Thus the scientist is interested only in factual propositions or in the factual component of ethical propositions: "science is interested in sentences only with regard to their verification" (*Administrative Behavior*, p. 249). The scientist looks at what can be looked at scientifically; he makes sentences that can be verified in the approved scientific fashion. Simon studies communication patterns in five-man groups; [108] he constructs a "logic theory machine" capable of discovering proofs for theorems in symbolic logic; [109] he makes models of imaginary ratlike organisms living in an imaginary world of cheese and space; and so forth. He believes and asserts that studies like these will contribute to an understanding of broader issues, though he says very little about that aspect of his enterprise.[110] Unless the reader shares Simon's unquestioning faith in science, he is likely to wonder whether there is any good reason to believe that these minute pellets will add up to any significant contribution to social science. He may even suspect that the intriguing complexity of the scientific apparatus has diverted attention from important human problems. Simon insists in his book of mathematical essays, "My concern has been with social science, and I have not allowed myself to be diverted from social science by the interesting mathematical questions that suggested themselves in the course of the investigations" (*Models of Man*, p. ix). Even if this is granted (and it is not always easy to grant), much of Simon's concern with "social science" has been directed to the relatively narrow range of questions that will submit to the scientific methodology. He is not unaware of this criticism; and although he has engaged in an increasingly narrower and more technical range of

[108] Harold Guetzkow and Herbert Simon, "The Impact of Certain Communication Nets Upon Organization and Performance in Task-Oriented Groups," *Management Science*, April-July 1955.
[109] Allen Newell and Herbert A. Simon, "The Logic Theory Machine: A Complex Information Processing System," *IRE Transactions*, vol. IT-2, no. 3, September 1956.
[110] That there is a connection between these narrower studies and the broader statement of the problems in *Administrative Behavior* is not to be denied. There has, indeed, been a remarkable consistency in Simon's work which is not always recognized. The trouble is that the basic approach leads away from important problems. Simon's recent attempt at something like a comprehensive view, in *Organizations*, illustrates the point very well. One of the main defects of older administrative studies which led him to write *Administrative Behavior* was their failure to catch and set down in words "the real flesh and bones of an organization" (*Administrative Behavior*, p. xlv). It is not unfair to say that *Organizations*, whose elaborate and highly refined structure of numbered propositions and hypotheses can scarcely conceal the emptiness it contains, is a good deal more remote from "the real flesh and bones of an organization" than *Administrative Behavior* and than the writings of Gulick and Urwick themselves.

studies, he emphatically denies that his science confines him to the study of trivia.

I hope it is clear that I do not accept the dilemma of either studying unimportant matters scientifically, or important ones by common sense. The third route—studying important matters scientifically—is a steep and rocky one, but the only one, I am convinced, that leads to our destination.[111]

The question is, how does Simon know what is important and what is not? Science does not tell him. Science "is interested in sentences only with regard to their verification," not their importance. Simon needs some substantive standard of importance, as well as the scientific standard of verification. Nor does he need this only in his capacity as "practical scientist," as one with a prescriptive (and therefore admittedly value-laden) interest. He needs it as much in his capacity as a theoretical scientist interested in pure scientific description, for it is only by means of such a standard that he can differentiate raw behavior into that worth describing and that not worth describing.[112] Given Simon's premises, however, any substantive standard must remain in the shadows. Thus he says in *Administrative Behavior* that "a scientifically relevant description of an organization" is one that "so far as possible, designates for each person in the organization what decisions that person makes, and the influences to which he is subject in making each of these decisions" (p. 37). But a description of only a very small range of decisions—for example, those made at coffee-break time—might be equally relevant *scientifically*.[113] Moreover, it is difficult to believe that Simon really intends his readers to take seriously the proposition that every decision (even "so far as possible") made by every person be designated and described. He relies on the common sense qualifications that any sensible reader will provide. It would be as mad to try to describe an organization by designating every decision made by every person and all the influences bearing on them as it would be for a decision-maker to try to conceive of every behavior alternative and of all the consequences of each of these alternatives. Clearly anyone wishing to describe an organization is interested in only a certain range of decisions, the significant or relevant or important ones. Simon says as much in the introduction to the second edition of *Administrative Behavior*:

111 *Public Administration Review*, Winter 1958, p. 61.
112 Thus the most obvious difference between the "old" and the "new" Simon—that the former often used normative language, while the latter purports only to describe—is not fundamental. Banfield concedes too much when he says that "now, so far as 'good' administration is concerned, [Simon] has no basis for judging what criteria [of decision] are relevant and what are not." *Public Administration Review*, Autumn 1957, p. 284. Without some notion of "good" administration, Simon has no criteria for deciding what is worth describing scientifically. See below, pp. 147-148, 317-318.
113 But it would not, Simon might reply, be a description of an organization. To consider the merits of that reply we would have to know what an organization is, but Simon does not tell us. If he had done so it might also be possible to penetrate the meaning of his phrase, "administrative organization," which suggests that there are other kinds.

one needs a vocabulary and concepts that focus upon the significant and dismiss the irrelevant. The reader can decide whether the vocabulary and concepts proposed here enable him to deal with organizational problems in a more fundamental way than is permitted by the homely wisdom that has passed for organizational analysis in the past [p. xxii].

How do we know whether a vocabulary points us to "the significant" while dismissing "the irrelevant"? A vocabulary serves this purpose if it enables us "to deal with organizational problems in a . . . fundamental way." How can we know that? Only by knowing what the problems are. An understanding of problem solving, which is the main concern of Simon's science, is altogether dependent upon an understanding of problems.[114]

"The first condition of organization is a problem. . . . Problems giving rise to organizations are as varied as the whole spectrum of human needs . . ." (*Public Administration*, p. 26). In his principle of bounded rationality Simon asserts, it will be recalled, that human problem solving capacity is very small "compared with the size of the problems whose solution is required for objectively rational behavior in the real world . . ." (*Models of Man*, p. 198). What is wrong with this principle is that, on Simon's premises, the size and scope of "the problem" is not something that can be objectively determined; there are not "human needs" but only "human wants." The problem can be defined and expanded or contracted as the actor likes, and it is just this flexibility that is made to tie up the satisficing model of rationality. It is most important to bear this in mind in considering what Simon regards as "a major, challenging task of organization theory: to find the ways of organizing that will cultivate foresight, and that will build into the administrative structure sensory organs and organs of reflection and action capable of anticipating and dealing with future emerging problems." This is "the principal *terra incognita* of organization theory today." Research in the area of "non-programed" decisions is, according to Simon, the great need of the future; we need to consider "how to construct administrative organizations that can act with a foresight and planfulness commensurate with the magnitude and importance of the issues they face" (*Research Frontiers in Politics and Government*, pp. 42, 44).[115]

Simon has worked out some of the formal aspects of this problem in great

[114] Simon's present preference for characterizing "the human organism" as "a complex information-processing system" is consistent with his movement away from "objective" rationality and towards a psychological explanation of human behavior. But even in his later work, the problem of "problems" reappears, as for example when he defines substantive programs as "the structuring of the problem-solving process that comes about as a reflection of the structure of the problem to be solved." *Organizations*, pp. 9, 179; see also pp. 188, 201. Simon's attempt to explore human rationality by experimenting with programs for digital computers—which are complex information processing systems—suffers from the same fundamental difficulty. See below, n. 115.

[115] Simon's recent preoccupation with digital computers is partly explained by his conviction that experiments with the computers will throw light on this problem—and, indeed, have

detail and with great sophistication, but he has dealt less adequately with the underlying question which his own theory throws up for consideration: what is a "problem" or an "issue"? [116]

Much additional research is needed on the relation between organization structure and perceived problems. Research is even more urgently called for—there has been virtually none at all—on the relation between the manner in which problems are perceived and what the problems "really" are. If we refer back to the example of the Department of Agriculture, we may well ask: Did emphasis in the department shift from production to marketing because production has ceased to be the *real* problem of agriculture, and marketing had become the *real* problem? Or did the problems remain the same, while public understanding of them changed? It is easy to see that, unless there is at least partial truth in the first viewpoint, the justification of one set of organizational arrangements in preference to another becomes extremely difficult [*Research Frontiers in Politics and Government*, pp. 37-38].[117]

Before we can search into the relation between perceived problems and what the problems "really" are, we need to consider whether we can possibly concede even "partial truth" to the viewpoint that there are real problems without abandoning the fundamental premise of Simon's science? His quotation marks around "really" warn us that there is something unreal about problems, and his theory certainly carries that implication. But throughout his writings, there is the assumption that there are real problems. He refers to "the crucial problems of our age" and "the recognition of new problems as they emerge." These would be problems, presumably, even if they were not recognized as such. As he explains in *Public Administration*,

before a governmental activity is undertaken, a problem must exist not merely in fact, but in people's minds as well. . . .

First, a few persons recognize the problem in its early stages and begin to write and talk about it. Their efforts may be fruitless over a considerable period of years,

---

already done so. For a broad statement of his activity and expectations in this field, see Herbert A. Simon and Allen Newell, "Heuristic Problem Solving: The Next Advance in Operations Research," *Operations Research*, January-February 1958. Here Simon predicts that "in a visible future . . . the range of problems [machines] can handle will be coextensive with the range to which the human mind has been applied." This will "force man to consider his role in a world in which his intellectual power and speed are outstripped by the intelligence of machines"; but in Simon's opinion "the new revolution will at the same time give him a deeper understanding of the structure and workings of his own mind." Simon confesses his own "personal hope that the latter development will outstrip the former . . ." (pp. 8-10). Cf. Harold D. Lasswell, "The Political Science of Science," *American Political Science Review*, December 1956, pp. 976-977.

[116] For an examination of the ground and background of this question see Joseph Cropsey, "What Is Welfare Economics?" *Ethics*, January 1955, pp. 116-125.

[117] Curiously, Simon does not consider the possibility that the problem might have remained the same, while public understanding of it *improved*, under which circumstances there would be no great difficulty in justifying one set of organizational arrangements in preference to another. Cf. his discussion of "Planning and Innovation in Organizations" in *Organizations*, ch. 7.

but if the problem persists, and particularly if it becomes intensified, a larger and larger segment of the public becomes aware of it [p. 31].

But Simon cannot consistently say that a problem exists *in fact*, because a problem always exists essentially in the realm of values. A decision about what is a problem, as distinct from a decision about how to solve a problem, is absolutely dependent on values. One of Simon's examples is the "problem" of the blind, which Helen Keller helped to bring to the attention of the public. Why was this a problem? Only because people held or acquired certain non-rational preferences that defined a certain situation as problematical. According to Simon's assumptions, if no one had held such values there would have been no problem. If there are no objective or "real" values there are no "real" problems.[118] And if there are no real problems, the basis of the science of problem solving is destroyed, as Simon himself comes very close to admitting in the above remarks.

The fundamental difficulty caused by the subjective basis of problem solving manifests itself also when we consider the status of rationality or efficiency (which is science applied to administrative decision-making), and of science itself. Efficiency is introduced in *Administrative Behavior* as a "principle"; later it is said to be a "definition of what is meant by 'good' or 'correct' administrative behavior. It . . . merely states that . . . maximization *is* the aim of administrative activity. . . ." Efficiency "*must be* a guiding criterion in administrative decision." "Efficiency, whether it be in the democratic state or in the totalitarian, is the *proper* criterion to be applied to the factual element in the decisional problem" (*Administrative Behavior*, pp. 39, 65, 184, italics supplied). Elsewhere efficiency is called "a basic value criterion of administrative decision" (p. 120); and in *Public Administration* the implication of treating efficiency as a value criterion is made explicit.

It is an observable fact that persons in administrative situations frequently *do* employ the criterion of efficiency in making choices, and it is for this reason that an understanding of the criterion is so important. Whether, or to what degree, administrators *should* employ this criterion is a question of values whose answer lies outside the science of administration [p. 491].

---

[118] Nor is it tenable, on Simon's premises, to assert the "reality" of problems in the much narrower sense that non-rational preferences may carry certain necessary implications and therefore create "real problems." Such an argument would have to assume that there is or ought to be some consistency or logic in preferences. It would involve saying, for example, that if your preferences lead you to think that everyone should have an elementary school education, they ought also to lead you to think that provision should be made for giving blind children such an education. But as we have seen, Simon has no basis for saying that inconsistent preferences are less rational than consistent ones. For the same reason it is not even possible, on Simonian principles, to talk about "real problems" in what at first might seem an acceptable sense, that is to say, "if he had known X then he would have preferred Y." For even assuming that the missing information was something the actor absolutely could not have had (otherwise his failure to know was the result of his preference for doing something else instead of persisting in searching for information), no one can possibly know what he would have preferred under different circumstances.

Given the distinction between the factual and value aspects of decision, two contrary conclusions seem to follow: (1) the factual aspects ought properly to be treated in terms of efficiency; (2) we cannot say how they ought to be treated, since *that* is a value judgment. The former is the conclusion most often (but not always) drawn or implied in *Administrative Behavior*, and it is on that basis that the administrative analysis rests. The latter is the conclusion most often (but not always) implied in Simon's later work; but while the one most consistent with his basic assumptions, it is devastating not only for administrative analysis but also for the notion of efficiency or rationality itself. Ultimately a commitment to rationality or to any value providing the necessary basis for rational behavior (such as consistency) is a value commitment like any other. The inevitable, if paradoxical, consequence of Simon's theory is that a man is no less rational if he spurns rationality altogether. It is wholly within a man's province to decide whether or to what extent to commit himself to the sober, efficient pursuit of stable and consistent preferences rather than to the excitement or the ease of doing what seems pleasant at this moment with no thought for the next. If arbitrariness sets the ends, arbitrariness also determines the means.

What, then, of science itself? Given Simon's premises, must one conclude that a commitment to science and to the understanding of the distinction between facts and values on which that science rests is a value commitment as arbitrary as any other? At first sight, it would appear that the answer is no. Simon *knows* that there is no basis in reason for ethical statements, or values, or preferences; and his argument takes the form of a logical demonstration: you can't deduce an "ought" from an "is." What, then, is the basis of this logic which is the foundation of the science? Simon does not answer, and apparently his disinclination to examine certain kinds of questions protects him from discomfort even in the face of a grave difficulty. On the one hand, he asserts that "as to whether [the principles of administration] should be logical or illogical there can be no debate" (*Administrative Behavior*, p. 44). This implies that the determination to be logical is inherently legitimate, while a contrary determination is not, in which case no sane enlightened man could choose to be illogical. That is as much as to say that a man ought to be logical, and it is therefore an exception to the apparently impregnable fact-value distinction. On the other hand, the philosophical position of which the fact-value distinction is an expression seems to demand the adoption of the position held by A. J. Ayer, that logic is nothing but "our determination to use words in a certain fashion." [119] In that case, science rests on no different basis than those metaphysical doctrines about values which are the outcome of a determination to use words in some other way, and it is no genu-

[119] A. J. Ayer, *Language, Truth and Logic* (New York: Dover Publications, Inc., 1946), p. 84; see pp. 31, 74-77. Simon points to Ayer's book as one of the sources of the reasoning on which his philosophical premises are based. See *Administrative Behavior*, pp. 45-46.

ine science. It is, that is to say, not entitled to use the words "true" and "false" (*Administrative Behavior*, p. 248). Luther Gulick's sly paradox, " 'should' is a word political scientists should not use in scientific discussion!" [120] shows a more subtle appreciation of the scientist's difficulty than Simon has ever evidenced.

CONCLUSION

Simon's original intention was to apply scientific method to the problems of government. He was emphatically not interested in merely "theoretical concepts devised by academicians," but in "practical tools by means of which practical legislators and administrators can meet the practical need of choosing between alternative courses of action." [121] In this respect he was in perfect harmony with his predecessors in the study of administration. Neither his conception of science nor his perception of the unsatisfactory state of the science of administration was new to students of administration, although the vigor with which he presented his views lent weight to the idea that he was making a fundamental break. As we have suggested, his criticism was, generally speaking, justified: the old vocabulary was imprecise and nonoperational, the tools of analysis were dull, the alleged scientific principles were nothing but more or (usually) less refined proverbial wisdom. Simon's criticism was largely justified, and he was right to point to the need for a more than commonsensical understanding of administration; but he mistook a symptom for the cause of the sickness of administrative studies.

Men like Gulick were without doubt vague and imprecise as scientists, but that was not due primarily to a lack of understanding of the scientific premises or to a lack of ability to reason from them. It was rather because, in addition to a certain *method* of investigation, these men were consciously guided by a sense of the needs or problems of government and other organizations. If the method provided by science did not fit the problems thrown up by administration, as often happened in the most interesting and important cases, the pre-Simonians were likely to resort frankly to common sense qualifications and adjustments. While their science, thus qualified, was neither pure nor sometimes even especially useful, it was usually directed at significant administrative problems. These men sought to maintain a proportion between administration and their study of it. Simon, on the other hand, committed himself, perhaps as strongly as a man can who actually wishes to engage in social studies, to the pursuit of science. His prescription for the ills of administrative study was to follow the demands of science wherever they led, and his willingness to swallow great quantities of this medicine

[120] *Papers on the Science of Administration*, p. 192.
[121] *The Annals of the American Academy of Political and Social Science*, September 1938, pp. 20-25.

distinguishes him from his predecessors. This is both his strength and his weakness. Compared with his predecessors, he certainly exhibits a better understanding of the fundamental grounds of the scientific method; he is better aware of its demands; and he is far more determined and sophisticated in putting it to use. But for these very reasons his failure, which is at bottom the same as theirs, is all the more emphatic. He does not even gain in precision and consistency what he loses in relevance.

Simon correctly points out the inadequacy of a merely commonsensical understanding of administration and of human behavior; but the result of his strenuous activities has been to leave the water a good deal muddier than it was before. Instead of accepting common sense as a guide and seeking to clarify its assumptions and to pursue its implications, he rejects it as fundamentally defective. He attempts to make an entirely new language that, because it is scientific, will be free of the defects of common sense. The attempt fails. Science remains dependent, both for its definitions and for its standards of significance and relevance, on a common sense grasp of the phenomena to be investigated.

Wherever Simon's science is probed, it is found to depend upon some pre-scientific divination of the nature of man and the world. Simon does in practice assume that there are real problems which would exist even if they were not regarded as problems. He assumes that there are important problems and unimportant problems, and therefore important decisions and unimportant decisions. He believes that men ought to act rationally and that their preferences should at least have that degree of consistency and stability necessary to the exercise of rationality. He believes that the pursuit of common goals is a higher endeavor than the pursuit of merely individual satisfaction and that, in either case, it is better done efficiently than inefficiently. He believes that logic is better than, say magic. His description and analysis of administration depend absolutely on these beliefs, but on his own premises they are beliefs for which there cannot be any reasonable basis. They are the unarticulated value judgments on which the allegedly value-free science rests, to which it resorts for guidance, and from which it draws whatever relevance it has to the real world of administrative behavior.

III

THE GROUP APPROACH

Arthur F. Bentley

by LEO WEINSTEIN

THE SCIENTIFIC STUDY OF GROUPS

WHILE THE importance of groups, of interests, and of group pressures in the political process has long been affirmed to be of primary importance, the past decade has witnessed the appearance of an ambitious series of efforts to place the group interpretation of politics on a firm basis. In texts, monographs, and programs of research a significant effort has been made to achieve a "meaningful conception of the role of political groups in the governing process," [1] or to articulate "a theory of political action believed to be implicit in the group theories." [2] These efforts at systematic statement and theoretical formulation would appear to be the mark of a growing maturity in an important section of political science, an indication that a summing up and a theoretical structuring of the rich body of specific studies of interest groups is forthcoming, or at least in the state of active preparation.

It comes as no surprise that by far the greater number of the more ambitious works in this field explicitly take their orientation from Arthur F. Bentley's *The Process of Government*.[3] While there have been some qualifications and reservations,[4] Bentley's announced intention in *The Process of Government*, "to fashion a tool," is the banner under which the studies of Truman, Gross, Peltason, and Monypenny have appeared. According to the almost universal testimony of students of group politics, Bentley's preliminary exploration of the field continues to set the pattern. He has, then, at least the claim on our attention of a revered pioneer.

[1] David B. Truman. *The Governmental Process* (Copyright 1951 by Alfred A. Knopf, Inc.), p. 13.
[2] Phillip Monypenny, "Political Science and the Study of Groups: Notes to Guide a Research Project," *Western Political Quarterly*, June, 1954, p. 183. See Bertram M. Gross, *The Legislative Struggle* (New York: McGraw-Hill Book Co., Inc., 1953); Donald C. Blaisdell, *American Democracy Under Pressure* (New York: The Ronald Press Company, 1957); Jack W. Peltason, *Federal Courts in the Political Process* (New York: Doubleday & Company, Inc., 1955).
[3] (Chicago: University of Chicago Press, 1908). Unless otherwise noted, succeeding references to this work will be to the reprint of 1949 published by The Principia Press of Trinity University (Tex.), San Antonio, Texas. Used by permission.
[4] Perhaps the best known is Merle Fainsod's objection to Bentley's neglect of the "amount of independent power" held and exercised by government personnel and by the agencies of government in the group struggle. "Some Reflections on the Nature of the Regulatory Process," *Public Policy*, I (Cambridge, Mass.: Harvard University Press, 1940), p. 299. See also the comments of Earl Latham, *The Group Basis of Politics* (Ithaca: Cornell University Press, 1952), p. 38, n. 39.

Even a preliminary investigation of Bentley's contributions quickly discloses some striking facts. A single reading of the first, "ground clearing," part of *The Process of Government* reveals Bentley's opposition to the use of "motives," "feelings," "ideas," and other such "entities" as if they were meaningful units for either theoretical or empirical analysis of government, as well as his contention that fundamental errors about the data and scope of social science are entertained by most if not by all social scientists. Briefly, the first of these errors consists in the effort to "explain," causally or teleologically, the course of political or social action. Efforts to explain why a given event comes to pass, or why it happened as it did, are in Bentley's view beyond the ken of social science. The search for a "why" has to be replaced by the search for "hows"; and the "hows," despite an infinite variety of superficial appearances, are all reducible to forms of activity, the activity of men in groups. In place of spurious and untenable explanation, social science must seek empirical description. The full description will be the complete science (*The Process of Government*, p. 209). To ask for more is to transcend the boundaries of science or, what is the same thing, to lapse into the inadequacies of everyday discourse.

Directly connected with the first error is the habit, held by Bentley to be indefensible, of seeking causes or determinants of action in the realm of feelings, ideas, or in the innate nature of men. Within the Bentleyan formulation, feelings, ideas, and moral and intellectual characteristics of men are nothing more than inferred "mind stuff" or abstractions spun out by students from their observations of the only data accessible to them, namely, human activity. It is by lapsing into the use of everyday language and common sense distinctions that a feeling or idea or a part of the character of man is made to serve the purposes of explanation. Common sense may serve to point to areas of significance, to activities whose further investigation may be worth undertaking, but once such investigation is begun common sense, common sense distinctions, and ultimately the everyday language of everyday life must be abandoned (*The Process of Government*, p. 165-172). In their place, the tools forged by Bentley must be used. With the use of such tools, the likelihood of fruitful progress is said to be great. It is necessary to stress the insistence Bentley places on full commitment to the views presented here (*The Process of Government*, pp. 465-480). Social science will continue to fall short of the promise it holds until it proceeds in "full system," that is, until the Bentleyan apparatus is made the instrument of social research. In his later works, Bentley finds "approximations" to the kind of science he is laboring to create in physics, physiology, and to a smaller degree, experimental psychology.[5] A reference to Lundberg brings sociology, or at least one

[5] Arthur F. Bentley, *Inquiry into Inquiries*, ed. Sidney Ratner (Boston: Beacon Press, 1954), pp. 348-353.

sociologist, within the sanctuary of partly approved work. There are no references to political scientists. This silence is consistent with Bentley's characterization of political science as a "dead" science. His use of political data for study is an expediental one, based on the more direct approach to group interests which is possible through a political analysis. But from political science as a discipline Bentley expected little. He considered it "a formal study of the most external characteristics of governing institutions," occasionally touched up with an "injection of metaphysics"; and in *The Process of Government* he disposes of it in seven paragraphs (p. 162). The practitioners of living disciplines fare little better. Whether it is Einstein, in whom Bentley asserts he found the means to make relativity an operating principle in social research, or the series of writers he surveys in outlining the development of group interpretation, Bentley strongly criticizes the shortcomings he attributes to the failure to embrace fully the approach of his own work.[6] In the large catalogue of writers he examines for purposes of illustration and support, there is not a single one who escapes serious attack for resorting to ideas or feelings, or any of the "things" derived from them.

In the light of this situation one wonders whether the failure of other researchers to do more than achieve "approximations" to the scientific study sketched in Bentley's work may be due to something in that work itself, something which prevents its full utilization in the manner Bentley prescribed. But there has been no serious effort to analyze Bentley's major work as a whole and in its own terms.[7] This would be of little moment if *The Process of Government* were an isolated and neglected item in the literature of political science. As we have seen, this is not the case. Leaving aside the incidental reliance placed upon Bentley by scholars in other fields, we have a growing number of studies in political science which present themselves as carrying Bentley's work a step nearer completion or as extending it to topics he only incidentally handled.

An examination of these studies re-enforces the question raised in connection with Bentley's criticisms of his contemporaries: is there something

[6] Arthur F. Bentley, *Relativity in Man and Society* (New York: G. P. Putnam's Sons, 1926), pp. 3-16; 157-168. See also *The Process of Government*, pp. 465-480.

[7] Neither David Easton's *The Political System* (New York: Alfred A. Knopf, Inc., 1953) nor Bernard Crick's *The American Science of Politics* (Berkeley: The University of California Press, 1959) attempts to deal with Bentley in his own terms. The former suggests using parts of Bentley's scheme as elements in a broader situational analysis without inquiring whether anything properly Bentleyan remains if parts are removed. Crick's work touches on Bentley as a member or representative of the progressive movement in the United States, an identification which has been made before. Cf. Henry Steele Commager, *The American Mind* (New Haven; Yale University Press, 1950); Richard Hofstadter, *The American Political Tradition* (New York: Alfred A. Knopf, Inc., 1948); and the interesting characterization of Bentley by E. Pendleton Herring in *Group Representation Before Congress* (Baltimore: The Johns Hopkins Press, 1929), p. 294, to which reference is made below, p. 221.

in Bentley's work that precludes the achievement of more than "approximations" to the proper study of government and society as Bentley conceived it? For it is clear that the current exponents of Bentleyanism present what, from Bentley's point of view, would be "approximations" at best. Among contemporary students of group politics, Bentley is cited as a model, standard, or inspiration guiding research in which, nevertheless, concepts and entities prohibited by Bentley occupy central positions. Even the most enthusiastic proponents of the Bentleyan approach to political science find it difficult or impossible to contain their observations and analyses within the explicit limits set by *The Process of Government*.

In his study of the federal judicial process, for example, Peltason identifies his orientation as "Bentleyan, behavioristic, actional, and non-motivational" (*Federal Courts in the Political Process*, p. 1). He gives his own reasons or purposes for undertaking the study and analyzes, with fair clarity, the motives of judges for the light they shed on their behavior as decision-makers. Judge Edgerton's willingness to support administrative adjudication as well as Judge Hutcheson's opposition to administrative adjudication are understood as consequences of their respective support of, or opposition to, the ideas of administrative competence emphasized in the New Deal era (pp. 16-17). Peltason characterizes such support or opposition as the "reflection" of interests playing on or pressing for expression through the judicial process, and this hypothetical identity of interest between judge and "group" is presented as the Bentleyan orientation. But the short excursions into intellectual biography are evidently needed by Peltason to lay the basis for the conclusion that judicial decision-making is an accurate index of the interest affiliations of the judges involved. What emerges from this part of his study is the conclusion that decision-writing can be considered an index of interest affiliation only after one has independently ascertained the beliefs or political opinions of the judges involved. The truth, adequacy, or novelty of Peltason's views are not our present concern. What we are concerned to show is that adherence to the Bentleyan orientation is possible only at the cost of operational abandonment of the "non-motivational" characteristic of that orientation, a cost Peltason was compelled to pay.

Again, Richard W. Taylor's examination of Bentley's methodology assumes that *The Process of Government* does provide a workable framework for research and proceeds to a discussion of selected contemporary group activities without further analysis of Bentley's work.[8] Characteristically, however, Taylor is unable to proceed very far before he departs from the Bentleyan requirements. He introduces the concept of "role" to explain why the observed behavior of men in given positions conforms to a pattern not of their

[8] Richard W. Taylor, "Groups and the Political Process: A Study of the Methodology of Arthur Fisher Bentley" (Unpublished Ph.D. Dissertation, Department of Political Science, the University of Illinois, 1950).

own making.[9] The "role" proves to contain a set of standards which pattern and direct the behavior of individuals. It must be repeated that we are not concerned with the adequacy or inadequacy of the supplementary concept we are offered, but rather with the fact that the concept of "role" is offered. This "spook" or bit of "mind stuff," in Bentley's terms, is needed to bridge the gap which is evidently present, in Taylor's judgment, between the parts of Bentley's work he wishes to use. Taylor is unconcerned with the fact that the bridge is constructed of materials which Bentley would have rejected with scorn. At the very least, a non-Bentleyan concept is introduced in order to make the Bentleyan concepts workable.

Perhaps the best known of the current Bentleyans is David Truman, who praises *The Process of Government* for having "given the subject much of what systematization it has so far received," and who goes on to say that "Bentley's 'attempt to fashion a tool' has been the principal bench mark for my own thinking." Truman presents "an evaluation and resulting synthesis that will give an explanation of group politics" (*The Governmental Process*, p. ix), in terms familiar even to casual readers of Bentley: group, interest, and activity; potential group and potential activity; the "rules of the game" and the "habit background." Negatively, there is a familiar argument against the notion of a common interest or national interest, a denial that a nation is a group, and a rejection of evaluation as part of the "scientific understanding of government or the operation of society" (p. 38).

Yet despite his explicit reliance on Bentley, his adaptation of the very title of Bentley's book, and his use of Bentleyan linguistic tools, Truman devotes a section of the first part of his *The Governmental Process* to "norm" formation in informal groups (pp. 14-44). Data taken from the behavior of small groups and from public opinion polls are held to provide, to all intents and purposes, the basic information on how norms are formed and how they influence behavior in "groups" like the American Federation of Labor or the Congress of the United States. Quite apart from what might be said about generalizing from such limited data,[10] it is abundantly clear that "norms" and "attitudes" which somehow come into existence and limit or channel

---

[9] *Ibid.*, pp. 51-52. Taylor says: "Bentley really views groups, not as an association of individuals, but as a synthesis of members' *roles*. . . . individuals participate in many groups, play many parts—often conflicting—and it becomes, therefore, convenient not to consider concrete persons as members of groups, but, rather, to consider *roles* as exemplified in activity of persons participating in groups." It is not clear from Taylor's remarks whether the role is the name given to whatever behavior we find manifested by "persons participating in groups," or whether the role is an expected pattern of behavior to which individuals conform. Taylor's discussion indicates that he has the latter alternative in mind. See also Taylor's "Arthur F. Bentley's Political Science," *Western Political Quarterly*, June 1952, pp. 214-230; esp. p. 216, where Taylor sees Bentley as using a "heuristic interest-group theory," and p. 224, where "concepts" make their appearance.

[10] See David B. Truman, "The Impact on Political Science of the Revolution in the Behavioral Sciences, "*Research Frontiers in Politics and Government* (Washington: The Brookings Institution, 1955), pp. 228-229.

behavior are, like Taylor's "roles," precisely the kinds of entities denied any meaningful place in the Bentleyan corpus.

As for the old-fashioned feelings and ideas . . . they are irresponsible and un-measurable, giving indeed an animistic semblance of explaining society, but actu-ally, to use their own method of speech, blocking explanation as much as the animism of the forest would block the study of nature. It is necessary to come to close quarters with them and to annihilate their false pretenses, before attempting to build up an interpretation out of the underlying facts which they dimly hint at, but never actually define. . . .

My concern is at no time with psychology, but always with the process of social life, and this, while it is always psychic, can at no time be understood or explained with the catchwords and verbal toys of psychology as the starting-point [*The Process of Government*, p. 3].

How Truman's "norms" and "attitudes," drawn from the findings of social psychology, are supposed to be compatible with Bentley's requirements is never explained. Why a dimension of explanation rejected as animistic and toylike by Bentley has to be used as a starting point by Truman is a perplex-ity demanding explanation before any structuring of group-interest data into a consistent and meaningful body of knowledge is possible. However, the fault is not all, or even mainly, Truman's. This disharmony between Bentley and those who regard themselves as his exponents is, more fundamentally, an expression of a disharmony within Bentley's work itself. Bentley *is* the father of the prevailing "group approach" to politics, including its essential inconsistency. It is precisely for this reason that we must turn back from the contemporary studies—full of interesting information as they are—to Bentley himself. First, however, it may be helpful to clarify this point by continuing briefly the consideration of the most illustrious of Bentley's followers.

When Truman turns to the anti-Bentleyan notions of "norms" and "atti-tudes," he is responding to a difficulty which he inherited from Bentley him-self, namely the difficulty arising from the restriction of scientific inquiry to manifest behavior or activity. In Bentley, the difficulty is met by the postula-tion of "potential" activity, or tendencies of activity which, while not evident, are said by Bentley to be just as "real" as the visible activity accessible to sight.[11] In Truman, the same limitation leads to the same attempted solution:

In the scientific study of society only frustration and defeat are likely to follow an attempt to deal with data that are not directly observable. Even the most insistent defenders of the scientific position, however, admit that, although activity is the basic datum of social science, a "becoming" stage of activity must be recognized as a phase of activity. There are, in other words, potential activities, or "tendencies of activity" [*The Governmental Process*, pp. 34-35].

11 See below, pp. 163-164.

Where, as we shall see, Bentley postulates his potential activity on the basis of an introspective self-analysis and of the reports conveyed to him by others, Truman relies for his postulation on "modern techniques for the measurement of attitude and opinion." But these techniques rest finally on what people say, on "talk activity," to use Bentley's phrase. And talk activity is considered a distorted and distorting "reflection" of interest, not the source of valid information about actual or potential interest.

Truman is concerned in the part of his argument we are reviewing here to present his understanding of "group." He begins by distinguishing between "categoric groups," which are "any collection[s] of individuals who have some characteristic in common," and groups simply. But groups simply are difficult to define. Truman stresses the importance of "shared attitudes" as the prime characteristic of groups as he understands them, but he blurs his meaning by speaking of the interactions among members of a group as another primary consideration, going so far at one point as to say the "interactions or relationships . . . are the group, and it is in this sense that the term will be used" (*The Governmental Process*, pp. 23-24). If the group is a set of individuals with shared attitudes who interact with or above a minimum frequency, we have one focus of discussion, one in which it would be interesting to discover what the "sharing" of attitudes means. If the group is a set of interactions or relationships, the focus of inquiry is no longer on the individuals in the group, but on "interaction" or "relationship." Here the teasing query is to discover how an interaction or a relationship is distinguished from random behavior if "activity is the basic datum of social science." Only by the uninforming assumption that all activity is "in system" can all behavior be called interaction or relationship. This is an assumption explicitly made by Bentley (*The Process of Government*, p. 285) and apparently shared by Truman. This assumption, however, dissolves the distinguishing characteristic of groups. With everything "in system," interaction ceases to be the specific feature of some things.

Truman's difficulties are compounded when he moves to "potential groups" and "potential activity." Except for a change in the identity of the legitimating sciences, Truman's constructs of potential activity and potential groups provide no more solid bases for the weight he places on them than do Bentley's. Whereas physics, chemistry, and biology provide the authority to legitimate Bentley's departure from his explicit assertions, more recent studies in psychology and social psychology perform the same function for Truman. He relies on "the most insistent defenders of the scientific position" to insist simultaneously on "activity as the basic datum of social science" and also on the need to postulate the existence of inevident activity in a "becoming" or "potential" stage. Truman never explains how his authorities enable him to discover activity where there is no manifest or evident action to guide him in his search. He resorts instead to an uncritical adoption of "becoming" and "potential," never showing how a science which is assertedly based on activity as its fundamental datum can accommodate "becoming" within its framework, to say nothing of finding room for "potential." The terminology of Greek philosophy sounds strange in a discourse which denies the basic tenets of philosophy altogether. Moreover, the science which welcomes "becoming" and "potential" may have to come to terms with the issues raised by "being." For example, it must make clear how or why current opinion can be used as the legitimator of its fundamental assertions. Truman admits the danger of attributing activity or interest to individuals or groups where there is no evident activity to support the attribution, but, as we have noted, he claims to find the authority to do so in "the modern techniques" for the measurement of attitude and opinion." [12] Nevertheless, our doubt persists. If interest is known only from the interactions of individuals, can a profession of faith, even faith in modern techniques, provide support for the asserted existence of "interests that are *not* at a particular point in time the basis of interactions among individuals . . ." (*The Governmental Process*, p. 34, italics supplied)?

Truman suggests another ground for the notion of potential interests and potential groups, but he does not explore it. In speaking of the distinction between categorical groups and "groups in the proper sense," Truman comments on the overlap in the senses in which the word "group" is understood.

In fact, the reason why the two senses of the term "group" are so close is that on the basis of experience it is expected that people who have certain attributes in common—neighborhood, consanguinity, occupation—will interact with some frequency. It is the interaction that is crucial, however, not the shared characteristic [p. 24].

For present purposes we suggest that the crucial factor is not interaction, which admittedly may or may not be present, but the "experience" appealed to in Truman's comment. The notion of potential groups and potential interests has its origin in the common sense observation that people who have certain attributes in common are expected to have common interests. As in Bentley, where the potential group is constituted by Bentley's discernment of common characteristics among some of the people he observes, so in Truman, the potential group is a number of people who have certain traits in common (whether "shared" or not is an open question) and who, on the basis of these similarities are expected by Truman to have similar interests—their potential interests.

What is clearly being circumvented in this discussion is the role of the evaluating observer. In this, the procedure and the problem are Bentleyan. *The Process of Government* warns against endowing groups with meanings

[12] Truman's remarks in The Brookings Lectures, 1955, cited above, should be considered at this point. They lend support to his note of caution if not to the procedure discussed above.

or values that are objective or "clothed in oughtness" (p. 213). Bentley, nevertheless, does speak of organizations which "genuinely" represent a mass of "indifferent taxpayers" (p. 226).[13] Truman is led into the same difficulty by adopting the same premises on the status of evaluation in social science.

Seen in these terms, is an interest group inherently "selfish"? In the first place, such judgments have no value for a scientific understanding of government or the operation of society. Schematically, they represent nothing more than the existence of a conflicting interest, possibly, but not necessarily, involving another group or groups. Judgments of this kind are and must be made by all citizens in their everyday life, but they are not properly a part of the systematic analysis of the social process. Secondly, many such political interest groups are from almost any point of view highly altruistic. One need only recall those groups that have consistently risen to defend the basic guarantees of the American constitution, to improve the lot of the underprivileged, or to diffuse the advantages stemming from scientific advance. Evaluations such as these may be made of particular groups, depending on the observer's own attitudes, but . . . they will not facilitate one's understanding of the social system of which the groups are a part [*The Governmental Process*, p. 38].

These remarks call for two sets of comment. First it will be useful to juxtapose two sentences which appear in the paragraph above:

In the first place, such judgments have no value for a scientific understanding of government or the operation of society.

Secondly, many such political interest groups are from almost any point of view highly altruistic.

Whether Truman means by "almost any point of view" to exclude the scientific one is not clear. He had earlier warned against "an excessive preoccupation with matters of definition," and had approvingly quoted Bentley: "Who likes may snip verbal definitions in his old age, when his world has gone crackly and dry" (p. 23). Is it an excessive preoccupation with definition to ask whether Truman does or does not believe that meaningful evaluations of group interests can be made? If they can, he and his science depart (reasonably, one may add) from Bentley's contrary assertion. If they cannot, how does Truman know that some groups do rise to defend Constitutional liberty? What are the credentials of an authentic defense of liberty as distinguished from deceptive self-pleading? We suggest it is Truman's notion of the potential interest of a given community or group which supplies him with the answer. He does not present, however, a reasoned defense of his choice of interests. There is instead condescending inattention to what he identifies as the citizen's obligation.

If we return to the quotation above and concern ourselves with the altruistic

[13] See below, pp. 190-191.

activities Truman does recognize, we meet another consequence of his (and Bentley's) effort to avoid evaluative judgments. Suppose we did know of a social system with no Constitutional guarantees, which did not consider the lot of the underprivileged to be a subject of common interest, and which opposed or restricted the diffusion of the advantages stemming from scientific advance. Would such knowledge, provided it were accurate, tell us nothing to "facilitate one's understanding of the social system of which the groups are a part"? If such knowledge is neither important nor useful, how are we to regard one of Truman's own statements of purpose: "A conception of the political process broad enough to account for the development and functioning of political groups is essential to a reliable evaluation of the alleged mischiefs of faction. To work out such a basis of interpretation is the purpose of this book" (p. 13). Or, in what light are we to read his evaluations of the Constitution of the United States: "The Constitution of the United States has lived to magnificent maturity. . . . It was well and wisely drawn" by "the skillful statesmen of the eighteenth century" (p. 480). How, finally, are we to view the concern with "morbific politics" which supplies the theme for the concluding part of *The Governmental Process?* If we consider Truman's writing to be his "activity" or "interest," we find in it an unrelaxed search for evidence capable of yielding the evaluations he seeks. The science he uses differs from the science he describes precisely in that the former incorporates what the latter explicitly rejects. Truman is torn between his role as a citizen making the kind of evaluations he admits are necessary and his role as a scientist above the battle. A confusion between impartiality and indifference clouds his understanding of scientific objectivity and adds an unnecessary burden to his role as a citizen.

A reading of Bentley will show the same inability to maintain the posture assertedly demanded by scientific study.[14] Truman in this respect, as in so many others, does no more than uncritically repeat, with different illustrations, the assertions of Bentley; the result is a repetition of Bentley's inability to maintain the posture assertedly demanded by scientific study. Once again we are pointed to the need of an analysis and evaluation of Bentley's own work as he presented it. The effort to provide such an analysis is made in this essay. Except for incidental references, we shall deal with Bentley alone, primarily with *The Process of Government.* In this way, perhaps, we can achieve one of the goals Bentley set before us, a "ground clearing" which will enable subsequent work in this area to proceed on a sounder basis, more fully aware of what he sought to teach.

[14] See below, pp. 178 ff.

BENTLEY ON SOCIAL SCIENCE AND POLITICS

Bentley begins his positive argument in the second part of *The Process of Government* with a question: "What are the raw materials of government?" (p. 175) His answer is two-fold and occupies the remainder of the book. Here the "tool" which is to be his primary instrument of research is both forged and used. He presents, that is to say, more than descriptions and definitions to identify and characterize the raw materials of government. He also indicates how the raw materials should be investigated and gives a sketch of the results he believes would follow from the investigations he recommends.

At the outset, it will be useful, indeed necessary, to present an outline of Bentley's exposition. The outline is required because his is a doctrine "which . . . cannot be criticized step by step according to the order in which its author puts it, for its characteristic is that, in order to state itself, it has to take for granted popular notions which it afterwards shows to be unmeaning." [15]

The "raw material of government," Bentley holds, is to be found in the action or activities of men. Not man alone, or even man added to man, but the action of "many men together" is the raw material (*The Process of Government*, pp. 175-176). It cannot be found in constitutional documents, or in lawbooks, or in writings and speeches on forms of government, but only in the "actually performed legislating-administering-adjudicating activities of the nation and in the streams and currents of activity that gather among the people and rush into these spheres." Typically we will find "the people striking at somebody or something along lines that tend to produce purer food, safer insurance, better transportation facilities, or whatever else—that is the raw material of our study" (p. 180).

We are to understand talking and writing as kinds of activity, related to other kinds of activity by a process of reflection or representation (p. 179). Ideas, creeds, and theories appear actively as words, and there is no idea "which is not a reflection of social activity" (p. 177). What we have before us to study is "one great moving process . . . and of this great moving process it is impossible to state any part except as valued in terms of the other parts. This is as true of the talk activities as of any other activities" (p. 178). Instead of attributing a ruling or dominating power to ideas and to words, "at every step we must regard them as activities and nothing else. We must hold fast to what we can observe and examine . . ." (p. 184). Our material for study will be "strictly empirical," although it is true that "in one sense" science is "all conception, not perception . . ." (p. 245).

Now, activity limited to the "motions of the body" does not give us "good

[15] T. H. Green, *Works*, ed. R. L. Nettleship (London: Longmans, Green & Co., 1885), vol. I, p. 132.

material to study." To "manifest, or evident, or palpable activity . . . must be added under the same term, activity, certain forms which are not palpable or evident to the same extent at the stage of their progress in which we have to search them out." These "are activities which can perhaps be pictured by the use of the word 'potential.'" Or, an analogy between them and the motions of physics or chemistry can be used: potential activity is like molecular motion and "palpable or external activity corresponds with molar motion." Or, again, by making "a half-compromise with everyday speech," we can call these inevident actions "tendencies." This is permissible so long as "we remember every time we use the words that these 'tendencies' are activities themselves; that they are stages of activity just as much as any other activity" (pp. 184-185).

The raw material, then, is "a mass of men . . . all of them thinking-feeling men, acting." And "political phenomena are all phenomena of these masses." But "in the complex modern state," it is rare that the masses we study are physically separate from each other. More often the men we study are involved in two or more "functions." For example, an individual who is a resident of New York City is also a resident of New York State. For some political purposes it is necessary to distinguish between the individual as a resident of the city and as a resident of the state, and "we must keep them distinct in their two functions." We thus find such individuals in "two groups, which must be separated in our analysis. The same physical men are among the components of both, and perhaps find themselves in one group pulling against themselves in another group." A nation, or "the nation" is to be pictured "as made up of groups of men, each group cutting across many others, each individual man a component part of very many groups . . ." (pp. 203, 180, 204).

"Group," the key word, so to speak, of the Bentleyan position is characterized as follows: "It means a certain portion of the men of a society, taken . . . as a mass activity, which does not preclude the men who participate in it from participating likewise in many other group activities." Bentley warns against thinking of a group "as a physical mass cut off from other masses of men," stressing instead the possibility of multiple group membership for any individual. In addition, the "technical sense" in which Bentley uses "group" puts heavy emphasis on action: "It is always so many men, acting, or tending toward action—that is, in various stages of action" (p. 211). Bentley's characterization or description of "group" achieves another purpose in addition to that of describing the phenomena gathered under the term; it serves to introduce the first of two synonyms which can be used interchangeably with "group." The first equivalent is "group activity" or "action"—"group and group activity are equivalent terms." By this equivalence or equivocation, Bentley takes the first step toward maintaining his initial definition of the "raw material" as "action," while at the same time endowing that "action" with meaningful content. As he says earlier, "We must get our raw material before us in the form of purposive action, valued in terms of other purposive action" (p. 179). The transition is completed to Bentley's satisfaction when he adds the final equivalent of group and group activity. This is the term "interest."

There is no group without its interest. An interest, as the term will be used in this work, is the equivalent of a group. We may speak also of an interest group or of a group interest, again merely for the sake of clearness in expression. The group and the interest are not separate. There exists only one thing, that is, so many men bound together in or along the path of a certain activity [p. 211].

If we try to take the group without the interest, we have simply nothing at all. We cannot take the first step to define it. The group is activity and the activity is only known to us through its particular type, its value in terms of other activities, its tendency where it is not in the stage which gives manifest results. The interest is just this valuation of the activity not as distinct from it, but as the valued activity itself [p. 213].

Two dangers need to be avoided in using the term "interest." First "is the danger of taking the interest at its own verbal expression of itself, that is to say, the danger of estimating it as it is estimated by the differentiated activity of speech and written language which reflects it." The second danger "is that we disregard the group's expressed valuation of itself and that we assign to it a meaning or value that is 'objective' in the sense that we regard it as something natural or inevitable or clothed in oughtness" (p. 213). Between these two dangers is the safe course marked out by the group's activities. "The interest is nothing other than the group activity itself" (p. 271). Activity is a key to interest; "indeed the only way to be sure we have isolated an interest group, is to watch its progress." And Bentley adds:

The interest I put forward is a specific group interest in some definite course of conduct or activity. It is first, last, and all the time strictly empirical. There is no way to find it except by observation. . . . [T]he interest is merely a manner of stating the value of the group activity . . . [pp. 214-215].

Bentley does not say who "states" the value or meaning of the group activity as a "strictly empirical" matter. We do know that "ideas" and "feelings" are not part of the raw materials except as they are "reflections" of "brain motion" (p. 182). But whose brain motion or reflection are we able to see? Our own? Then is the value or meaning of the group activity what we as observers or perhaps as critics think it to be? Or does the brain motion and its reflection belong to the group? How then are we to decide whether to accept the group's self-evaluation or to seek another evaluation, one which is more accurate but not yet damned as objective or natural? No answers are given, only an admonition. We are to "hold fast to the practical reality, and accept the interests that it offers us as the only interests we can use, studying them as impassively as we would the habits or the organic functions of birds, bees, or fishes" (p. 214).

What this practical view shows us is the following. The groups we are concerned with are of various kinds. Close to the "surface of society" are the political groups, primarily the agencies and organs of government (p. 209). Government is to be understood as "a differentiated, representative group, or set of groups (organ, or set of organs), performing specified governing functions for the underlying groups of the population." The "underlying groups" are arranged in depth. Closest to the government are "organization" and "discussion" groups which are involved in government in "an intermediate sense." Government in the intermediate sense is what we get "when we have clearly passed beyond the limits of the differentiated governing activities, but are still among phenomena that are specialized with reference to the government, or, let us say, among political phenomena" (p. 261). An illustration makes clear what Bentley's effort at definition leaves vague: political parties are the primary examples of groups involved in government in the intermediate sense.

Below the parties are the electorate and "semi-political groups" (p. 423). The electorate, which is never the same as "the whole citizenship," "reflects" or "represents" the interests of the citizenship and also of noncitizen groups in the population. Bentley realistically notes that we cannot find the electorate simply by consulting a list of constitutional rights. The electorate in his view is that part of the population of a regime which effectively determines the choice of officials. Examples of "semi-political groups" are the press and organizations like a "protectionist league," "a civil service reform organization," and "citizens' associations." Bentley notes in passing that most of his examples are "taken from a single country, and that a country in which the rights of free association and free speech are guaranteed by law." But while these guarantees are said to be important from an unspecified "technical standpoint," Bentley insists the guarantees "do not produce any vital difference in the human process. They simply describe and help to maintain the group process as it is actually proceeding" (pp. 431-433). The difference, which would appear to be vital, between "describe" and "help to maintain" is not pursued. The essential features of constitutional democracy are assumed to be the conditions in which American groups, and apparently all groups everywhere, act.

Deeper still in society are the fundamental "underlying groups," the "wheels within the wheels," the givers of motion to the process of government (p. 117). No examples of these ultimate or fundamental groups are offered for our examination, but we do gain a hint as to what these ultimate or fundamental groups may be from a later remark about "the environment as a condition of the group formation." We learn that there are "groups rest-

ing on mines, farms, fisheries, cattle herds, city lots; we have groups related
to steam power and to electricity" (p. 462). It would not be a great gamble
to hazard the view that the underlying groups are economic groups, or, to
adopt a somewhat older terminology, that the deepest underlying groups are
determined by the relations of men to the conditions of production.

Bentley centers his attention on "political groups and other groups that
function in the specifically social process" (p. 212). In this process we typically find groups in conflict or competition with each other. We find that
"the phenomena of government are from start to finish phenomena of force,"
but to avoid "metaphysical quagmires," Bentley proposes the substitution of
"pressure" for "force."

Pressure, as we shall use it, is always a group phenomenon. It indicates the push
and resistance between groups. The balance of group pressures *is* the existing state
of society [pp. 258-259].

All phenomena of government are phenomena of groups pressing one another,
forming one another, and pushing out new groups and group representatives (the
organs or agencies of government) to mediate the adjustments [p. 269].

With these amplifications of what "government" means, we are able to
round out the "senses" in which Bentley speaks of government. Government
"in the broadest sense . . . is the process of the adjustment of a set of interest
groups in a particular distinguishable group or system without any differentiated activity, or 'organ,' to center attention on just what is happening" (p.
260). Bentley is referring to "societies showing adjusted interest groups without a differentiated 'government,'" but he gives no examples. He also includes within the meaning of "government in the broadest sense" the "adjustment or balance of interests" in a family, a church, or a corporation (p.
268). Government "in the narrowest sense" is "a differentiated, representative
group, or set of groups . . . performing specified governing functions for the
underlying groups of the population." Here the institutions and agencies of
formally organized governments are intended. Between these two senses is
the "intermediate" one noted above, the sense we get "when we have clearly
passed beyond the limits of the differentiated governing activities, but are
still among phenomena that are specialized with reference to the government, or, let us say, among political phenomena." In addition to political
parties, "the part [a] corporation will take in the next political campaign" is
offered as an example of government in the intermediate sense (p. 261). What
appears to be intended here is that range of organization and activity which
seeks to direct the choice of personnel and policy of the formal agencies and
organs of government.

For all of the senses of government, the same general assertion is made:

The interest groups create the government and work through it; the government,
as activity, works "for" the groups; the government, from the view-point of certain

of the groups may at times be their private tool; the government, from the view-point of others of the groups, seems at times their deadly enemy; but the process is all one . . . [p. 270].

From the observation of the multiplicity of groups in society, together with the asserted identity of interest and group or group activity, Bentley reaches a familiar conclusion: "I think I am justified in asserting positively that no such group as the "social whole" enters into the interpretation in any form whatever." What is proclaimed as the interest of the whole or as the common interest will prove on examination to be "merely the group tendency or demand represented by the man who talks of it, erected into the pretense of a universal demand of the society." But in fact, what we find in any society is "always some parts of the nation . . . arrayed against other parts" (p. 220). The existence of a "conflict phase" (p. 289) establishes to Bentley's satisfaction the nonexistence of a social whole or interest of the whole. For something to be "the interest of all the people," it has to be desired by all of them. By this criterion, not even murder can be said to be "against the social interest." For, to say nothing of the "recurring crimes of passion, and the murders by professional thieves" (which apparently demonstrate the difference of interest between murderer and victim and thereby establish the nonexistence of a social whole or a common interest), "there is a vast amount of homicide in routine features of our commercial life, such as railroad operation, food manufacture, sweat-shop clothes-making, and so on. And such murders answer to existing interests" (p. 221).[16]

Although there is no social whole and no common interest, Bentley does recognize that group activity may be regarded as proceeding in "a great sea of social life," in which any particular group activity "is but a slight modulation." Taking this view, "we shall get the conception of a 'habit background' in which the group activity operates." However, for Bentley the significance of the "habit background" or "rules of the game" does not lie in its serving to indicate what the common interest is, but in its non-controversial character: it is "not at all a subject of discussion by the man who calls it an interest of society as a whole . . ." (pp. 218, 220).

The habit background may usefully be taken into the reckoning as summing up a lot of conditions under which the groups operate, but reliance on it is apt to check investigation where investigation is needed, or even become the occasion for the introduction of much unnecessary mysticism. By appealing to the habit background we must not hope to get away from the present in our interpretations. Just as ideas and ideals are apt to give us a false whirl into the future with our in-

---

[16] In driving his point home, Bentley's humanitarianism, together perhaps with his scorn for law books, appears to get in the way of his concern with clarity of definition. "Homicide" is supposed to equal "murder" and the continuation of such "murder" to prove that there is no common interest.

vestigations, so in somewhat the same way the habit background is apt to carry us back into the past and thus away from our raw material [pp. 218-219].

We now have the general outline of Bentley's position before us. The basic material for study is a multiplicity of groups in conflict, each group pursuing its interest, and the interest known only from the activity. The phenomena of government are the activities of groups pressing toward an adjustment or balance of an undisclosed kind. Any agency of government is to be understood as the reflection or representation of the group struggle at a given time. "The balance of the group pressures *is* the existing state of society" at any given time.

In Bentley's own view, the final product of his endeavor would be a fuller understanding of government seen as the balance or adjustment of group pressures. That is, if we emphasize the tone which sounds most clearly in his writing, and do not stress the admission of another purpose to be considered below, we will regard his work as a contribution to the scientific understanding of government. He was convinced and has apparently convinced a sizable following that a full analysis or "statement" of the groups would be the full science of government.

When the groups are adequately stated, everything is stated. When I say everything I mean everything. The complete description will mean the complete science, in the study of social phenomena, as in any other field [pp. 208-209].

The comprehensiveness of Bentley's claim is manifest in his ringing assertion. What has not been sufficiently emphasized by his students is an admission Bentley makes repeatedly in *The Process of Government*, the admission that neither there nor elsewhere does he attempt a full "statement" of the groups. He does not give or attempt to give an analysis of government, but attempts, as the prefatory slogan in *The Process of Government* indicates, to "fashion a tool." While firmly convinced that "there is no other way to get a unified picture of the whole process except by reducing it to such groups," Bentley straightforwardly admits, "I do not pretend here to state them [the groups] completely . . . but only to indicate by way of illustration, how such a problem must be approached." He was not "attempting so much to get results as to indicate methods . . ." (pp. 373, 434).

One note is perhaps in order at this point. A reader familiar with Bentley's position may miss, in the survey we have presented, the liveliness and polemic enthusiasm which are surely in his work. To the extent that this lack detracts from the essentials of Bentley's presentation, one can only plead one's limited capacity. Bentley's "eloquent reiteration," his anxiety "to seem factual and tough-minded," his wish to supply "an antidote to various forms of political humbug," [17] should be, and herewith are, expressly noted. In defense of the

[17] W. J. M. Mackenzie, "Pressure Groups: The 'Conceptual Framework,'" *Political Studies*, October 1955, pp. 249, 251.

relatively colorless outline we have attempted, it may be said that the great desideratum in the study of Bentley is to move beyond "eloquent reiteration." Bentley's phrases appear at times to serve as prose equivalents of exclamation points in writings where elucidation, analysis, or demonstration rather than the fervor of certitude are required.[18] Our present task, in W. J. M. Mackenzie's phrase, is to determine "how much would be left if his vigorous language were analyzed prosaically." [19] This we propose to do. The analysis can best begin by returning to Bentley's statement on the raw materials of government.

THE RAW MATERIALS

In *The Process of Government*, the first two pages of the chapter on the raw materials exemplify the procedure Bentley uses in developing his position as well as the difficulties to be faced in analyzing and evaluating that position. Bentley begins his positive argument, it will be recalled, by asking a question: "What are the raw materials of government?" "The morning paper," he says, "tells me that the Standard Oil Company has been indicted on some thousands of counts for violating the federal laws." Earlier, the newspaper had told him of "many employees of one of the executive departments of the government . . . scurrying over the country gathering facts about the way in which that company had conducted its business with the railroad companies." Earlier still, the newspaper had told him of a Congressional resolution ordering the investigation. A final retrospective glance at the newspaper would have made it possible to "read of the excited activities of many men which came to a climax in the passage of the law under which these indictments have been found" (p. 175).

Beyond what the newspaper told him, Bentley also knows what the papers will tell him in the future. In "a few months . . . I shall read of the trial in court, of the punishment which will perhaps be imposed, and in part of the effect which the punishment has, or, alternatively, which the indictments even without punishment have, on the company's business methods." Furthermore, Bentley adds, "I have reason to think also that I shall soon hear a certain leader of a great portion of the people announce fresh steps to be taken toward the introduction of improved methods of controlling such corporations . . . and that this will sooner or later be followed by a renewed assertion by another popular leader that the present methods of control will be applied so vigorously as to secure the desired change in conditions without further legislation."

[18] See Taylor, *Western Political Quarterly*, June 1952, pp. 214, 217, 225; see also Ratner's "Introduction" in Bentley, *Inquiry into Inquiries*.
[19] *Political Studies*, October 1955, p. 250.

"Here," we are told, "is some of the raw material for the study of government. There is no other kind."

It is first, last, and always activity, action, "something doing," the shunting by some men of other men's conduct along changed lines, the gathering of forces to overcome resistance . . . or the dispersal of one grouping of forces by another grouping. The writing and talking and speech-making are activity just as much as any of the other facts I have mentioned [p. 176].

"Action," or "activity" is the raw material. It is men in motion, doing something, going somewhere. Two qualifying provisos are immediately added by Bentley. The action of men, not man alone or men alone, is the raw material. This material cannot be "found in one man by himself, it cannot even be stated by adding man to man. It must be taken as it comes in many men together." What is meant by this, Bentley adds, is that "the 'relation,' i.e., the action, is the given phenomenon, the raw material; the action of men with or upon each other." This absorption of the individual into a relationship of "many men together" rests, apparently, on Bentley's earlier assertion that "we know men only as participants in such activity" (p. 176). The conclusion toward which these observations lead is finally expressed in the following way: "The individual stated for himself, and invested with an extra-social unity of his own, is a fiction" (p. 215). Bentley is silent on the natural or phenomenal unity of the individual as an individual, but insists that if we are to see the raw material as it is, man must be reduced to social matter in motion, the social matter to be seen as "masses of men" and not as individuals.

Not only does the raw material, men in action, present man in the only form accessible to us, as "the cloth, so to speak, out of which men in individual patterns are cut" (p. 176), but these men or this human material is "composed of thinking and feeling actors." What we are to "see" under Bentley's direction is men in action, "many men together," who are "thinking and feeling actors," who "act through a thought and feeling process." At this point we can but recall Bentley's claim that the material as he presents it is "strictly empirical." This claim, together with the question how thinking and feeling are "seen" in, or as, action, will be returned to presently.

Bentley's examples consist of several parts. First there is a series of newspaper accounts of the course of an investigation, indictment, and trial of a corporation for violation of federal laws. There is in addition a set of predictions, made by Bentley, of the probable future efforts to control corporations like Standard Oil by regulatory legislation, together with a prediction of the likely course of political party debate on the issue of regulatory legislation. There is, finally, reference to reading material containing "many criticisms of everybody and everything concerned, both in current periodicals and in books of all degrees of remoteness from the hottest spots in the conflict." Newspaper accounts, predictions which Bentley has "reason to think" would be confirmed, and a body of critical literature. These are what Bentley calls the "raw material for the study of government," and beyond which he asserts there is no other kind.

On turning the page we find this material characterized as "first, last, and always activity, action, 'something doing.'" Now it must be observed that Bentley does not present us with "action" or "activity." He does point to reports of "something doing." The distinction is vital. "Something doing," a phrase taken from the everyday vocabulary of everyday life, points to a particular identifiable event or series of events, and calls it or them to our attention. But reports of "something doing" cannot be labeled "action" and left at that. Taken strictly, and despite the assertion that the raw material is "strictly empirical," what Bentley does is to present us with a structured account of a set of events, followed by a set of predictions about events which have not yet transpired and whose probable appearance is vouched for only by Bentley's assurance that "I have reason to think. . . ." This is not to draw his judgment into doubt. The entertaining satire of his predictive sentences should not be permitted to obscure the knowing familiarity with American political practices manifested in these sentences. What is intended is a query about and a dissent from the conclusion Bentley reaches about the nature of the material he has isolated as the raw material of government.

We have been offered a sample of political activity to be sure, but the initial characterization of the sample as "first, last, and always activity" or "action" is incomplete. A vital part of the sample is omitted, or more properly stated, surreptitiously included in the phrase "something doing." Bentley is able to bring his sample to our attention because it is structured, because it is identified as a "something" of political significance by means of factors other than the movement or activity he stresses. The newspaper stories are not sufficiently discussed by Bentley to permit one to judge whether he agrees with the whole report or not, but from what he has said, he clearly places his reliance on an unidentified writer's account of what is relevant in reporting the Standard Oil investigation and indictment. There is, moreover, a prior judgment that the investigation and indictment themselves are at least newsworthy and perhaps important as events in the political life of the nation, and this judgment, too, is accepted by Bentley.

The first question that must be put is, why, out of the infinity of happenings, or out of the indescribable "chaos" of activity which confronts the naked eye, are these particular items presented for our consideration? What criterion of significance guided the selection of the newspaper items? Stated as a "how" question, the problem is, how was a particular "something" isolated and identified when supposedly there is visible to us nothing but action, a constant flux, which, as action, carries no indicators of significance or relevance attached to itself? Bentley has not presented "action" or "strictly em-

pirical" material as the raw material of politics, but has instead taken as his
first sample an organized description, based on an unspecified criterion of
significance. At the very outset of his enterprise, when he seeks to find a unit
of activity to serve as an example, Bentley shows himself and his method to
be entirely dependent on what an organ or agency of public opinion says is
relevant. Bentley "sees" in short, with the aid of, or in the perspective of,
current opinion.

Now, political life does move on the plane of action. But to make politics,
even the raw material of politics, no more than "action," with analogies to
the movement studied in physics (pp. 176, 214, 185) or in biology (p. 189)
is to obscure by far the greater part of political life. What results is a vagueness of statement where precision greater than that found in everyday life
was promised. Bentley's statement retains an air of solid familiarity because
it incorporates under "talk activity" the outlook and the distinctions of everyday political life. But this incorporation is purchased at a high cost. The roles
of thought, feeling, and opinion in political life are almost entirely obscured.
The planning and judgment, the desires, passions, and irrationalities which are
essential parts of political life remain virtually unexamined, apparently because Bentley regards them as but shaky hypothetical inferences from action.
So too, do the criteria of significance of the observer, the student of government, remain unexamined. These are all subsumed under "action."

Nevertheless, Bentley fails to adhere to the program he has outlined even
in the very effort to present the raw materials as action. He points to relevant
material in an informed way. His predictions are based on his knowledge of
American regulatory legislation and of American party characteristics. His
awareness of the relevant literature on the subject of corporation control and
administrative regulation further indicates what steps he knows need to be
taken if one is to "see" the events discussed in as comprehensive a manner
as possible. Yet none of this knowledge is made the object of examination. In
order to "see" political action the observer requires equipment which his
mere looking does not supply. Above all he requires an understanding of the
"political" to serve as a standard against which to judge the relevance of
events to the purposes of investigation. Bentley uses an understanding of
"political" which he does not discuss or define. As we have indicated, this
understanding is supplied by current opinion, by the unexamined perspective
supplied by the "everyday purposes of everyday life."

Bentley's raw material also is endowed, after its initial presentation, with
the ability to think and feel and to direct itself purposively; the raw material
is "composed of thinking and feeling actors" who are before us in the form
of purposive action (p. 179). Bentley's example affirms what his assertions
deny: the phenomena cannot be understood within a framework limited to
action or activity. Only by a gradual expansion of the meaning of "activity,"
to encompass thought and feeling, and finally purpose as well, is Bentley able

to select his material and to describe it in a fashion that corresponds roughly to what it is.

To repeat, we are presented on one page with an articulate and informed general account of a set of events and an informed set of conjectures about probable future developments. On turning the page we are told we have before us "action," or "activity," vague entities whose use largely empties the designated material of interest to the citizen and makes it unintelligible, if not indeed undiscoverable, to the student of government. Action is undeniably to be included among the "phenomena" of government, but action is certainly not the whole even of Bentley's presentation, other than in the trivial sense that men are animate beings and what they do can thus be subsumed under animation or action. This needs but to be stated for its inadequate vagueness to be seen. Men act. How they act, what the object of their action is, why they single out one object and not another, are questions not answered by a repeated invocation of "action" or "activity."

Telescoped into the initial presentation of the "raw materials" is the crux of the Bentleyan difficulty: his unwilling reliance on current opinion as the basis of his observation as well as the source of his assumptions about the characteristics of the material he observes. We have our attention called to subjects of interest to public-spirited, or at least politically interested, citizens. The issue is initially described and discussed in terms familiar to the citizen and on the basis of judgments of significance or relevance shared by citizens. Having fixed the object of attention firmly before us, and having called upon the host of associations the citizen recognizes, Bentley then characteristically fixes upon one dimension of the event and seeks to reduce all discussion to derivatives of it. But as we have seen, in presenting his examples, Bentley's statements have what meaning they possess by virtue of distinctions drawn from the everyday vocabulary of everyday life, a vocabulary consistently depreciated by Bentley. His proposed contribution, the reduction of all phenomena of government to action, leads to vagueness, not clarity.

Can it be said, in defense of the procedure Bentley follows, that one has to start somewhere; that all Bentley has done is take newspaper accounts of events as the easiest and most directly accessible material to talk about; that the events reported and not the reports are what Bentley means when he calls the raw material of government action or activity? Could he as easily have presented his own account of the raw material and thereby escaped the questions directed to the selection, organization, and evaluation of the accounts he took from newspapers?

The answer appears to be no. If Bentley had presented a straightforward account of political activity, there would be some changes. The predictions would have to be dropped; events which have not yet transpired are not "activity" or "something doing," and this remains true even after Bentley later introduces the concept of "potential" activity or "tendency." We would then be left with the equivalent of the newspaper stories. What characteristics would Bentley's account have? Limiting himself to a description of movement or action, without aid from the concepts, distinctions, and evaluations supplied by the vocabulary of everyday life or by the comments of practicing politicians, what could Bentley tell us? It is difficult to see how anything more than pointing could show us our "raw material" simply as activity, and in the pointing itself, one would still require a criterion of selection to direct the pointing to one act or movement rather than to another. If Bentley were to grant that he thinks or believes that the raw material of government is composed of purposive human beings seeking to achieve or to prevent reform through legislation, he would have a statement that adequately described his example. In such a statement, action or activity would appear as a means toward an end or ends determined by purpose and channeled within the institutional framework of a particular system of government. As our discussion will presently show, this is in effect what Bentley does, but he does it while talking of action as his sole datum. "Activity" remains prominent as a term in his discussion, but shrinks in significance in his analysis.

Satisfied that the raw material of government is activity, Bentley moves to a statement of where this material is found. It will not be found, we are told, in lawbooks, or in the proceedings of constitutional conventions, or in "essays, addresses, appeals, and diatribes on tyranny and democracy." These are the apparatus of that "dead" political science Bentley dismissed with brevity and contempt. Nor will the raw materials be found in the "character of the people," nor in their specific "feelings," "thoughts," or "minds." These are the spurious entities Bentley attempts to reject in the first part of *The Process of Government*. "The raw material can be found only in the actually performed legislating-administering-adjudicating activities of the nation and in the streams and currents of activity that gather among the people and rush into these spheres." Furthermore, we must not seek the raw materials in the "motives" of the people. A concern with motives would serve only to introduce complexity, "and the more you deal with them the more complex they become. And with them you go into the labyrinth, not into the light." Not motives, but action is the source of our data: "The people striking at somebody or something along lines that tend to produce purer food, safer insurance, better transportation facilities, or whatever else—that is the raw material of our study" (pp. 179-180).

We cannot find the raw material in lawbooks, proceedings of constitutional conventions, or essays on tyranny and democracy, but we can find it in legislating, administering, and adjudicating activity and in the streams and currents of activity that flow into these spheres. One must ask how Bentley finds the American tripartite constitutional division of powers when he looks at activity unless he has first consulted or attended to those who have consulted the American Constitution and the content of American lawbooks. It does not take a highly acute realism in politics to recognize that the actions described in American constitutional terms are in part the result of a constitutional structure which channels actions into these "streams"; in part the result of laws that define, sometimes in uniquely local ways, action as legislative, or administrative, or judicial; and finally, in part the result of habits and convictions among the citizens of the nation that the "currents" forming among them should flow into legally constituted and legally defined channels.

So too, while Bentley depreciates motives, he nevertheless uses motives to give content and direction to the activities he describes. "The people" strike at somebody or something. Their striking is not blind, at least not according to Bentley's report, for he tells us that they strike "along lines that *tend* to produce purer food, safer insurance, better transportation facilities" (italics supplied).[20] A more candid and a more fruitful statement here would read: "The people strike along lines that *are intended* to produce purer food, safer insurance, and better transportation facilities." Certainly the large catalogue of abuses and outrages that can be compiled from the examples Bentley consistently uses in his work could not be as easily gathered if the striking of the people in the past had tended of its own accord to the results Bentley describes. "The people" may "strike" but they do not inevitably achieve reforms. Bentley's ambiguous statement only partly obscures the clarity of purpose and uniformity of direction he apparently saw in such efforts. Or, if he were to persist in seeing reform as the natural "tendency" of action, we would be forced to observe that the action he stresses in so lively a fashion is very slow-paced indeed. Evolution, and progressive evolution at that, would then appear to be the "activity" Bentley sees as the raw material of government. The burden of our argument is that progressive evolution is indeed one of the assumed goals of "the process of government" as Bentley sees that process, but this goal is never made the object of examination by him: progressivism apparently could safely furnish a perspective from which to observe and criticize railway abuses, the "murder" that is routine in industry, and the "excrescences of the tariff" (pp. 221, 237, 349). Yet progressivism was apparently too fragile to bear the weight of being the expressed principle of selection in seeking the raw materials of government.

What becomes visible in this review of Bentley's effort to designate or identify the raw material of government is the continued reliance he places on depreciated or ostensibly rejected factors. A constitutional and legal framework, rejected as not part of the raw material of government, is immediately reintroduced as the criterion for identifying and discussing relevant phenomena of government. Motives, thrown out because they are too complex

[20] The introductory sections of Truman, Peltason, and Gross (as cited above, p. 153) are similarly instructive on this point. Each delves into the motives of the actors he is purportedly observing. Each also shows the Progressive orientation which so strongly colors Bentley's discussion.

and because they lead us into the dark, are immediately reintroduced to supply the criterion for identifying the purposes of political action. Bentley's criteria for the discovery and identification of relevant data are supplied by current opinion. He understands the political to be what current opinion regards as political. He sees the motive or purpose of political action to be what "the people" express as the purpose of their political strivings. Why, one is driven to ask, is there this unsatisfactory and transparent effort to deny his reliance on current opinion, to ignore or neglect the motives, the legal procedures, and the institutional framework which the citizen recognizes as the commonplace characteristics of political life? What is it Bentley seeks to gain, or to avoid, in his circuitous statements and descriptions?

We are pointed toward an understanding of Bentley's procedure by the recurrence throughout the constructive or positive part of *The Process of Government* of the same quarrel which is so prominent in the earlier destructive critique. Summarizing the "ground clearing" part of the book, Bentley says that the argument "amounts to about this: that the 'feelings,' 'faculties,' 'ideas,' and 'ideals,' are not definite things in or behind society, working upon it as causes, but that they are—or rather what is meant by them is—society itself stated in a very clumsy an inadequate way" (p. 165). "When 'ideas' in full cry drive past, the thing to do with them is to accept them as an indication that something is happening; and then search carefully to find out what it really is they stand for, what the factors of the social life are that are expressing themselves through the ideas" (p. 152). The ideas are a kind of sieve; they are "there," but only as an exit point for "factors of social life" which express themselves through the ideas. What Bentley denies "is that the separation of feelings and ideas, looked on as individual psychic content, from society or from social institutions or from social activity, is a legitimate procedure in the scientific investigation of society." Such a separation exists "wherever feelings or ideas are given independent value as factors in interpretation. . . ." Further, it is Bentley's contention "that such a separation, when built up into a system of interpretation, collapses of its own defects, and brings down the whole system in a crash" (p. 166).

Bentley is emphatic, however, in insisting upon what his argument does not deny:

I have not denied the existence of a real, living, intelligent human social material which is indicated when feelings and ideas are mentioned.

I have not denied that this feeling, thinking, ideal-following material is the stuff we have before us in interpreting society.

I have not denied that the ordinary statement of this material from the individual view-point, in terms of our current vocabulary, is fairly adequate for the purposes of everyday life. I have no more desire to interfere in that region than I have, for instance, to deprive some unhappy being of the anthropomorphism that suits his needs.

I have not denied that this same ordinary statement has an aesthetic value, any more than the physicist would deny color when he studied wave-lengths. That form of statement has a clear value for fiction and poetry . . . which for all I know, or care, it will retain forever [pp. 165-166].

It is clear from these remarks that, although the feeling and idea system breaks down, some kind of feeling, thinking, and ideal-following survives the collapse to remain part of the material Bentley identifies as "the stuff we have before us in interpreting society." We learn, indeed, that "of course, even though the feeling and idea system breaks down, the feelings and ideas still have a meaning in the social interpretations in which they are used, and fill there a function." What is this function? What remains for the thus-far always discredited and sometimes annihilated feelings and ideas to do? "They are used because they bring a certain amount of order into what would otherwise be a chaos. In casting them out we must be very careful not to cast out that meaning, that order, with them. . . . [W]e must be careful to retain the practical realities of our lives . . ." (pp. 166-167).

To suggest that a "spook" is at work to spirit back what had just been rejected would unjustly minimize the achievement we witness here. A whole pantheon of spirits would be kept busy carrying back in vessels marked "meaning" and "order" the entities which had been thrown out under the labels of "feelings" and "ideas." And this, we are told, must necessarily be done in order to avoid confrontation with what would otherwise admittedly be a chaos of unintelligible movement. The nearly miraculous event Bentley's denials and affirmations achieve is this: ideas are cast out, but their "meaning" and the "order" they bring are somehow retained. And all this is done so that we can retain the practical realities of our lives.

SCIENTIST OR COMBATANT IN THE GROUP STRUGGLE?

The unresolved debate in the first part of *The Process of Government*, between the Bentley who throws out ideas and feelings as "just nothing at all" and the Bentley who takes them back for the sake of the "order" and "meaning" they introduce into the "chaos" of activity, appears in the tool-fashioning part of the book as a tension between Bentley's scientific, essentially descriptive orientation and the citizen or partisan orientation.

At first blush Bentley's purposes would seem to have been stated adequately when we cited his assertion that the "complete description will mean the complete science, in the study of social phenomena, as in any other field" (p. 209). He seeks "a view as objective as possible" of the group process. The raw material he sets before us is said to be "strictly empirical" and empirical in the toughest sense possible. Bentley will have as little to do as possible with the misleading phenomena presented in words about government.

These, he tells us, are but "color flashes" on the "surface" of society. He seeks to penetrate behind the "appearances" to discover and demonstrate the "reality" or "realities" of the governmental process. He is willing to admit that "in one sense all science is 'up in the air,' " that "it is all conception, not perception. . . ." He apparently regards these admissions as compatible with his empirical outlook, as an assurance that science "does not have absolute validity" (p. 245). Some of these admissions would establish, if rigorously pursued, that Bentley's raw material is not simply a description of the phenomenal world, but a description guided by conceptions which enable him to discriminate between phenomena of "appearances" and phenomena of "reality," or between the secondary and primary qualities of social matter. Whatever the effect of such admissions on the character of the science Bentley sought to advance, they add force to the characterization of his endeavor as a scientific or theoretical one, addressed to the understanding. He believed in and sought scientific accuracy and scientific objectivity. "We are not," he said, "conducting a propaganda" (p. 263).

There is, nevertheless, a special problem which Bentley does not succeed in bringing under the control of his scientific outlook, the problem posed by words, by "ideas," and by "feelings." We have already had occasion to note Bentley's attack on efforts to understand or to learn the "why" of social phenomena in the "ground clearing" chapters of *The Process of Government*. Talk activity and theoretical statement are depreciated as "thin, bloodless" (p. 114), and remote from the realities of the group process. Bentley included his own theoretical statement in such depreciation. The theme recurs with greater emphasis in the part of *The Process of Government* now before us. For his own positive or constructive purposes, Bentley asserts, " 'ideas' and 'feelings' are words we use to emphasize certain phases of men's participation in the actions" (p. 176). It is the status of thought and feeling, or ideas and feelings, as words, that must now be explored. What Bentley wishes to avoid is briefly indicated in the following remarks:

When we follow everyday theories and set the "feelings" and "ideas" off by themselves as the "causes" of the activities, we arrive at once at an enormous overvaluation of the forms of activity which appear in words. To the words are attributed a sort of monopoly of intelligence. Ideas, creeds, theories, and other such abstractions, all of them appearing actively as words, are supposed to rule the world, other things being merely ruled. One can get anywhere from primitive magic to "laissez faire" or a theocracy by this system [p. 180].

Bentley is engaged throughout in a dispute with the view that thought rules the world. Thought, as a generic term for ideas and feeling as expressed in words, is precisely what Bentley seeks now to reduce to a form of activity similar to, if not on a par with, other kinds of action. For present purposes it is not necessary to rehearse the series of assertions encountered in the first part of *The Process of Government* which are part of the reduction attempted here. It is sufficient to point to the quotation just given, where the conclusion that ideas do not rule is drawn from the observation that erroneous ideas have been and are being held.[21] On talking and writing activity generally, we find a remarkable paragraph on the "fashion" of overvaluing such activity.

It is no doubt because that particular form of activity which consists in the moving of the larynx or the pushing of a pencil has a direct value relation with such a very large proportion of all our activities that it has gained this extravagant attribution of importance. And then, too, the pencil-pushers naturally value their own activity most highly, and, as they have by far the best opportunities to make their valuation known, they have set a fashion of speech about it [p. 181].

Pencil pushers naturally value their own activity highly, and, having the best chance to make their views known, have set a fashion about it—the fashion of valuing it highly. One can all but hear the cry of "vested interest" as the summary explanation of the overvaluation of pencil pushing presented here. "Interest" is self-interest in a narrow, indeed, cynical sense.

Now, in addition to the observation that not all pencil pushers value their own activity so highly that they take all opportunities to set a fashion in favor of it,[22] one would have to inquire into the assumed state of fact Bentley reports in these sentences. If the pencil pushers can set a fashion through words, then words would appear to have some of the ruling power Bentley wishes to deny. Moreover, one would expect an analysis and not depreciation of so interesting a phenomenon. As an observation datum, speech and writing enjoy an extravagant attribute of importance. Why? What is the "direct value relation" of talking and writing to "such a very large proportion of all our activities"? Instead of answering these queries, Bentley makes an effort to reduce words and the use of words to activity, to a "technique" of action no different basically from other techniques.

Muscle is one form of technique for the groups, deception is another, corruption is another; tools of war fortify muscles, and tools for trickery are also to be found. Oratory and argument count as technical agencies at their proper stages in governmental development [p. 442].

As technique, words must be referred back to the activity they "reflect." "The ideas can be stated in terms of the groups; the groups never in terms

[21] Note that the errors indicated—primitive magic, *laissez faire*, theocracy—have the same quality as the earlier examples had: they are the kinds of error a liberal reformer would want replaced by enlightenment. One of the characteristics of the tool Bentley is forging appears to be its utility as an instrument of reform. How Bentley conceived of himself as a reformer will emerge later.
[22] Plato *Phaedrus passim*, esp. 275 D ff. Bentley's own views, too, would appear to argue against the naturalness with which pencil pushers place high value upon their own work, but greater consistency of viewpoint would have to be manifested before Bentley's testimony on this point could be given its proper weight.

of the ideas" (p. 206). The fact that Bentley never once does what this sentence claims puts no barrier in the path of its assertion. The relationship between words, ideas, feelings, and group activities is never given a clear consistent formulation by Bentley. The ideas and feelings are presented to us as words which are "reflections" of something more fundamental; this is as close to a definite position as Bentley comes. The foregoing discussion has already indicated the status of "reflection" as a key term in Bentley's exposition, serving as a bridge between all that men express verbally and how they act in pursuit of their interests. "There is no idea which is not a reflection of social activity" (p. 177). With such emphasis and reliance argumentatively placed on "reflection," one would expect a clear statement of what "reflection" is and how it works. None is given. There is instead this astonishing footnote:

I see no reason for offering definitions of the terms, reflect, represent, mediate, which I shall use freely all through this work. They indicate certain facts that appear directly in the analysis of social activity; the very facts indeed that I am especially studying. My epistemological point of view is admittedly naive, as naive, I hope, as the point of view of the physical sciences . . . [p. 177, n. 1].

Epistemological naïveté may or may not be a virtue in physical science. Without further information about what physical science naïveté meant to Bentley, we are unable to appraise or even to understand his assertion. We are similarly at a loss to gain understanding of the "facts" assertedly present in the study Bentley says he is making. The footnote does convey, however, the authoritative power that "science," especially "physical science," has for Bentley. If a part of his enterprise is somehow similar to physical science, that in itself is sufficient warrant for its soundness.

The question of how speech is a "reflection" of action cannot be abandoned despite the unwillingness of Bentley to aid in discovering his meaning. While we shall not succeed in finding a definition of "reflection," we shall be able to gain a measure of understanding of the term in Bentley's argument and thereby advance a step toward clarifying the focus of attention or the object of *The Process of Government*.

Writing activity is a reflection of group activity. This, we are told, is true for all writing having any bearing on political life:

When a man writes a book to advance some particular theory about society, he reflects in it a certain phase of the social process, more or less truly. If his book has any bearing, however remote, on political life, it falls within the field before us. Now the reflection of a phase of the social process is the same thing as the reflection of some group interest or set of group interests. His "theory" is such a reflection. It is such an act of "representation" [p. 428].

This assertion bears a certain resemblance to a view made current in recent decades in the sociology of knowledge. Men's opinions are determined by their "social coordinates." [23] Man is a "product" of his time and place. We are not now concerned with the difficulties this view raises, nor with its genealogical relation to Marx's statement on the relation between the conditions of production and the political "superstructure." [24] What is significant in these sociological and historical arguments is the reservation of an undetermined or relatively undetermined position from which it is possible to make the observation that all other views are socially determined. Whether it is the fortunate membership one has in a "socially unattached intelligentsia," [25] or the near-miracle of a "portion of the bourgeoisie . . . who have raised themselves to the level of comprehending theoretically the historical movement as a whole," [26] these positions provide, at least in their intention, for the possibility of viewing the process or the phenomena from an undetermined or free perspective.

Bentley's position, in contrast, does not provide this opportunity. There is no Archimedean platform from which the Bentleyan social scientist can apply his analytical lever to the world. In that case science would appear to be impossible. There would instead be a relativity of perspectives, each determined by group interest. And relativity was in fact what Bentley retrospectively asserted he had worked toward. In his next book, *Relativity in Man and Society*, Bentley points to Einstein's theory of relativity as a sign of the direction social study would have to take if it were to achieve scientific standing. But Einstein's relativity, even in Bentley's description of it, has a feature which is incompatible with the kind of social science relativism seen in Bentley's work. Bentley knew that physical relativity assumed a constant as the reference point for the observations it makes: the constant velocity of light.[27] While measurements or observations will differ under different conditions, equally competent observers will report the same measurements or observations under a specified set of conditions. By contrast, there is the question whether a Bentleyan equivalent for "equally competent" observers can be found. In his expressed, as opposed to his operating, position competence is compromised, if not made impossible or meaningless, by the insistent characterization of all talk, words, argument, reasoning, and observation as "reflections" of group positions, to be understood by reference to group interest and not by reference to a constant criterion of any kind. Members of different groups would not see or report the same phenomena because they would

23 C. Wright Mills, "Language, Logic and Culture," *American Sociological Review*, October 1939, p. 678.
24 Karl Marx, *A Contribution to the Critique of Political Economy* (Chicago: C. H. Kerr, 1904), pp. 10-12.
25 Karl Mannheim, *Ideology and Utopia* (New York: Harcourt, Brace & World, Inc., 1946), p. 137.
26 Karl Marx, *Selected Works*, ed. V. Adoratsky (Moscow: Co-operative Publishing Society, 1935), vol. I, p. 216.
27 *Relativity in Man and Society*, pp. 10-12; 223-224.

not see with the same eyes. There might be an accidental conjunction of group views, but there would be no criterion to serve as a measure for all observers. When we add to this the admission, to be considered below, that group members may be mistaken in their "reflection" of the group interest, the parallel between physical science relativity and Bentley's relativism evaporates.

Near the end of *The Process of Government*, again in a footnote, Bentley informs us: "In the case of my own variation of group interpretation, I think that any experienced reader can easily determine its representative character in terms of American life of the last decade" (p. 479, n. 1). Bentley is, by his own intention and in his own awareness, a participant in the group struggle, a combatant and not an observer. This does not mean merely that as a scientist Bentley holds views opposed to those held by other scientists attempting to understand the same social phenomena. What is involved here is the tying of social science to the "process" of group struggle: "the works [of social scientists] as they stand do but reflect phases of the group process, . . . they have value and meaning only as they reflect phases of it with accuracy, and . . . even the most accurate reflection has value only as process through which the underlying interests work somewhat more smoothly . . ." (p. 479). The quotation brings us full circle. We end as we began, with a dual focus: a quest for, and belief in, objectivity or accuracy, together with the conviction that every statement has meaning only as a reflection of a phase of the group process. While we do not know what reflection fully means to Bentley, the intention to convey the view that man's thought is determined by group membership and by group interest is clear. There is no autonomy for reason, not even for the reason which seeks to set this conclusion before us.

Comment on the position Bentley has thus established is difficult to order. If we are to be consistent with Bentley's view of political life as an endless struggle of groups in which all men are committed as partisans, we must evaluate his work as a shot or thrust in a partisan battle. This conclusion, however, would make impossible a science of social interpretation that is objective, empirical, and not "a propaganda." The notion of "reflection" as Bentley uses it tempts one to speculate that he thinks the "social process" has advanced to the point where men "no longer need to seek science in their minds; they have only to take note of what is happening before their eyes and to become the mouthpiece of this." [28] But Bentley's affirmation that science "is the construction of the scientist's mind," and that it is "all conception, not perception" (p. 245), seems to dispose of this suggestion. Nevertheless the dual commitment to the group struggle and to the pursuit of a science above the struggle remains.

As a group participant, we note, Bentley is somewhat shy about stating his

[28] Karl Marx, *The Poverty of Philosophy* (New York: International Publishers, 1939), p. 106.

position. His examples, however, enable us to identify it with reasonable accuracy. His concern with railway rate abuses, wage slavery, municipal and corporate corruption; his linking of totemism, *laissez faire*, and theocracy, all point in one direction. Bentley appears as a proponent of progressive enlightenment. It is a shrinking and perhaps disenchanted progressivism, which does not go to the length of stating its goals explicitly. One might go further and note in the stress on the economic basis of political life and on the group antagonisms which are ultimately economic antagonisms, a faint echo of Marxism, a Marxism with the ultimate goal left out. But since Bentley does not adhere to his announced "representative" status as a group participant any more consistently than he does to his announced scientific intentions, the further pursuit of this question would not add to our understanding of his political views or purposes.[29]

Our conclusions must stress the dual purposes articulated and maintained by Bentley. He alternates between two views, each stated explicitly and repeatedly in the course of his work. At times he appears to favor the view which is least favorable to his enterprise: he is a participant in the struggle of groups in American politics, on the side of the progressives at the turn of the century. His work might therefore be considered a partisan statement made by a participant in the political struggle. Alternatively, he asserts that he is articulating a scientific method, a method which will disclose a view "as objective as possible." The full description yielded by this method will be the full science with nothing left out. His scientific purpose appears to be limited to description but, however it might be stated finally, it would be emphatic on one point: it would differ in purpose, as in method, from the purposes and procedures of everyday life, including everyday political life.

The impasse between Bentley's two purposes is the result, as we have shown, of his desire to avoid giving ruling power to "words," and to the ideas, feelings, and opinions "reflected" in talking and writing activity. The depreciation of talk activity and of common opinion, the attempted reduction of thought to "reflection" of activity or interest, results in a conflict which makes a consistent statement of Bentley's major purposes impossible. The conclusion we reach here would serve to dismiss Bentley's work as a reasoned statement of a scientific method. But Bentley sought to outline a method of analysis, not to present "a mathematical sort of elegance" [30] in closely reasoned analysis. The question remains, then, whether, despite the weaknesses in reasoned statement made along the way, Bentley succeeds in producing a useful tool for social science analysis.

[29] See below, pp. 242 ff., 322-323.
[30] W. J. M. Mackenzie, *Political Studies*, October 1955, p. 254.

THE TOOL EXAMINED

THE EXTENDED CONCEPT OF ACTIVITY

What emerges from Bentley's analysis of "activity" is not a "strictly empirical" description of action, but is instead a construct or concept that enables him to bring selected items from everyday life within the sweep of his description of the raw materials of politics. Bentley discriminates among the "phenomena" of political life, selecting "reality" and rejecting "color flashes" or "appearances" without informing us what basis there is for his selection and rejection. The phenomena are apparently divided into phenomena proper, or phenomena of reality, which Bentley takes as his raw material, and epiphenomena, which he rejects as spooks or as surface coloration, without political significance (*The Process of Government*, pp. 178, 183). When we turn to his selected items, they prove to be some but not all of the items common opinion holds to be significant in politics. This applies to his understanding of "political" and his usage of "government" in the "narrow sense," as well as to the specific actions he brings to our attention. "The people" striving for reform of abuses, seeking safer insurance or purer food, and channeling their strivings into legal courses of action are examples.

Bentley's "activity," as we have seen, is not to be understood as the mere phenomenon of movement of men in masses. The men who compose the raw material are "thinking-feeling actors," who act through a "thought-and-feeling process" (p. 176), with thinking and feeling to be understood as "words" used to emphasize certain phases of men's participation in the actions. Purpose is similarly made part of the activity (p. 179). Thus Bentley is willing to admit that men do think and feel, but the admission as he wishes it to be understood would amount to no more than repeating, in a new way, that men in action are the phenomena accessible to us as students of politics. That is, we know the ideas and feelings only as they are "reflected" in action. But the use of "reflection" as a bridge between talk activity (ideas and feelings) and other activity obscures a difficulty. How is the transition between idea or feeling and action made? How does Bentley know what designation to apply to the action? "We know nothing of 'ideas' and 'feelings' except through the medium of actions." This declaration lies at the base of Bentley's statement that " 'ideas' and 'feelings' are words we use to emphasize certain phases of men's participation in the actions." Beyond the phenomena of action directly visible to us, we are in the realm of words, of hypothesis, theory, and shaky inference (pp. 176, 177, 182, 187). The course of action provides the one safe guide toward an understanding of political life. For this reason, we must handle language carefully, skeptically, and with an eye on the action that alone gives it sound meaning. But the action itself is called by a specific name. Bentley does not present us in *The Process of Government* with a full vocabulary which is to furnish the linguistic basis for his discussion.[31] He instead uses a wide range of terms drawn from everyday speech. Despite his frequent warnings about the incapacity of everyday speech to supply the needs of scientific description, Bentley proceeds as if his everyday terminology were adequate for his purposes. What basis is there for this assumption?

An answer to part of our question is most directly gained by turning to Bentley's explanation of why he fixes on political groups as the focus of his study. He had earlier presented us with a rough outline of his group concept, in which the political groups were seen as close to the "surface of society." Below them were the underlying interests of which the political group activities were reflections and representations. Bentley himself observes that at first glance it would seem more reasonable to begin with fundamentals, with the underlying groups, and to proceed from them to the more superficial ones. But this is not the course he follows. He tells us instead, "we are to confine our attention to the process of politics, and the political groups are the only ones with which we shall be directly concerned" (p. 209). In thus confining our attention, Bentley admits that the "economic basis of political life must, of course, be fully recognized," just as he admits his own primary interest to be a desire to understand "the economic life." But he is convinced that he can "gain a better understanding of the economic life" by studying political groups. Why? Bentley's answer is perhaps the most startling disclosure in a book full of surprises:

it is my conviction that political groups, highly differentiated as they are, can well be studied before the other groups; and that indeed one has a better chance of success in studying the political groups first than in studying other groups first. The very fact that they are so highly representative makes it easier to handle them. They are in closer connection with "ideas," "ideals," "emotions," "policies," "public opinion," etc., than are some of the other groups. . . . And as the same psychic process, including all its elements, is involved in the facts which enter into the interpretation of all forms of social life, we have better prospects of successful work in a field in which we can get it, I will not say in most direct, but in most manifest, most palpable, most measurable form [pp. 209-210].

After the flood of tirade, contempt, and irony in which Bentley so often washed ideas and feelings, he now turns to ideas and feelings as the best

---

[31] The successive stages of Bentley's effort to provide such a vocabulary may be seen in his publications: "The Units of Investigation in the Social Sciences," *Publications of the American Academy of Political and Social Science*, no. 149, June 18, 1895, pp. 87-113; *Relativity in Man and Society* (1926); *Linguistic Analysis of Mathematics* (San Antonio, Tex.: The Principia Press of Trinity University [Tex.], 1932); *Behavior, Knowledge, Fact* (San Antonio, Tex.: The Principia Press of Trinity University [Tex.], 1935); (with John Dewey) *Knowing and the Known* (Boston: Beacon Press, 1949); "Kennetic Inquiry," *Science*, December 29, 1950, pp. 775-783. An overview of Bentley's program is provided by Sidney Ratner in his "Introduction" to Bentley's *Inquiry into Inquiries*.

material for his study. The former "color flashes" and "thin, bloodless" cries are now the most manifest, most palpable, and most measurable forms of the "psychic process" Bentley identifies as his object of interest. But this turn-about, remarkable as it is, is capped by the last sentence in the passage quoted above, in which we learn that "the same psychic process is involved in the facts which enter into the interpretation of all forms of social life."

We have moved one step toward an understanding of the transition from feeling to action with the discovery of a uniform "psychic process" which Bentley assumes to be present in all forms of social life. Bentley has no intention here of positing a "social mind." In fact he twice launches lengthy attacks against proponents of this notion (chs. 3 and 9). The "same psychic process" Bentley is talking about is present in the "thinking-feeling actors" who are the raw materials of his study. We have, in short, a common "psychic" nature, if not a common human nature, as a fundamental assumption in Bentley's construct of "activity." How is this assumption used? Bentley affirms that "certainly no man has any direct experience of the feelings or other mental states of other men." At best, men may make "very useful" inferences about the "feelings, and so forth, of other men. . . ." But Bentley is not interested in the merit of particular inferences. What he wishes to know is how we have any knowledge of other men's feelings and ideas. His answer is as follows: "I know myself, so far as I have any knowledge that is worth while, by observation of my actions, and indeed largely not by my own observations, but by what other people observe and report to me directly or indirectly about my actions" (p. 187). We have previously remarked on how often Bentley is led by common opinion. Here we find him not simply led by common opinion, but, as it were, constituted by it, by what "other people report" to him about his own actions.

This does not, however, bring us to the end of our inquiry. Even if we were to lend credence to the admissions made here, they would not suffice to answer the question we have set: what is the transition between feeling and action? It is highly unlikely that all people who reported to Bentley about Bentley would convey the same messages about his actions, especially if his earlier assertion about group membership determining the content of talk activity is true. How then does Bentley know what to believe, or in his terms, how does he gain "any knowledge that is worth while" about his actions? By "observation," we are told. "I know myself . . . by observation of my actions," or "by what other people observe and report. . . ." Now "observation" in this context suffers from the same vagueness we have found at other critical points in Bentley's statement, and the vagueness is due to the same cause, Bentley's unwillingness to grant "rule" to thought. He puts himself into the position of receiving a multiplicity of reports (aural or ocular impressions) about himself and others with no means to discriminate between accurate and inaccurate or relevant and irrelevant reports. Yet he asserts that by this means he gains "knowledge that is worth while." The opposite conclusion appears to be the more reasonable. Without criteria of significance to guide the self-observation or to evaluate the reports of others, he would be left staring blindly at himself; but no criteria are offered. We are left with an assumption of a common human psychic nature, with a fairly rich vocabulary of political life drawn from common opinion, and Bentley's manifest involvement in the politics of his day. How are we to understand these items?

Bentley makes the transition from feeling to action by using the assumption of a common psychic process in all men as the basis for generalizing from his own psychic processes, or from his own thought and feelings to the thought and feeling of other men. The content of his generalizations is supplied by current opinion. The ideas, ideals, opinions, and policies offered by some political groups are the ideas, ideals, opinions, and policies that Bentley incorporates into his raw material. They are the means he uses to give to activity the richness of content it would otherwise lack. The search for relief from abuses, excrescences, and corruption that current opinion sees as the means to improvement in political life is taken by Bentley as the content of activity that is significant for understanding "the economic life" or the "realities" of the political process. An introspective psychology informed by "what other people observe and report" thus provides the transition between feeling and action. This at once permits Bentley to assume that other men think and feel as he does and to assign words taken from everyday life to the phenomena he includes under the caption "activity."

If the foregoing analysis is tenable, it leads to the conclusion that thought, especially thought informed by common opinion, provides the foundation of Bentley's construct. This conclusion would be trite in the analysis of an argument that lived more comfortably with common opinion and the everyday purposes of everyday life, or in an argument which unequivocally fixed on theoretical clarity as the object of its pursuit. It comes as a shattering critique to an argument which seeks to escape the "rule" of words and the "monopoly of intelligence" (p. 180). Activity is made a meaningful rubric by endowing the actors with ideas and feelings. Observation is made possible by similarly endowing the observer. Yet neither of these is willingly done in the presentation we have surveyed.

Our analysis also enables us to turn to another aspect of Bentley's "activity" construct of which mention has been made. "Potential" activity or "tendency" is introduced when we "look a little closer at a specimen of . . . activity with its thought-feeling coloring." The closer look shows us that from "the motions of the body" alone "we do not get good material to study." Despite the injunction laid down three paragraphs earlier that "we must hold fast to what we can observe and examine," we must now add to external activity and "under the same term, activity, certain forms which are not palpable or evident to the same extent at the stage of their progress in which we have to search them out." Such inevident or impalpable activities are what is "pictured by the use of the word 'potential.' " Or, by making "a half-compromise with everyday speech" we can call such activities "tendencies." However they are designated, Bentley insists that he is dealing with "stages of activity just as much as any other activity" (pp. 184-185).

The following observation is suggested by Bentley's assertion. If we must "hold fast to what we can observe and examine," no amount of words, especially in a work radically critical of the pretentions of language, can make inevident and impalpable forms into "stages of activity just as much as other activity." [32] If we are limited to what we can see and feel, to what is visible and palpable, we have no way of knowing whether there is anything at a "stage" other than the stage of manifest activity, unless it is present in the contemplation of the observer. But again, contemplation, the office of thought, is officially rejected in Bentley's statements.

Let us see what gain the use of potential activity represents to Bentley, what tempts him into the territory of the kingdom of darkness. His examples cover two ranges of data. There is first the problem posed by dissimulation in action. If a man dissembles his anger, to take Bentley's illustration, he is nevertheless acting in a certain way. His "action" is described as follows: The dissembling man may delay taking the next step to which anger would ordinarily lead. One must suppose it is Bentley's sharing in the "same psychic process" with other men that enables him to know what this next step would be. In any event, the angry man may wait for a "more fitting time for the blow"; he does nothing to show his anger. Nevertheless, if we see as Bentley wishes us to see,

we find literally the man's body, the whole man, not merely his abstract "soul," but all of him, poised as if to spring. He is directed toward some further activity which will be more palpable, but no more truly activity [p. 188].

The fanciful physiology aside, there is nothing in this statement to show how the angry man, while he is dissembling, acts in a way to make his anger or his dissimulation visible to Bentley. We come then to Bentley's second source of information. He can only know at what "stage" the "whole man" is by contemplation, or by reflection in the non-Bentleyan sense of this term. Only by contrasting with the visible behavior before him what he knows or believes should move a man to anger and what he thinks the manifestation of anger should be, can Bentley speak of dissembled anger at all. In so doing, however, he makes use of the "psychic process" he assumes is the same for all men and generalizes from his own thought to the "soul state" or "psychic

[32] See above, pp. 159-162. Truman replaces the concern with language by, as it proved, a short-lived certainty that modern techniques of opinion and attitude measurement furnish the means to overcome the difficulties posed by "potential" and "tendency." It cannot be said that Truman's assertions are an improvement on Bentley's.

process" of the man he observes. "Potential" activity in this instance is the construct enabling Bentley to "make sense" of an individual as a whole: "the whole man" does not emerge meaningfully if Bentley confines himself to the observation of external action. A man's "potential" or "tendencies" are possibilities or capabilities of action, discerned by Bentley and judged by him to be appropriate in given circumstances.

Bentley shows the political application of "potential" activity in the following illustration. He speaks of a city in which a group of taxpayers organize to work for the adoption of a regulation "to prescribe the width of wagon-wheel tires in proportion to the load carried, so as to save the pavements from the injury caused by narrow tires and heavy loads." The organized taxpayers will lead others. But the task of leadership will be difficult because "these others . . . although actually suffering in equal degree will be indifferent and often really ignorant of the fact that any such movement is under way." Success will further be delayed because the "team-owners will strenuously resist the adoption of the regulation." But Bentley is undeterred:

Nevertheless the movement, or some substitute for it, is bound to win after a greater or less time. It will win because the organization that leads it genuinely represents the mass of indifferent taxpayers. It will win because it will be clear that those indifferent taxpayers are potentially comprised in the group activity. There is a tendency to action among them. If sufficiently goaded they will certainly come to "know" their own interest [pp. 226-227].

This account is rich in features to give us pause. We could inquire how men who are "indifferent" are known to be "actually suffering": or how Bentley knows the mass to be "really ignorant" of a movement when he had earlier asserted "the only way to be sure we have isolated an interest group is to watch its progress" (p. 214); or what basis there is for his certainty that all "genuinely" represented groups achieve their purposes in time. But our concern here is with the "potential activity" or "tendency" to action Bentley finds in the mass of indifferent taxpayers. From his account the mass is clearly not acting or even beginning to act in a way to support the proposed traffic regulation. Bentley tells us it is clear the indifferent taxpayers are potentially comprised in the group activity. To whom is it clear? He knows this on the basis of his own assessment of the situation. There is a potential for action, or a tendency, when, in his judgment, men capable of acting a given way are present and when reasons for action are discernible—when men "come to 'know' their own interest." The potential or tendency is a possibility of action discerned by an observer who predicts what may, can, or should happen if the necessary materials and necessary conditions are present. Again, leaving aside the sanguine view of how political reform is achieved, what we have here is a violation by Bentley of his former requirements. We were told earlier we must not attempt to understand a group's interest by assigning it a "value

that is 'objective' in the sense that we regard it as something natural or inevitable or clothed in oughtness." [33] Yet this is precisely what Bentley does,
and has to do, to find the potential activity or tendency in the social phenomena before him. The indifferent taxpayers are clearly "potentially comprised in
the group activity." That is, they ought to be comprised in it because it
"genuinely represents" their interests; they are naturally comprised in it because men will act in pursuit of "their own interest" when they come to
know their interest; finally, there is an "objective" value to what they may
do because it is in the interest of the mass of taxpayers, that is, in the interest
of the city as a whole, to maintain its pavements in working order and
equitably to regulate their use.

The foregoing discussion shows Bentley's "potential activity" as a construct
used for two purposes. It is used to give coherence to the "whole man," to
see the individual, at rest and in motion, as endowed with the range of ideas
and feelings that Bentley's "psychic process" informs him is the equipment of
normal men. We find here no talk about the individual as a "fiction" or as
known only as part of the activity of masses. Neither fiction nor mass is
permitted to obstruct Bentley's pursuit of "the whole man . . . all of him . . ."
(p. 188).[34]

"Potential activity" is also used as the cover under which Bentley makes
his assessments of the relevant factors present in whatever sample of social
life he selects for study. We are not centrally concerned with the content of
his judgment, but rather with the demonstration that it is *his* judgments we
are given, not the "facts" present in "stages," for these "stages" are not manifest, evident, or palpable as activity. Bentley's judgments rest upon the
"underlying interests" or "deeper lying groups" that he asserts are the basis
of the phenomena he studies, but that remain inevident throughout his
work. We shall return to these phantom groups below.

THE EQUATION OF ACTIVITY, GROUP, AND INTEREST

In addition to extending "activity" to include ideas, feelings, and potential
activity, Bentley takes one further step to enrich "activity" as the raw material
of politics. It consists of the effort to equate "activity" with "group" and with
"interest." "Group" first appears formally as a supplement to Bentley's account of activity. It will be useful to recall Bentley's "technical" characterization of "group."

The term "group" will be used throughout this work in a technical sense. It
means a certain portion of the men of a society, taken, however, not as a physical
mass cut off from other masses of men, but as a mass activity, which does not
preclude the men who participate in it from participating likewise in many other

[33] See above, p. 165.
[34] See also pp. 176-177.

group activities. It is always so many men with all their human quality. It is always so many men, acting, or tending toward action—that is, in various stages of action. Group and group activity are equivalent terms with just a little difference of emphasis, useful only for clearness of expression in different contexts [p. 211].

In the light of our foregoing discussion we are able to shorten the inquiries we have to make about the meaning of this statement. Despite the entangling immersion in language seeking to keep the emphasis on concrete individuals, or on "masses of men," the group is primarily an analytical concept and not an empirical datum for Bentley. He is fairly explicit on this point but unhappily not consistent. He tells us that "every classification of the elements of a population must involve an analysis of the population into groups" (p. 206). Here the primacy of analysis is clear. He goes on to tell us that no single classification of a population into groups can be "so comprehensive and thorough that we can put it forth as 'the' classification of the population." He gives two reasons why such a comprehensive classification is impossible, each pointing toward a somewhat different conclusion. First, "the purpose of the classification must always be kept in mind." Classification is guided by purpose, the purpose of the classifier. Since purposes may vary, the classification of men into groups may vary; the same men who appear in one classification for one purpose appear in another classification when the purpose is different. This despite the fact that we are dealing with the same men. "Group," understood in this light, is similar to "potential" activity; both are concepts or constructs setting forth the observer's judgments on the possibilities, or capabilities, of a given body of material. The variety of possible classifications is determined by the observer's judgment of the number of relevant ways a given set of individuals may be arranged. A classification of the women of the country into a blonde group and a brunette group is possible, Bentley tells us, but such groups would not be relevant for any purposes of social study that he can conceive. Somewhat strangely he also says that "one would be hard put . . . to justify emphasis on a distinction between Germans and English in treating the local politics of a city like Chicago" (p. 208). The same would be true of any other classification in which groups are "distinguished from one another by the race test alone, and acting as such in the political field." But the main point in this line of discussion is the stress on groups as analytical concepts, classifications of men determined by the purposes and "practical considerations" of the investigator.[35]

Bentley's rejection of purposes and "practical considerations" as the basis of a comprehensive classification of groups appears to derive from his conviction that no analysis can be "objective." He does not, however, pursue this theme alone in moving toward his conclusion about the impossibility of a

---

[35] See above, p. 159, for Truman's treatment of this issue.

comprehensive classification of groups. He presents a second reason to doubt the possibility of such a classification when he writes of his masses of men as if they were divided into a "limitless criss-cross of groups," shifting his emphasis to the affiliations or organizational memberships of specific individuals as the source of the difficulty he sees. He is puzzled to understand how a man or a mass of men can be in two such entities at the same time, and he adds to the confusion by writing of men who "perhaps . . . find themselves in one group pulling against themselves in another group" (p. 203).

The only "pulling against themselves" possible would be in the form of intellectual or emotional tension, but with ideas and feelings outlawed as spooks, Bentley is forced into clumsy physical imagery. Despite the repetition of such language, the difficulty presented is a minor one once the language is seen as part of the effort to persist in the use of physical terminology (as an analogue to empirical data) accompanied by an analytical reliance on groups as objects of contemplation. However, by assimilating affiliation or membership to something like physical presence, and making such membership a key discriminant of groups, Bentley does raise another barrier against any comprehensive classification of groups.

There is a more substantial confusion which results from Bentley's use of group to refer to formal organizations like the "protectionist" league and the political parties mentioned in the preliminary outline.[36] In place of a "technical sense," Bentley lapses into the use of "group" as "a handy and intelligible colloquialism. . . ."[37] As a colloquialism, "group" may refer to a number of individuals who share certain attitudes or purposes and are aware of sharing them—the members of the Prohibitionist Party, for example. But "group" may also refer to a number of persons, or things, that share in a common characteristic discerned by the observer. Bentley's blonde women are an example. Colloquial usage applies the same term, "group," to both cases. Our present difficulty stems from Bentley's use of "group" in its compounded colloquial meanings while raising claims for it as a technical term.

Bentley's procedure in the quest for clarity has been commented upon before. He attacks the everyday vocabulary of everyday life on the ground of its vagueness, the insufficiency of its distinctions for scientific purposes. He then seeks to destroy common sense distinctions, but does not replace them with sharper scientific distinctions. Instead he offers still more vague uses of the everyday vocabulary and at times adds further to the confusion by making "half-compromises" that are neither more meaningful than everyday speech nor expressive of the limited but rigorous meanings of scientific terminology. His treatment of "man," "feelings," "ideas," "activity," "potential," and "group" demonstrates his shortcomings in this respect. A further rehearsal of Bentley's analytical weaknesses would do little more than repeat our earlier

[36] See above, p. 166.
[37] Mackenzie, *Political Studies*, October 1955, p. 247.

observations and conclusions. It is more instructive to follow Bentley as best we can as he proceeds in the development of his position.

"Group," then, is to be seen as an equivalent for "activity." It is a means to indicate the particular activity called to our attention, or to indicate that political activity is not a unitary movement, but is instead characterized by conflict and competition or by the possibility of conflict and competition.

From this development it is but a short step to the next equivalence Bentley seeks to establish, the equivalence of "group" and "interest." "There is no group without its interest. An interest, as the term will be used in this work, is the equivalent of a group." Bentley insists that "the group and the interest are not separate. There exists only the one thing, that is, so many men bound together in or along the path of a certain activity" (p. 211). This last remark illustrates Bentley's shift from group as an analytical concept to group as an empirical aggregate of men bound in or along a certain course of activity. If this latter were strictly so it would not be possible to have men as members of one group "pulling against themselves as members of another group" because at any moment any particular group of men would be committed to "a certain activity," not to two or more contrary activities at the same time. But this aside, we have only advanced part of the way to the full equation Bentley is building. Group and interest are equivalent; this adds a synonym to our vocabulary and nothing else. A gain is made when "activity" is introduced.

The group is activity and the activity is only known to us through its particular type, its value in terms of other activities, its tendency where it is not in the stage which gives manifest results. The interest is just this valuation of the activity, not as distinct from it, but as the valued activity itself [p. 213].

We are now on familiar ground. Interest is a form of activity, more specifically of talk activity. The interest is the talk activity that reveals the "particular type" of activity we have before us for examination. In short, our data come bearing their own labels, they are self-identifying. We have sufficiently disposed of this assertion in the analysis of "potential" given above. What may be instructive now is to consider the problem posed by identifying interest with the valued activity itself, or the group's valuation of itself.

Bentley tells us that we must neither accept the interest "at its own verbal expression of itself" nor bring to the interest a "meaning or value that is 'objective' in the sense that we regard it as something natural or inevitable or clothed in oughtness." What course is open to us in these circumstances when we "cannot take words for our test" and when we also "cannot take 'bed-rock truth'" as our test? Bentley's answer is familiar:

The interest I put forward is a specific group interest in some definite course of conduct or activity. It is first, last, and all the time strictly empirical. There is no way to find it except by observation. . . . [I]ndeed the only way to be sure we have isolated an interest group, is to watch its progress [p. 214].[38]

Manifestly, Bentley's answer is insufficient. Taken literally, it would require us to accept the valuation a group places on its own activity, since observation in the sense of looking at motion would tell us nothing, and observation in the sense of listening to the group's talking activity would convey meaning only if we believed the group's evaluation of itself. But this latter alternative is a course against which common sense cautions and which Bentley forbids. If we were to accept another group's evaluation of the group we were observing, we would still be accepting a self-evaluation, since every verbalization is a "reflection" of a group's interests and none is objective or natural or inevitable. But Bentley nevertheless insists on watching the "activity" of a group as the sole guide to knowledge about the group. Activity is as close to a self-evident truth that is not "bed-rock truth" as Bentley permits himself to come. But the identification or equation of interest and activity is neither rationally defensible nor useful as a common sense procedure. If the interest of a labor union, for example, is the repeal of the non-Communist oath provision of the Labor-Management Relations Act of 1947, the union's activity cannot by any stretch of terminology be called the repeal of that provision. To achieve the change, the union may send petitions to Congress, or union representatives may appear at Congressional hearings, or the union may form a political action association to organize voters to reward or punish particular Congressmen or particular parties. The union may talk to the press, presenting its views on the inequity of the law, or argue that loyal American labor does not need such legislation to keep its organizational house in order. But none of these activities nor any combination of them is the same as the interest of the group engaging in them. The changed law, the interest, is a goal toward which other activities are directed. We may be able to understand why a group acts the way it does by understanding its interest; we would be returned to unintelligible movement of the kind Bentley called chaos if we attempted to see activity and interest as identical. Bentley manifestly requires intelligence, the function of thought, in his material, and in himself, to gain an understanding of "interest." Characteristically, however, he paralyzes analysis and would reduce directed action to random movement by his unwillingness to admit the nonidentity of thought and action. He will not admit the thought to be the father of the act. His is a conception in which purpose and means become one.

Especially in the context of politics does Bentley's faith in activity as the sole sound guide to valid knowledge strike one as unwarranted. Bentley flees to action as a way to escape from the dissimulation he finds in "talk activity." He does not seem to take seriously the possibility that dissimulation may

[38] Cf. above, p. 165.

occur in manifest activity as well as in words. A legislator who introduces a bill late in a legislative session, certain that the bill will neither be considered nor enacted, may be acting in a way to impress uninformed constituents with his effort to make good a campaign promise. The need to be aware of what action means is as great as the need to know what "talk activity" means. Neither one, by itself, can be taken at face value as the "worth while" knowledge Bentley seeks.

A further understanding of interest is telescoped at great cost into Bentley's construct. At one point in his discussion, he gives the following account of an election in which an incumbent office-holder is defeated as an illustration of interest as activity, in this instance, voting activity.

When he ["the representative in the formal sense"] loses elections or falls below what is expected of him, he is judged as undesirable in the party group. When he abuses public office too grossly, wastes too much public money, tolerates too much injurious discrimination between citizens, he is judged by large sections of the citizenship in subparty groupings, and with him his party is judged, so that the subparty interest dominates the party interest in a certain proportion of the outlying party members, leading to a desertion at the polls by the "independent" vote, and to possible loss of a good part of their power by both boss and machine [p. 230].

Leaving aside the question of what "public" means in this account, or what group view allows Bentley to know whether there has been abuse, waste, and discrimination, or whether instead the defeated candidate is the victim of spurious tags and labels, we have to ask what the word "interest" means in, and contributes to, Bentley's account. We learn that the representative is judged by many citizens who, on the basis of their judgment, refuse to vote for him. Bentley describes this by saying "the subparty interest dominates the party interest." While there might be an excuse for reading "interest" to mean "group" here—a group of citizens dominate by their votes the votes of a group of party workers—to say the interest dominates obscures the situation. What dominates, from Bentley's own account, is the judgment of these citizens. A representative found wanting because of abuse, waste, and discrimination will or, a more guarded realist might say, may be defeated at the polls. Stated thus directly we have a possible observation on American party politics. When stripped of its group husk, the statement is a very rationalistic and optimistic expectation of voting behavior and comes as a surprise in a tough-minded description of the political process. One may, perhaps, suspect that Bentley's progressivism is at work coloring his expectations. More to the point, Bentley's shift from "judgment" to "interest" in the account above obscures what his observation or expectation most strongly conveys, namely, that the judgment of performance governs the citizens' support of candidates and parties. There may be an interest directing the judgment, but from Bentley's account that "interest" would appear to be the opinion that abuse of office, waste of funds, and discrimination among citizens are not meritorious activities. Opinon, and judgment based on opinion, thus emerge as the factors of basic importance in guiding many citizens at the polls. To speak of their behavior as interest is a way of obscuring the "rule" of "words," in this instance the domination of opinion in society.

THE COMMON INTEREST

Interest, then, emerges as a "manner of stating the value of the group activity" (p. 215), but what is decisive about the "manner" of statement is that the value or meaning is assigned to the activity by Bentley; it is not the activity itself. Beyond this fundamental service that interest performs in the tortured exposition of it Bentley presents, there is another service it is intended to perform. This is to carry to completion his argument against the idea of common interest, to establish the conclusion that there is no common interest or no "group interest of the society as a whole" (p. 222).

The phenomena of social life Bentley has thus far pictured are, as we have repeatedy noted, primarily phenomena of conflict, "the people striking at somebody or something." The people, however, are not to be considered as the citizen body as a whole. He is certain a "conflict phase" will be found if a given activity is pursued far enough.

As for political questions under any society in which we are called upon to study them, we shall never find a group interest of the society as a whole. We shall always find that the political interests and activities of any given group—and there are no political phenomena except group phenomena—are directed against other activities of men, who appear in other groups, political or other. The phenomena of political life which we study will always divide the society in which they occur, along lines which are very real, though of varying degrees of definiteness. The society itself is nothing other than the complex of the groups that compose it [p. 222].

Bentley argues from the presence of conflict to the conclusions that there is no society as a whole and that there is no interest of society as a whole. The lapses from his own requirements need but be noted in passing, since by this point his incapacity to adhere to the assertions he makes should require no extended documentation. A "social whole," as a nation, or in other forms, frequently appears in his own remarks. In respect to primitive societies, Bentley admits that "the most intense interest will be that of the whole tribe . . ." (p. 331). In discussing American politics, Bentley speaks of some American Presidents who were "fully authorized representatives of the nation" (p. 344); of the "fate of a nation" turning in some rare cases on a leader's fitness or unfitness; and of the "legislating-administering-adjudicating activities of the nation . . ." (p. 180). But dismissing these as we do the nods of Homer, let us consider the explicit argument.

Not even in war, when a nation is pitted against another nation, can we speak of each nation as a whole with an interest of the whole.

It is true that if we have two nations at war we can treat for the purposes of the war, though only to a certain limited extent, each nation as a separate group; but it is clear that under such circumstances neither nation is the "social whole"; it takes the two together to make the society whose processes we are at the time studying [p. 220].

As it is true that neither nation alone is the "social whole" we are studying, so it is equally true, apparently, that "the two together . . . make the society whose processes we are studying." Bentley asserts a unity, a strange and strained one, in order to deny more familiar and, it must be confessed, more meaningful unities. Paradoxically, while the conflict of war somehow makes a larger society, conflict within a "nation" is supposed to prove the absence of a social whole and therewith the absence of a common interest. He continues:

There are always some parts of the nation to be found arrayed against other parts. It is only by passing from the existing, observed, actual interests to the "objective utilities" I have mentioned . . . that we can drag in the "social whole," and there we are out of the field of social science.

But if there are only parts arrayed against other parts, how does he know they are parts of "the nation"? His example takes for granted the soundness of the legal definition or the political decision which discriminates one nation from another, and only within this secure but unexamined unit does he deny the existence of unity.

In addition, Bentley's view of what is relevant to the study of politics masks if it does not obliterate some of the essential conditions of political life. He argues that if there "were such a comprehensive all-embracing interest of the society as a whole it would be an established condition, and not at all a subject of discussion by the man who calls it an interest of society as a whole . . ." (p. 220). Bentley considers the noncontroversial as irrelevant or nearly irrelevant in the study of politics. The established conditions that are not the subject of discussion constitute, as we have seen, the "habit background" or the "rules of the game." To mix perspectives, it is the prominence of the background that Bentley ignores. He is willing to say "there is no savage tribe so low but that it has its rules of the game, which are respected and enforced" (p. 218). What is true of the savage tribe in this respect has not been shown to be untrue of "the complex modern state." The rules of war which Bentley cites as examples of the habit background are one instance that we might expect him to consider at length. "Modern battle," he admits, is not fought "with complete abandon, but under definite limitations." He lists some of the limitations but does not consider their significance. Modern nations, Bentley says, conduct war subject to prohibitions against the use of explosive bullets, or of the poisoning of springs, or the firing on Red Cross parties. But Bentley does not consider that such nations conduct war to achieve particular purposes. The "habit background" which limits conflict to means short of "complete abandon" is the group interest of the international society as a whole, part of the noncontroversial agreement that destruction and suffering may be necessary for certain purposes but not as ends in themselves.

Bentley's original statement of the raw materials shows us people seeking to prevent or to punish corporation abuses by recourse to law. The "streams and currents of activity that gather among the people," Bentley tells us, "rush into" the spheres of legislation, administration, and adjudication. The attack on the corporation, like the war Bentley mentions, is not conducted with "complete abandon." The "streams and currents of activity" of reformers and antireformers alike flow into these channels guided by the opinion that correction or punishment by legal means are "rules of the game" which ought to be "respected and enforced" in a healthy republic as well as in a savage tribe. The pursuit of interest by legal means is "not at all a subject of discussion" precisely because it is "a comprehensive all embracing interest of the society as a whole." But since Bentley dismisses the noncontroversial as unimportant, he does not consider what his own examples could tell him about the conditions under which the activities he stresses are pursued. More important, he does not see the need to be concerned with these noncontroversial interests in order to understand why the activity he observes takes the form it does. Bentley's ultimate optimism lies in the unexpressed assumption that the nation as a whole is automatically self-sustaining. The "rules of the game" that guide and limit domestic conflict in the United States (from which Bentley draws most of his examples) were framed or stabilized by an earlier group of men who presented an institutional plan and an argument addressed to their compatriots. But Bentley will not regard those rules, either as originally intended or as now understood and followed, as representing judgments of how the common interest may best be served.[39]

Another dimension of Bentley's attack on the idea of common interest takes the form of asserting that government, too, must be seen as serving the interests of particular groups, and this despite his counterassertion that government is the "balance" of group interests, with every interest somehow "represented" (pp. 264-271). His views emerge in the course of his discussion of law and of legislation. Of law he says:

[39] The same problem, dealt with in the same offhand manner, is touched upon in Truman's comments on "morbific politics," and in Gross's concern to push back "the laws of the jungle."

Any classification of laws into those which hit at evils and those which work constructively for public welfare is fundamentally wrong, or, rather, it pretends to be fundamental, when actually it is superficial. This is true of, I care not what, laws. Suppose we have quarantine regulations "to promote public health": they strike at certain objectionable activities of men. Take a campaign by the state to protect crops against some insect pest: it proceeds by striking against certain careless activities of men. . . . The striking done by the law is not anything negative which exists merely for the striking's sake. But it is never, on the other hand, a pure matter of everybody's welfare. However much any of it may be ennobled and glorified in the speech that accompanies and represents it, the conflict phase can be found when the whole range of the society in which it exists is taken into account [pp. 288-289].

We note at the outset that there is a whole before us for consideration: "the society" whose "whole range" we must examine. We note too that certain activities are "objectionable" or "careless" and that neither of these evaluations bear quotation marks. We may wonder whether law is never a "pure matter of everybody's welfare." Even the purveyor of impure food, for example, benefits from legal assurances of the purity of the food he buys for his own consumption. Still, there is no denying that conflict is a massive factor in political life. There would be no need for law if men's social behavior were as natural as digestion; law implies, that is to say, the possibility of disobedience and hence nonunanimity.

The phenomena of conflict that Bentley stresses do exist; but he fails to convey a balanced assessment, and this despite the recurrence in his work of the view of government as the balance of interest. But more than balance is lacking. Bentley's conviction that the public welfare or common interest is nonexistent is so powerful that he is forced to trivialize some of his most important observations. He notes, for example, that in many public debates on economic policy there may be "a huge 'consumer's group' on one side and a 'trust interest' on the other side." Bentley insists that

there is no essential difference between them for all of that. It is a little easier for the vague groups to talk about themselves as "the people," and a little more difficult for the well-organized groups to prove that they are "unselfish"; but that is a detail of technique [p. 429].

Why is it "a little more difficult" for a "trust interest" to prove itself unselfish? What difference in "technique" does Bentley envisage? Does he mean that with sufficient dissimulation any position can be successfully presented as in the common interest? Such success would prove nothing against the observation that the purposes of the trust interest as trust interest cannot be publicly defended. "The people" may be naïve or ill-informed, but what they seek, at least in the sanguine examples furnished by Bentley, needs no disguise to present itself as in the common interest—purer food; safer insurance; better transportation facilities; relief from abuse, waste, discrimination, and corruption. There is no "difficulty" in stating these goals publicly. But this important difference in the activities he discerns is not explored. Certain goals or purposes can be publicly presented. These are ordinarily the staple items in the agenda of politics. These are items in the pursuit of the common interest or public welfare.

Admittedly, there is a grave difficulty in the search for the common interest. Even with the best effort, men differ about what the common interest is. They may be mistaken in what they so identify. They may dissemble their purposes. There may be situations where the alternatives are equally acceptable as serving the common interest, and the decision to accept one alternative rather than another turns on contingent factors, like the ease of gaining votes or other support for one of the alternatives. We may agree, for example, on the need to produce an adequate food supply as in the common interest of this nation. Whether we get it by measures to keep the marginal farmer in production or by encouraging large-scale agriculture is a tangential issue from this viewpoint. There may be other desirable goals achieved in the choice of one of the alternatives and this may decide the issue. The support of marginal farmers may help to preserve satisfaction with that part of the "habit background" in which the assumption of the value of rural life is contained. That the issue is complex does not demonstrate that the common interest or public welfare is nonexistent or that its statement is necessarily a cover for the particularistic greed of some segment of the citizen body.

But in Bentley's view, "the very nature" of the legislative process is "give and take," or "trading" (p. 371). Bentley's words sound familiar, and indeed they are, for his discussion is one source of the idea of "brokerage politics" which is now so popular. In seeking to remove the "opprobrium" from the practice of "log-rolling," Bentley performs a useful service in putting the stress on compromise as the characteristic form of legislative activity in this country. But even in presenting his useful observations he proceeds by creating a contrast unsupported by his examples or by common observation. Thus, he tells us, when log-rolling is condemned,

it is only by contrasting it with some assumed pure public spirit which is supposed to guide legislators, or which ought to guide them, and which enables them to pass judgment in Jovian calm on that which is best "for the whole people." Since there is nothing which is best literally for the whole people, group arrays being what they are, the test is useless, even if one could actually find legislative judgments which are not reducible to interest-group activities [pp. 370-371].

There are several things one has to inquire about in respect to these remarks. Is there a necessity that "a pure public spirit" be the guide to the common good? If Bentley means by this a spirit unaffected by any narrower, particular interests, he has not shown why a legislator, or anyone else, might not judge that his particular interests depend on the maintenance of a broader interest and therefore demand certain legislation. The opposition Bentley constantly makes between the common good and selfishness is unwarranted. It may be the height of self-interest rightly understood that tells a man it is in the common interest, including his own interest, to have an administrative agency staffed with personnel able to perform their legally assigned tasks without regard to the special pleadings or blandishments offered by himself. The unpredictability of the results of irregular procedure, if nothing else, may convince him that equal treatment is in his own best interest as well as in the best interest of the community. Bentley's irony or cynicism at the sight of selfishness is a moralistic blinder. Realists of the stripe of Machiavelli, Hobbes, Adam Smith, or the authors of the *Federalist* could show him that far from being indubitable proof of the nonexistence of a common good, selfishness properly understood, properly motivated, and properly directed may be the means best able to achieve the common good. This is not to argue that private vices are necessarily public virtues, but simply to indicate that the invocation of "realism" or of the facts of "group arrays being what they are" does not dismiss or even adequately state the issue Bentley has raised.

If Bentley means by his "pure public spirit" and "Jovian calm" that a genuine common good would have to be pursued by men unsullied by contact with the conflict of political life, the argument is equally unsupported. A legislator might be as tough-minded as Bentley would like, but nevertheless judge that certain legislation is necessary to maintain or attain the goals of the community. On the basis of the crassest experience possible, a legislator might decide that it is in the public interest to expand the merit system for civil service employment rather than to continue the wasteful and disastrous use of patronage. He might decide that no regulatory agency could perform the task for which it was created if every decision of the agency were subjected to attack and criticism by Congress on the basis of unsubstantiated or previously disproved charges, and he might decide this was in the public interest despite the evident advantages his party could gain from continued attacks on appointive officials selected by an earlier administration of another party. There does not, in short, have to be a "thin, bloodless" or spiritually pure or unrealistic basis for the invocation of the public interest. Bentley refuses to argue the issue directly but, instead, rests his disbelief in a common good on caricature and *non sequiturs*.

Group arrays as Bentley has pictured them are divided arrays. Insoluble disagreement on what is the common good or a perpetual selfish seeking for advantage are the conclusions he draws from these facts, or asserted facts. But neither the existence of disagreement nor of selfishness disproves the contention that there is a common interest. Indeed, one of the admissions he makes about his groups would appear to apply with equal force to the society as a whole. Bentley, as we have seen, insists that every group has its standard or interest; only the nation as a whole, or society has no common interest. One might inquire why "the nation" or the "whole society" alone of all units identified by Bentley cannot have a common interest when every other "group," potential or actual, is said to have, or to be constituted by, a common interest.

However there is a more pointed observation to be made, one the students of Bentley are strangely silent about. When speaking of leadership, Bentley says "the leadership which one group performs for another or for a set of other groups is not dependent upon the express adhesion of the full membership of the represented groups" (p. 225). Some of the members may be unwillingly "represented," that is, these members may not share the group interest. From what we have said to this point, and from what is normally said by Bentley, the expected conclusion would be that such members are not part of the group, since their "activity," their dissent from the group purposes, would not show them as "reflections" of the "real" interest of the group. But Bentley does not reach this conclusion. Instead he goes on to make a passing observation which richly deserves fuller attention:

Dissent by a member of the group may not take him out of the ranks. Under some circumstances it will, or rather it represents his actual transfer to another group position; but under other circumstances *dissent may be a wrong expression of group position* . . . [italics supplied].

There is dissent within groups. But if this is admitted, what is the group interest? From what point of view, with what "Jovian calm" does Bentley decide one "reflection" to be the "real" one, another to be a "wrong expression"? All he can see is men in movement. To call some of their movements the authentic group interest and others a wrong expression is not possible within Bentley's framework. Furthermore, and more fruitfully, if dissent does not remove a man from the group ranks but instead may be an indication that the man is mistaken, then dissent or conflict does not take the groups out of society as a whole and does not prove that there is no interest of the whole. The errors in everyday explanations of politics were the primitive facts that launched Bentley on the search for a scientific social interpretation. Instead of moving toward the replacement of error by knowledge, which he at points recognizes as the scientific or theoretical enterprise, Bentley propounds an argument in which the distinction between truth and error is destroyed, absorbed into the activity that all but blinds him to the significant problems.[40] His incapacity to come to rest on the meaning of interest is one consequence of this dissolution into vagueness. Hence his emphatic remarks lose their assertive power. When he declares that "so long as murders exist to give meaning to laws against murder, the social welfare as a whole expressing itself

[40] Cf. the case of Herbert Simon; see above, pp. 123 ff.

in laws against murder will be a fiction, not a fact" (p. 157), we have reason to remain unpersuaded. The murderer may be in error in thinking his activity on an equal plane with that of the judge who condemns him.

While there may be men in politics, or observers of politics, who knowingly and wilfully would injure others in the pursuit of their own desires, Bentley clearly is not one of them. In spite of his formal onslaughts on common interest, his writing is informed throughout by "pure spirit," by a standard based on the genuine national needs of the country as he understands them. When he writes of "the excrescences of the tariff," or of inadequate service, or of illiberal treatment, or of corruption, he adopts the perspective of the public-spirited citizen disturbed by actions or conditions opposed to the national interest. Unfortunately, his concentration on the divisive nature of group conflicts and his assumption of vulgar greed as the basis of group interest divert him from consideration of the possibility that there may be a "group" made up of men whose interest is the common interest and who remain members of this group despite their disagreement over the content of this interest. The fact that groups are in conflict does not establish the absence of a larger group which comprehensively contains the contending parties. This conclusion is opposed neither to Bentley's democratic sympathies nor to his aspirations toward a realistic social science. In the words of Rousseau:

It appeared . . . that in the midst of murder, proscription, and civil war, our republic only throve: the virtue, morality, and independence of the citizens did more to strengthen it than all their dissensions had done to enfeeble it. A little disturbance gives the soul elasticity; what makes the race truly prosperous is not so much peace as liberty.[41]

Except for their toughness and the need, possibly, to substitute "psychic process" for "soul," these remarks by an earlier seeker of a new social science should be entirely acceptable to Bentley.

To repeat, without a notion of the general welfare or of the common interest, Bentley is unable to present an articulate or coherent statement of the most elementary facts of political life. His practice as distinct from his protestations confirms this need. He takes guidance from current opinion to discern relevant subjects for study or action, but fails to examine the content of the opinion which makes his enterprise possible. What is missing in his statement is an argument or reasoned discussion of what his understanding of current opinion is, what, for example, the "genuine national needs" of the United States are. Admittedly the articulation of these needs is a most difficult task. And to adopt a phrase from Taylor,[42] it is still possible to write books

[41] *The Social Contract*, iii, 9.
[42] Richard W. Taylor (ed.), *Life, Language, Law* (Yellow Springs: The Antioch Press, 1957), p. 5.

on politics without raising the question of the common interest. But where it is raised, one looks for a fuller, more reasoned, and more richly illustrated presentation than the one we are given in the piecemeal and inconclusive assertions in *The Process of Government*.[43]

THE TOOL IN USE

THE UNDERLYING GROUPS

According to Bentley, it is of fundamental importance to know what the underlying groups and the underlying interests are, as the precondition for understanding ideas, government, and the other more superficial and pretentious groups and group activities. The goal toward which Bentley's examination of the raw materials of government and his attempted equation of activity, group, and interest point is set before us in the following way:

And above all we find that the great need at every stage in our examination of the process is for a careful analysis of all the group operations, and for a thorough-going statement of the most superficial and pretentious in terms of the deeper-lying and most fundamental [p. 422].

Idea activities—to use another term in place of discussion groups for the moment—represent underlying interests, and so do government activities. Both are differentiated structures through which the interests work. Both are agencies for some of these underlying interests as they strike at others. Neither ideas nor governments in their limited immediate statement reflect fully the whole situation. They cannot be understood for what they are till they have been functioned in the social process; and to function them means to reduce them to terms of the underlying interests which give them their strength and their social meaning and value [pp. 441-442].

The argument of the latter two-thirds of *The Process of Government* can gain strength and persuasiveness only by showing an underlying stratum of groups and group interests of which all the phenomena in everyday political life are but the manifest or superficial reflections. Indeed, it is only by suspending judgment and argumentatively granting the existence of these fundamental groups and interests that we can give partial meaning to the particular assertions Bentley makes as he canvasses the traditional categories of political science with his constructs of activity, reflection, and interest. Yet when we inquire what these underlying interests and groups are, we are met with silence. In a brief chapter on "The Underlying Conditions," we find this surprising first paragraph:

I have talked repeatedly about the "underlying groups" without attempting to specify them systematically. I conceive that these groups must be taken as they

43 See below, pp. 322 ff.

come, in each country and period as they are there and then found. I do not think they have as yet been worked out in sufficient detail for many countries to justify any attempt at a general classification of the types of underlying groups which enter into political life. I wish here only to show in a general way some of the conditions of the formation of these underlying groups, more by way of indicating how such matters lie outside the scope of this volume, than to make any positive contribution to their understanding [p. 460].

With but two small modifications, Bentley's own words in this paragraph are the best possible comment on his achievement. He does indeed repeatedly talk about the "underlying groups." They are pointed to as the "wheels within wheels," the implied source of movement in the social process (p. 117). We read in an earlier chapter that the underlying groups and interests create the "technique" (pp. 223 ff.)—that is, the discussion and organization groups—which is on the surface of society. Bentley asserts that a full statement of the underlying groups would wholly absorb the discussion and organization groups, so that no independent need to talk about these latter would remain (p. 445).[44] But it is not quite true to say, as he does, that he has not attempted to specify the underlying groups systematically. He simply has not specified them at all. Nowhere in *The Process of Government* or in any of Bentley's subsequent works do we learn more about them than we do here.

In addition, it is beside the point to say the underlying groups have "not yet been worked out in sufficient detail for many countries." The question is, for what country have they been worked out at all? At the risk of undue repetition, we must emphasize that the answer is, "We do not know." In place of a specification or identification of the underlying groups we are given a set of conditions or factors that may, but need not, be "taken into account in the analysis of the underlying groups" (p. 464).[45] The factors prove on examination to be a people's material conditions of life, including the "biologically described man," that is, the physical adaptations of men "on one side to the perils of tropical jungle and on the other side to the no less serious perils to the health from crowded city life" (p. 460). When these conditions—the environment, the wealth forms of the population, the techniques of industry, the state of communication and transportation, and the

44 Cf. pp. 271, 442-443.
45 When later writers like David Truman or Oliver Garceau use Bentley's approach, their incorporation of his loose notion of "group" involves them in the ambiguities and unfulfilled promises detailed here. Furthermore, it involves them and their critics in a fruitless debate about whether or not political life can be understood entirely in terms of the group approach, or whether the groups may but need not be the exclusive basis of their analysis of politics. Cf. Oliver Garceau's review of Bernard Crick, *The American Science of Politics*, and H. Marks Roelofs' reply, in *American Political Science Review*, December 1959, pp. 1117-1119, and June 1960, pp. 496-497; also, Stanley Rothman, "Systematic Political Theory: Observations on the Group Approach," *American Political Science Review*, March 1960, pp. 15-33, and David Truman's communication to the same journal, June 1960, pp. 494-495.

"organization of the underlying factors" (p. 463), which means "organization as we see it in corporations and in labor unions"—when these are taken into account, we have, "most crudely put, . . . groups resting on mines, farms, fisheries, cattle herds, city lots; we have groups related to steam power and to electricity" (p. 462). As we indicated earlier, these tentative and strangely guarded comments impress one as a weak statement of the view that the "underlying groups" are those constituted by the material conditions of production and that the discussion and organization groups, represented by parties, the press, and the formal agencies of government are but the ideological apologists of the dominant economic interests of a country.

It is fruitless, at this point, to inquire into Bentley's debt to Marxism. He presents so haphazard an account of his theoretical or political intentions that to trace them to a single source would be to burden that source with an unwarranted load.[46] At any rate, he draws the conclusion that material conditions generally and economic conditions more particularly are what we find "when we go down to the group statement" and "get down below mere reasoning to the very basis of reasons" (p. 241). That it is reason which tells us we are "down" to the underlying group level Bentley will not admit, although as we have seen the admission is necessary for his enterprise, as is the admission of the role of reason in observing and evaluating the activity, the ideas, and the feelings. But these considerations have, we hope, been sufficiently explored in the earlier parts of this essay. Our present task is to see what kind of results Bentley achieves with the "tool" he has been forging.

The incomplete character of Bentley's presentation of the foundation of his understanding, which we discussed above, is matched by his repeated admissions that he is not "attempting so much to get results as to indicate methods" (p. 434) and that he has only "sketched . . . in broad outlines, without tracing the activity back very far" (p. 377).[47] These admissions apply to each of the aspects of government Bentley examines. There is an initial attempt to identify "the raw materials" of government and to explain how group, group activity, and group interest are equivalent ways of designating the same material. Then this apparatus is brought to bear, as we have seen, on some of the traditional categories of political science analysis, on public opinion and leadership, on political parties, on the electorate, on the organs, agencies, and procedures of government, with the tripartite American constitutional system serving as the basis of comparison and the point of departure for the surveys Bentley makes. Each of these categories is seen as a "reflection" or "expression" of conflicting groups and interests. If one therefore inquires what, for example, the executive is, the answer is returned as a formula. There is, to begin with, Bentley's warning: "I am no more here

[46] See the comments of Myron Q. Hale in "The Cosmology of Arthur F. Bentley," *American Political Science Review*, December 1960, p. 956.
[47] Cf. also pp. 209, 211, 339, 347, 367, 373, 383, 384, 434, 459, 460, 465.

than elsewhere in this volume making an attempt to cover systematically the field of government . . ." (p. 339). This is followed by the core assertion of his work, made specific for the topic at hand: "The key to the whole situation is to be found in the interest groups . . ." (p. 351). "The history of the presidency . . . has been the history of the interests which chose it as their best medium of expression when they found other pathways blocked" (pp. 344-345). There is finally an indication of how events are to be understood, or at least viewed, from the group-conflict perspective, together with the candid admission that

I do not make any pretense of having worked out this problem in terms of the groups involved so as to be able to give positive proof. I am interested here in illuminating the group process through the presidency, and I merely choose the most probable of the explanations of the special fact . . . [p. 347].

While this method comes as a disappointing vagueness where one had sought increased clarity, it does offer a single compensation. Since the method and the rationale are the same in each of the traditional divisions of political science Bentley handles, it is possible to make an assessment of his work with great brevity. With this in mind, we propose to look at an illustration to see what the group approach, as Bentley uses it, tells us.

THE GROUPS IN ACTION

We start then with group interests seeking expression, in a course of struggle with other interests, but subject to the limitations "implied" in "the habit background in which the struggle proceeds" (p. 372). The interests "create" government or "work through" it, as the case may be. In their creation or work a variety of "techniques" may be employed. These include the familiar discussion and organization groups considered as "technique" for achieving the group purposes, but may also include deception, the appeal to numbers, to force, or to law (pp. 215-217). The fundamental point is that "always and everywhere our study must be a study of the interests that work through government; otherwise we have not got down to facts" (p. 271). Subject to the qualification that he does not trace out any of the interests in detail, Bentley asserts he uses this method to understand what is happening in politics and that he gains an understanding from it far superior to that gained from attention to the discredited ideas and feelings or to the content of the arguments, programs, policies, or plans of the contending groups. He illustrates his procedure most frequently with examples drawn from American politics and we will follow him as he analyzes one of these examples. It is drawn from "the legislative process." "A piece of legislation like the statehood bill passed in the spring of 1906" which "provided for the admission of Oklahoma and Indian Territory as one state, and of Arizona and New Mexico as another," is analyzed in two steps (pp. 372-373). First there is an outline of the everyday or common sense approach. This is followed by the group-interest analysis.

The ordinary, and from Bentley's point of view inadequate, way to find out what happened would be to consult newspapers, the *Congressional Record*, committee reports, and

a very large amount of reasoning as to why the territories should or should not be combined into two states, some personal material about Senator Beveridge's long study of the situation, similar facts about the way in which other members of Congress "made up their minds," a great mass of objectively stated facts about the territories, put forth as the basis upon which minds were to be "made up," and some occasional accounts of the activities of lobbies of Arizona mine-owners or other persons.

If we tried to "reduce all this information to order," Bentley says, "we should soon find ourselves compelled to infer a great deal about the meaning of different parts of it, or else go outside it or rather through and behind it to get its value in the legislative process." And if we could not do this, we should "have to wait for the outcome of the voting in the two houses of Congress to get an idea of the relative strengths, and even then we should have but a superficial understanding of the forces."

This is the sum of the everyday procedure as presented by Bentley. No purpose for inquiry is expressly stated, although several are implied in Bentley's account. Would the records, facts, and opinions be studied with a view to deciding whether we as citizens, or the Senators as our representatives, should admit these territories as states? This is a possibility. Or is the everyday interest directed toward understanding why and how various legislators decided to vote when the statehood bill reached the Senate floor in 1906? This too is hinted at. Bentley ventures back into the forbidden "metaphysical quagmires" to tell us we would "have but a superficial understanding of the forces" determining the relative voting strengths if we confined ourselves to the information and procedures found in everyday life.

Leaving purpose aside, it is important to assess what the common sources of information and everyday procedure provide. There is, first, the identification of the topic, although this itself raises a problem. We learn from other sources that Bentley's description is not very accurate. There was no "piece of legislation . . . passed in the spring of 1906" which "provided" for the admission of these territories as states. A series of bills to admit all of these territories as states, with various specific proposals for how many states should be formed, was debated in Congress from 1902 to 1911. A bill to admit Oklahoma and Indian Territory as a single state was passed in 1906, but a similar bill to admit the Arizona and New Mexico territories as a single state was defeated.[48] But despite the misstatement, we learn from Bentley's account

[48] Claude G. Bowers, *Beveridge and the Progressive Era* (Boston: Houghton Mifflin Company, 1932), pp. 233-235; cf. pp. 182-184, 189, 193-201.

of everyday information that proposed legislation dealing with the admission of new states is the topic before us. We have, in addition, official documents, ranging from the *Congressional Record* through committee reports and other "objectively stated facts about the territories" to statements by legislators on their studies and conclusions. And finally there is the record of the votes in Congress. To reduce this information to order, although no ordering principle or purpose is indicated by Bentley, everyday procedure would attempt to draw inferences from the materials and in addition search for "the meaning of different parts of it," in order "to get an idea of relative strengths" and "forces" moving toward a vote.

What does Bentley's group analysis yield? He is certain at the outset that "in all this material there is nothing from the stump speeches to the votes on final reading of the bill that cannot be reduced to what it stands for in the term of groups of men, and there is no other way to get a unified picture of the whole process except by reducing it to such groups" (p. 373). Although most of this remark is properly seen as an introductory claim, not yet subject to the need for supporting argument and analysis, one question must be raised. What is the "whole process" of which the group method will produce a picture? "Process" has appeared repeatedly in the citations from Bentley but never with proper credentials. A guide is given by the descriptive terms with which Bentley qualifies "process." The "legislative process" appears to be the procedure used by Congress or by another legislature in pursuit of its formal purposes, together with efforts made with a variety of techniques by men outside the Congress to influence a particular outcome or result in legislation. Then is the focus of Bentley's interest in the statehood bill on the processes, ranging from "stump speeches to the votes on final reading of the bill," used by Congress in doing its work? Let us see if the succeeding parts of Bentley's presentation support this guess.

In group terms, we have first of all "the locality groups, the four territories." Following these we have the "organized party interests, Democratic and Republican, having a special eye to the senatorships to be created." Then follow the "Arizona mine-owners, possessing certain present privileges, and fearing their loss." Next there are "transportation interests directly involved, because of the probability of controlling the senators who would be chosen from the more westerly of the two proposed states." There is "also a wider grouping of industrial interests looking toward a similar end, and finally a widespread but comparatively weak interest of Americans in avoiding the creation of 'rotten-borough' states . . ." (pp. 373-374).

If we ask what has been gained in the account just presented, the answer is, very little. And that little is simply a fuller statement of the everyday information Bentley presented in condensed form as part of the ordinary knowledge he depreciates. Bentley attempts to disarm such an evaluation as this with a familiar explanation: "To describe these groups I am using loose language in compromise with current methods of speech, but I have solely in view the group activities which were forging ahead through the political process." But by this point in his work these remarks are inadmissible, or are admissions of nonperformance. The "groups" described are the organizations and populations said to be concerned with the statehood bill. They are described in terms taken from current speech, with no greater precision than is commonly found in such speech. Bentley's "compromise with current methods of speech" leads to neglect of at least one of the "interests" he is so eager to reveal. He is strangely silent about the kind of interest or group represented by Senator A. J. Beveridge. Beveridge was articulately aware of the Arizona mine-owners, and was much more specific than Bentley about their "possessing certain present privileges, and fearing their loss." Beveridge opposed admission of the Arizona-New Mexico territory unless adequate provision for taxing the mining industry was contained in the statehood bill:

> I don't want anybody ever again to tell me about the high moral tone of wealthy men when their pocketbook is touched. These fellows are indulging in the crudest kind of scoundrelism. They are inspired by nothing in the world except a desire to escape taxation. The mining corporations of Arizona have taken out of the territory over $400,000,000 of mineral wealth; and they have paid the Territory nothing in the way of taxes.[49]

Certainly there is enough realism about greed, as well as sufficient toughness of outlook in Beveridge's remarks to exempt him from the scorn Bentley heaps on "the man of wisdom," with his "thin, bloodless" cries (pp. 349, 114). There is in addition a concreteness of detail sorely lacking in Bentley's initial group statement.

Pursuing the statehood bill further, Bentley deals next with the fate of the parts of the bill which provided for the admission of Oklahoma and Indian Territory as a single state and the admission of the Arizona-New Mexico Territory as another single state.

> Oklahoma and Indian Territory as locality groups quickly proved themselves weak. . . . There was some vigorous leadership of the locality groups in both of the territories, but it made little headway. No strong allies were found, and the local demonstrations succumbed easily to the pressure of the Republican party interests, backed up by the wider anti-rotten-borough interest.
>
> In Arizona and New Mexico the case was very different. . . . [H]ere, although the Republican party interest in preventing double statehood with double sets of senators was even stronger than in the preceding case, there were strong allies for the separation movement, and the locality interests presented themselves as the central point of the whole dispute. Just how much appearance and how much reality there was in this prominence of the locality interests would be a matter for exact research, but the fact that the group interests involved were very much larger

[49] *Beveridge and the Progressive Era,* p. 233.

and very much stronger than the locality interests is well enough established [p. 374].

What do we learn from these paragraphs? The remarks about the relative strengths of the "locality groups" or "locality interests" circle around, but do not touch, the bit of information they seek to convey, namely, that a bill to admit Oklahoma and Indian Territory as a single state was carried, while a similar provision to admit the Arizona and New Mexico territory as a single state failed to pass.

Bentley's explanation seems to base itself on the relative strengths of "locality groups" and other "group interests," the former winning in one case, the latter in the other. But his very language, all questions of accurate information aside, creates confusion and vagueness. In the Arizona-New Mexico case he opposes "the locality interests" to "the group interests." But what are locality interests if not group interests? This discussion began with the assertion that "first of all there were the locality groups." If it is said Bentley means that some groups or interests other than locality groups or interests prevailed, we may grant this. But his remarks do not tell us what these other interests or groups were. Furthermore, in his statement, "locality" appears as something other than, and opposed to, "group interests." He has mentioned mineowners, "transportation interests," "a wider grouping of industrial interests," and "a very widespread but comparatively weak interest of Americans in avoiding the creation of 'rotten-borough' states." We do not learn which of these or which combination of these prevailed over the locality interests, and in addition we are told that "exact research" would be needed to determine how much of what appeared to be locality interest was "reality" and how much "appearance." Further, we observe that Bentley's use of "group" or "interest" does not remain stable for the length of a single example. He spoke at the outset of "the organized party interests, Democratic and Republican." This suggests that we have to do with two "interests" or "groups"—the Republican party and the Democratic party. But when he tells us that "the Republican party interest" in preventing double statehood with double sets of senators was "even stronger" in one case than another, "interest" no longer means the Republican party as a group; it means a goal or purpose of the Republican party, presumably the goal or purpose of maintaining a majority in the Senate. This is not the end of the difficulty. Group or interest at times means the organized entity—the legally defined territories and states, the two major political parties, the mine-owners. Interest begins to loosen in meaning, and hence analytical utility, when it begins to include "wider groupings of industrial interests" that are not further identified. We know these "wider groupings" are industrial "interests," but whether this means the owners and managers of industrial corporations, the nonmanaging stockholders of such corporations, or the employees of such corporations or whether the remark refers to "potential" industrial enterprises we do not learn. The vagueness is increased when we move to the "widespread but . . . weak interest of Americans" opposed to the creation of rotten-borough states. For here we are confronted with the fact, discoverable from newspapers or the *Congressional Record*, that a number of prominent Republican Senators were leading critics of the original statehood bills on the ground that the bills would create rotten-borough states. It is not clear from Bentley's account, and it is never made clear, whether we are to consider the Republican party as one "interest" and the opposition to rotten boroughs another interest. Certainly it is possible to do this, but not without further specification of what "Republican party interest" then means. Bentley, in short, is obliged to present us with far greater information than he has presented before we would be in a position to say whether the construct of "interests" as he uses it is able even to reproduce, to say nothing of improve upon, what we can discover with greater ease and greater illumination from the sources he depreciates.

Our difficulties do not end here. Bentley goes on to tell us what the committee reports and the Senatorial votes meant. Reports and votes alike were "nothing more than . . . the medium through which the various group interests could state themselves." Any particular report simply "set forth the adjustment between these various group interests to the best of its representative ability." So, too, the arguments preceding the votes showed us "discussion groups reflecting all the elements of the process through a technique peculiarly their own."

We do not learn what the content of any particular report or argument was, but are instead assured that "just so far as these arguments reflected group positions, and served to develop them and make clear the lines of the contest, so far they may be said to have counted in the result." The now completely vague and unidentified group interests are said to be at work and all else is to be understood as the reflection or representation of these interests. Bentley will entertain no exception: "If we cannot reduce an argument to group interest on its face, we may know we can reduce it to similar interests indirectly, and make it appear but a mask for those interests" (p. 376). Bentley's position certainly has this merit: it will permit no view opposed to his to intrude on his interpretations. But what does the direct or indirect reduction of argument to interest achieve for the student of politics? It makes an a priori assertion or dogma the basis of social interpretation. This dogma is capable of assertion in all political contexts but is incapable of test, understanding, or measurement in any context. If we are required to say that all is interest or the reflection of interest, we are driven to an abstraction so airy it is useless in the study of government. Coming at this late point, after the primacy of interest has been stated in numerous combinations, one begins to despair of understanding by this method. One wonders why the interests themselves are not identified or described, why their techniques are not presented in sufficient detail in a single instance to provide some support for the structure of assertions we have been given. Nowhere does Bentley provide such an example. There is instead a final statement that completes Bentley's comment on the statehood bills. After the generalized and now nameless interests have been presented as working their way through committees and reports and after the requirement is introduced that all argument be reduced, directly or indirectly, to group interest or a mask for group interests, we reach the final stage of the legislative process. "Out of it all we come in the end to the voting, and there if our study has been full enough we can trace back the group interests, and even on the rough votes, each a crude lump of pressures, we can make our analysis with fair accuracy" (p. 377).

With all due respect, it is submitted that we learn nothing new in the "analysis" we have been given. Indeed, if we forget the everyday sources of information which identify and structure our example for us, we are in a position where we literally cannot discover what happened in the debates and votes on the statehood bills. It is all the more remarkable, therefore, to find Bentley summarizing his achievement in the following language:

> I have sketched this bit of legislation, not exactly as it happened, but in broad outlines, without tracing the lines of activity back very far, either into party organizations or into the "public-opinion" activities. But it is enough if I have made clear how the coarsest phenomena, so to speak, the crudest, largest, broadest, are really the most important in social interpretation, and how instead of trying to reduce them into fine theoretical elements, we should always aim to reduce the fine-spun theories into them, if we want to get on the track of a reliable interpretation [p. 377].

The degree of detail into which we have entered in examining this example is necessary to forestall the suspicion that claims as great as Bentley's could not be raised on such a frail basis. But this is indeed the case. The example enables us, however, to learn a little more about Bentley's use of his tool.

We are able, to begin with, to add somewhat to our understanding of how he uses his group concept. It was noted above [50] that "group" appears to be an analytical construct for Bentley; the number and kinds of groups he describes will be determined by the purposes of a particular investigation. Yet in the example before us this does not seem to be entirely true. Here Bentley begins with concrete "groups" that are legally defined or whose presence is affirmed by current opinion communicated in the mass media. The "locality groups" or interests are simply identified as the four legally defined territories, whose future status is in issue. The Republican and Democratic parties are identified as organization and discussion groups, but this, in the example before us, simply tells us that debate and argument occurred among men publicly identified as Republicans or Democrats. There is no examina-

[50] See above, pp. 191-192.

tion of what these labels mean, of the range of viewpoints and purposes contained under each of them, or of the divisions which make it treacherous to rely on American party labels as indicators of individual interest or purpose. On the contrary, one gains the impression that the Republican and Democratic parties are treated as formal organizations with contours almost as clear as the legally defined boundaries of the Oklahoma and Indian territories. In any case, "group" in these instances identifies some of the units defined either in law or in common opinion. Their relevance to the legislative process is assumed on the basis of their prominence in public discussions of the issue under review.

There are in addition the Arizona mine-owners, whose common group characteristic lies in "possessing certain present privileges, and fearing their loss." Here the basis of the group identification is the assumption by Bentley that all mine-owners shared a common interest in preserving their present privileges. The fact of ownership is presumably easy to determine. The assumption that "mine-owners" as a group shared the same desire and the same fear is not documented, but rests on the assumption that, "group arrays being what they are," self-interest will "reflect" itself in a common position on the statehood bills. This is not an unreasonable assumption as a first approximation; but self-interest is far more complex than Bentley recognizes. One wonders, for example, what he would make of the letter Beveridge sent to Gifford Pinchot in which he told how, while in the Territories,

I quite accidentally—quite accidentally—met an Indianian who also accidentally owned a mine, and when I got back he accidentally sent me a block of stock in the mine. Well, I just as accidentally returned it to him—damn him.[51]

Even if one were to put the worst interpretation on Beveridge's behavior and assert him to have been moved by self-interest, it would remain true that it is a step toward vagueness to identify self-interest with greed without further qualification. A difference between intelligent greed and unintelligently directed greed "reflects" itself in different activities, but Bentley does not inquire into the possibility of such differences among the actors here, including the mine owners. The difference between self-interest as material greed and self-interest as the desire for honor introduces further possibilities of special relevance to political life which Bentley does not entertain. He has chosen one possibility and dogmatized it into a certainty.

Possibility enters also into the next example of groups Bentley gives us, but in a different form. He speaks of the "transportation interests" as "directly involved" because of the possibility of their controlling the new senators. The possibility here appears as Bentley's surmise about the reason that drew the transportation interests into the statehood controversy. Again, his guess is a defensible one, but, again, the status of the "interest" is not made clear. The

[51] *Beveridge and the Progressive Era*, p. 216.

transition from groups or interests as formal organizations whose presence in a given political situation is observed, to interests as purposes or reasons why numbers of men with one or more characteristics in common may or should be concerned with a particular political development, is made without attention to the different meanings that the word "interest" serves. The lack of clarity results from Bentley's vacillation between the viewpoint of the citizen and the viewpoint of a social scientist attempting a statement as "objective as possible." The current attractiveness of scientific status needs no comment. Joined to the assumption of a scientific posture, however, is a sufficient amount of unexamined everyday information and current opinion to lend concreteness and familiarity to Bentley's discussions. Strict adherence to his scientific program would result in the empty generalizations we have detailed above. His combination of scientific posturing and reliance on common opinion yields a formula—seek the interest—which is at once a reasonable, although not a new, warning and a form of statement capable of uncheckable application everywhere: "If we cannot reduce an argument to group interest on its face, we may know we can reduce it to similar interests indirectly, and make it appear but a mask for those interests."

We do not intend to deny the importance of the stress on interest, even on interest narrowly and selfishly understood, which Bentley makes. "This policy of supplying, by opposite and rival interests, the defect of better motives, might be traced through the whole system of human affairs, private as well as public." [52] The qualifications we do wish to enter are the following. First, Bentley's use of interest, or group, or activity "reduces" everyday political distinctions to a common denominator that, as he presents it, is more vague and less precise than the everyday distinctions with which he begins. His "strictly empirical" phenomena, furthermore, are seen on examination to be constructs whose very meaning is supplied by fragments of common opinion put together on the basis of a conceptual criterion that is never made clearer than his own admitted primary interest in "the economic life" and the supporting conviction that "the economic basis of political life must, of course, be fully recognized . . ." (p. 209). Now, again, there is no intention to depreciate the role of conceptualization or of thought or even of economics in social science analysis. But Bentley's contempt for, and depreciation of, theory, the "man of wisdom," and ideas and feelings is far more evident than his reliance on concepts. The remark we quoted from Peltason, that his orientation is "Bentleyan, behavioristic, actional, and nonmotivational" [53] is the result with which we are concerned. The conviction that "Bentleyan" means nonmotivational results in a carelessness about fundamentals, a lack of interest in understanding why a particular political phenomenon is worth study, and a futile effort to describe the phenomenon without attention to

[52] Alexander Hamilton, James Madison, and John Jay, *The Federalist*, No. 51.
[53] See above, p. 156.

the purposes of either the observer or the participants. Bentley saves his effort from complete futility at the cost of coherence and consistency. So do Peltason, Truman, and the rest. Indeed, Bentley's contemporary attractiveness is due largely to that very vagueness which can contain, even if it cannot reconcile, the prestige of science and the good sense of common opinion. But while consistency has sometimes been put down as the last refuge of small minds, it does have its virtues. It might have enabled Bentley and his followers to break out of the ever-repeated "compromise" they have to make with the everyday vocabulary of everyday life. It might have enabled them to communicate something instructive about politics.

These general considerations, however, should not divert us from the purpose at hand. We have surveyed one of Bentley's group analyses. In it the unachieved goal was the presentation of the political process, in this case the legislative process, as the effect or reflection of streams of interest flowing through, or represented by, the men who alone are directly visible to us in mines, corporations, the electorate, the political parties, and the branches of government. A metaphor based on pressure and movement is presented as the concrete reality and as the best way to describe that range of political life covered by legislation. In fact the metaphor barely approximates the commonplaces of everyday discourse. The supporting "analysis" cannot be said to achieve even this.

THE ASSUMPTION OF ORDER

One final consideration and we are done. Bentley's discussion leaves us with a continuity of activity as the fundamental phenomenon of social life generally and of political life more particularly. Except to the extent that it is used to convey meaning, in "compromise" with everyday speech, the idea of purpose is abandoned as a useful concept in the study of government. Group conflicts remain before us. There is, it is true, a "habit background" which sets limits to the techniques of conflict, but the habit background, the rules of the game, as well as the "social whole" in which these unexamined elements are present, are given serious attention only as objects of depreciation or attack. At best they are grudgingly admitted to convey the minimum of structure Bentley needs to call a "social something" to our attention and to indicate, but not to explain, why certain forms of activity are or are not found in particular situations. Group pressing on group in a conflict of interest thus appears as the sum and total of the process of government. If we ask what maintains this process or what it can tell us about society, the answer we get is: "The balance of the group pressure is the existing state of society" (pp. 258-259). "Balance," like "process," is never described or defined, but Bentley's discussion does offer a guide to his meaning. He assumes the existence of a peculiar order that purportedly characterizes the group process. In an early remark on the group struggle, Bentley tells us that "one opposition appears and adjusts itself and another takes its place . . ." (p. 217). A rotation of group oppositions is assumed, in which, after a particular opposition "adjusts itself," another takes its place. Leaving aside the mystery of group "adjustment," we inquire how we know that this order or pattern of rotation is present and what guarantees its continuance. Bentley offers a twofold answer. There is, first, a most reassuring picture of "modern society":

Is mobility of individuals increasing? Are income conditions changing? Are important new group relations forming among women, or including women? Are nuisances and dangers growing out of disjointed families? There will be a shoving aside of the old ordering of the interests, and an establishment of a new ordering with groups of all grades of depth, of all degrees of representativeness, functioning away in a great whirl. . . . Order is bound to result, because order is now and order has been, where order is needed, though all the prophets be confounded [p. 267].

Order is bound to result because order is needed. One is at a loss to know whether to stress the unwarranted hopefulness of these remarks or their question-begging circularity. As we shall presently see, the hope needs emphasis. But at the moment the question is, what can this order or "new ordering" be, or mean? The indicated meaning of order is "system"; "system" is an inherent characteristic of all activity:

It is of the very definition of activity that it is systematized. Even the simplest motion with which the physicist deals is part of a system of motion. . . . Behavior is a word biologists are now using of the very simplest reactions of the simplest organisms, and except as system it cannot be comprehended at all [p. 285].

We meet again the authoritative power of physical and biological science, but, as before, we are not more enlightened by his reference to practices in these sciences. The physicist in 1908 may have referred his "simplest motion" to the system of classical mechanics, or he may already have been wondering why the classical system could not account for certain phenomena he observed. In any event, he, as well as the biologist, worked with a conceptual outlook which sought to interpret data in the light of a particular system, the system of classical mechanics or the enzyme system, as the case might be. "System" by itself is too vague to tell us much more than what we have previously touched upon, namely, Bentley's assumption that all activity is "by very definition" ordered or systematic. This conveys an assurance, not a meaning. We do not learn what particular system or order is assumed in Bentley's descriptions of group conflict. And his stress on relativity of judgment compounds the difficulty. The quotation above continues as follows:

All the actions that enter into the behavior of an idiot are correlated, much more all the activities of a mentally competent person. True enough, we can choose many special points of view from which we will say that a certain lot of activity is not systematized, but here we are merely adopting a group's position as our own position from which to view the world, and we are judging along the lines of that group's activity; and the denial of systematization so uttered is a limited denial of a limited form of system, no matter how vehemently or how absolutely phrased. It is a representative activity, reflecting certain group interests along certain lines, but not capable of elevation for use in broader fields.

If the denial of system to some activity is itself a "representative activity . . . not capable of elevation for use in broader fields," so for the same reason the affirmation of system must also be "representative," limited, and, to say the least, untrustworthy. Bentley's efforts at systematic statement ends in a return to group relativism, which, as we have earlier seen, makes objective or "elevated" statement impossible. But the consequences of this relativism are veiled by Bentley's second assumption: group conflict has a self-adjusting or systematically rotating character. As a realist, Bentley admits there may be "hurts" as well as benefits to the participants in the group struggle. His final conviction, however, is as hopeful as it is truly astonishing:

And moreover the hurts and the benefits so loudly proclaimed are never permanent things; they are small in comparison with the deeper-lying benefits; and if the most powerful movement . . . seems dangerous to the "liberties of the state" or to any other fiction, we may be sure that it will trickle away in driblets with access to power. For the very nature of the group process (which our government shows in a *fairly* well-developed form) is this, that groups are freely combining, dissolving, and recombining in accordance with their interest lines. And the lion when he has satisfied his physical need will lie down quite lamb-like, however much louder his roars were than his appetite justified [p. 359, italics supplied].

Bentley's citizenship, indeed, his ardent patriotism, shines in his certainty that the very nature of the group process is essentially a somewhat noisy but beneficial rotation of groups. After all the depreciation of forms of government, of reliance on law, on constitutions, and on common opinion, "our government" is the final security for Bentley's conviction that the ultimate yields of the group struggle are "deeper-lying benefits." The progressive impulse here leads to the view that the politics of a healthy constitutional democracy are in their "very nature" the undirected but finally self-restrained conflict of groups, and as such can be generalized into the characteristic process of all government. To recur to Bentley's imagery for a moment, politics everywhere is seen as the process by which lions, after having eaten a sufficient number of lambs, become themselves lambs. In his political zoo Bentley looks for a miracle to supply the restraints earlier realists had expected from the fox.[54]

[54] Cf. above, pp. 53-54; 105-109.

CONCLUSION

A sense of unfulfilled promise pervades *The Process of Government.* To Bentley this is as it should be, for as he says in the last lines of his work, "Whatever tools of method we devise . . . can only prove their value in the using—in the using by many workers, not by one, or by two, or by three" (p. 484). The number of field hands using the Bentleyan tools must now be as large as Bentley could have hoped. Yet the result has been nothing but a multiplication of the mere "approximations" to the proper study of government as Bentley understood it. The tools have been put to use diligently, but they are defective. The achievement of a science depends critically on the clarity with which its object is defined; the utility of a method depends largely on the clarity with which it is set forth. On both these grounds we find Bentley's work sorely lacking. Without imposing a consistency that is not present, it is impossible to state his object, or to indicate how he intends his method to be applied. Both difficulties flow from the same source, Bentley's unresolved confusion about the purposes of his endeavor.

The generally received view of Bentley's purpose is that he sought to create an objective science of social interpretation, or at least to show how contributions to such a science could be made. We have seen that this is indeed one of his stated purposes. The complete science, with nothing left out, will result from the strictly empirical descriptions of group activity which his method will enable us to obtain. We are to view our data—the activity of men in groups—"as impassively as we would the habits or organic functions of birds, bees, or fishes" (p. 214). Instead of taking sides in the conflicts which constitute the centrally significant phenomena of politics, we are to remember that "we are not making a propaganda." But Bentley's view of human action rests on the primacy of "interest." Now, despite whatever difficulties there may be, and there are serious ones, in understanding Bentley's conception of "interest," he seeks to maintain the assertion that all actions, including "talking and writing activity," are "reflections" of group interests. In his explicit address to this point, he admits of no exception to this view:

When a man writes a book to advance some particular theory about society, he reflects in it a certain phase of the social process. . . . If his book has any bearing, however remote, on political life, it falls within the field before us. Now the reflection of a phase of the social process is the same thing as the reflection of some group interest or set of group interests. His "theory" is such a reflection [p. 428].

Bentley saw no reason to define what he meant by reflection. Nor did he indicate how one was to know which interpretation of a theory was the accurate reflection of group interest, or how, considering his admission that a group member may be mistaken in his reflection, we are to know whose interpretation to fix upon in seeking an understanding of group interest. But he did insist that there was no exception to the status of talk and writing as a reflection of group interest. He pointedly includes his own work within the sweep of his generalization, presenting it as the reflection or representation of certain group interests active in American politics at the turn of the century.[55] With this admission, however, he appears to withdraw the earlier claim he had made—the claim to be seeking the complete science of social interpretation—and to substitute a brief in behalf of the particular political program his own group affiliations compel him to "reflect." If, then, his purpose is not objective scientific research but political action, what can be said of it?

Somewhat strangely, Bentley is shy about stating what specific political interest or purpose he conceives himself to be pursuing through the medium of The Process of Government. His examples, however, abundantly compensate for the want of a more explicit statement. The indignation over the excesses of the industrial system, the cynicism about the achievements of representative government, and the irony about progress identify Bentley as a liberal critic of late nineteenth-century American life, especially of economic organization and practice. His comments convey a desire for, and a surprisingly optimistic expectation of, progressive reform in the United States. To this writer's knowledge, the first notation of this aspect of Bentley's enterprise was made by E. Pendleton Herring, who listed Bentley in a bibliographic note among those writers who were dissatisfied with things as they were.[56]

Surely practical political reform may be a legitimate goal of political science and of political scientists. Bentley's understanding of the conditions of human action, however, raises the question whether reform is a possible goal of action. His view of himself and of all other men as group-bound and group-determined in their views does not furnish a basis for discovering the difference between genuine reform and mere random change, or between accurate and inaccurate statements of relevant political problems. More significantly, the group-reflection argument also destroys the possibility of that science of social interpretation which Bentley alternatively presents as his guiding purpose. If description and analysis cannot reasonably seek to be objective, or if the pursuit of objectivity is known in advance to be a futile quest, we are offered an invitation to a Babel where many interests replace many tongues as the insuperable barrier to the erection of a tower of human achievement, whether of scientific description or of practical reform. In Bentley's work the

[55] See p. 479, n. 1.
[56] Group Representation Before Congress, p. 294. W. J. M. Mackenzie, whose incisive article on pressure group theory is too little known in this country, sees Bentley as a would-be reformer who "boldly hitches himself into his system by his own boot-straps. . . ." Political Studies, October 1955, p. 255. Bernard Crick's recent characterization of Bentley has been mentioned above, p. 155, n. 7.

aspiration toward a strictly empirical description and an analysis which is as objective as possible stands side by side with the assertions that objectivity is impossible for citizen and scientist alike. In the failure to pursue this problem or, more generally, in the failure to pursue analysis of any kind, lies the single greatest shortcoming of The Process of Government, considered either as a scientific work or as part of a program of progressive reform.

In the failure to pursue analysis, in the willingness finally to rest content with contemporary public accounts of political issues, Bentley's science of social interpretation does not rise to, and certainly does not rise above, the level of that citizen debate which he so often dismisses with contempt. There is no clearer analysis of the issues in debate, nor is there the description of a single example with sufficient thoroughness to permit one to agree that Bentley's method is able to achieve the articulation of a significant political observation in new form.

What suggests itself as a plausible explanation of the strange position Bentley takes is the implicit democratic assumption on which his work rests.[57] Every view, in science or in politics, is entitled to statement on a basis of equality with every other view. Every opinion, as the statement of a group position, is necessarily as good as any other statement, since there is no "monopoly of intelligence," no ruling position from which group-free evaluations or statements can be made. Democratic equalitarianism is in this instance fortified by its close analogy to science as Bentley understands science. The "system" he finds at work in physics or biology assumes a unity in which there is a meaningful relation or "balance" among each of the parts. This situation he also finds in the process of government. There is no part that is critical, no part rules or is sovereign; every part has an effect on every other part, every part counts. There is thus a democratic order at the foundation of science as well as of politics. Bentley's "equilibration of interests" or "balancing of groups" (p. 274) puts the some positive value on the contribution of each part in the system as does a democratic orientation in politics. Multigroup analysis, pluralism in this restricted sense, appears to unite Bentley's view of science and of politics. The scientific universe is a pluralistic one, and the pluralistic universe is a democratic one. We submit that Bentley, no more than James, whose relevant work[58] appeared a year after The Process of Government, succeeds in rescuing this view from buzzing confusion.

If, in place of asking for the purpose of Bentley's investigation, we inquire as to its method, the answer is a modification of the injunction: "Seek the interests." Here the familiar image of Bentley as a tough-minded student of politics comes into its own. His basic conviction that humbug or deception characterizes much of the debate about political purposes leads him to seek a means to cut through the deception to the verities or realities of political life.

[57] See below, pp. 322 ff.
[58] William James, A Pluralistic Universe (London: Longmans, Green & Co., 1909).

The means he suggests is the discovery and description of the conflicting interests seeking expression in a given community. Bentley insists upon "activity" as the key to an undeceived understanding of interest. His illustrations and examples convey with adequate clarity what his comments seek frequently to deny, namely, that interest cannot be understood simply as observed activity. On the contrary, interest is sometimes understood by Bentley as the consciously held or shared purposes of an individual or group and sometimes as the assessment of individual or group needs made by a practicing politician or by an observing student of politics.

His illustrations and examples also make two further points clear. The first is that, while Bentley often identifies interest with greed, he does not always give it that meaning. Bentley will speak cynically of the man who, "being the possessor of no traction securities," becomes a "municipal-ownership advocate" (p. 115), but he will as often cite instances of men who escape narrow interest domination to "reflect" interests on "broader lines" or who act in behalf of a "great group interest" which neither knows nor cares what its needs are (p. 352). The admission does further violence to the notion of "reflection" as an automatic and impersonally determined response of individuals to the mysteriously vague "deeper-lying interests," but it accords well with what observation shows us.

Similar observations support our second point, namely, that Bentley's arguments against the idea of a common interest either are not supported or are flatly contradicted by his own subsequent discussions. Thus, his conclusion that there is no common interest does not follow from the observation of group conflicts in a country. The examples he so often cites of groups convinced they must seek their ends by legal means lend substance to the vague "deeper-lying benefits" he sees resulting from adherence to the covenanted procedures of "our government." The noncontroversial agreement to pursue ends by legal means is part of the common interest, hidden in Bentley's discussion by its unexamined inclusion in the "rules of the game" or the "habit background." So too, his own description of log-rolling as "the most characteristic legislative process" (p. 370) is qualified by the contrast he draws between the "typical" procedure and the "genuine national needs" whose absence he deplores. What is lacking in Bentley's appraisal of this dimension of politics is, strangely enough, a sufficient degree of toughness. Fearful of a "monopoly of intelligence" and perhaps too easily moved by the plight of the underdog, Bentley's sentiments divert him from his search for "what goes on in society." He is not tough enough to sustain the inquiry.

Nevertheless, Bentley's stress on seeking the interests as the key to the understanding of politics emerges as the source of his contemporary stature and attractiveness to students of politics. The call for realism, or for a disenchanted firmness, as the proper attitude for the study of politics is, subject to the qualifications we have noted, an appropriate appeal. In a way, Bentley's skeptical toughness is an approximation to the sense of wonder with which all serious inquiry is said to begin. If we add to this toughness Bentley's humanitarianism or progressivism, we have the specific combination that characterizes his most enthusiastic students. One is tempted to say that hard-headed progressivism appears today as the equivalent of justice in a view of politics which no longer expressly concerns itself with justice.

IV

SCIENTIFIC PROPAGANDA

Harold D. Lasswell

by ROBERT HORWITZ

SCIENTIFIC POLITICAL THEORY

One aspect of the task of the systematic student of politics is to *describe* political behavior in those social situations which recur with sufficient frequency to make *prediction* useful as a preliminary to *control*.[1]

IN THESE LINES, his first to be published, Harold D. Lasswell succinctly states the intention of his entire work: description, prediction, control. During the decades following this statement of intention, Lasswell has gained international fame as a pioneer in the methodology of the social sciences. He has been widely acclaimed for his contribution to the development of research techniques in a broad variety of areas, including the study of propaganda and public opinion, content analysis, communication theory, decision-making, and the policy sciences. Typical of the testimonials to his accomplishments is that of Heinz Eulau, who contends that while "concern with methodology has not been a hallmark of political science," "the only persistent and consistent discussion of methodology can be found in the work of Harold D. Lasswell. . . ." [2] Somewhat more critically, Bernard Crick also discovers Lasswell's major contribution to American social science to consist of his numerous, often bewildering, "conceptual frameworks."

Professor Lasswell is not a settler, he is a pathfinder and a border scout. . . . He has blazed the trail for small armies of settlers, but, as the wagons stop moving and the ploughs are dragged out, he always gallops off to yet more virgin soil, leaving the Social Science Research Council to organize a Territorial Government. . . . His originality, width of knowledge, energy and his refusal to become "hidebound" in his thinking are admirable, but his movements do become a little bewildering for those who want not merely to do "research," but to do research with the latest concepts and the newest tools. They are apt to appear outmoded before they have had time even to unpack.[3]

---

[1] Harold D. Lasswell, "Chicago's Old First Ward: A Case Study in Political Behavior," *National Municipal Review*, March 1923, p. 127, italics supplied.
[2] "and there," continues Eulau, "it is scattered through numerous books and articles of three decades." Heinz Eulau, "H. D. Lasswell's Developmental Analysis," *Western Political Quarterly*, June 1958, p. 229. See also Richard Christie and Marie Jahoda (eds.), *Studies in the Scope and Method of the Authoritarian Personality: Continuities in Social Research* (New York: The Free Press of Glencoe, Inc., 1954), p. 22.
[3] Bernard Crick, *The American Science of Politics* (Berkeley: University of California Press, 1959), pp. 180-181.

This widely held view that the unique importance of Lasswell's work lies in its unending concern with the methodology of the social sciences gains support from a basic distinction that Lasswell, himself, has drawn for over a quarter-century, the distinction between "scientific political theory" and "political philosophy." A lucid, early statement of this distinction may be found in his famous *Politics*, which was published in 1936.[4] Here, he distinguishes between "the science of politics," which "states conditions," and "the philosophy of politics," which "justifies preferences" (p. 13). The science of politics, or scientific political theory, "calls for the systematic statement of theory and the use of empirical methods of gathering and processing data" (p. 187), as Lasswell re-emphasizes in his 1958 "Postscript" to the *Politics*. The importance of this distinction is reiterated in his most recent major methodological treatise, *Power and Society*, which is explicitly described as "a book of political theory." [5] Here Lasswell and Abraham Kaplan vigorously assert that scientific "theorizing, even about politics, is not to be confused with metaphysical speculation in terms of abstractions hopelessly removed from empirical observation and control" (p. x). *Power and Society*, maintain the authors, contains "no elaborations of political doctrine, of what the state and society *ought* to be," for "historically . . . such doctrines have served chiefly to justify the political philosopher's own preferences (and, of course, those of the groups with which he identifies himself)" (p. xi).

This distinction between "the science of politics" and "the philosophy of politics" appears to rest on fundamentally the same grounds as the fact-value distinction of contemporary social science positivism. Though Lasswell is distinctly restrained in the use of this terminology,[6] it is clear when he argues that political philosophy "justifies preferences," that he does not intend to suggest that it provides thereby a sound mode for evaluating different ethical or political systems. Rather, political philosophy "justifies preferences" in the sense of providing rationalizations for them. It is, in short, ideology. Still, this should not be taken to suggest that Lasswell rejects the data of political philosophy as simply meaningless. The scientific political theorist, if he is to state all of the relevant conditions within a given society, must take account of its value preferences and their ideological or philosophical façade.

This understanding of the character of political philosophy reveals the de-

4 *Politics: Who Gets What, When, How* (New York: McGraw-Hill Book Co., Inc., 1936). This work was republished in 1951 in *The Political Writings of Harold D. Lasswell* (New York: The Free Press of Glencoe, Inc.), and again in 1958 (New York: Meridian Books, Inc.) with an extended "Postscript." All page references to the *Politics* in this essay are to the 1958 edition.
5 Harold D. Lasswell and Abraham Kaplan, *Power and Society: A Framework for Political Inquiry* (New Haven: Yale University Press, 1950), p. ix.
6 As, for example, in his recent praise of Woodrow Wilson as a student of politics who "could distinguish between celebrating a value and designating an event." Foreword to the 1956 program of the American Political Science Associaton meeting, Washington, D. C., September 1956.

cidedly unequal status of political philosophy and scientific political theory. It is the latter which is intended to be all-encompassing, for it establishes the framework within which political philosophy is to be understood. An example may prove helpful in clarifying this point. A scientific political theorist engaged in studying French society during the last decades of the eighteenth century would, in Lasswell's view, be required to take account not only of such factors as changes in class structure, in leadership elites, and in property ownership, but also of the role of the Rousseauan "ideology" with its doctrines of "the rights of man," the social contract, and so forth. The scientific political theorist would seek to determine the social function of Rousseau's thought considered as a preference-justifying ideology. He would, at the same time, reject as patently absurd Rousseau's own understanding of his teaching as a true understanding of politics and society. In summary, the traditional claim of political philosophy to architectonic status, the status that it enjoyed during the extended period from Socrates to Rousseau, is explicitly rejected by Lasswell. Scientific political theory, having occupied the throne of the deposed queen, reduces her to mere ideology.

The fashion in which scientific political theory incorporates the function of traditional political philosophy may be partially explained by consideration of a related distinction which runs through Lasswell's work, the distinction between contemplative and manipulative analysis. The scientific political theorist acts from what Lasswell terms "the contemplative standpoint" in seeking to describe the social process and to predict its development (*Power and Society*, p. xii).[7] While such analysis is absolutely essential for the scientific political theorist, it is not sufficient. "The purely contemplative standpoint . . . fails to maximize the relevance of inquiry to the richest potentialities and most pressing needs of society in the given situation." [8] That is to say, the scope of *contemplative analysis* does not extend beyond description and prediction, the initial objectives of the systematic or scientific student of politics. Scientific description is required for prediction, but prediction, in turn, is necessary for effective and intelligent social control. Of the three elements in this progression, the objective of social control is ultimate and governing. This shift from description and prediction to control is described by Lasswell as a movement from the contemplative to the manipulative standpoint. From the manipulative standpoint, a "problem is formulated in terms of courses of action leading to the *goal*. The elements of the situaton are analyzed and appraised in terms of their bearing on the formation of policy" (p. xi, italics supplied). Accordingly, "the result of inquiry is a warranted

---

[7] From the contemplative standpoint, "propositions state the existence of functional co-relations (in the form Y is a function of X)."

[8] Lasswell adds that the recognition of the necessity for going beyond contemplative analysis constitutes "what is sound about the emphasis on 'unity of theory and practice' in pragmatism and the traditional literature of Marxism."

statement of the way in which an actor in the situation can increase the probability of occurrence of a specified state of affairs . . ." (p. xii).[9] The simultaneous adoption of the manipulative and contemplative standpoints is identified by Lasswell as "configurative analysis," and this approach has characterized his work almost from its very beginning.[10]

Lasswell recognizes that the objective of configurative analysis, the merging of the goals of description, prediction, and control into a unity of "theory and practice," raises for his own work certain of the questions associated with "the philosophical tradition in which politics and ethics have always been closely associated" (p. xiii). For here "the functions of the scientist overlap and interact with those of the policy maker. As a citizen, a moral person, the scientist has his own preferences, goals, values; all his acts, including his acts of scientific inquiry, are subject to self-discipline by moral aims." Such aims, "in turn, stimulate and fructify his science." [11] Postponing for the present further consideration of the relationship between the "scientific" and "valuational" aspects of Lasswell's social science, we may recapitulate the argument of this introduction by emphasizing the inadequacy of the view that the central and unifying meaning of Lasswell's work lies in his extensive concern with methodology. Important as his methodological contributions have been, such a view does justice neither to his avowed intention nor to his broad accomplishments. Just as the objective of the "contemplative standpoint," namely, description, is subordinate to his ultimate interest in social control, so his social science positivism is subordinate to the goals of prediction and political reconstruction.

POSITIVE LIBERALISM

It is evident that the introduction of the "manipulative standpoint" necessarily raises the question of the ends or purposes to which social control is to be directed. These ends, as they are conceived by Lasswell, may be most directly grasped by examining a cross-section of his early writings, for it is here that he has most simply and directly stated his political objectives. Such an examination quickly reveals his fervent commitment to a certain understanding of democratic liberalism, "*positive* liberalism," as we may term it, following Lasswell.[12] His devotion to the cause of positive liberalism has helped to give his work its unique shape and character, and it provides a

[9] "To produce Y (or: To make Y most likely to occur), do X!"
[10] See Harold D. Lasswell, *World Politics and Personal Insecurity* (New York: McGraw-Hill Book Co., Inc., 1935), pp. 4 ff, for an early discussion of the purpose of the "configurative method of political analysis."
[11] Lasswell argues here that he escapes the error of the philosophical tradition by "giving full recognition to the existence of two distinct components in political theory. . . ." To this question we must return in the concluding section of this essay.
[12] See his "Political Policies and the International Investment Market," *Journal of Political Economy*, June 1923, pp. 380-400. (Copyright 1923 by the University of Chicago.)

sound starting point for thoroughgoing analysis. The ultimate objective of positive liberalism, in the most general sense, has remained constant, currently finding its expression in the assertion that "we are concerned with the dignity of man. We want to participate in the realization of human dignity on the grandest possible scale." [13] According to Lasswell, twentieth-century societies, without exception, have fallen far short of this goal. The domestic and international scenes alike have been dominated by tensions and overt conflict—to the detriment of human dignity. To understand more specifically the character of these strife-producing tensions and the main tenets of Lasswell's positive liberalism, which aims at their elimination, we turn to three representative writings.

Lasswell's first extended consideration of domestic political tensions, *Labor Attitudes and Problems*, appeared in 1924. It begins with a statement of the perennial political theme: the struggle between the "haves" and the "have-nots." The opening paragraphs of this early work state the problem neatly:

Yesterday morning as I rode downtown in a streetcar, I sat beside a man who was clad in a blue shirt and overalls. The headline on the front page of my newspaper read: "CARPENTERS REFUSE TO RETURN TO WORK." The man at my side glanced at the headline and exclaimed: "Refuse to return to work! Those contractors won't let them go back to work. No self-respecting man will slave for starvation wages. . . ."

On the way back home I found myself occupying a seat with a man who was clad in a conservative gray business suit. I chanced to inquire, "When do you suppose those carpenters are going back to work?" "Say," he replied hotly, "Nobody knows. Why, do you know that those fellows get a bigger salary than school teachers? Those building trades fellows are all alike; they want everything they can get their hands on, and they loaf half the time, at that. . . ."

Now, just how am I to account for these two men? Both of them are Americans. Both of them live in my own city, and went through grammar school here. They read the same newspapers; they go to see the same moving pictures. Why do they think so differently? . . . In the case of the two men on the streetcar we feel that the sharp contrast in opinions is not purely a personal matter, that it reflects a general difference in outlook in some way related to the difference between business suits and overalls.[14]

[13] Harold D. Lasswell, *The World Revolution of Our Time: A Framework for Basic Policy Research* (Hoover Institute Studies: series A, no. 1; Stanford, California: Stanford University Press, 1951), p. 5. While considerable emphasis has been placed on Lasswell's earliest writings in order to establish the character of his positive liberalism, the reader should not infer that his work as a whole is to be treated chronologically. Specifically, Lasswell's socio-historical analysis will be considered prior to his psychological analysis, despite the fact that he manifested a keen interest in Freud a few years before he afforded comparable consideration to Marx. It is in his synthesis of the Marxist, Freudian, and Propagandistic elements that the guiding intention of his work may be discerned; hence its chronological development is substantially irrelevant.

[14] Willard E. Atkins and Harold D. Lasswell, *Labor Attitudes and Problems* (New York: Prentice-Hall, Inc., © 1924), p. 3.

The political implications of the struggle between the man in the gray business suit and the man in overalls are brought immediately to the reader's attention. "By their votes" the men in blue shirts and overalls "can exert pressure upon political leaders . . ." (*Labor Attitudes and Problems*, p. 4). Writing in 1924, Lasswell and his co-author, Willard Atkins, foresaw some of the chief areas in which the growing political effectiveness of American labor was to manifest itself in coming decades. As they anticipated, legislation has been enacted to safeguard workers in such matters as the settlement of labor disputes, the adoption of old-age pensions, the granting of injunctions, and the provision of adequate educational training. Well taken is their argument that an understanding of the workers' outlook and the enlistment of their cooperation in government "is of vital necessity."

Less sympathetic and extensive consideration is given to the objectives of management, which are somewhat tersely summarized as the securing of profits (p. 442). Despite this imbalance in treatment, the general perspective from which the opposed claims of labor and management are discussed here may be characterized as that of the concerned citizen seeking enlightenment on a vitally important question of public policy. "In a field in which controversy and disagreement are the distinguishing features, it is well to weigh the merits of particular methods and points of view" (frontispiece to Part I). The questions raised, even the vocabulary with which they are discussed, reflect the outlook of the citizen. For example, in dealing with the critical question, "Who Are the Workers?" the authors reject a number of specialized definitions in favor of the commonplace, citizen understanding, which tells us that " 'workers' may be defined as all those who are supposed, and commonly considered by the community as a whole, to be workers." They grant that this is "a somewhat ill-defined and changeable standard"—and, we may note, a nonideological standard; unlike the Marxian definition, "it is not open to the charge of including superintendents as workers, and of excluding the craftsmen who own their own tools. The community does define and place individuals, even though it does the task unconsciously, and the interesting fact is that people tend to accept the community judgment" (p. 10). The citizen's viewpoint is no less relevant to the authors' consideration of the crucial question to which their study points: " 'what is to be done . . . ?' " (p. 500) The welfare of the community or the public interest provides the standard. The public interest must be protected "against the injuries inflicted by contending groups of capital and labor." This protection may be partially achieved "by some intelligent community policy which could anticipate, and perhaps prevent, the culmination of the crisis" threatened by labor-management conflict (p. 503). While "labor groups" and "employing groups" may be understood in some respects as "special interest groups," we are told that "it should not be supposed that *all* special interest groups are opposed to the public interest . . ." (p. 471, italics supplied).

Nevertheless, the fact remains that the tensions between capital and labor are especially acute in the contemporary world. Why is this the case? "While it may be true that the machines have, on the whole, conferred large benefits upon humanity, there is a growing feeling that these benefits have not been so great or so well distributed as might naturally have been expected" (pp. 501-502). What then must be done to achieve a more natural distribution of the fruits of technology? We must achieve social progress comparable to the advances made in science and technology: "*progress should be defined in terms of human welfare*" (p. 501). Still, this argument simply moves the question back a step, since capitalists and workers disagree substantially in their understanding of "human welfare." Revealingly, the authors seem to resolve this difficulty by embracing the position which carries with it at least the weight of numbers. They contend, somewhat ambiguously, "not that the workman is the only person whose rights must be considered in an industrial enterprise; but in the intricate problems of what to change and what to conserve in our present system, it should never be forgotten that the factory exists for man and not man for the factory . . ." (p. vi).[15] This "frankly democratic" view requires that the evils of inequality be eliminated through social controls designed to achieve at least equality of opportunity. Such "equality is secured to some degree today through certain services rendered by the Government,"[16] for "an indirect consequence of the spread of these public services and the principle of 'ability to pay' in taxation has been the tendency toward the equalization of wealth" (p. 506). By subsequently endorsing this principle, the authors appear to pass judgment in favor of the rightness of the position of the workers. Progressive taxation, the "taxation of the industrially privileged," finds its theoretical justification "on the ground that a dollar to a rich man means less than a dollar to a poor man, because the rich man has more dollars." The plea of democratic liberalism for greater equality, a plea which has consistently characterized Lasswell's work,[17] calls for positive assistance to the "have-nots" in their struggle with the "haves." The tension between the man in the conservative business suit and the man in overalls is resolved in favor of the latter.

Turning to another area of political conflict, Lasswell early considered "Political Policies and the International Investment Market," about which he wrote in 1923. Here again he moves incisively toward the heart of the political problem. The struggle which we have observed between the "haves" and "have-nots" on the domestic scene finds its international parallel in the conflicting positions of the "lending states" and the "borrowing states."

[15] Cf. John Dewey, *Human Nature and Conduct* (New York: Holt, Rinehart and Winston, Inc., 1944), pp. 270 ff.
[16] Cf. John Dewey, *The Public and Its Problems* (Chicago: Gateway Editions, 1946), pp. 63 ff.
[17] Cf. especially, *National Municipal Review*, March 1923, pp. 127-131.

Possibly the broadest generalization about the movement of capital throughout the world is that it tends to flow from the industrialized to the non-industrialized areas. At one time the political policy of the undeveloped countries was the suppression of foreign economic intercourse, and it was not until the political power of the industrialized states was exerted against them that the world was open for investment. The net effect of these conflicting political forces has been, therefore, to break down the barriers against investment and to facilitate the international transfer of capital.[18]

Lasswell describes in some detail the "political weapons" used by such countries as Imperial Germany, Italy, Britain, and France. There is some weighing of the merits and limitations of the techniques typically used by "lending states": the use of pressure to secure concessions, intervention by armed forces, and devices of dual-citizenship and extraterritoriality. The techniques used by "borrowing states" to encourage or to retard the importation of capital are then discussed. Resort to such "political weapons" by both the "have" and "have-not" states produces those political tensions that manifest themselves in various forms of international strife, including war.

The political tensions produced by the operation of the international investment market might be controlled in one of two ways, Lasswell argues. The most obvious and direct way would be to restrict such investment. Certain practical difficulties would, of course, arise in the implementation of such restrictions,[19] but Lasswell has a much more fundamental objection to this approach. He places himself firmly on the side of "the men of the steam age [who] have refused to defer to the scruples of oriental or ethiopian civilizations." In discussing certain doctrines of international law designed to prevent one state from intervening in the affairs of another to enforce contractual obligations, he contends that "even though such a policy were practicable it would, by discouraging investors and removing the fear motive as a spur to the adoption of machine technology by the backward nation, delay the exploitation of the resources to which the entire world has a just claim." But what principle of justice requires that the resources of the world be exploited? No clear answer to this question can be discovered in Lasswell's early writings, though it appears that the principles of positive liberalism require the worldwide dissemination of modern technology. Accordingly, Lasswell recommends that a substantial part of the royalties paid by concessionaires for the exploitation of natural resources "be applied to the improvement of technical education or to the expansion of productive enterprises" in the backward areas (pp. 392, 396, 398).[20]

[18] *Journal of Political Economy*, June 1923, p. 394.
[19] See, for example, Lasswell's discussion of certain of President Wilson's policies aimed at restricting investment, pp. 390 ff.
[20] One is tempted initially to understand Lasswell's proposals for the betterment of "oriental or ethiopian civilizations" as some variation on the theme of "the white man's burden." But no. There are ethical implications underlying that position which are

Having contended that the scope of the international investment market should be broadened, Lasswell turns to a consideration of the forms of control to which it should be subjected, if any. Here he tells us us a good deal more about the specific objectives of social control. He severely condemns the modes of control established under the League of Nations, for "under the administration of the civil servants of the power exercising the 'sacred trust,' notorious abuses have cropped out." Indeed, "in the islands of Samoa the Chinese are said to be working in practical slavery, and on an unjustifiable pretext the Hottentots in former German Southwest Africa have been massacred." The Mandate system established by the imperialistic, colonial powers, he continues, has clearly led to grave abuses. But there is an alternative which can prevent such abuses, while still securing an expanded international investment market: "a consortium policy, ought to be adopted from the outset for the purpose of dealing with backward countries." Why? Because "under the consortium it becomes theoretically possible to decide whether or not a borrowing government is sufficiently representative of the people to justify support, and to establish definite provision, requiring that the loan be used for development projects of general social benefit." This requires, according to Lasswell, "the provision of some means by which all states wishing to participate may do so as of right. . . . If many nations are represented [in a consortium] it may be expected that the wider clash of interests will check the aggressiveness of the few, make for publicity of deliberations, and give the liberal sentiment of the world an opportunity for bringing pressure to bear on behalf of weak peoples" (pp. 399, 397, 398).[21] In the name of the liberal sentiment of the world, unqualified by the use of quotation marks or other caveats, Lasswell calls for the exercise of substantial social control "on behalf of weak peoples." Again, the principles of positive liberalism call for protection of the "have-nots" against exploitation by the "haves."

Further insight into the principles of Lasswell's positive liberalism is provided by an article in which he deals with the social problem that has been of greatest concern to him throughout his career, securing international amity. In discussing the problem of "Prussian Schoolbooks and International Amity" in 1925, he reminds us that " 'the reconciliation of peoples' became one of the official ends of German education when . . . the Constitution of

---

unacceptable to him. Thus his proposals do "not rest upon any assumption as to the inherent superiority of western civilization; it rests content with assuming its apparent inevitability" (p. 398). But neither does Lasswell rest long on the notion of historical inevitability, as we shall observe in the subsequent discussion of his formulation of the thesis of historical materialism.

[21] Even so, grants Lasswell, disagreements may arise, in which event "it appears equitable, also, that disputes arising over the interpretation of the contract negotiated between the consortium and the borrowing state should be subject to automatic arbitration before the International Court of Justice . . ." (p. 399).

1919 was accepted." [22] He accordingly undertook an extensive and penetrating analysis of Prussian schoolbooks "with the express purpose of searching out any material which might be regarded as dangerous for international reconciliation. . . ." His investigations were specifically designed "to uncover anything which presents any foreign nation or all foreign nations as an enemy; which puts foreigners in an unfavorable light; which exalts war by glorifying military heroes and military successes; which tends to feed national vanity by direct or strongly implied assertions of superiority." The tenor of Lasswell's questions are, for present purposes, more important than his findings, which may be simply summarized. "It is only fair to say that these German reading books are, on the whole, quite free from matter which perils international understanding" (p. 720). It is worth noting in passing that this study represents Lasswell's initial experiment with the technique which has come to be termed "content analysis." The claims made here in behalf of this technique are quite modest, and there is no great concern with methodological complexities. The author explains merely that "an attempt is made in every case to indicate by some quantitative measurement the importance of the item to which reference is made" (p. 718).[23] None of the quantitative measurements are reproduced, nor do they appear to have been utilized in formulating the study's conclusions. These conclusions are invariably expressed in distinctly qualitative terms and in a vocabulary familiar to the citizen and statesman, who, presumably, are most directly concerned with them. For example, in speaking of the Treaty of Versailles, Lasswell maintains that "when a controversial subject is touched upon at all, it is absolutely essential to insist that both sides of the question be given, and to condemn a one-sided effort to create a festering sense of injustice in the minds of the young by hateful insinuation and underhanded innuendo" (p. 721). Such judgments are expressed throughout the study, often in such familiar terms as "proper balance," "entire objectivity," and a "nice sense of proportion." While the perspective within which these judgments are made remains that of a liberal citizen-reformer, Lasswell manifests growing doubts about the capacity of the citizen-statesman to deal with the social tensions that give rise to the deadly malady of war. This concern with the problem of effective social control leads him to call for the assistance of like-minded social scientists:

It is important for the cause of international reconciliation that a method be worked out and an appropriate organization be set up for the critical comparison of the textbooks of the nations of the world. The writer of the present article in-

[22] Harold D. Lasswell, "Prussian Schoolbooks and International Amity," *Journal of Social Forces*, May 1925, p. 718.
[23] Lasswell notes that "the investigator used a rather elaborate method for keeping his records as detailed and objective as possible, but it is beyond the scope of the present article to give anything more than the end results."

vites correspondence from those interested in the technical or the material sides of this problem [p. 722, n. 11].

This plea points to a decisively important aspect of Lasswell's work: social control through science. Throughout his career, he has become increasingly preoccupied with the techniques for realizing such control, while affording less concern to the delineation of the goals themselves. It is only in his early writings that he describes these goals at any length, and, as we have seen, the results are not altogether satisfactory even here. It is clear, however, that Lasswell's initial motivation was supplied by a citizen's concern with the achievement of a more just and stable social order. The manner in which he identifies and addresses himself to these political issues, even his vocabulary, is characteristically that of the citizen, or, more precisely, the citizen-reformer. This may be characterized as a pre-scientific, or, in his terms, a pre-"systematic" understanding of politics, within which methodological and terminological considerations remain subordinate to political concerns.[24] Each of the early writings examined thus far reveals an observed or implied conflict between the "haves" and the "have-nots." Lasswell does not neglect to take note of the claims of the "haves," but he appears to be more immediately and deeply impressed by the claims of the "have-nots." [25] His suggestions for the resolution of these conflicts invoke standards of community welfare, domestic or international as the case may be, but these standards remain rather general in character. His substantive political objectives may be summarized as a plea for greater equality, freedom from various forms of economic exploitation, and the minimization of social strife through intelligent social action designed to maximize the welfare of the many and reduce human suffering.[26] Lasswell's political objectives, as revealed by his early writings, are those of the humanistic, liberal American citizen of a broadly Wilsonian persuasion.

Neither in his early writings nor at any subsequent point in his career has Lasswell submitted these political goals to sustained analysis, though they have, in one form or another, remained the axiomatic objectives of his social

[24] See below, pp. 316 ff.
[25] For Lasswell's most thoroughgoing consideration of the problem of economic monopoly and some of its social implications, see his two studies carried out under the auspices of the Committee for Economic Development: *World Politics Faces Economics* (New York: McGraw-Hill Book Co., Inc., 1945), esp. pp. 87 ff.; and *National Security and Individual Freedom* (New York: McGraw-Hill Book Co., Inc., 1950), pp. 70 ff.
[26] There is some connection between Lasswell's liberalism and Utilitarianism, as he, himself, occasionally suggests. This theme remains largely undeveloped in his work, as do most questions that point to political philosophy. See below, pp. 300-304. For some of Lasswell's major hints on this connection, see especially, *Power and Society*, p. 61, n. 6; and *Power and Personality* (New York: W. W. Norton & Company, Inc., 1948), p. 240, where he writes that "under the impact of behaviorism the older 'pleasure-pain' postulate is often rephrased as 'abolishing stimuli' in modern systems of psychology. Unconscious as well as conscious dimensions are included, and in this way equivalency is achieved with the Benthamite 'calculus of felicity.' "

science. Being unconcerned with political philosophy, the discipline through which he might have analyzed these objectives, he turned rather toward the problem of their scientific realization. Indeed, the defect of the older liberalism, in Lasswell's view, lay not so much in insufficient clarity about its objectives as in its failure to grasp the necessity for positive governmental action based on a new and more adequate political science. From his analysis of domestic and international political issues, Lasswell early concluded that the doctrines of that flourishing liberalism which informed and directed world transformations for over a century had languished and fallen into disrepute. Not only had the doctrines of the nineteenth century, or negative liberalism, failed to eliminate political strife, they had come to stand in the way of effective social reconstruction. The resounding defeat of Wilsonianism on the world scene, and in American domestic politics as well, provides a focal point for understanding Lasswell's dissatisfaction with the older liberalism.

I do not need to remind you of the tragic end of the last war, of the concessions reluctantly given by President Wilson in the hope of saving an instrument of permanent rehabilitation, and of how even this instrument was struck from his hand and from that of his successors. Today we believe in the positive and permanent role of America in the world.[27]

The League of Nations did not insure the peace, nor was it able to liberate the subject peoples of the world from their nondemocratic, imperial masters. Why did the League fail in its progressive mission of liberation and democratization? Because of the failure, argues Lasswell, of the "so-called Liberals of the modern world" to understand that government in the twentieth century must no longer submit to business domination or maintain neutrality toward the "dollar exporters."

It is fatuous to bemoan the fact that "politics interferes with business" and demand the "emancipation of business from politics," for when maladjustments in a social situation are due to a particular balance of forces, political or economic, the only recourse is to work for a more adequate adjustment of these forces, not for their abolition.[28]

It follows that removal of trade restrictions, laissez faire in industry, and nonintervention in international relations do not constitute adequate policy. The "Cobden dream of evolutionary progress to world fraternity and democracy in one big market has been rudely interrupted. It has been interrupted by the fact of giant private monopoly and the fact of global war, neither of which were foreseen or explained." In short, while "the ideal of human dignity is positive, it entered the stage of the large-scale modern state clad in the

[27] Harold D. Lasswell, "The Communications Front: Strategies of Political and Moral Warfare," Vital Speeches of the Day, October 1, 1942, p. 763.
[28] Journal of Political Economy, June 1923, p. 400.

scanty garments of negativism. Private businessmen were out to get government out of the market." [29]

Negative liberalism has failed. Mounting crises of depression and war have given rise to destructive strife on both the domestic and international scene. Such are the political facts of our time, as reported by Lasswell, and these facts cry out for positive governmental action. Still, can the demands of positive liberalism be met through the tenets of orthodox democratic theory? Can traditional democratic practices and institutions provide adequate solutions to the pressing problems of the twentieth-century world? Lasswell remarks that "as long as the democrats were in opposition, they were free to belabour the fact of an infallible though almighty king with the fantasy of an all-wise public. Enthrone the public and dethrone the king! Pass the sceptre to the wise!" [30] Yet, the democratic public has hardly proved to be "all-wise," finds Lasswell, and the sanguine expectations of an earlier day have gradually given way to a spirit of critical evaluation of democratic theory and practice. Along with other thoughtful or impatient liberals, Lasswell has accordingly been led to seek the causes of the shortcomings of democracy. While agreeing in substantial measure with the diagnosis suggested by certain friendly critics of democracy, he differs markedly with respect to the cure. The key ingredients in his own prescription are incisively presented in his review of Walter Lippmann's famous work, *The Phantom Public*, which merits quotation in its entirety.

When Walter Lippmann wrote on the problem of public opinion in politics in 1922 he concluded that controversial questions ought to be threshed out before government commissions in order that "a public opinion in the eulogistic sense of the term might exist" (*Public Opinion*, p. 405). Today he doubts whether a public opinion can ever deserve a eulogy. "I set no great store on what can be done by public opinion and the action of the masses" (*Phantom Public*, p. 199). He now says that the public is incompetent to decide with wisdom and justice upon the substance of policy, because it is doomed to act from outside upon those who have inside knowledge and responsibility. The public should not concern itself with settling disputes according to what it thinks right; it ought to recognize its own incapacity for substantive choice, and to favor those who conform to a procedure.

"For the purpose of social action, reasonable behavior is conduct which follows

[29] Harold D. Lasswell, "The Prospects of Cooperation in a Bipolar World," *University of Chicago Law Review,* Summer 1948, p. 900; and "Policy and the Intelligence Function," in Daniel Lerner (ed.), *Propaganda in War and Crisis* (New York: George W. Stewart, 1951), p. 56. This article is reprinted from *Ethics,* October 1942, where its title was "Ideological Intelligence and Public Policy," and it is also reprinted, but not in its entirety, in *The Analysis of Political Behaviour* (London: Routledge & Kegan Paul Ltd, 1948), pp. 120-131.
[30] Harold D. Lasswell, *Propaganda Technique in the World War* (New York: Alfred A. Knopf, Inc., 1927), p. 4. This work was reprinted in 1938 (New York: Peter Smith), with identical pagination.

a settled course whether in making the rule, in enforcing it or in amending it." "It is the task of the political scientist to devise the methods of sampling and to define the criteria of judgment. It is the task of civic education in a democracy to train the public in the use of these methods. It is the task of those who build institutions to take them into account." (P. 145.)

It is superfluous to pay lengthy tribute to the cogent and spirited qualities of this tract. Mr. Lippmann amply sustains his reputation as a creative thinker about the fundamental nature of democracy, and the fact that his conclusions fly in the face of accepted dogma gives them new pith and point. There is some reason for believing, however, that if he has succeeded in escaping from the ditch in which the orthodox democrat flounders, it has been to fall into it again farther upstream. He begins with the very sound proposition that it is not good to demand more from the public than it can reasonably be expected to perform. "The ideal of the omnicompetent, sovereign citizen is, in my opinion, such a false ideal. It is unattainable. The pursuit of it is misleading. The failure to achieve it has produced the current disenchantment" (p. 39). What he has done has been to picture the public as spasmodic, superficial, and ignorant, and then he has proceeded in his constructive prescriptions to exhort this wreck to exercise the superlatively difficult virtue of self-restraint. He says that it should disinterest itself from the substantive content of policies and confine its participation to the reading of signs to determine whether certain procedures have been observed.

Now the plain facts are that the public (or more properly the plurality of publics) is marked by active sentiments and conceptions about right and wrong, the desirable and the undesirable, and that part of its essence is to opinionate about policies, projects, and panaceas. That the total number of issues about which this is true is likely to be exaggerated by the orthodox democrat may be admitted; but that Mr. Lippmann can hope for any fundamental change in the state of affairs by exhorting the public to quit meddling when it feels an impulse to interfere is to set out upon a crusade which has no prospect of consummation within a predictable future.

Mr. Lippmann seems to flinch from drawing the conclusions to which the logic of his own brilliant studies into the nature of opinion seems to lead. Inasmuch as the public verdict is "made to depend on who has the loudest or the most entrancing voice, the most skilful or the most brazen publicity man, the best access to the most space in the newspapers," as he said in *Public Opinion* (p. 401), it would seem that those who want to control the public in the interest of what they conceive to be sound policy ought to outbrazen the rest. If the intelligentsia and the academics shrink at first from participating in or supporting such a continuing body of agitation, and if they have erected this infirmity into a taboo, it is perhaps easier to overcome this taboo of a minority than to remold the entire electorate in the patterns of restraint.

Sign systems and intelligence bureaus may help the few to make up their own minds, but the mobilization of the many depends upon other means.[31]

Lasswell does not flinch from drawing the conclusions to which Lippmann's reflections are said to point. Disagreement on important political issues, he

[31] *American Journal of Sociology*, January 1926, pp. 533-535. (Copyright 1926 by the University of Chicago.) See above, p. 49, n. 73.

reiterates, is "marked by active sentiments and conceptions about right and wrong, the desirable and the undesirable. . . ." Such questions require careful and mature reflection; but, if the public is, in fact, "spasmodic, superficial, and ignorant," then it is foolish—even dangerous—"to exhort this wreck to exercise the superlatively difficult virtue of self-restraint." Can one, Lasswell asks, reasonably expect such political partisans as union leaders, capitalists, or dedicated pacifists voluntarily to disengage themselves from direct, active involvement in politics and permit political control to be exercised by others?

Lasswell's critique of Lippmann's reflections on democratic theory points him to further delineation of the ultimate objective of the systematic student of politics—social control. The passing request for scholarly assistance in the task of international reconciliation, noted in the study of Prussian schoolbooks, is here expanded into the suggestion that "those who want to control the public in the interest of what they conceive to be sound policy ought to outbrazen the rest." The reluctance of the "intelligentsia and the academics," who erect the infirmity of democracy into a taboo, must be overcome if "the many" are to be properly guided in our mass democracies of the twentieth century. "Democracy has proclaimed the dictatorship of palaver, and the technique of dictating to the dictator is named propaganda." [32] "Propaganda" in this context is not to be understood in the vulgar sense of "the making of deliberately one-sided statements to a mass audience," [33] although Lasswell does use the word both in this popular, narrow sense and as a summary expression of the search for effective social control. This "management ideal" does not consist in the attempt to " 'put something over,' but to find out what will stay put in social practice," to find solutions to the pressing social tensions and conflicts of the twentieth-century world.

> With respect to those adjustments which do require mass action the task of the propagandist is that of inventing goal symbols which serve the double function of facilitating adoption and adaption. The symbols must induce acceptance spontaneously and elicit those changes in conduct necessary to bring about permanent adaptation. The propagandist as one who creates symbols which are not only popular but which bring about positive realignments of behavior is no phrasemonger but a promoter of overt acts.[34]

Lasswell here exposes most clearly the nerve of his entire work. It is veritably from this locus that one is obliged to trace every major aspect of his construction. The all too common misunderstanding of Lasswell's work—that

[32] Harold D. Lasswell, "The Theory of Political Propaganda," *American Political Science Review*, August 1927, p. 631.
[33] See Harold D. Lasswell, "Propaganda and Mass Insecurity," *Psychiatry*, August 1950, p. 284.
[34] Harold D. Lasswell, "Propaganda," *Encyclopedia of the Social Sciences* (New York: The Macmillan Company, 1934), vol. XII, p. 527. To be referred to later in the text as *Ency. Soc. Sci.*, XII.

its chief concern is with methodology, that it is unintelligible, that it is in-consistent—stems from the failure of his readers to relate its different parts to this central theme. The ultimate responsibility is not Lasswell's, for a careful consideration of the entire body of his writings can hardly fail to reveal the central significance of propaganda and the propagandist.

LASSWELL'S POLITICAL SOCIOLOGY

A NEW SCIENCE OF POLITICS

Lasswell contends that the effective propaganda required for the achievement of the goals of positive liberalism depends upon science. Specifically, it de-pends upon bringing the findings of a broad array of contemporary social sciences—sociology, history, economics, psychology—to bear in the analysis of the political facts of our day. These developing social sciences must replace the outdated and inadequate American political science which has provided the ideological foundations of traditional or negative liberalism. In order to understand the character of Lasswell's propaganda and the new social science on which it rests, we must first consider his criticisms of the traditional po-litical science which it is intended to replace.

According to Lasswell, "the vocabulary of American public life is legal, ethical, and theological, rather than analytical; and, where it is analytical, it is personal and partisan rather than impersonal" (*World Politics and Per-sonal Insecurity*, p. 214). These deficiencies are said to stem from the fact that "the United States has been relatively free from the play of the inter-national and of the interclass balance of power"; they are also "partly assign-able to the belated struggle over slavery."

The problems arising from the institution of slavery on the plantation preoccupied Americans at the time when modern industrial capitalism was making its bow on the world stage. The struggle over the position of the slave distracted the atten-tion of Americans from the class implications of modern industrialism by creating a united front of employers and wage earners against the plantation owner. . . .

The polemics of the slavery controversy were legalistic, ethical, and theological. No one succeeded in injecting into the vocabulary of the time a full-blown eco-nomic analysis of all social institutions, laying bare the role of modern industrial-ism in driving a wedge between capital and labor. The symbol of the proletariat or of the bourgeoisie was eclipsed by language about plantation owners, freemen, and slaves. Since to the northern factory worker the slave was somebody who was black and Southern, the ringing call of the Communist Manifesto awoke but a feeble echo on this side of the water, where factory hands were identified with their employers in a common crusade against the slave system [p. 216].

The upshot of the parochialism, moralism, and legalism of American public life and social science is that Americans have had "no book that performed the role of intellectual orientation which has been played by *Das Kapital* in Europe. Almost the only legacy from the political past of the United States is the *Federalist*," which, according to Lasswell, "repeats the classical language about the rich and poor, but rises to no masterly heights of analysis of the peculiar formations of emergent capitalism. This new and portentous phenomenon thus remains verbally 'uncontrolled' " (p. 217). This persistent theme is reiterated more broadly in the *Politics*, where Lasswell finds that the "non-Marxist literature on government and administration has tended to minimize the elite consequences of institutional practices by considering relative 'efficiency' or by using universalistic terms like 'liberty' or 'obedience' " (*Politics*, p. 216).[35] While American social scientists have lagged behind, some thinkers in Europe have been "coming to grips with the momentous changes in its technique of production, and forming a vocabulary capable of designating the new world generated by these innovations. . . ." Social phenomena in Europe have been subjected to the "corrosive sublimate of historical materialism," which "reduces all the traditional gods to puppets by exposing the wires which lead to the profit makers" (pp. 217, 215). Marxism rejects, as does Lasswell, "the ideology of the ruling elements of the West." "The ideologies of the nonsocialist world have been in a bruised and battered condition in recent times." They have "offered no coherent explanation of big-scale war or big-scale monopoly," and "have been unequal to the task of arriving at a consensus on the nature of the historical process in which they find themselves." [36] On the other hand, the Marxist forecast gained in influence as it grew in plausibility:

For a century a war for the minds of men has been fought in the name of Marxism against feudalism and capitalism. For a century Marxist analysis has been vilified and denied; and yet the plausibility of the socialist diagnosis has borne itself in upon more and more men and women the world over.

This is not solely attributable to zealous propaganda. The Marxist analysis has won its way because it has seemed to be vindicated by so many facts.

For instance, Marxists take credit for having made the forecast that crises of

[35] Lasswell notes in *World Politics and Personal Insecurity*, p. 4, n., that the "modern conceptions of the 'elite' and of 'ideology' derive from the Marxist literature as critically elaborated by Sorel, Max Weber, and Pareto." See also Harold D. Lasswell, *World Revolutionary Propaganda* (New York: Alfred A. Knopf, Inc., 1939), pp. 9-10, n. 12. Cf. the view of David Easton ("Harold Lasswell; Policy Scientist for a Democratic Society," *The Journal of Politics*, August 1950, p. 463, n. 28), who argues that "Lasswell consciously adopts [Pareto's] elitist principles of analysis as an alternative to quasi-Marxist class analysis." The adequacy of Easton's view may best be judged by considering the fact that Lasswell devotes virtually an entire chapter of the *Politics* under the heading of "Class" to a discussion which must be understood as nothing other than "quasi-Marxist class analysis." Furthermore, Lasswell has seen no difficulty in drawing on *both* Marx and Pareto in his discussion of those "World Revolutions" "which inaugurate new principles of elite recruitment and new reigning ideologies in the political life of humanity" (*World Politics and Personal Insecurity*, p. 4).
[36] *University of Chicago Law Review*, Summer 1948, pp. 878, 900.

unemployment would get graver. Who is to deny that this is, to say the least, plausible? Marxists take credit for forecasting that private monopolies would become steadily more powerful in capitalistic countries. And who, in view of international cartels and the history of our Antitrust Act, will assert that this is wholly fantastic? Marxists also take credit for the assertion that businessmen, when they feel threatened by proletarian leaders, will support the liquidation of democracy. And who, with Italian fascism, German nazism and Spanish falangism in mind, will declare that this has nothing to support it? [*Power and Personality*, pp. 179-180]

CONFIGURATIVE ANALYSIS

Valuable as Marxism appears to be for understanding the political facts of our time, Lasswell finds it insufficient in certain respects and erroneous in others. Although he has never attempted a detailed critique of Marxism, he does reject certain of its tenets, and he revises still others by incorporating them into "configurative analysis." Configurative analysis, it will be recalled, consists "in the adoption of *contemplative* and *manipulative attitudes* toward political change," and "in the use of concepts of *development* and *equilibrium*" as well (*World Politics and Personal Insecurity*, p. 5). It is to the latter two concepts that we must now direct attention.

The application of equilibrium analysis may be most clearly seen in *World Politics and Personal Insecurity* and the famous work based on it, *Politics: Who Gets What, When, How.* In the latter book, Lasswell describes in exhaustive detail the respective amounts of "*deference, income, and safety*" and other "values" enjoyed by various elites at different times (*Politics*, pp. 13 ff). He expends considerable effort and ingenuity in constructing and manipulating the seemingly limitless categories of equilibrium analysis. For example, we are told that "shifts in the volume and distribution of values are affected by overt acts of conscious *striving*, like fighting, negotiating, adjudicating, persuading, boycotting, rewarding, or propagandizing." Furthermore, "since these overt acts," in turn, "are modified by the particular *symbols* with which they are associated, the scope of political inquiry" in the form of equilibrium analysis "must be broadened to include such symbols. Fighting, spending, and ceremonial conduct are affected by the spread of identifying symbols like 'nation,' 'state,' 'class,' 'race,' 'church.'" Finally, "the growth of demands, as for 'security,' 'equality,' and 'supremacy,' has some effect on what is sought in the name of symbols of identification" (*World Politics and Personal Insecurity*, p. 7). Equilibrium analysis, which describes these manifold interactions, is an unending task of the social scientist, for modern societies are in constant flux.

Nevertheless, although equilibrium analysis occupies a substantial portion of Lasswell's work, the data that it provides are seen by him to be essentially static and inconclusive. For that matter, equilibrium analysis goes little beyond the "idle and rather misleading" conflict metaphor, which, despite its popularity among many social scientists, provides nothing more than an "approximately accurate picture" of the way in which events may be conceived at a given time. "But this static version of events at one phase is no explanation of how they came to pass," [37] or where they are going. The data of equilibrium analysis acquire substantial significance for Lasswell only as they are subjected to developmental analysis.

In developmental analysis Lasswell seeks that historical orientation, the lack of which has constituted one of the alleged defects of American social science. It is here, too, that "the systematic student of politics" lays the basis for prediction that is "a preliminary to control." The political cause of "positive liberalism" depends upon such historical orientation, for even the best-intentioned social action is doomed to failure if it is out of harmony with the "trends" of its historical epoch. But a fundamental question immediately presents itself; namely, whether a scientific analysis of history is possible, or whether it can provide the basis for prediction. Lasswell replies in the affirmative, though with considerable qualification.

The attention of one who wishes to analyze social relationships must play back and forth continually between the events that have receded into history, and to the future events destined to become history.... His problem is to characterize the significant social structures of the future as well as the past, since, after all, future and past are only aspects of one and the same comprehensive, overlapping manifold. For if the future were not according to its *nature*, a new edition of the past, and thereby a partial manifestation of a cosmic repetitive compulsion, a critical thinker would probably never solve his problem and never become oriented in the future, even with the help of developmental constructs which he has obtained from the past. Possibly an examination of the past in the perspective of developmental constructs will provide the key to understanding the outcome of conflicting social movements; of antithetical structures, which might in the course of time be identified as the most likely ones; but it is completely inadmissible to assume, as Marx did, that historical examples of a change through "development by leaps and bounds" [dialectical change?] allows us to generalize a scientific law of change for inevitable future development.[38]

[37] Harold D. Lasswell, "The Function of the Propagandist," *International Journal of Ethics*, April 1928, pp. 267-268.
[38] Harold D. Lasswell, "Psychoanalyse und Sozioanalyse," *Imago*, 1933, no. 3, p. 377, italics supplied. The foregoing translation and others below from the same article have been checked for accuracy by Professor Lasswell. Lasswell's argument would appear to be consistent with what Marx and Engels wrote of the possible outcome of past class warfare. For example, there is the famous passage in Part I of the *Communist Manifesto* in which Marx and Engels, describing the history of class struggles, find that the fight between oppressor and oppressed culminates "either in a revolutionary reconstitution of society at large, or in the common ruin of the contending classes" (Part I, 2d paragraph, italics supplied). Lasswell argues that Marx and Engels may have been mistaken in their forecast that the class struggle between bourgeoisie and proletarians would end in the inevitable victory of the world proletariat because the "possibility was overlooked that the terrific

Lasswell agrees with Marxism in postulating historical uniformities, but he takes issue with what he understands to be the claim of dialectical and historical materialism to provide an absolute law of historical prediction. Postponing consideration of Lasswell's criticism of the Marxist dialectic, we may note here his argument that one reason for Marx's exaggerated claim is his failure to consider that "in forecasting human affairs a factor enters which is absent from predictions about non-human relations" (*The World Revolution of Our Time*, p. 4). The very act of prediction introduces the now familiar problem of the self-fulfilling or self-denying prophecy. Historical insight may affect future conduct, inasmuch as it changes the context of action "by altering the current meaning. Since the laws of social relations are about meanings, they are subject to change *with* notice (with insight)." Historical forecasts or predictions cannot be properly characterized as fully scientific in view of the indeterminism which stems from human choice. Strict prediction must give way to what Lasswell terms probability hypotheses, or "developmental constructs." These constructs rest on a foundation which is provided by developmental analysis (pp. 4-5), and we must consider this foundation at some length.

Through developmental analysis Lasswell attempts to relate equilibrium data "to tentatively held conceptions of the elite-symbol changes [changes in the ruling class and its ideology] toward which or away from which events are moving," especially such events as those "world revolutions . . . which inaugurate new principles of elite recruitment and new reigning ideologies in the political life of humanity" (*World Politics and Personal Insecurity*, pp. 5, 4). Lasswell does not find it necessary for his purposes to extend this consideration of history to the nonwestern world, geographically, or beyond the feudal period, temporally. Within these limits he identifies the historical movements and trends which have progressively modified the justification for rule "from the 'divine right of kings' to the 'rights of man,' from the 'rights of man' to the 'proletarian dictatorship.'" These are said to "have been the principal vocabulary changes in the political history of the modern world" (*Politics*, pp. 114-115). Stated in somewhat different terms, Lasswell's historical analysis proceeds through the identification of certain focal points in history, which parallel those of classical Marxist analysis. France is said to have been "the center of a world revolutionary upheaval in 1789 and the years following." Again, "in 1917 Russia was the seat of another world revolutionary transformation, this time in the name of the world 'proletariat' against the world 'bourgeoisie' (and feudality)" (*Power and Society*, p. 282). Through the revolution in France "the monarchical system was

tempo of technoscientific expansion would put the controlling few on opposite sides of frontiers and unleash a war in which the globe itself would vanish or both warring power constellations would suffer unprecedented losses (two Carthages; not one Rome)" (*Power and Personality*, p. 211).

liquidated," [39] and the hold of those who ruled from hereditary seats of power in caste-bound societies was severely shaken as "the masses were organized around the symbols of democratic nationalism and sought emancipation from dynasticism and feudalism" (*World Politics and Personal Insecurity*, p. 120). The new elite which then arose is sometimes identified by Lasswell as the upper bourgeoisie. Although it ruled "in the name of the rights of man," it is seen in fact as representing a plutocracy, an elite skilled in bargaining (*Politics*, p. 115). Businessmen especially have been the dominant element in the ruling elites during the period of democratic nationalism. "Policies favorable to the growth of commerce and industry were instituted by rearranging the system of tariff and taxation. Individual proprietorship was encouraged by transforming peasants into landholders." This world revolutionary movement was subjected to the historical process of diffusion and restriction following its eruption in 1789. The French armies "went charging across the continent of Europe in the name of the universal good." They were followed by the sometimes more subtle agents of economic imperialism and other agencies of "indirect diffusion." Nevertheless, "democratic nationalism" was finally restricted, and thus "fell short of creating a world state, or a world community of states, bound by a common mythology and relinquishing the monopoly of violence to a harmoniously circulating elite." This failure of democratic *nationalism* is of considerable theoretical importance in Lasswell's developmental analysis. What was it, he asks, that underlay the inability of democratic nationalism to create a world state or an effective community of states? "This failure is to be attributed to the dialectical processes arising to block the expansion of authority from any one local area, regardless of the inclusiveness of the symbols used by the authority." Those whose actions were guided by the thesis of democratic nationalism certainly succeeded in creating "many nationalisms and much local democracy," but the very fact of their "partial successes" then operated dialectically to produce antithetical or restrictive forces in the form of "heightened parochialism" (*World Politics and Personal Insecurity*, pp. 120, 122). Thus, while "many details of the French pattern of 'democracy' were adopted and adapted," the net result of this historical epoch was such that the theory, institutions, and practices which were "legitimized in the name of the rights of man" became "cemented in walls of intense nationalistic sentiment" (*Politics*, pp. 116, 115).

Democratic nationalism having run its course, the beginning of a new historical era, our historical era, was signalled by the eruption of a competing world historical movement in Russia in 1917, where "a significant political movement of protest arose in opposition to the property system which had benefitted by democratic nationalism." It was Marxism which "outcompeted

---

[39] Harold D. Lasswell, "The Scope of Research on Propaganda and Dictatorship," in Harwood L. Childs (ed.), *Propaganda and Dictatorship: A Collection of Papers* (Princeton: Princeton University Press, 1936), p. 120.

the 'utopian' socialists and the anarchists, and furnished the dominant language in the name of which counter-elites sought to supersede the established order." The symbols and practices of the revolution of 1917 are said by Lasswell to be undergoing a process of diffusion and restriction which parallels that of the revolution of 1789. Just as the earlier "revolution in the name of humanity is treated as the *French* revolution . . . a revolution in the name of the world proletariat is treated as the *Russian* revolution" (*Politics*, pp. 117, 120). Bipolarization has occurred in space, not by class, thereby bringing into question Marx's prediction of the rise to power of a transnational proletariat. Orthodox Marxism's failure in prediction is seen to stem in part from its inadequate psychology, in particular from its failure to take account of the powerful and deep-seated forces of parochialism.[40] Accordingly, Marx was mistaken in his prediction that the national identifications of the proletarian class would wither away upon exposure to the searing blasts of his transnational ideology. In this respect, Marx showed himself not merely a poor psychologist but, even more importantly, an inadequate student of propaganda.

Lasswell does not rest his criticism of this aspect of the Marxist analysis solely on psychological or propagandistic grounds. He has repeatedly expressed doubts that the revolution of 1917 was "a true 'proletarian' revolution. Did the class consequences of the revolution benefit the whole proletariat as much as it contributed to the rise of certain other class formations?" Lasswell thinks not. He appears instead to take the position that the revolution of 1917 signified the rise of the lesser bourgeoisie, or the "middle-income skill group," as he often terms it. By the same token, he argues that many seemingly incompatible political movements of our historical epoch, including American New Dealism, "would become intelligible" if understood as manifestations of the "same basic process by which all power goes to the lesser bourgeoisie." Even "the struggle of Trotsky against Stalin may have this historical significance" (*Propaganda and Dictatorship*, p. 118).

The common factor in the seeming political confusion of our time is the rise to power of the middle-income skill group. Despite the contraditions and the aberrations of Russian Communism, Italian Fascism, and German National Socialism, a new world-revolution is on the march. In the name of the "proletariat," the middle-income skill groups are rising to power at the expense of aristocracy and plutocracy. This is the larger context against which political developments in the United States are to be understood.[41]

Since Lasswell does not indicate in any coherent fashion the basis for this portion of his developmental analysis, it is difficult to state his teaching here

[40] See below, pp. 252 ff and, especially, *World Politics and Personal Insecurity*, pp. 122 ff.
[41] Harold D. Lasswell, "The Moral Vocation of the Middle-Income Skill Group," *International Journal of Ethics*, January 1935, p. 127.

with precision. He does, however, provide us with a clue in his enthusiastic review [42] of Ruggiero's classic analysis of *The History of European Liberalism*. According to Ruggiero, expressing a view which was subsequently embraced by Lasswell, the crisis of liberalism stemmed from

the increasing growth of new middle classes, equidistant from the great capitalistic *bourgeoisie* and the proletariate, due to the ever-increasing specialization of industrial and agricultural activity, and destined to play a part somewhat analogous to that formerly played by the *bourgeoisie* as a whole in its relation to the aristocracy and the lower classes.[43]

Lasswell includes in these new middle classes, or "the middle-income skill group," engineers, lawyers, government officials, and others who are distinguished from the proletarians primarily by the fact that they possess education. The acquisition of such education involves the sacrifices of immediate enjoyment in behalf of long-range goals, adds Lasswell, hence "there is an inner psychological attitude in common among those who make sacrifices to acquire skill . . ." (*Politics*, pp. 19-20).[44]

Thus Lasswell argues that the world revolution of our time may be understood as "the rise to power of the 'intellectuals' who successfully allied themselves with the manual toilers in their common struggle against the aristocracy and plutocracy" (*Propaganda and Dictatorship*, p. 118).[45] In keeping with the general character and objectives of his positive liberalism, he expresses the hope that the middle-income skill groups can be brought to recognition of their "moral vocation," "to a sense of the reflective and critical value of their own activity, and a recognition of the universal character of their historical mission." [46] The essence of this mission, according to Lasswell, is the realization of the most completely democratic society attainable in the present historical epoch. Although perfect democracy cannot be achieved under present conditions, rule by the middle-income skill group is thought by Lasswell to be far more just than the "dictatorship of the proletariat" prescribed for our historical epoch by classical Marxist analysis. The class warfare demanded by orthodox Marxists would be unnecessary if the middle-income skill groups could overcome their present failure to find unity and a clear-cut understanding of their historical purposes (*World Politics and Personal Insecurity*, p. 7). Effective propaganda may provide the largely peaceful

---

[42] *American Journal of Sociology*, January 1929, pp. 730-731.
[43] Guido de Ruggiero, *The History of European Liberalism* (New York: Oxford University Press, 1927), p. 439.
[44] See *American Journal of Sociology*, November 1932, p. 466.
[45] He adds in the *Politics* that "common resentment against a social order which does not invariably apportion high rewards to skill draws the small professional man, businessman, farmer, and skilled worker away from the social forms which preserve plutocracy" (p. 20).
[46] Ruggiero, *The History of European Liberalism*, p. 440. Cf. Lasswell's appeal to the "intelligentsia and the academics," above, p. 241, and his specific appeal to lawyers, below, pp. 281-282.

means through which the middle-income skill groups can achieve political hegemony,[47] although Lasswell tells us little about the devices through which rule would be attained or exercised.

Lasswell's developmental analysis can carry us no further, for it eschews historical prediction. Speculation about the future is a function of his developmental constructs,[48] through which he attempts peacefully to move mankind toward a social objective that approximates in many ways the ultimate goal of the "radical democrat," as expressed by Engels. As Lasswell puts it:

It should not be denied that the long-run aim of societies aspiring toward human freedom is to get rid of power and to bring into existence a free man's commonwealth in which coercion is neither threatened, applied nor desired. This is the thread of anarchist idealism that appears in all uncompromising applications of the key conception of human dignity. When Engels wrote of the eventual "withering away of the state" he was voicing the hope, though not necessarily the certainty, of the radical democrat. In our day, however, the probability that we can reduce power to the vanishing point seems very remote indeed. The urgent task is to chasten and subordinate power to the service of respect [*Power and Personality*, p. 110].[49]

While it is evident that Lasswell's developmental analysis parallels the findings of orthodox Marxism in substantial measure, it nevertheless differs in certain important respects. The key to both the similarities and the differences may be found in Lasswell's application of the fundamental Marxist concept of historical materialism. Although he finds this concept extremely useful, he accepts it only with a certain restraint and is led to add important modifications. For example, in explaining the existence of "common trends in the development of the major states of the world during our historical period," Lasswell suggests that "growing similarity in the methods of production throughout the world increases the likelihood of similarity in experience, perspective, and institution among the major states." Hence, "modern technology is no longer confined to western Europe and the northeastern United States, and it is improbable that the trend toward dispersion will be reversed. Methods of production determine the division of labor; the division of labor has a profound effect upon the focus of attention, and hence upon experience, perspective, and institution." [50] Again, "large changes in the composition of the elite may be treated as functions of large changes in the prevailing division of labor," since "the probability of elite alterations will be increased if the processes of production have notably altered" (*World Politics*

[47] See below, pp. 274 ff.
[48] See below, pp. 286 ff.
[49] Cf. Marx and Engels, *The German Ideology* (New York: International Publishers Co., Inc., 1947), pp. 22, 70.
[50] Harold D. Lasswell, "Toward a Skill Commonwealth: A Workable Goal of World Politics," in Lyman Bryson, Louis Finkelstein, R. M. MacIver (eds.), *Approaches to Group Understanding* (New York: Harper & Brothers, 1947), p. 290.

and Personal Insecurity, p. 5). Accordingly, the growth of new classes, like the growth of new skills, is intertwined with the appearance of new means of production. "Likelihood," "probable," "profound effect upon," "intertwined with"—it is clear that Lasswell is restrained in his statement and application of the concept of historical materialism. But what are the grounds of this restraint?

Some part of the answer to this question may be discovered by noting Lasswell's emendations to the associated thesis of cultural lag. Though agreeing with classical Marxism that "changes in the division of labor or other nonsymbolic conditions will effect changes in ideology" (*Power and Society*, p. 124), Lasswell insists that "a change in the material environment does not necessarily precipitate immediate awareness of its implications . . ." (*World Politics and Personal Insecurity*, pp. 60 ff). For example, the aforementioned failure of the "middle-income skill group" to achieve its proper position in society stems in part from its having been "the victim of a *psychological* lag behind changes in economic practice." [51] Although the conception and application of the thesis of cultural or psychological lag is not itself in conflict with Marxism, Lasswell's emphasis on "psychological" rather than "cultural" factors points him to a reconsideration of the relationship between material and ideological aspects of society. He is led to challenge as an extreme and oversimplified position the *Communist Manifesto's* characterization of ideology as mere superstructure,[52] while Trotsky is cited with approval for having taken "recognition—'in principle'—of nonenvironmental determinants of behavior" (*Power and Society*, p. 5). Classical Marxism has failed to recognize that "the relations between . . . material and ideological . . . are manifold and complex" (*World Politics and Personal Insecurity*, p. 60). These relations are said to be still insufficiently understood, despite the fact that "the problems of interplay" between them have been "given great currency by the political resonance of Marxist socialism." Marx's failure to understand the relationship between "the psychological and material factors connected with the processes of power" led to his incorrect prediction of the inevitable collapse of capitalism. The sanguine Marxist "prophets of world unity did not attach enough importance to the counter-tendencies which were bound to be stimulated by the very tendencies on which they pinned their hope. In this sense, their thinking was 'undialectical.' " [53]

The crux of Lasswell's criticism of classical Marxism is that it concentrates

---

[51] *International Journal of Ethics*, January 1935, p. 131, italics supplied.
[52] See Part II of the *Communist Manifesto*, where Marx tells the bourgeoisie that "your very ideas are but the outgrowth of the conditions of your bourgeois production and bourgeois property, just as your jurisprudence is but the will of your class made into law for all, a will whose essential character and direction are determined by the economic conditions of existence of your class."
[53] Harold D. Lasswell, "Sino-Japanese Crisis: The Garrison State versus the Civilian State," *China Quarterly*, Fall 1937, p. 647.

attention on economic and historical concerns at the expense of the psychological dimension of human life. This excessive narrowness underlies the failure of Marxism to supply adequate description of the forces at work in society as well as its oversanguine "prophecy." For example, classical Marxism, according to Lasswell, has virtually neglected such psychologically powerful bonds as patriotism. Underestimating the strength of such "identifications," it has mistakenly restricted its analysis of dialectical movement to class conflict. Moreover, it has failed to see that those who would direct society to new goals must actively concern themselves not merely with class conflict but with the reshaping of the human psyche. Classical Marxism has improperly assumed that man's potential rationality was such that his insight at a certain point in historical development would lead him to an understanding of his true situation—the famous claim of the *Communist Manifesto* [54]—and would thereby enable him to pass quickly through the final stage of his "prehistory" into the realm of freedom or the Free Man's Commonwealth. These mistakes suggest to Lasswell the need for "a more adequate frame of reference for the analysis of the social process than the Marxist system was able to provide." [55] Adequate developmental analysis, concludes Lasswell, requires an "intensive" psychological dimension to supplement sociohistorical analysis.

LASSWELL'S POLITICAL PSYCHOLOGY

PSYCHOLOGICAL DIALECTICS

Part of the early impact of Freud was to re-emphasize the importance of personality in the social process, thereby modifying the simple timing conceptions of the kind that had so often misled Marxist prophets of imminent revolution [*The State of the Social Sciences*, p. 113].

Freud's chief significance is that he has pointed the way to "the discovery of *intensive* methods of observation as a supplement to the *extensive* ones." [56] "The psychoanalytical interview which extends over a long period of time is the intensive method. . . ." Today, "thanks to the discoveries of psychoanalysis it is possible . . . to set up a more comprehensive theory of social change," and thereby complete "the dialectic methods of procedure." Proper integration of the psychological element, particularly by one who appreciates the significance of psychoanalysis for a "general theory of a social event," promises a

[54] See Part I of the *Communist Manifesto*, where Marx argues that mankind "is at last compelled to face with sober senses his real conditions of life and his relations with his kind."

[55] Harold D. Lasswell, "Impact of Psychoanalytic Thinking on the Social Sciences," in Leonard D. White (ed.), *The State of the Social Sciences* (Chicago: University of Chicago Press, 1956), p. 112.

[56] *Imago*, 1933, no. 3, p. 377. The similarity of the presentation in this early article and Lasswell's review of the "Impact of Psychoanalytic Thinking on the Social Sciences" in *The State of the Social Sciences* almost twenty-five years later is quite striking.

more "fruitful dialectic relationship between intensive and extensive observation methods. . . ." Lasswell illustrates this as follows:

Psychoanalysis has greatly increased our knowledge of the dialectic relationship between the symbols. Changes in the economic situation modify the distribution of labor, shift the focus of attention of many people and thus hasten the changes in their egos, which for their part again determine the economic relations of the superego and the id.[57]

While the addition of a psychological dimension increases the complexity of the Marxian dialectic, its usefulness, if any, cannot be ascertained until one determines more precisely the meaning of the Freudian terminology. Assistance is furnished by Lasswell's article entitled "The Triple-Appeal Principle: A Dynamic Key."[58] Here he reports that Freud, "the epochal figure" in the development of psychoanalysis, has divided the personality "into three main divisions." These divisions, along with their Freudian names and general connotations, may be indicated as follows:

"socially acquired inhibitions"	superego	conscience — mores
"testing of reality"	ego	reason — expediences
"biological needs"	id	impulse — countermores

According to Lasswell, "the meaning of any social object to any particular person is to be interpreted in terms of its appeal to one or more of these main divisions." The "essential principle" is that "prolonged ego and super-ego indulgence produces redefinitions in directions gratifying to the id; prolonged ego and id indulgence produces redefinitions in directions gratifying to the super-ego" (*The Analysis of Political Behaviour*, pp. 181, 180, 194).

The social application of this principle involves the search for "the dialectical process through which uniformities may be developed from dissimilarities," that is to say, an inquiry into "how the existing differences in ideology and in material situation can be transmuted into ideological and material uniformity" (*World Politics and Personal Insecurity*, p. 128). In keeping with this objective, Lasswell attempts to analyze the psychological implications of the Marxist ideology itself. He finds that "the Marxist symbolism" provides "the most rapidly growing body of unifying mythology. For seventy-five years Marxism has been spreading over the earth," so that "Marxism is today the strongest protest symbolism with revolutionary demands and

[57] *Imago*, 1933, no. 3, p. 381. He adds that "since the complexity of these interrelations was not fully comprehended by Marx, the time periods which might be concerned with a possible appearance of socialism were always underestimated." This appears to explain the meaning of Lasswell's phrase "simple timing conceptions," and is another statement, one gathers, of the concept of cultural or psychological lag.
[58] In *The Analysis of Political Behaviour*, pp. 180-194. It is reprinted from the *American Journal of Sociology*, January 1932, where the title is "The Triple-Appeal Principle: A Contribution of Psychoanalysis to Political and Social Science."

universal claims." Application of psychological dialectics to the successful spread of Marxism reveals that at the level of the superego it has presented a challenge to the mores, or socially acquired inhibitions, of precapitalistic or capitalistic countries. "In common with all emancipation symbolism, Marxism inflicts deprivations (attacks, 'castrations') upon the symbols and practices of constituted authority. . . ." Such attacks take advantage of those characteristic "ambivalences toward authority" which have often been revealed by psychoanalysis. This Marxist attack on the mores is supplemented at the level of the ego by "an elaborate theory of history and social change," thereby introducing considerations of expediency, which appeal to the reason. Furthermore, the Marxist castigation of capitalist society as immoral, dehumanizing, and inequitable finds support within the id by appealing "to some of the deepest impulses in the personality." It "implies the violation by the social environment of the 'implied social contract' by which the child renounces the direct gratification of his impulses on the tacit promise of ultimate gratification" (pp. 128-129, 130, 133 ff).

Having effectively destroyed the hold of the mores and released the forces of the countermores within the id, Marxism attempts to provide symbols for new identifications. Its success in this quest is again governed by the complex "dialectical relations between material and ideological conditions" (p. 128). Whatever the outcome of its application within the Soviet Union,[59] its chances elsewhere are seen to be heightened by several noteworthy characteristics, especially the "scientific" form which it assumes, its claims to "objectivity," and its all-encompassing, though vague, formulation of the future society.[60] This very "ambiguity of the future frees the omnipotence cravings of the individual," while the "vagueness of the classless society symbol permits it to take on color according to the deeper yearnings for the reinstatement of that happy time in infancy when one was the center of the world . . ." (p. 134).

There is evidently a provocative application of Freudian terminology in the foregoing description. By viewing history through the Freudian as well as the Marxian glass, Lasswell is able to see Marxism itself in its role as myth serving certain psychological functions; he purports to see Marxism more clearly and fully than Marxism could ever see itself. But Lasswell is content to paint with a broad brush. He does not attempt to develop this particular formulation of "psychological dialectics" beyond the foregoing sketch. The well-known case histories of his books *Psychopathology and Politics* and *Power and*

[59] Lasswell is led to comment that "the dialectical analysis of the 'dictatorship of the proletariat' has been neglected by revolutionary theorists" (*World Politics and Personal Insecurity*, p. 128, n. 1). Lasswell's reinterpretation of the meaning of the revolution of 1917 and his middle-income skill group analysis may be understood as one aspect of his attempt to rectify this deficiency in contemporary Marxist analysis.
[60] Cf. Lasswell's formulation for an American *Das Kapital*, below, p. 286, n. 107.

Personality, which are based upon intensive psychoanalysis, will be considered later.[61] For the present, it is sufficient to note that these case histories do not carry Lasswell's psychological dialectics beyond the suggestive but scarcely convincing sketch that we have just considered. They do not carry Lasswell from the realm of individual psychoanalysis to a broadly useful social psychology.

There is, one concludes, something in Freudian psychology which resists fusion with the Marxian dialectic. The basic difficulty quickly reveals itself, for it does not require profound reading of Freud's works, especially those in which he explores the philosophical underpinnings of his psychology, to perceive his view that the fundamentally individualistic nature of man stands as an insuperable obstacle to his thoroughgoing socialization. These doubts are most strongly expressed in *Civilization and Its Discontents*, a work which Lasswell, quite understandably, finds "disappointing." A brief consideration of certain theses of this work may assist us in understanding the reason for the disappointment to which Lasswell gives expression in reviewing it for the *American Journal of Sociology*.[62] In the first place, Freud questions the applicability of his psychological concepts, derived as they are from clinical diagnosis and treatment of individuals, to analysis of social problems.

I would not say that such an attempt to apply psycho-analysis to civilized society would be fanciful or doomed to fruitlessness. But it behooves us to be very careful, not to forget that after all we are dealing only with analogies, and that it is dangerous, not only with men but also with concepts, to drag them out of the region where they originated and have matured.[63]

It is quite true that Freud himself makes use of just such analogies in this work and others,[64] but many of these analogical speculations are disappointing to Lasswell. According to Freud, "it can be maintained that the community . . . develops a super-ego, under whose influence cultural evolution proceeds" (*Civilization and Its Discontents*, p. 100). Just as the individual superego is open to criticism for failing "to take into account sufficiently the difficulties in the way of obeying it," so "the same objections can be made against the ethical standards of the cultural super-ego. It, too, does not trouble enough about the mental constitution of human beings; it enjoins a command and never asks whether or not it is possible for them to obey it." The key question of *Civilization and Its Discontents* is "how to dislodge the greatest obstacle to civilization, the constitutional tendency in men to aggressions against one

[61] See below, pp. 263-274.
[62] September 1931, pp. 328-331.
[63] Sigmund Freud, *Civilization and Its Discontents*, trans. Joan Riviere (New York: Doubleday Anchor Books, 1958), pp. 103-104.
[64] See Freud, *Group Psychology and the Analysis of the Ego*, trans. James Strachey (London: Hogarth Press, 1949) and *Totem and Tabu*, trans. James Strachey (New York: Norton, 1952).

another; and for that very reason the commandment to love one's neighbour as oneself—probably the most recent of the cultural super-ego's demands—is especially interesting to us." Although this commandment is "the strongest defense there is against human aggressiveness," it is unfortunately "impossible to fulfil"; and anyone who tries to fulfil it only puts himself at a serious disadvantage. "What an overwhelming obstacle to civilization aggression must be if the defense against it can cause as much misery as aggression itself!" (pp. 101-103) [65] These considerations, as Lasswell points out in his review, lead Freud to put "the fateful question of the human species," namely, "whether and to what extent the cultural process developed in it will succeed in mastering the derangements of communal life caused by the human instinct of aggression and self destruction" (p. 105).

The evident pessimism lying behind this question is unacceptable to Lasswell, who emphatically argues that "although the instinctive nature of man is in principle non-social and in important particulars antisocial, man is capable of socializing his destructive impulses to a very high degree." [66] Lasswell has never entirely abandoned Freudian language, but he has found certain basic elements of the Freudian psychology inadequate. In a 1939 summary of Freud's contribution to the social sciences, he observes that some of Freud's "tentative 'applications' of psychoanalysis to society have already been superseded. . . . His distinctive terminology is already in process of liquidation as his work merges with the broad stream of scientific development." Significantly, "it has been a sociologist with psychoanalytical training who has coped most boldly with the problem of putting the psychoanalytical procedure itself in explicit relationship to the cultural-historical setting in which it originates and survives." Erich Fromm undertakes to demonstrate, according to Lasswell, that Freud's "conscious liberalism of outlook is associated with an unconscious negative preference for those impulses which are tabooed by bourgeois society. Hence Freud is said to stand as the representative of an order of [bourgeois] society which demands obedience to certain specific prohibitions and prescriptions." [67] Just as Freudian psychology can understand the Marxian sociology better than Marxism understands itself, so also, it appears, this psychology requires inspection under the sociological glass.

Freud provided the basic point of departure from which Lasswell has attempted to provide that intensive analysis which he has found lacking in

[65] Freud goes on: " 'Natural' ethics, as it is called, has nothing to offer here beyond the narcissistic satisfaction of thinking oneself better than others. . . . I should imagine that as long as virtue is not rewarded in this life ethics will preach in vain." As we shall see, this is a lesson that Lasswell has taken very much to heart.

[66] Harold D. Lasswell, "Conflict, Social," *Encyclopedia of the Social Sciences*, vol. IV, p. 195. To be referred to later in the text as *Ency. Soc. Sci.*, IV.

[67] "Contribution of Freud's Insight Interview to the Social Sciences," the *American Journal of Sociology*, November 1939, pp. 375, 385.

the Marxian dialectic, but Freud's psychology proved to be of questionable applicability to the social problem—or, if applicable, incapable of providing a satisfactory solution to it. Lasswell has therefore found it necessary to modify the Freudian psychology in order to avoid the pessimistic Freudian conclusion. Following the lead of certain post-Freudian psychologists, Lasswell has sought a more promising social psychology.

In the study of interpersonal relations it is useful to examine the ego for the purpose of discovering "the self system." The self system in turn comprises three main sets of patterns: identifications, demands, expectations. When we refer to ourselves in the privacy of meditation we are aware of such subjective events as feeling a strong sense of "I" or "me" or "we." The primary symbols are the "I," "me," and "Harold Lasswell"; and they are linked with such secondary symbols as "family, friends, neighbors, nation" and the like. The "others" who are included in the "I-me-we system" are part of the identifications belonging to the self system as a whole. The "others" who are not so included are not part of the self.[68]

According to this formulation, men, who are by nature destructive and in important respects antisocial, are attached to one another by means of the largely unexplained and ever so vague mechanism of "identification." We are told only that somehow the primary self system, the "I, me," becomes "linked with such secondary symbols as 'family, friends, neighbors, nation' and the like" in such a way that they become "part of the self system as a whole." Except for "identification," it would seem that this tangle of egoistic spider webs would give rise to nothing but conflict and tension. Yet precisely how competing imperialistic self systems are socialized by identification or how the assumed psychic mechanism of identification is supposed to operate is never explained by Lasswell. Indeed, the concept of identification serves as no more than a restatement of the problem it purports to solve. Lasswell's failure to subject this concept to sustained analysis or to put it to use, except incidentally, may be taken as evidence that it does not really provide the solution to the social or political problem, however useful it may be in a merely descriptive social psychology.[69]

[68] Harold D. Lasswell, *Democratic Character*, in *The Political Writings of Harold D. Lasswell* (New York: The Free Press of Glencoe, Inc., 1951), p. 481. Lasswell notes here that the term "the self system" is that of Harry Stack Sullivan "in his later articles," and that his classification of "identifications, demands and expectations" follows "the general frame of thinking made current by several scholars, notably George Herbert Mead, whose contributions are today receiving such active recognition in the textbooks of social psychology. *The Political Writings of Harold D. Lasswell* will later be referred to in the text as *The Political Writings*.
[69] Herbert Simon's discussion of "identification" is scarcely less rudimentary. See above, pp. 93-95. In *Psychopathology and Politics*, (Chicago: University of Chicago Press, 1930, pp. 242-246, Lasswell does take note of Hans Kelsen's "sharp, and in many ways devastating, criticism" of the foundation of Freud's social psychology, here identified by both Kelsen and Lasswell as the theory of "social 'parallelism.'" The heart of Kelsen's criticism of Freud's theory of "identification" appears to be the telling point that "if one really wished

POLITICIZED PSYCHOLOGY

Another way in which Lasswell attempts to deal with the problem of man's antisociality is by shifting the emphasis from the subjective "instincts" underlying human behavior to the values toward which that behavior is directed —that is to say, to the things that men overtly want and seek. Despite his well-deserved reputation for having introduced Freud to American political science, Lasswell rises rather quickly and often from the murky and unchartable depths of the Freudian unconscious to the surface of human life. Much of the time, he has been concerned with recognizable political phenomena, although this concern is, as we shall observe, only a prelude to his own attempt finally to reach beneath what he takes to be the superficialities of political life for a genuine solution to the political problem.

The general character of Lasswell's politicized psychology may be seen most clearly in his famous *Politics*. This work, which has been mentioned as an outstanding example of Lasswell's "equilibrium analysis," is concerned with the question of "Who Gets What, When, How"—in short, with the distribution of "values" directly sought by mankind. Anything and everything that men want is described by Lasswell as a "value." The first question, then, is what do men want? To this question Lasswell has provided various answers, but running through them all is a common core. His most famous formulation is found in the well-known passage with which he begins the *Politics:*

The study of politics is the study of influence and the influential. . . . The influential are those who get the most of what there is to get. Available values may be classified as *deference, income, safety.* Those who get the most are *elite;* the rest are *mass* [p. 13].

An earlier formulation of the values sought by mankind differs slightly. In a 1931 article on "Social Conflict," he reports that individuals are "always widening or narrowing the sum of their claims on society for life, liberty of movement, property and deference" (*Ency. Soc. Sci.,* IV, p. 194). Here Lass-

---

to consider the state as consisting of a community of consciousness . . . then, in order to avoid inadmissible fictions, one would have only to be consistent enough really to consider the state as formed only by the contents of those whose consciousness had shown the necessary agreement. One would be bound to realize that community of will, feeling or thought, as a psychological group manifestation, fluctuates tremendously at different times and places. In the ocean of psychic happenings, such communities may rise like waves in the sea and after a brief space be lost again in an ever-changing ebb and flow." (Lasswell is here quoting from Kelsen's "The Conception of the State and Social Psychology," *International Journal of Psycho-Analysis,* January 1924, pp. 1-38.) Lasswell attempts to answer this criticism with the argument that the state must be understood as occupying "a time-space manifold of similar subjective events." By thus reintroducing certain of the traditional determinants of the state, namely, temporal span and geographical location, Lasswell inadvertently confirms Kelsen's criticism of the inadequacy of the concept of "identification" or "social 'parallelism.' "

well adds "deference" to the three "claims" that Americans have been taught by John Locke to regard as their natural rights. For reasons he does not specify, Lasswell apparently prefers the formulation of Locke's great predecessor. Discussing the meaning of "deference" or "respect," he explains that "respect is the value of status, of honor, recognition, prestige, the 'glory' or 'reputation' which Hobbes classes with gain and safety as one of the three fundamental human motivations". (*Power and Society*, p. 56). It is in the *Leviathan* that Hobbes writes "that in the nature of man, we find three principal causes of quarrel. First, competition; second, diffidence; thirdly, glory. The first maketh man invade for *gain*; the second, for *safety*; and the third, for *reputation*." [70] Income, safety, deference.

This famous trilogy is expanded on occasion into lists of some six to eight values. In the most extensive, current formulation, as found, for example, in *Democratic Character*, Lasswell finds it "convenient to operate with . . . the following eight terms . . . *power, respect, affection, rectitude, well-being, wealth, skill, enlightenment*" (*The Political Writings*, p. 474). "Equipped with some such list of categories, we are in a position to consider any community according to the old formula: *Who gets what (values) when and how?*" (p. 475) Lasswell hastens to assert the equivalency of the current and the older formulations by adding that "in my *Politics* (1936) . . . I spoke of safety, income and deference as 'representative' values. Safety can be treated as equivalent to well-being, income to wealth, and deference, if desired, to the sub-divided list comprising power, respect, affection, rectitude. This list is still to be taken as 'representative' rather than 'definitive'" (p. 475; n. 20).[71] "Representative." A more ambiguous term could hardly have been chosen: "Representative" in what sense? "Representative" of what? Lasswell never answers these questions "definitively." He deliberately refrains from any attempt at a final statement of human values. Times change, conditions change, men change; and so do the values that men seek. Yet, it is as clear as anything ever is in Lasswell's ambiguous discussion that amidst all this change the desire of men for safety, income, and deference remains fundamental, whatever the specific content of these values at any particular time and place.

The famous question—"who gets what, when, how?"—when applied to the individual is stated by Lasswell in terms of a formula of "indulgence" and "deprivation." Although the formula is put in quasi-psychological terms, it

---

[70] *Leviathan*, i, 13, italics supplied. Hobbes goes on: "The first use violence, to make themselves masters of other men's persons . . . ; the second, to defend them; the third, for trifles, as a word, a smile, a different opinion. . . ." One important contrast between Lasswell and Hobbes lies in their different estimates of the importance of the value of "deference" or "reputation."

[71] This distillation seems to leave out "skill" and "enlightenment," but it is fairly clear from Lasswell's discussion that these are valuable only as instrumental to one of the three basic values.

is important to see its close connection with the political formulation of the *Politics*. To the extent that an individual gains safety, income, and deference, he is "indulged"; to the extent that he fails to secure them, he is "deprived." In short, "indulgence and deprivation are general terms for any improvement or deterioration in value position or potential" (*Power and Society*, p. 61). The relative success or failure of an individual in the quest for value indulgence is formulated by Lasswell as the "Indulgence/Deprivation" or "I/D" ratio. It is not insignificant that Lasswell shifts the terminology of his formulation from that associated with the political arena within which men openly and actively struggle with one another for "safety, income, and deference" to that associated with the psychology laboratory within which passive and controlled organisms are indulged or deprived.[72] In any event, the description rests on an underlying principle which Lasswell terms the "maximization postulate." This proposition asserts that "human activity is self-directed within the limits of capability, on the basis of expected net value advantage." [73] The implications of this view of human activity may be best weighed by examining Lasswell's discussion of that value which seems to fit least comfortably into the "maximization postulate," namely, "rectitude."

It will be recalled that Lasswell suggests that the basic value of "deference" may be considered as consisting of the components of "power, respect, affection, rectitude." In the ordinary understanding of "rectitude," the understanding which reflects the unsophisticated view of ordinary people, rectitude is considered a moral virtue. For example, such men as Lincoln, Wilson, and Gandhi are often described as men of rectitude. The quality of rectitude is ascribed to individuals. Rightly or wrongly, the commonplace understanding of rectitude presupposes an important difference, a difference of intention or motive, between the moral virtue of rectitude and the pursuit of such values as safety, income, and deference. Yet Lasswell lists rectitude as a subdivision of the value "deference." What is Lasswell's understanding of rectitude? In *Power and Society*, the work in which he manifests the greatest concern with clarity and adequacy of definitions, we are told that "*rectitude* comprises the moral virtues—virtue, goodness, righteousness, and so on" (p. 56). Here Lasswell's understanding of rectitude appears to be much like the commonplace understanding. He uses the term remarkably little considering its wide compass, reaching, as it does, concerns of religion, temperance, fortitude, and goodness knows what—a veritable potpourri of moral values. What is more significant, when he does use the term it has a distinctly different significance

---

[72] Whereas "who gets what, when, how?" suggests that it is the individual who is trying to "get" values, the "Indulgence/Deprivation" formulation suggests that men are being indulged or deprived by someone else. This shift in emphasis points to the culmination of Lasswell's psychopolitical argument. See below, pp. 274 ff.

[73] Harold D. Lasswell, "The Value-Institution Analysis of Mass Communication," unpublished manuscript. A large part of Herbert Simon's work consists of an elaborate investigation of this proposition. See above, pp. 69 ff.

from what appears in the definition. Thus Lasswell says in another place that "*rectitude* is the value of morality" (*Power and Personality*, p. 17). But the Lasswellian question is: of what value is morality? "In many cases uprightness (a *reputation* for *rectitude*) is a basis of power. A vital step in many political careers has been the *reputation* for moral integrity . . ." (p. 29, first and last italics supplied). It follows that a shrewd politician will seek a reputation for rectitude if his quest for "power" is thereby facilitated. A banker will seek a reputation for rectitude in order to gain and hold the money of his depositors, that is, facilitate his quest for income. The far-sighted, value-grasping individual will cultivate the appearance of rectitude, nothing more:

The bold, frank aggrandizement of self is rarely tolerated in society, for "the greatest power manifests itself as collective power," and the man who cherishes power must achieve some measure of socialization or he is outlawed. Although in principle no warm-hearted lover of his fellow-men, he must keep his contempt to himself or feign expansive sentiments of group loyalty [*Psychopathology and Politics*, p. 50].[74]

Rectitude is valuable because it is useful to the "aggrandizement of self," to the pursuit of safety, income, and deference. More precisely what is valuable is a reputation for moral integrity; whether the reputation is deserved is irrelevant. We seem to have been carried a long distance from the initial emphasis on the "moral virtues." Yet Lasswell has not shifted his ground, quite the contrary. Behind each of his formulations, either stated or implied, is this purely instrumental view of rectitude. Those in search of safety, income, or deference must judge whether a reputation for rectitude will help or hinder them in their quest. Should they judge that such a reputation will be useful to them, they will then conform to whatever standards society happens to have approved as "right." The man of rectitude in the Soviet Union will seek guidance from *Pravda* and similar spokesmen for the current party line. In the United States, where the current and prevailing social "myth makes articulate a demand for a sense of personal and collective responsibility for perfecting a free society" (*The Political Writings*, p. 477), the man of rectitude will regulate his moral standards accordingly.[75] Rectitude is nothing more nor less than the successful adjustment to the current demands of those dominant in a given society. However, while many political careers have been built on

---

[74] In the same way that the value-grasping individual disguises his motives behind the mask of rectitude, rapacious governments conceal their motives behind the claim of "justice." Lasswell's political realism leads him to correct—with a simple "sic"—the formulations of Aristotle who, in Book III of his *Politics* and elsewhere, naïvely assumes that justice is meaningful: " 'governments which have a regard to the common interest are constituted in accordance with strict principles of justice (*sic*) and are therefore true forms . . .' " (*Power and Society*, p. 231).

[75] Lasswell recognizes, but does not resolve, the obvious difficulty of the possibility of disagreement within a given society regarding the standards of "right" conduct. Who, or what part of the society is to be regarded as the authoritative spokesman?

a reputation for rectitude, Lasswell does not fail to recognize that "there are careers that have been furthered by a reputation for unscrupulousness . . ." (*Power and Personality*, p. 29). It follows that the shrewd man will have to judge whether in a given situation a reputation for rectitude or for unscrupulousness will further his career, his acquisition of safety, income, deference.[76] No matter how much men may purport to concern themselves with "moral virtues," Lasswell's analysis unfailingly reveals the value-grasping individual acting according to the "maximization postulate."

Lasswell perceives, then, an unrelenting struggle among men for safety, income, and deference, a struggle which generates untold hostility and destructiveness. Infinite chains of political tension are initiated by men intent only on maximizing their indulgences and minimizing their deprivations.

The banker who makes a commercial loan in the ordinary course of business, the board of directors that retains a monopolistic advantage for the company, the trade union that condones restrictions of production, the pressure group or trade association that sustains a trade barrier may unwittingly contribute to a wave of happenings that spell collective inflation and collapse. A social practice is destructive which provokes intense concentrations of destructive impulse, although most of the process occurs under circumstances in which the participants neither see nor seek these results [*Power and Personality*, p. 111].

What are the political consequences of this view of destructive self-seeking? Would not action in accordance with "the maximization postulate," if men lived "without a common power to keep them all in awe," lead to "that condition which is called war; and such a war, as is of every man, against every man?" [77] Under such circumstances there would be, in the well-known words of Hobbes, "no society; and which is worst of all, continual fear, and danger of violent death; and the life of man, solitary, poor, nasty, brutish, and short." According to Hobbes, man's passions lead him to an awareness of the necessity for achieving peace, without which he cannot live well, if at all. Man's reason enables him to understand the necessity for creating civil society and to agree to the institution of a commonwealth. The sovereign thus created is *necessarily absolute*, Hobbes tells us, whether it be termed a monarchy, democracy, or aristocracy.

It goes without saying that Lasswell does not accept the Hobbian conclusion; it was hardly for the sake of such a political order that he sought to overcome Freud's pessimism regarding the possibilities of the thoroughgoing socialization of mankind. Yet it is not only, not even mainly, Hobbes' absolute sovereign to which Lasswell objects. The analysis of "who gets what,

---

76 Said Machiavelli to the prince: "it is well to seem merciful, faithful, humane, sincere, religious, and also to be so; but you must have the mind so disposed that when it is needful to be otherwise you may be able to change to the opposite qualities." *The Prince*, ch. 18.

77 *Leviathan*, i, 13.

when, how?"—the analysis of conflict between men in their struggle for values or indulgences—is no more than equilibrium analysis. It is, of course, an indispensable part of the social scientist's enterprise, for it is important to know what values men strive for, what form these values take, and how they are distributed at a particular time and place. Taken by itself, however, the "conflict metaphor" of equilibrium analysis tends to be idle and misleading precisely because it does not, in Lasswell's view, lead anywhere. Equilibrium analysis, such as that which is the chief concern of Lasswell's *Politics*, constitutes only one component of his political science. It is only through developmental analysis that it is possible to move in the direction of the *resolution* of pressing political problems. So far as Lasswell is concerned, Hobbes' absolute sovereign provides no more than an especially clear example of the impossibility of providing a satisfactory solution to the political problem at the political level.

HOMO POLITICUS

The reason, in Lasswell's view, for the fundamental inadequacy of social analysis and action that remains on the merely political level is best seen in his analysis of power. The struggle for safety, income, and deference is, in its most general statement, the struggle for power. "The concept of power is perhaps the most fundamental in the whole of political science: the political process is the shaping, distribution, and exercise of power (in a wider sense, of all the deference values, or of influence in general)" (*Power and Society*, p. 75). The full description of the political process—who gets what, when, how?—is the first step towards fundamental social analysis and manipulation. The second step consists of the thoroughgoing investigation of the political personality, "whose principal value is the pursuit of power. The essence of power is understood to be the capacity, and usually the will, to impose one's own values as permanent or transitory motives upon others" (*Psychopathology and Politics*, p. 50).[78] Although the "pure" political type, with its "bold, frank aggrandizement of self," is rare, this urge to dominate and shape the character of others manifests itself in every field of human activity: science, economics, art, social life, religion. In the political sphere proper, however, the pursuit of power reveals itself most massively and destructively.

The ascendency (the "charisma") of many so-called natural leaders turns out to be that of the successful delinquent. No one can look at the psychological structure of the tyrannies of recent world politics without recognizing that such political leadership is juvenile delinquency on a colossal scale. In the immediate

---

[78] This definition of 1930 was restated in "decision-making" terminology in *Power and Personality* in 1948, where Lasswell describes the power relation as follows: When "policies are expected to be enforced against an obstructor by the imposing of extreme deprivations, we have decision, which is a power relation. The offender can be deprived of any or all values" (p. 18).

struggle for power, one set of delinquents fights it out with another set, and with one another individually; and the balance of power is tipped by the weight of the psychic-castrates whom the successful delinquent is able to intimidate into accepting him as a hero [*Power and Personality*, p. 167].

Lasswell's famous reports of psychoanalytical case studies of the political type need not detain us long. The basic intention is clearly expressed in *Psychopathology and Politics*, where Lasswell reports that "we want to discover what developmental experiences are significant for the political traits and interests of the mature. This means that we want to see what lies behind agitators, administrators, theorists, and other types who play on the public stage." Beyond this, "we want to see whether the intensive investigation of life-histories will in any way deepen our understanding of the whole social and political order" (pp. 8-9). Lasswell makes no serious attempt to justify this initial selection of "agitator, administrator, theorist" as the political types. He tells us merely that he is following the lead of Eduard Spranger, "the distinguished educational psychologist of the University of Berlin, [who] has developed a morphology of personality on an original basis." Lasswell refers to the Old Testament prophets as illustrations of "the 'pure-type' agitator." Karl Marx is said to have been a pure "theorist," while the pure "administrator" is exemplified by the American president, Herbert Hoover. Among the examples of "mixed" types, we find Thomas Hobbes, who "was a theorist and an agitating pamphleteer" (pp. 49, 53).[79]

With this typology before him, Lasswell turns to the analysis of some twenty case histories in order to determine the developmental experiences which were significant in creating the political traits and interests of political man. Given this intention, one might have expected case histories of individuals who had enjoyed outstanding political careers or at least extended political experience "on the public stage." However, of the twenty individuals studied intensively, only one, a Mr. "R," was at any time elected to public office. Lasswell reports that "he was elected to various local offices, and then to Congress. He was reputed to be an impractical dreamer, and enjoyed making rather fanciful speeches. His legislative career as recorded in the *Congressional Record* was undistinguished." Mr. "R." is placed by Lasswell in the category of "theorists," perhaps because following his abrupt departure from Congress, "he practiced law desultorily . . . and devoted himself to study and writing. His one published volume is a vague disquisition on human affairs, which accurately reflects the indeterminate, rhetorical, and meliorative

[79] Lasswell does not explain the principles by which Hobbes is classified as "an agitating pamphleteer," as well as theorist, while Karl Marx, who authored such avowedly agitational tracts as the *Communist Manifesto* and countless articles designed to shape political activity, is classified as a pure "theorist." One must wonder whether such seemingly absurd classification points to a misunderstanding not merely of the intention of Marx and Hobbes, but also of the distinction between ideology and political philosophy. See below, pp. 300 ff.

quality of his thinking." One gathers that the "fanciful" quality of his think-ing became rather pronounced as he "elaborated a private form of religion." "His ideas were that he had been chosen to work out the salvation of the world, and that he had been endowed with unusual, indeed supernatural, understanding of men's motives, and special power to heal insanity" (pp. 170, 169).

Lasswell also describes a Mr. "C," a verbose crank and "paranoid" who ran for president "on a minority ticket." This would seem to exhaust the politically relevant information on Mr. "C," unless one includes the ex-tended reports of his paranoid fantasies, many of which had political con-tent of a sort. For example, Mr. "C" "announced that he was going to be the next president of the United States of America. . . . On the next inaugu-ration day he will take charge by divine power, and after that his red-headed wife will be given full authority" (p. 113).

Among the remaining case histories we note a few individuals who spent at least some period of their lives in "administration." Mr. "F," for example, was a member of the secret service for a few years. His administrative career was rather abruptly ended during World War I when he insisted that he had "found ground glass in the bread served to men in camp. When the laboratory did not confirm his findings," he contended "that he mixed ground glass with flour and submitted a sample to the laboratory, which reported no ground glass, thus confirming his suspicions that the laboratory staff was composed of aliens—a German, an Austrian, and a Turk." His "administra-tive" career terminated, Mr. "F" turned his talents and energy to "agitation." "His patriotic and religious lectures became famous among the smaller com-munities of the land" (pp. 120, 118).

In working his way through nearly a hundred pages of such fascinating details, the reader is likely to forget that the purpose of this "intensive in-vestigation of life-histories" is to "deepen our understanding of the whole social and political order" (pp. 8-9). What is most significant is that Lasswell devotes almost all his attention to infinitely detailed description of "devel-opmental experiences," while hardly touching on the political traits and interests of the mature person. Of one "administrator," a Mr. "H," we are treated to some eight pages of vivid description of his sexual development, while almost nothing is said about the character of his administrative activi-ties or responsibilities. One of the few political allusions running to more than a sentence is found in the case history of a Mr. "K":

For some years he was in the forestry service, where part of his duties was to mark the trees that might be cut by private lumbermen. The lumbermen naturally argued that the straight, sound trees should be cut and the damaged ones left for seed. K. took a variety of other factors into account, and spent days measuring and estimating position, growth rates, and shade area, exasperating the lumbermen with his everlasting and often superfluous scrupulousness. He keenly felt his responsibilities as a public servant, and disliked the very appearance of succumbing to private pressure [pp. 142-143].

For these pains, "K" is described by Lasswell as "a pedantic official," after which the political dimensions of the case history are dropped entirely. Their place is taken by some eight pages of "developmental history" that concludes with the observation that "from one point of view, 'K's' character may be summed up by saying that his overscrupulous performance of duty was an elaborate effort to demonstrate his potency. . . . His genital difficulties testify to the intensity of the castration conflict, and show the passive-oral regression" (pp. 150-151). But there is no convincing evidence whatsoever that these difficulties were in any way connected with what Lasswell has termed an "overscrupulous performance of duty." For that matter, such evidence as is furnished by the case history indicates that Mr. "K's" performance of his public duties was "overscrupulous" only from the point of view of those private lumbermen who were intent on getting as much first-rate timber from the public domain as quickly as possible, regardless of the long range and sound development of the forest. The standards applied by Mr. "K," to judge from Lasswell's account, appear to be none other than those accepted as generally sound by professional foresters. Private lumbermen acting in terms of "the maximization postulate," that is, intent on securing maximum profits, may well have challenged the propriety of Mr. "K's" standards, but such disputes would seem to require reference not to the alleged pathological genesis of Mr. "K's" views, but to recognized criteria of forest management and economics and to other considerations pertinent to resolution of the not uncommon tensions between public and private interests.

Lasswell's most sustained attempt to establish the connections between the political views and activities of mature individuals and pertinent aspects of their "developmental histories" may be found in his consideration of a variety of socialist and anarchist "theorists" and "agitators." The developmental roots of anarchism are almost unfailingly connected with hatred of the father, while in the case of socialism it is the brother who is identified for this purpose. Of Lasswell's various illustrations of this theme, the most substantial is that of a Mr. "M," whose case history was taken by Dr. Wilhelm Stekel of Vienna and is reproduced, at least in part, by Lasswell. Mr. "M" is described as

a prominent socialist who agitated for an economic brotherhood of man, and whose most important private motive in this particular was a bitter hatred of his own brother. Most of this hatred was displaced from his brother on to capitalistic autocracy, and overreacted against by a social ideal of fraternal equality. His hatred of his own brother was not entirely disposed of by this displacement, and it was necessary to keep at a distance from him, and from many of his traits. . . .

M spent the years agitating at home and abroad, spending a year and a half in prison. Thus he succeeded in gratifying his masochistic desire to be punished for his hatred by provoking society to avenge itself on him [pp. 157-158].

One is struck by the readiness with which Lasswell accepts Stekel's "explanation" of "M's" socialism. No account is taken of the fact that of the multitude of individuals who hate their brothers, only a small portion have chosen socialism as a means of "displacing" their hostilities, or of the fact that there are many socialists who have no brothers. Stekel and his followers have asserted a relationship between two facts about Mr. "M" without supplying any evidence that the relationship is meaningful. They do little more than to play with the words "brother" and "brotherhood." All other considerations aside, one would think that the beginning point of any explanation of a given individual's adherence to socialism or any other political doctrine would have been to ascertain the major tenets of that doctrine. The word "socialism" is as sweeping as perhaps any term to be found in the vocabulary of politics. One has only to read Section III of the *Communist Manifesto* to gain a rudimentary notion of the vast differences between some of the contending schools of socialism. Lasswell can hardly be unaware of these differences, yet he indiscriminately lumps together such "socialists" as an insignificant preacher, who is described as an obscure "agitator," with a "prominent" European "theorist." We are told a great deal about the alleged brother-hate of this strange pair, but virtually nothing about the similarity or differences in their political views (pp. 82, 92-94, 157-158).

The initial stage in a scientific approach to politics, Lasswell has consistently asserted, is accurate description. Description of relevant data gives rise to the categories required by scientific prediction and control. It is contended at the beginning of *Psychopathology and Politics* that the case histories supply just such descriptive data; they are intended to provide a representative sample. For this reason,

some of the life-histories which are summarized in this monograph come from mental hospitals. Others have been collected from volunteers who were outside mental institutions and who were aware of no serious mental pathology. They have been undertaken on the understanding that our knowledge of human nature in politics would be advanced if "normal" individuals were studied with the same care which is often bestowed on the abnormal [p. 6].[80]

But we are hard pressed to find the "normal" individuals within Lasswell's sample. He says that "the purpose of this venture is not to prove that politicians are 'insane' " (p. 7), but where, we must ask, are the examples of *sane*

[80] It is noteworthy that Lasswell places "normal" in quotation marks, while omitting them for abnormal. This is consistent with the understanding of psychological realism that what is taken in everyday life to be "normal" must be understood in the light of something deeper. According to this approach, it is in studying those conditions which most men characterize as "sick" that psychological realities are most often to be discovered.

politicians? Of the twenty case histories presented, the only two individuals who ran for or served in elective office were (or became) severely paranoid. No less than eight of the twenty individuals within the total sample are identified by Lasswell as "psychotics." At least six others are described as "neurotics," or as individuals whose case histories were derived during the course of therapeutic psychoanalysis. Of the remaining six cases, only one, the "agitator," Mr. "A," is identified as having volunteered for psychoanalysis in the interest of "the progress of science" (p. 79). (And what was behind *that* we can only guess.) Lasswell's description of the remaining five individuals indicates that they were obvious candidates for therapeutic analysis, even though they are not clearly labeled "neurotics" or "psychotics."

At the very least, it is clear that most or all of these individuals are, from Lasswell's own viewpoint, "immature." Yet their histories are studied for the purpose of determining "what developmental experiences are significant for the political traits and interests of the mature" (p. 8). The same problem presents itself with respect to the three minor judges whose case histories are presented in fragmentary form in *Power and Personality*. The very fact that these "cranks," "neurotics," and "psychotics" were incapacitated for any serious or sustained role on the public stage would seem to make them marginal for the purposes of *political* analysis. Such a collection of case histories might yield data of some importance to clinical psychologists, but there is no evidence that it has deepened Lasswell's "understanding of political personalities" or led him or others to the development or significant delineation of "political types."

The general character of Lasswell's case studies is sufficiently clear, and further examination would serve only to re-enforce what has already been said here or elsewhere in this volume.[81] Lasswell does not establish that the political opinions of these individuals are "rationalizations" of subconscious drives. He does not establish the meaningfulness of the connections he finds between certain political opinions and certain facts of an individual's psychological history. He does not establish the relevance of the psychological history of these peripheral or extreme political types to the generality of men active in political life. It is necessary, however, to take account of Lasswell's warning that "these studies are admittedly incomplete. . . . The number of documents on hand is limited. Caution would counsel deferred publication of even these materials" (p. 13).[82] Yet, in a much more recent work, *Power and Personality*, which was published eighteen years after *Psychopathology and Politics*, we discover the same basic categories and typologies, although the "administrators" are now termed "bureaucrats," while the "theorists" are

[81] See above, pp. 22-31; see also Crick, *The American Science of Politics*, pp. 197 ff.
[82] *Psychopathology and Politics* was reprinted (with pagination, identical to that of the original 1930 edition) in *The Political Writings* (pp. 1-282) and again in 1961 (New York: Compass Books).

now identified, not inappropriately, as "detached characters." It is suggestive of the real role which case studies play in Lasswell's understanding of *homo politicus* that the twenty case histories of *Psychopathology and Politics* are replaced by only three in the latter work. The case histories serve at most as faint illuminations of a typology adopted prior to research.

As has been noted, Lasswell acknowledges his indebtedness to Spranger for this conception of the political man, the *homo politicus*. "Spranger's subtle comments in elaborating this simple, central conception" are said to be "among the most valuable in the literature of society." The nucleus of Spranger's thinking on this point is summarized by Lasswell as follows. "The *homo politicus* is characterized by the following relationship between desire, method, and success: desire to control the motives of others; methods varying from violence to wheedling; and success in securing communal recognition" (*Psychopathology and Politics*, p. 52). Lasswell has found it convenient to restate Spranger's conception in notational form, a form in which it has come to be well known: $p\} \ d\} \ r = P$. Lasswell explains this formula, "which expresses the developmental facts about the fully developed political man" (P), as follows:

The first component, p, stands for the private motives of the individual as they are nurtured and organized in relation to the family constellation and the early self. . . . [P]rimitive psychological structures continue to function within the personality long after the epochs of infancy and childhood have been chronologically left behind. The prominence of hate in politics suggests that we may find that the most important private motive is a repressed and powerful hatred of authority. . . .

The second term, d, in such a formula describes the displacement of private motives from family objects to public objects. The repressed father-hatred may be turned against kings or capitalists, which are social objects playing a role before and within the community. . . .

The third symbol, r, signifies the rationalization of the displacement in terms of public interests. The merciless exploitation of the toolless proletariat by the capitalists may be the rational justification of the attitude taken up by the individual toward capitalism [pp. 74-75].

The political type is infantile, immature. It is because Lasswell knows or assumes this prior to clinical investigation that he can rest content with case histories of individuals who do not seem to the psychologically unsophisticated eye very representative of the political type. Not only that, given this assumption, it might be said that the sicker or more infantile the individuals whose cases are examined the better for purposes of research, for they will reveal more clearly what is being sought. At any rate, *"it is not too far fetched to say that everyone is born a politician, and most of us outgrow it"* (*Power and Personality*, p. 160). Yet many do not, as the political tensions and crises of our time and all past ages testify. As a perfect illustration of "the true political type," Lasswell offers us the example of Napoleon, "with his insatiable craving for gestures of deference to his ego from his fellow men. . . . He sought the balm of success for his wounded ego, and he was forever licking his self-inflicted mutilations" (*Politics*, p. 141).[83]

How does it come about that the political type develops this insatiable craving for deference? What is it in the background of political men that preserves such "primitive psychological structures"? Lasswell's typical answer is found in his "social-anxiety hypothesis."

The most drastic form of the social-anxiety hypothesis applied to politics is that *men can only be free when they are free of social anxiety*. The appearance of a tyrant is an extreme sign of mass demands for the devalued self to depend upon someone else. So long as these dependency demands are generated in the lives of men, the masses will force themselves upon potential tyrants, even though at first glance it looks as though the tyrants were forcing themselves on the masses [*Power and Personality*, p. 163].

Both those who rule and those who are ruled, then, are mentally ill. The tyrant is no less so than his subject; in any event, both suffer from dependency demands. These dependency demands are generated by inadequate modes of child training, among other things. It is "withdrawal of the nipple," which precipitates "one of the major crises of growth. Weaning is the first substantial loss which is inflicted upon the individual after birth, and the way in which it is met establishes reaction patterns which may serve as important prototypes for subsequent behavior" (*Psychopathology and Politics*, p. 102). Deprivations of a similar kind follow, which, according to Lasswell, block "the outflowing energies of the personality," thereby frustrating "the primary ego" (*World Politics and Personal Insecurity*, p. 154). This results in regression of the personality and the reanimation of autoerotic dispositions.

How may such regression be prevented? Lasswell's diagnosis, as set forth in the social-anxiety hypothesis, suggests a relatively simple remedy. Stated crudely, if deprivation is bad for the human organism, then indulgence must be good for it. Lasswell's later writings especially are replete with suggestions that the indulgent treatment of human impulses strengthens personality and fosters the development of that self-confident individuality which he associates with the healthy or "democratic" character.[84]

Our basic postulate in examining human activity is that the "maximization principle" applies in accordance with which the tendency is to maximize the indulgences of the system as a whole. It is evident why the reduction and avoidance

[83] Cf. *Psychopathology and Politics*, pp. 126, 183, 264.
[84] See especially *Power and Personality*, chs. 3, 7, and *Democratic Character* in The *Political Writings of Harold D. Lasswell*, pp. 502-514.

of anxiety (an acutely dysphoric set of events) occupies such a pivotal position in the evolution of the personality [*The Political Writings*, p. 512].

Past psychic damage to an individual may be partially rectified by psycho-analysis, which is designed "to stimulate the individual to the reconstruction of values, not on the basis of imposed authority, but through prolonged scrutiny of the self as a process." Such analysis may provide the individual with "relief from disproportionate feelings of futility, despondency, persecu-tion, and omniscience" (*Psychopathology and Politics*, p. 218). Potential psychic damage to the individual may be at least partially prevented by pro-tecting him from both subjugation to and exercise of power in such a way as to produce "low estimates of the self." It is in this sense that Lasswell should be understood when he contends that the urgent task of our time "is to chasten and subordinate power to the service of respect" (*Power and Per-sonality*, p. 110).

Such a psychologically healthy individual is also understood by Lasswell to be the free man. The psychological and political meaning of freedom and power are merged. Lasswell is therefore led to comment that

Spranger is right in saying that, when one succeeds in penetrating the psychology of the search for power, it becomes comprehensible that he whose nature is bound up in the pursuit of authority is most keenly sensible to the limits of his own freedom, and consequently suffers so keenly from nothing else in life than his own subordination. Sensing this, the Stoics long ago contended that the essence of liberty is the self-sufficiency which makes no demands on others. Ascendency in-volves dependence, a reciprocal relationship which has been exhaustively de-scribed by Simmel [*Psychopathology and Politics*, p. 52].

Helpful as psychoanalytic techniques may be in restoring some individuals to psychic health, the broader problem posed by Lasswell is that of creating and maintaining societies in which no destructive power relations exist. The unhealthy, power-oriented states of the past have produced psychic cripples faster than psychoanalysis can cure them. Very simply, "the long-run aim of societies aspiring toward human freedom is to get rid of power and to bring into existence a free man's commonwealth in which coercion is neither threatened, applied nor desired" (*Power and Personality*, p. 110). This aim cannot be achieved by traditional political methods:

The time has come to abandon the assumption that the problem of politics is the problem of promoting discussion among all the interests concerned in a given problem. Discussion frequently complicates social difficulties, for the discussion by far-flung interests arouses a psychology of conflict which produces obstructive, fictitious, and irrelevant values. The problem of politics is less to solve conflicts than to prevent them; less to serve as a safety valve for social protest than to apply social energy to the abolition of recurrent sources of strain in society.

This redefinition of the problem of politics may be called the idea of preventive politics [*Psychopathology and Politics*, pp. 196-197].[85]

Lasswell's conception of preventive politics, or of social psychiatry, as he often terms it, is the capstone of his social-psychological analysis. As such, it represents an open and decisive break with the approach and methods of conventional politics. "The political methods of coercion, exhortation," as well as discussion, improperly "assume that the role of politics is to solve conflicts when they have happened." Not only have past attempts by political men to solve social problems by these means been necessarily self-defeating, but they have contributed to an increase in social tensions and strife. This vicious cycle must be broken. It is "the ideal of a politics of prevention . . . to obviate conflict by the definite reduction of the tension level of society . . ." (*Psychopathology and Politics*, p. 203).[86]

Such a task cannot be entrusted to those political types considered in Lasswell's famous formula: "$p\} d\} r = P$," for such politicians, by displacing their private affects on public objects increase rather than decrease the tension level of society. These politicians, as well as their followers and the societies which produce them, are too sick even to see their real interests, much less to take effective action in their own behalf. He continues: "The findings of personality research show that the individual is a poor judge of his own interest. The individual who chooses a political policy as a symbol of his wants is usually trying to relieve his own disorders by irrelevant palliatives" (p. 194). The attempt to solve any fundamental human problem by conventional political means is characterized by Lasswell as

a magical solution which changes nothing in the conditions affecting the tension level of the community, and which merely permits the community to distract its attention to another set of equally irrelevant symbols. The number of statutes which pass the legislature, or the number of decrees which are handed down by

[85] Lasswell has never tired of suggesting that the technique of "free association" popularized by Freud for treatment of the mentally ill, should be more generally utilized in the political realm as "a special technique of enlightenment" or insight. In *Power and Personality* he contends that "quite apart from its utility as a means of therapy, it is only beginning to be understood that free association is a method of using the mind on a par with reflective thinking, and that, like any true method, it can be deliberately cultivated" (p. 196). Such illustrations of this technique as one finds in Lasswell's work do little to demonstrate its usefulness, although some of its political implications are clearly consistent with the general character of his teaching and buttress it. For example, he suggests that "the Greeks settled many public affairs by argument and the mode of talking and thinking appropriate to this sort of activity was developed into the principles of dialectic. . . . Today we are dimly aware that too much emphasis has been given to dialectic, and that other ways of talking and thinking are needed to supplement it" (p. 197). This and other considerations "raises in more acute form than ever the possibilities of reducing destructive tendencies throughout society by a combined therapeutic operation that employs many patterns of interpersonal intervention" (p. 198). See the discussion of "Psychoanalytocracy" below, pp. 286 ff.
[86] See also p. 265.

the executive, but which change nothing in the permanent practices of society, is a rough index of the role of magic in politics.

. . . Political symbolization has its catharsis function, and consumes the energies which are released by the maladaptions of individuals to one another.

. . . About all that can be said for various punitive measures resorted to by the community is that they have presently broken down and ceased to continue the damage which they began to inflict on society [pp. 195-196].

The traditional techniques of politics have compounded social problems, while the traditional terms used in stating and discussing them have obscured the real issues. "Our thinking has too long been misled by the threadbare terminology of democracy versus dictatorship, of democracy versus aristocracy." Our real problem, argues Lasswell, "is to be ruled by the truth about the conditions of harmonious human relations, and the discovery of the truth is an object of specialized research; it is no monopoly of people as people or of the ruler as ruler" (p. 197).

The most pressing problem of social reconstruction is the reshaping of those institutional and other arrangements based on unequal distribution of power, for it is the exercise of power that generates the psychic tensions described by Lasswell's social-anxiety hypothesis. The heightened tension level generates strife which, in turn, increases the exercise of power. This destructive cycle can be broken, Lasswell argues, only through the creation of basically egalitarian societies within which the exercise of power will be minimized. "In our day," writes Lasswell, "the probability that we can reduce power to *the vanishing point* seems very remote indeed," but the eradication of power is, nevertheless, the ultimate goal (*Power and Personality*, p. 110, italics supplied).

To summarize: Lasswell's account of the political and psychological history of mankind presents an unrelieved spectacle of destructive strife and tension, while past political theory consists of little more than infinite elaborations of the central error of prescribing merely political remedies for the ills of political life. Marxism, it is true, is a partial exception, for its vision of the communist society carries us beyond the realm of politics into the free man's commonwealth. However, Marxism's failure to take sufficient account of the "intensive" dimension of human life led it to be over-sanguine about the prospects of the realization of the trans-political ideal. The Marxian dialectic is, in Lasswell's view, defective—and, so far as the way to freedom through class warfare is concerned, too political. Lasswell looked to Freud to supply the missing psychological dimension of analysis. As we have seen, Lasswell's own political psychology is of the loosest and most general character, and it departs in fundamental respects from the Freudian original. However, Lasswell does attempt to lend substance to Marx's vision of man's end by specifying its psychological characteristics, an attempt which we shall consider in the concluding section. In addition, Lasswell borrows from Freud the figure of the psychoanalyst which, inflated far beyond its original dimensions, becomes the commanding character in Lasswell's propagandistic social science.

PROPAGANDA

As long as modern technology prevails, society is honeycombed with cells of separate experience, of individuality, of partial freedom. Concerted action under such conditions depends upon skilfully guiding the minds of men; hence the enormous importance of symbolic manipulation in modern society.[87]

Lasswell's chief concern has always been with the problem of "skilfully guiding the minds of men" rather than with the exploration of that "freedom" towards which men are to be guided; or, in terms of our initial statement of the problem, he has been chiefly concerned with the "positive" part of "positive liberalism." It is in his analysis and use of the many voices, the blaring trumpets, the gentle strings, and the insinuating oboes, of Propaganda that the inner consistency of Lasswell's work is to be found. He has always been acutely aware of the difficult problem of being understood by diverse audiences. His writing has therefore been characterized by great flexibility of style, extreme inventiveness in usage and vocabulary, along with changes in emphasis, as his attention has shifted back and forth between various aspects of a teaching that, while homogeneous in content, has been directed to a heterogeneous audience. Included among his specific addressees have been not only a broad range of academicians, including political scientists, sociologists, and psychologists, but also businessmen, lawyers, statesmen, journalists, psychiatrists, and substantial parts of the general public at home and abroad.

Lasswell's first comprehensive attempt to come to grips with the subject of propaganda was his 1926 doctoral dissertation, entitled *Propaganda Technique in the World War*, which was published the following year. The opening argument closely connects the study of propaganda with Lasswell's dominant scientific concern—effective social control. He sharply challenges the view of those "people who in the years before the War were disposed to accept the changing tides of international animosity and friendship as inevitable manifestations of the cosmic fate, which commanded the sun to rise or the rain to fall." Explanations of the causes of the Great War and sweeping social change are no longer to be sought through "supernatural" or "impersonal" agencies, for "a word has appeared, which has come to have an ominous clang in many minds—Propaganda" (p. 2).

This whole discussion about the ways and means of controlling public opinion testifies to the collapse of the traditional species of democratic romanticism and to the rise of a dictatorial habit of mind. . . .

[87] "The Garrison State and Specialists on Violence," *The Analysis of Political Behaviour*, p. 149, reprinted from the *American Journal of Sociology*, January 1941.

Familiarity with the ruling public has bred contempt. Modern reflections upon democracy boil down to the proposition, more or less contritely expressed, that the democrats were deceiving themselves. The public has not reigned with benignity and restraint. The good life is not in the mighty rushing wind of public sentiment. It is no organic secretion of the horde, but the tedious achievement of the few. The lover of the good life no longer consults Sir Oracle; he pulls the strings of Punch and Judy. Thus argues the despondent democrat. Let us, therefore, reason together, brethren, he sighs, and find the good, and when we have found it, let us find out how to make up the public mind to accept it. Inform, cajole, bamboozle and seduce in the name of the public good. Preserve the majority convention, but dictate to the majority! [pp. 4-5]

Propaganda has acquired unique importance in the modern, democratic, scientifically oriented world. "Propaganda rose to transitory importance in the past whenever a social system based upon the sanctions of antiquity was broken up by a tyrant." Its *ever-present* function "in modern life is in large measure attributable to the social disorganization which has been precipitated by the rapid advent of technological changes." [88] These "technological changes," or changes in the modes of production, which were considered in some detail as part of Lasswell's sociohistorical analysis, have contributed to the passing of "monarchy and class privilege" (*Propaganda Technique in the World War*, p. 222).[89] Dissolved also have been "the ties of automatic allegiance" by which men were bound to the ruling monarchs or aristocrats. Modern man is therefore faced with the problem of creating new allegiances, a problem complicated by the enormous size and the heterogeneous character of many of today's states.

Wherever the ties of automatic allegiance have been dissolved, men have relearned *the power of passions* in the life of society, and the potency of words, of news, of opinions, in the control of passions. They agree with the eighteenth-century publicist who wrote:
"The only Way therefore of dealing with Mankind is to deal with their Passions; and the Founders of all States and of all Religions have ever done so." [90]

[88] Harold D. Lasswell, "The Theory of Political Propaganda," *American Political Science Review*, August 1927, p. 631. Cf. "Propaganda," *Encyclopedia of the Social Sciences*, Vol. XII, pp. 523-524; also *Propaganda and Dictatorship*, p. 112, where Lasswell finds that "modern social development has nurtured insecurity by undermining ancient loyalties, and [that] possibly the chief meaning of the present epoch in world affairs is the struggle to relieve crises of insecurity by means of symbolic fundamentalism imposed by violence. Hence the truculence of proletarian socialism in the presence of surviving vestiges of monarchism, clericalism and capitalism; hence the urge to dissolve all lesser loyalties on behalf of one overmastering loyalty."
[89] Cf. "The Function of the Propagandist," *International Journal of Ethics*, April 1928, p. 261; also, "Policy and the Intelligence Function," in *Propaganda in War and Crisis*, p. 56.
[90] Harold D. Lasswell, "Propaganda in a Planned Society," in Findlay Mackenzie (ed.), *Planned Society, Yesterday, Today, Tomorrow* (New York: Prentice-Hall, Inc., 1937), pp. 629-630; the quotation is from "Cato" in the *London Journal*, July 29, 1721; italics supplied.

Manipulation of men's passions is necessary both in peace and war. Regarding the latter, "there is no question but that government management of opinion is an unescapable corollary of large-scale modern war. The only question is the degree to which the government should try to conduct its propaganda secretly, and the degree to which it should conduct it openly" (*Propaganda Technique in the World War*, p. 15). It is in times of war especially that the heterogeneity of the typical modern state presents to the propagandist the task of creating a new unity to replace the old bonds "sanctified by theocratic or aristocratic" leadership (*Ency. Soc. Sci.*, XII, p. 523).

In the Great Society it is no longer possible to fuse the waywardness of individuals in the furnace of the war dance; a new and subtler instrument must weld thousands and even millions of human beings into one amalgamated mass of hate and will and hope. A new flame must burn out the canker of dissent and temper the steel of bellicose enthusiasm. The name of this new hammer and anvil of social solidarity is propaganda. Talk must take the place of drill; print must supplant the dance. War dances live in literature and at the fringes of the modern earth; war propaganda breathes and fumes in the capitals and provinces of the world.
Propaganda is a concession to the rationality of the modern world. A literate world, a reading world, a schooled world prefers to thrive on argument and news. It is sophisticated to the extent of using print; and he that takes to print shall live or perish by the Press. All the apparatus of diffused erudition popularizes the symbols and forms of pseudo-rational appeal; the wolf of propaganda does not hesitate to masquerade in the sheepskin. All the voluble men of the day—writers, reporters, editors, preachers, lecturers, teachers, politicians—are drawn into the service of propaganda to amplify a master voice [*Propaganda Technique in the World War*, p. 221].

"Propaganda is surely here to stay. . . ." It has become indispensable for even the "normal" operations of government in this, the era of positive democracy. In peacetime, as well as wartime, "the displacement of cults of simple obedience by democratic assertiveness complicates the problem of eliciting concerted action." While democratization may not have released "the masses from ignorance and superstition," it has certainly made necessary "the development of a whole new technique of control, largely through propaganda" (*Ency. Soc. Sci.*, XII, pp. 526, 523).
What is propaganda? As defined most simply and conventionally by Lasswell, it is "*the use of symbols to influence controversial attitudes.*" [91] In this context, propaganda is said to be one of the four "chief instruments of policy in war and peace"; the others being diplomacy, arms, and economics.[92] One

[91] Harold D. Lasswell, "The Propagandist Bids for Power," *American Scholar*, Summer 1939, p. 353, reprinted in *The Analysis of Political Behaviour*, p. 175.
[92] "Political and Psychological Warfare," in *Propaganda in War and Crisis*, p. 265.

of Lasswell's most frequent illustrations of the use of propaganda as such an instrument of wartime policy is the atrocity story.

Are atrocity stories to be played up more in the future than in the recent past? Intelligence may report that if more atrocity stories are circulated among the wives of skilled workers, it may give them a more vivid sense of what war is and stimulate their aggressive interest in helping their husbands keep on the job. This estimate of the probable result may be supported by interview data collected in the field and by the results of an experiment in which more interest in the war is indicated after reports of Japanese atrocities [*Propaganda in War and Crisis*, p. 62].

This use of propaganda in the modern world is accepted and familiar, and Lasswell shows only passing concern with it. At this level, propaganda is clearly subordinate to such instruments of political policy as diplomacy, arms, and economics. But Lasswell argues that the function of propaganda need not and should not remain at this subordinate level. He reminds us that in the modern state, democratic or despotic, the functions of propaganda and diplomacy are often unified within what he terms " 'political' policy." Such unification points the way to Lasswell's expansion of the function of propaganda, an expansion which leads finally to its transformation. It is as an ingredient of " 'political' policy" that one may properly understand the function of "propaganda of the act," or "propaganda of the deed." This application of propaganda depends upon "the expected disproportion between the specific consequence and the general reaction," which, for example, lies "behind some political assassinations" (*Ency. Soc. Sci.*, XII, p. 522). Propaganda of the act or deed is far more likely to be effective than those forms of propaganda which depend primarily on the use of spoken, written, or pictorial symbols of mere ideological policy. As examples, Lasswell cites the dramatic action of the American government during the Civil War in sending a shipload of food-stuffs to mitigate the sufferings of unemployed English textile workers, the capture of symbolic cities during revolutionary movements, and such tactics as the bombing of London by the Germans during World War I. This last "isolated act of violence" was

intended to produce a powerful impression. The dropping of bombs upon enemy cities was less for immediate military and strategic purposes, than for propaganda purposes. It was supposed that civilian morale would crack under the strain of perpetual fear. This, besides the *propaganda of frightfulness* and other acts of frightfulness, was supposed to produce discouragement and defeatism [*Propaganda Technique in the World War*, p. 199, italics supplied].

The keenness of Lasswell's insight has been confirmed in subsequent years which have witnessed an intensification of "the propaganda of frightfulness" punctuated by such propagandas of the act as the murder of the Russian Tsar and his family, the liquidation of sizable segments of the bourgeoisie of Russia and other Eastern European countries, Stalin's and Hitler's "purges,"

Franco's mass murders of Loyalist officers, and the atomic destruction of Hiroshima and Nagasaki. What must be emphasized, however, is the comprehensiveness of propaganda, as Lasswell understands it: "the more successful propagandas will show how it is possible to obtain the neat coordination of censorship, information, violence and policy" (*Propaganda and Dictatorship*, p. 111). Within the sphere of "successful propagandas" we now discover virtually *all* of the "chief instruments of policy in war and peace," although propaganda was initially said to be only one of these instruments. Moreover, as the *coordinating* agent of the instruments of policy, propaganda comes to comprehend policy itself. Before turning to an examination of the highest all-embracing function of propaganda, however, it is necessary to consider the question of the place of the propagandist in the government and society at large.

Under some circumstances it is relatively easy to discover the relationship between the decision-maker(s) and the propagandist which will allow the latter full scope for the effectuation of his insights. For example, in Nazi Germany, "propaganda . . . was a party-government monopoly, and at the elbow of Hitler stood a remarkably gifted colleague, Goebbels, who had direct access to the ultimate decision-maker." Speaking specifically of the " 'symphonic structure' of Nazi propaganda against Britain," Lasswell writes that "the various instruments did not necessarily, or even typically, play the same notes or even the same harmonies. But the skilful counterpoint of the Nazi German composer-conductor imposed unity upon the whole." [93] Goebbels-Hitler, the "composer-conductor," faced especially severe difficulties in creating unity *within* Germany, but, thanks to effective propaganda (including no doubt "propaganda of the deed"), they succeeded. Hitler was generally in the forefront of attention and appeared most often to be the decision-maker as he stridently announced the policies of the Third Reich. But, from Lasswell's description of his relationship to Goebbels, one is led to wonder whether in certain decisively important respects his position was not subordinate to that of the propagandist who provided him with certain of his key goal symbols. While Hitler directed the orchestra, it appears to be Lasswell's view that others may have been instrumental in writing the score.

Whatever the precise factual relationship between Goebbels-Hitler, the important point, in Lasswell's view is their unity. The propagandistic decision-making function was not handicapped by serious divisions in practice. The discovery and implementation of equivalent "composer-conductor" relationships within nontotalitarian states is necessarily a more difficult matter, since "deep timidities complicate the task of translating democratic aspirations into compelling institutional terms" (*Propaganda in War and Crisis*, p. 67). Lasswell has manifested unceasing concern with this problem over several

[93] "New Rivals of the Press, Film and Radio," in Pierce Butler (ed.), *Books and Libraries in Wartime* (Chicago: University of Chicago Press, 1945), pp. 36, 48.

decades as he has examined a broad range of possible relationships between the propagandist and decision-makers within democratic society. In his doctoral dissertation he suggests that "there is no question of organization of more interest to the student of political science than the proper relation" between them (*Propaganda Techniques in the World War*, p. 37), and he examines in detail various alternatives adopted by the warring nations in World War I. The most relevant portion of his discussion is that dealing with the well-publicized clash between Mr. Creel's Committee on Public Information and the American Congress. This clash points to an extremely delicate problem in a democratic polity, namely, that the propagandist may find it expedient, even essential, to commit "the country in advance to a policy which the legislature has not yet decided upon" (p. 41). The propagandist who is subject to even indirect legislative control may thus find himself the object of extremely painful investigations. He may even suffer cuts in budgetary appropriations designed to restrict or to eliminate his functions. The attacks on Creel were so savage that he was led to complain that "the heavens may fall, the earth may be consumed, but the right of a Congressman to lie and defame remains inviolate" (p. 45).[94]

The Creel-Wilson team, unlike that of Goebbels-Hitler, appears to have suffered precisely from the fact that it was Wilson who embodied *both* the major functions of the propagandist and the formal decision-maker. Creel, the official propagandist, held a distinctly subordinate and ineffective position. It is true that in the short run "it was of no particular importance that Mr. Creel lacked prestige. The foreign policy of the country was made by President Wilson, and it happened to have great propaganda value" (p. 29). However, Lasswell implies that Wilson was concerned only incidentally with propaganda; he failed to recognize the full coordinating scope of propaganda and the propagandist. Even apart from this, Wilson was in a dangerously exposed political position. Such magic as his propaganda possessed was effectively destroyed by those legislators who, scorning his new "goal symbols," rejected his leadership. They then went on to undermine the institutional devices, such as the League of Nations, which were intended to implement these symbols. Both Creel and Wilson were destroyed politically, along with the bulk of Wilson's program, both foreign and domestic.

This fate, suffered at the hands of a fickle representative assembly, suggests to Lasswell the danger inherent in the propagandist taking formal responsibility for policy-making in a democracy. His real influence, which ought to be great and even commanding, need not—perhaps should not—be matched by equivalent formal authority and responsibility. Accordingly, "it is not necessary that the heads of the propaganda services should formally occupy ministerial or cabinet posts, but they should have ministerial or cabinet influence, in

[94] Citing George Creel, *How We Advertised America* (New York: Harper Brothers, 1920), p. 52.

fact" (p. 28). Under such circumstances the propagandist may be able to maintain the continuity of his work, even when the more exposed formal decision-makers fall victim to legislative or popular passions. Indeed, the most important service of the formally designated decision-maker may consist in taking upon himself the consequences of unpopular policies, thus helping, consciously or not, to maintain the influence of the propagandist.

Lasswell suggests that especially "during our present period of transition from a business-dominant to a government-dominant state," the relationship between formal decision-makers and propagandists should and "will be in a constant state of redefinition" (*Propaganda in War and Crisis*, p. 66). Finding a suitable locus of operations during wartime will not present too great a difficulty, for under such conditions, propagandists are likely to be sought out for service and given the necessary popular recognition and support. During peace time, however, the question of the institutional locus from which the highest function of the propagandist should be carried out in a democracy must remain open, and propagandists will be called upon to demonstrate every resource of creative imagination and tactical flexibility in adjusting to rapidly changing situations.

Lasswell is, of course, perfectly aware that the merely organizational question is only the most superficial part of the broad problem of the role of the propagandist. Particularly is this the case in representative democracies, where the propagandist must generally shun official responsibility and nurture the ambiguity of his own position if he is to survive at all. However effectively elected officials may serve as lightning rods to protect propagandists from the raging storm of representative democracy, the more basic, long-run problem is to foster a broad and deep acceptance of propaganda itself. Lasswell is keenly aware that democrats more orthodox than himself harbor lingering suspicions, even active distrust of everything associated with propaganda. Accordingly, he is impelled to take up the cudgels for his cause, to become a propagandist for propaganda. He has engaged in this activity at every opportunity, directing his message at both the purveyors and the receivers of that propaganda which, he believes, must penetrate to every corner of social life. The vocabulary in which he speaks is most often that of "social psychiatry."

In collective policy as in somatic medicine the problem is to improve the layman's judgment in selecting expert advisers and guides. It is no news that the layman is often the victim of misplaced confidence in choosing his physician and politician. . . .

Those who want to practice social psychiatry or fulfill any other of the functions appropriate to the policy scientists of democracy have the practical problem of winning lay confidence in their good intentions and ability [*Power and Personality*, pp. 131-132].

The prevailing public "image" of most candidates for this task—the psychiatrists, professors, and social scientists—is not an encouraging one from Lasswell's point of view. The general public has generally shown itself reluctant to entrust political responsibilities to eggheads and "brain trusters"; and the composite image of the "professor" is similarly "often concocted from those quaint articles of infrequent and slow-footed solemnity, the academic cap, hood and gown." Nor is the public entirely mistaken, argues Lasswell. While various professional groups, including social and natural scientists, physicians, clergy, and educators, have done "a job that is in many ways admirable, no group gives the community the full benefit of its judgment in clarifying democratic policy . . ." (pp. 133-134, 139). These groups have not, that is to say, shaken off their own inhibitions or recognized the range of responsibilities and opportunities which the era of propaganda or social psychiatry offers them.

Lasswell has directed considerable efforts to mobilizing the academic community and training it for its tasks, but we have not touched on a more immediate possibility: to make policy scientists—or social psychiatrists, or propagandists—of those professional people who are already influential. In this connection, he reports, "there is, of course, the lawyer" (p. 134), who may be said to exercise the broadest responsibilities in our society. Lawyers are usually dominant in state and national legislatures. They preside over the court systems that apply and interpret the work of their fellow lawyers. Furthermore, as key members of constitutional conventions, they were generally instrumental in shaping the judicial and legislative framework within which future generations of lawyers enjoy such large opportunities. "It should need no emphasis that the lawyer is today, even when not himself a 'maker' of policy, the one indispensable adviser of every responsible policy-maker of our society—whether we speak of the head of a governmental department or agency, of the executive of a corporation or labor union. . . ." It is as such an adviser that "the lawyer, when informing his policy-maker of what he can or cannot legally do, is, as policy-makers often complain, in an unassailably strategic position to influence, if not create, policy." [95] No less important, the lawyer is respected. Lawyers, like "physicians share the heavy dignity that comes of long acceptance" (Power and Personality, p. 134).

Lawyers clearly have broad influence, even authority. But the difficulty, contends Lasswell, is that they "have been trained for but a fraction of the task of the policy scientist or the informed leader of democracy." The conventional law school "turns out a specialist on predicting how an appellate court will respond if a controversy is put up to it." Even worse, "the usual training of the lawyer in our civilization leaves him indoctrinated with a set

[95] Harold D. Lasswell and Myres S. McDougal, "Legal Education and Public Policy: Professional Training in the Public Interest." Yale Law Journal, March 1943, pp. 208-209. With minor changes, this article appears in The Analysis of Political Behaviour, pp. 21-119.

of biases of the utmost danger for democracy." Among other things, "the weight of legal brains is on the side of monopoly clients," and lawyers have failed to point out to their clients when "a given line of policy will probably contribute to the concentration of control over wealth and in this way endanger democratic institutions . . ." (Power and Personality, pp. 136-138).

Lasswell's rumination on this problem has long since led him to propose radical reconstruction of law school curricula. His most dramatic and comprehensive proposals appeared during World War II, at a time when he found that "the law schools are in a state of abeyance" and "crisis compels people to clarify their objectives. . . ." Sufficiently bold and far-sighted action during the "propitious moment" presented by the war might forestall the otherwise strong probability that "in the rush of conversion from war to peace the archaic conventions and confusions of the past may win out over the vital needs of our civilization and the doors may open to admit the unwary members of an entire generation into a reguilded vacuum." Undoubtedly, "war is the time to retool our educational processes in the hope of making them fit instruments for their future job." [96] As always, the "major purpose" of this job

is to promote the adaptation of legal education to the policy needs of a free society. Therefore, our first principle is that all legal structures, definitions, and doctrines must be taught, evaluated, and recreated in terms of the basic democratic values. Not only the legal syntax but also all legal structures and procedures must be related to the larger institutional contexts, the factual settings, that give them operational significance.[97]

Of course, adds Lasswell, "in a democratic society it should not . . . be an aim of legal education to impose a single standard of morals upon every student. But a legitimate aim of education is to seek to promote the major values of a democratic society and to reduce the number of moral mavericks who do not share democratic preferences." [98]

Although this plea has perhaps not been without some limited effect, the law schools have not generally taken up Lasswell's proposals for the radical reconstruction of legal education. Though there is a growing interest in social science, most law schools, most of the time, still teach the law. From Lasswell's point of view, this may be partly due to the failure of those in authority to recognize the need or to seize the opportunity for reconstruction which war, that climate most friendly to propaganda, provided. But there is a deeper reason. Lawyers and law schools are in the nature of the case primarily concerned with the law as it is, not with its fundamental reconstruction. The influence of lawyers in the daily business of government—so long, at least, as it is a government of laws—makes it necessary to enlist them in the propa-

[96] Yale Law Journal, March 1943, pp. 292, 211.
[97] Ibid., p. 243, italics supplied.
[98] Ibid., p. 212.

ganda army; but, in spite of individual exceptions, most will find their places among the ranks of the junior and noncommissioned officers.

To fill the higher ranks, Lasswell looks less to the law schools than to the academic community, especially those members who are concerned with political and social affairs. Many of the academics will inevitably find themselves in comfortable staff positions: "in the future, the propagandist may count upon a battalion of honest professors to rewrite history, to serve the exigencies of the moment, and to provide the material for him to scatter thither and yon" (*Propaganda Techniques in the World War*, p. 53). But higher opportunities will also present themselves. It was as early as 1925, we may recall, that Lasswell invited the participation of the scholarly community in furthering one of the vital causes of positive liberalism.[99] The bolder restatement of this invitation in his review of Lippmann's *The Phantom Public* revealed yet higher vistas:

it would seem that those who want to control the public in the interest of what they conceive to be sound policy ought to outbrazen the rest. If the intelligentsia and the academics shrink at first from participating in or supporting such a continuing body of agitation, and if they have erected this infirmity into a taboo, it is perhaps easier to overcome this taboo of a minority than to remold the entire electorate in the patterns of restraint.[100]

Lasswell has endlessly reiterated this call to arms. Both from the campus and from the seat of government, he has carried messages of propaganda to the potential propagandists themselves.[101] In his presidential address to the American Political Science Association in 1956, he called for the creation of a force of scholars to guide mankind in its perilous journey into the scientific wonderland of the future.[102] It is to such a scholarly force, suitably led, that the fate of mankind should be entrusted, certainly not to conventional political leadership. Lasswell has sought, therefore, to awaken the imagination of the academics, the intelligentsia. He has castigated them with severe descriptions of their present impotence, while tempting them with glimpses of their potentialities for active direction of mankind's future.

Do we by lecturing and writing merely create others who lecture and write? Is there any evidence that those who talk or write in this vein will be marked by any homogeneity during crises of war or revolution? Do they stand out from the rank and file of the community during times of stress, or do they adapt their idiosyncratic vocabulary to the exigencies of instant and overwhelming necessity? Does

[99] See above, pp. 236-237.
[100] *American Journal of Sociology*, January 1926, p. 535.
[101] At the time of his proposals for radical reconstruction of law school curricula (1943), Lasswell was serving as Director of War Communications Research in Washington and was also a "Visiting Sterling Lecturer" at the Yale Law School.
[102] "The Political Science of Science," *American Political Science Review*, December 1956, pp. 961-979, esp. pp. 977 ff.

more knowledge of footnotes and vocabulary modify overt adjustments? Is there anything that carries over from theme writing, lecturing, listening, and discussing to paying, fighting, and the other overt acts of life?

However uncertain the answers may be to this series of questions, we may reflect that those who indulge in the exchange of descriptive-analytical words about world politics constitute a self-selected elite. They usually fire their barrages from the battlements of universities or allied institutions of the higher learning. . . . Indeed, the populace may conceivably acquiesce more and more in their technique of investigation, their questionnaires, their interviews, their physiological measurements. The act of emitting vocabulary in public places, like a university, creates a pattern which diffuses with greater or lesser rapidity along the channels of communication. Could their acts but elicit the requisite deference from the rest of the world, the meek, presumably the college professors in this field, might inherit the earth. . . .

It is indisputable that the world could be unified if enough people were impressed by this (or by any other) elite. The hope of the professors of social science, if not of the world, lies in the competitive strength of an elite based on vocabulary, footnotes, questionnaires, and conditioned responses, against an elite based on vocabulary, poison gas, property, and family prestige. For our encouragement, I may cite the elite which so long and so successfully maintained its position at the apex of the pyramid of the Roman Catholic Church, or I may refer to the Chinese mandarins . . . who so long survived.

We may be without conscious interest in our "power" position in society, but we cannot escape from the "power" implications themselves. . . . Those who declare that they want truth and are indifferent to control may, indeed, get truth; they are bound to have some control [World Politics and Personal Insecurity, pp. 19-21].

Let us share the enthusiasm of Lasswell's apocalyptic vision for a moment. Let us suppose that he succeeds in overcoming the "deep timidities" of the intelligentsia and academics, and that they show themselves willing to join the propagandist in the task of social control. Would not the greater and far more difficult task still lie ahead? Would not Lasswell still need to dispel the suspicion of the very masses for whom social control is necessary? As already noted, this would require "a propagandistic campaign designed to win public understanding, confidence and acceptance of the propagandist." Lasswell argues unceasingly that there is no incompatibility between democracy, as he, the "positive liberal," understands it, and the fullest development of propagandism. Not only can the propagandist strengthen democracy; he is indispensable to its very survival. Lasswell admonishes defenders of the democratic faith to reformulate their credo in the light of the inevitable, as well as the "indispensable," function of propaganda today: "an ethical system which is consonant with present practices must be capable of restatement in a form which sanctions propaganda. Ethical judgments of one sort may kick against the pricks of the unmodifiable; but their probable fate will be to lose out to another set of ethical rationalizations which harmonize with the facts." [103]

One of the major reasons for the distrust of the professional propagandist is the general conviction that he "is engaged in spreading convictions which bear no necessary relation to his private beliefs. . . ." In this respect, he is said to be at one with "the diplomat and the lawyer in flouting certain conventions of democracy, but he is an object of more intense distrust than they, since his goings and comings are still mysterious and therefore particularly ominous to the general public." But surely, argues Lasswell, these are insufficient and improper bases for distrust. Despite the disharmony between the private and public convictions of lawyers and diplomats, it is universally recognized that their services are required by even the most democratic societies. For that matter, "the diplomat and the lawyer are conspicuous and even honorable members of society," even though "there are many detractors who murmur against them." [104] Why should not the propagandist also be recognized as a conspicuous and honorable member of society?

It may be true that without the contributions of lawyers and diplomats, the American republic could hardly have been founded or preserved. But "America's debt to propaganda" is likewise "very great":

The propagandist of religion walked beside or a little in advance of, the explorer, trader and occupier of the broad acres of the New World. The natural reluctance of men to pull up stakes and settle overseas was overcome, in part, by the incessant use of propaganda. . . . "The land of opportunity" is a tribute to the tireless propaganda of the colonizing and shipping interests on both sides of the Atlantic Ocean.[105]

Is it not therefore unjust and unwise for democratic societies to deny to the propagandist that recognition and acceptance which has been accorded his fellow professionals, the lawyer and the diplomat?

The foregoing arguments by no means exhaust Lasswell's attempts to gain general acceptance of the propagandist. Such direct attempts [106] to garb the propagandist in the cloak of respectability constitute only one part, albeit an important one, of his long-run propagandistic campaign. Propaganda aimed

---

[103] International Journal of Ethics, April 1928, p. 261.
[104] Ibid., p. 259.
[105] "The Propagandist Bids for Power," American Scholar, Summer 1939, p. 350.
[106] For an interesting indirect attempt, see Lasswell's Democracy Through Public Opinion (Menasha, Wisc.: George Banta Publishing Co., 1941), in which some of the arguments on behalf of the propagandist which we have been considering appear verbatim—except for replacement of the words "propaganda" and "propagandist" by such terms as "expert on public relations," more acceptable to democratic public opinion. Cf. pp. 74-75 here with the article on "The Function of the Propagandist," International Journal of Ethics, April 1928, pp. 258-259. Cf. also Democracy Through Public Opinion, pp. 36-37, with "The Propagandist Bids for Power," American Scholar, Summer 1939, p. 350, or again with The Analysis of Political Behaviour, pp. 173-174, where the American Scholar article is printed under the different title, "The Rise of the Propagandist."

directly at legitimizing propaganda in a democracy is least effective in the most important case, that is, in the case of the highest and most comprehensive function of propaganda. At this level, the propagandist must engage in a kind of "propaganda of the deed"; he must go beyond talking about propaganda—and propagandize.[107] To this highest function of propaganda, which is at the same time the highest form of propagandizing on behalf of propaganda, we must now direct our attention.

THE MASTER PROPAGANDIST

THE DEVELOPMENTAL CONSTRUCT

The highest task of the propagandist is identified by Lasswell as "goal clarification." It is in the performance of this task that the most comprehensive purpose of propaganda, and of the teacher of propagandists, is revealed. The grounds of Lasswell's argument with respect to goal clarification may be summarized as follows: (1) He reiterates that his "regard for men in the mass rests upon no democratic dogmatisms about men being the best judges of their own interests"; the conventional democratic techniques of policy making are therefore more likely to complicate problems than to resolve them. (2) Neither can the formulation of sound social policy be based on some principal of seeking a compromise between the conflicting interests of individuals or groups. (3) Lasswell therefore finds it necessary to undertake the task of "goal clarification," which is nothing less than the discovery of the genuine—as opposed to the imagined—interests of mankind, the creation of appropriate policies for the implementation of these goals, and the invention of goal symbols designed to win consent (*Ency. Soc. Sci.*, XII, p. 527).

The first of these points requires little further amplification. We need only to remind ourselves of Lasswell's discussion of Lippmann's work, *The Phantom Public*, in which the public was characterized as "spasmodic, superficial,

---

[107] Cf. Lasswell's prescription for an American Capital:

"If we were to offer the specifications for an American Capital, they would run somewhat as follows: (1) The title must be a slogan. . . . (2) The book must be thick. Thickness conveys authoritativeness and discourages reading by the masses who must revere the book as a symbol. (3) The book must be systematic and quantitative ('scientific'). The analytic pattern of thinking has now become so current in society that the volume must appear to possess imposing categories and sub-categories. . . . (4) The vocabulary must be more than analytic. . . . (5) The selected 'facts' must allude mainly to American experience. . . . (6) The key words and the style must be invidious. Terms like 'unearned increment,' 'surplus value,' 'leisure class' can be handled with appropriate innuendo. (7) The volume as a whole should be ambiguous, obscure, and somewhat contradictory. This facilitates the redefinition of the book to serve the purposes of the self-selected revolutionary elite. (8) The style must be dull, in order to reduce the danger that the work will be extensively read or that the illusion of comprehension should sprout too widely and too readily without aid of centralized interpreters . . ." (*World Politics and Personal Insecurity*, p. 219).

and ignorant." [108] This early judgment is reinforced in Lasswell's subsequent discussion of the developing "human sciences," where "the modern propagandist, like the modern psychologist," is said to recognize "that men are often poor judges of their own interests, flitting from one alternative to the next without solid reason . . ." (*Ency. Soc. Sci.*, XII, p. 527).

If such be the case, then those who are responsible for the formulation of social policy will necessarily be involved in "much more than the estimation of the preferences of men. . . ." They will have to take "into account the tissue of relations in which men are webbed, searching for signs of preference which may reflect no deliberation and directing a program toward a solution which fits in fact" (*Ency. Soc. Sci.*, XII, p. 527). The propagandist rejects the passive view of the social process as "a parallelogram of forces" that are largely beyond control and assumes an active or manipulative posture, from which he asks:

How may existing culture-patterns be used to redefine the objects in which I am interested?
Thus the propagandist is constrained to think of society as a process of *defining and affirming meaning*. His chief preoccupation is with the modes of presentation which redefine meanings.[109]

In redefining meanings, the propagandist must, of course, begin by taking account of the "vested values" that are held by those individuals or groups to which and for which he is speaking, hence his need for equilibrium analysis (*Ency. Soc. Sci.*, XII, p. 524). This presents a great challenge to "the propagandist's creative ingenuity," for he must remember that the great masses of men, tending to be unimaginative, place great faith in the familiar and the traditional. It is therefore incumbent upon the propagandist, if he is to protect his handiwork from damaging suspicion and even outright rejection, to make use of familiar names of "values" as he redefines "the significance of social objects."

Thus, "with respect to those adjustments which do require mass action the task of the propagandist is that of inventing goal symbols which serve the double function of facilitating adoption and adaption. The symbols must induce acceptance spontaneously and elicit those changes in conduct necessary to bring about permanent adaptation." It is the task of the propagandist to "create symbols which are not only popular but which bring about positive realignments of behavior." As the "promoter of overt acts" required for social reconstruction, the Master Propagandist must be equipped with the tools of that sociohistorical and psychological analysis dealt with previously. Armed with such understanding, he will be sensitive "to those concentrations of motive which are implicit and available for rapid mobilization when the ap-

[108] See above, p. 240.
[109] *International Journal of Ethics*, April 1928, pp. 265-267, italics supplied.

propriate symbol is offered." This symbol may be discovered by the propagandist through sociohistorical and psychological analysis, after which he may
"direct his creative flashes to final guidance in action" (Ency. Soc. Sci., XII,
p. 527).

To understand this highest activity of the propagandist, indeed of Lasswell himself, we must return to his conception of the "developmental construct." Here we see the identification at the highest level of social scientist
and propagandist. Although the developmental construct is disciplined by
scientific "trend" and "equilibrium" analysis, which we have considered at
length, Lasswell emphasizes that it does not make possible exact prophecy:
"a 'developmental construct' is a speculative model." If "the Marxist conception of our epoch as one moving from capitalism to socialism were free from
dogmatic claims to embody scientific truth," we should have a developmental
construct.[110] Cognizance was taken earlier of Lasswell's discussion of "the
self-fulfilling prophecy" and the difficulty that this implies for the Marxist
claim of historical inevitability. This difficulty is not only recognized but is
ingeniously incorporated into Lasswell's social scientific propaganda. The very
creation and propagation of the developmental construct may become the
most important factor in bringing about those events "predicted" by the
construct.

As propaganda, developmental constructions are mythology. But such constructions are not always—or not only—propaganda. If tentatively and critically
held, they are means to the end of orientation.

Hence developmental constructions are related both to method and to myth.
And method must evaluate their potential effectiveness as myth [World Revolutionary Propaganda, p. vi].

Through the developmental construct, the Master Propagandist redefines
meaning, creates symbols designed to "bring about positive realignments of
behavior," and thereby promotes those "overt acts" required for social reconstruction. In this fashion the tremendous burden of responsibility for the
fate of mankind is shifted from the unfathomable and uncontrollable workings of mysterious history into the surer hands of the Propagandist.

[110] Harold D. Lasswell, "The World Revolutionary Situation," in Carl J. Friedrich (ed.),
Totalitarianism (Cambridge: Harvard University Press, 1954), p. 360, italics supplied. Cf.
Power and Personality, pp. 208 ff., where Lasswell writes that "Marx and Engels were setting up a developmental construct when they postulated the passage of history from capitalism to socialism. They rejected as 'mechanistic' the forms of thinking that had no place
for other than what we call scientific propositions. They made a mistake when they confused their developmental construct with a scientific law, imputing to it the 'inevitability'
of a proposition that summarizes data of observation. An assertion about the 'inevitability'
of future events is propaganda. . . ." Cf. also Lasswell's discussion of "prediction" and
"prophecy" in The Comparative Study of Symbols (Hoover Institute Studies: series C,
no. 1; Stanford: Stanford University Press, 1952), p. 6.

THE GARRISON STATE

Of the several developmental constructs created by Lasswell during the course of his long career, his "garrison state" construct has undoubtedly attracted the most persistent scholarly and popular attention and won the greatest acclaim. This construct, which was first sketched in a 1937 article in the China Quarterly and subsequently developed in more detail in the American Journal of Sociology, has acquired the status of a modern social science classic.[111] It further provides an important part of the framework for the extensive Hoover Institute Studies, Lasswell's single postwar venture into large-scale political research.[112]

Lasswell credits August Comte and Herbert Spencer for having originated the typology of the "garrison state." In one sense, the prototype of the garrison state is the "military state" of the past, whose "distinctive frame of reference . . . is fighting effectiveness" (The Analysis of Political Behaviour, p. 148). The past development and functioning of the military state is of little concern to Lasswell, for the purpose of the developmental construct "is to envisage the possible emergence of the military state under present technical conditions" (p. 147). Given the "technical conditions" of the modern world, the rulers of the contemporary military or "garrison state" will have to possess "a large degree of expertness in many of the skills that we have traditionally accepted as part of modern civilian management." For example, a concern with the morale of the populace will require the development of propaganda skills, and "there will be an energetic struggle to incorporate young and old into the destiny and mission of the state" (pp. 148-149). As we have learned from Lasswell's discussion of "propaganda of the deed," the use of coercion can have an important effect upon far more people than it reaches directly, hence "the spectacle of compulsory labour gangs in prisons or concentration camps is a negative means of conserving morale—negative since it arouses fear and guilt." Thanks to "recent advances in pharmacology," further control of the unskilled masses, along with any "counter-elite elements" can be furthered through "the use of drugs." Still, the ruling elites of the "garrison state" must "for the immediate future" at least "continue to put their chief reliance upon propaganda as an instrument of morale" (pp. 150-151).

Despite the probability of certain "equalitarian adjustments" in the distribution of some values, the political complexion of the garrison state will be distinctly despotic, rather than democratic. "The distribution of power will show the largest inequalities"; accordingly, the distribution of every other

---

111 "Sino-Japanese Crisis: The Garrison State versus the Civilian State," China Quarterly, Fall 1937, pp. 643-649; "The Garrison State and Specialists on Violence," American Journal of Sociology, January 1941, pp. 455-468, reprinted in The Analysis of Political Behaviour, pp. 146-157, which will be cited here.
112 See The World Revolution of Our Time.

value in the "garrison state" will be subject to manipulation and control by the power elite. Since power is not shared equally in the "garrison state," elections will be nothing more than the mockery of the propagandistic "plebiscite." Any rival political parties that dare present themselves will be liquidated, and government will be increasingly centralized and swollen as it absorbs the varied functions of all other associations. This concentration of power will mean that the masses will receive only a small portion of the material advantages made available by the technique of modern science. The elites of the "garrison state," like "the ruling elites of the modern business state," the bourgeoisie, will continue to hold "in check the stupendous productive potentialities of modern science and engineering." They "will most assuredly prevent full utilization of modern productive capacity for non-military consumption purposes" (p. 153). In the "garrison" or "totalitarian" state, "the essential characteristic of all institutions is that all values—power, wealth, respect, enlightenment, for example—are concentrated in a few hands and are subordinated to the supreme value—power." [113]

Although Lasswell does not equate the "garrison state" with fascism, one can hardly fail to be struck by their many points of resemblance. Moreover, his explanation of the rise of "garrison states" out of the crisis of "dilatory capitalism" [114] skilfully applies certain theses of Lenin's Imperialism, or, more generally, a latter-day Marxist explanation of the rise of fascism:

Tormented by their insecurities, businessmen and monopoly-politicians, when confronted by rival politicians who invoke a socialist vocabulary, are sorely tempted to embark on a war to "restore freedom" by opening up areas to the "world market" that have been excluded from it by political means. This alternative drives the genuinely competitive businessman and the civilian monopolist into the arms of the military and the police, whether in preparation for war, or in the attempt to administer "conquered" territory. Under modern conditions the active phase of fighting must be followed by prolonged military and police measures in order to protect a new regime against subversion. . . .

Dilatory capitalism, therefore, finds itself partly transformed into a political order, uncertain what to do next. One prognosis, at least, is highly probable: War will not restore business but consolidate the military and the police in a garrison-caste state [Power and Personality, pp. 215-216].[115]

---

[113] *Psychiatry*, August 1950, p. 285.

[114] See *Power and Personality*, pp. 212-216.

[115] Cf. Robert A. Brady, *Business as a System of Power* (New York: Columbia University Press, 1943). The major elements of this position have long been present in Lasswell's work. "The road to power in our civilization is by no means an exclusively governmental highway, for technical implements have scattered authority and created an industrial feudality. The directors of large corporations have to make decisions which are far more important for the daily happiness of mankind than most of the decisions of governments. Since government is so largely the agent of corporations, the government is hardly master in its own house" (*Psychopathology and Politics*, p. 47).

Understandably, Lasswell is passionately concerned that what he takes to be a "probable" drift of the world toward "garrison states" be reversed. While the "principle of preference for a free economy springs directly from the over-riding goal of human dignity" (*National Security and Individual Freedom*, p. 70), such an economy in practice is found to have led to monopoly and to the concentration of wealth, phenomena which have troubled Lasswell from the earliest expression of his positive liberalism. In the United States, the free economy waned around the turn of the century; industry became more monopolistic and wealth more concentrated.[116] "If the Americans of middle income can be brought to self-consciousness in the demand for the ruthless use of the income tax to eliminate incomes above a modest figure, the problems arising from the inequitable distribution of wealth will be less acute" (*World Politics and Personal Insecurity*, p. 232). However, the underlying problem of monopoly presents a more difficult challenge. "We must recognize . . . that from the point of view of a free society the objection to monopoly is less economic than political and moral" (*World Politics Faces Economics*, p. 87). For that matter, "monopolistic business is a form of politics, and is called 'business' by mistake or design. One result of the mistake or design is that the politicians who run monopoly business use the symbol 'business' to obtain support from what remains of genuinely competitive businessmen in the rivalry of monopoly-politicians with government-party politicians" (*Power and Personality*, pp. 137-138).

In Lasswell's view, "many factors, including the vastly increased capitalization required by modern industry, have so greatly heightened the tendencies toward the concentration of control that government must step in to prevent private monopoly, and must thereupon retain control in order to ensure the benefits of large industrial production" (*National Security and Individual Freedom*, p. 71). In some instances, mixed economies might provide the solution: "some economies can be not 'all-socialist' but 'socialist-primacy' economies; others can be not 'all-capitalist' but 'capitalist-primacy' economies" (*World Politics Faces Economics*, p. 85). The special circumstances of any given society would, presumably, determine the appropriate combination of state and private ownership of the means of production. In any case, sweeping changes in economic relationships, generally in the direction of socialism, will be required. "In nations possessing a long tradition of democracy," Lasswell suggests, "the likelihood that socialism can be combined with democracy is greatest" (p. 84). However, the objective is not the preservation or creation of any particular political institutions. Indeed, if those political institutions traditionally associated with democratic government were to present serious obstacles to economic and social reconstruction, they would have to yield in

[116] See Harold D. Lasswell, "Skill Politics and Skill Revolution," reprinted from *Chinese Social and Political Science Review*, October-December 1937, in *The Analysis of Political Behaviour*, p. 135.

favor of the more fundamental objectives. The need for social reconstruction might even require the replacement of the traditional institutions of representative government by a temporary "dictatorship." Such a change in institutions need not be considered undemocratic, Lasswell argues:

> It is convenient to use the term "dictatorship" for a temporary concentration of effective and formal power in a few hands. Thus capitalist or socialist dictatorships can be democratic if they are conceived as emergency suspensions of democracy, or as transitional steps toward democracy [p. 85].[117]

THE FREE MAN'S COMMONWEALTH

It is clear that Lasswell is fervently concerned with reversing the contemporary and, hopefully, short-term trend toward garrison states. But the positive objective of the Master Propagandist extends far beyond the mere modification of traditional economic, social, and political institutions, all of which are, fundamentally, institutions of power. Lasswell's ultimate objective is the utter annihilation of that sphere of life and discourse characterized by power. It is precisely for this reason that such great institutional latitude can be permitted during the period of transition to the power-free, universal democratic society.

[117] Since it is despotism, not dictatorship, which the social psychiatrist must combat, it is important for Lasswell to distinguish the two terms. He writes that "the word 'despotism' is here used to mean both tyrannies and absolutisms. That form of despotism or dictatorship in which a number of capitalistic institutions are found has often been called fascist. There is, however, no such agreement upon a term for despotism or dictatorship combined with many socialist institutions. Sometimes, when fascism is made a synonym of despotism, 'social (socialist)-fascist' is the term."

While there may very well be no *universal* "agreement upon a term for despotism or dictatorship combined with many socialist institutions," it is rather curious that Lasswell fails even to mention the generally used term, "dictatorship of the proletariat." Given this failure, the reader is left to wonder whether the U.S.S.R. is to be classified as "social (socialist)-fascist" or as a socialist-democratic (temporary) dictatorship. In 1945, when these definitions were published, Lasswell reported that "the Russian system is organized as a gigantic hierarchy, and there is a chain of command from top to bottom. . . . [D]evices of mass participation have been kept strictly within bounds by the tight, centralized discipline of the Communist party. In the future, as initiatives multiply from below, democratic centralism may come closer to democratic theory. And this largely depends on world political security" (*World Politics Faces Economics*, pp. 85-86). This hope appears to have faded by 1950, when Lasswell notes that:

"Through the years it has been slowly dawning upon the observers of Russia that the most important thing to be discovered about Soviet Russia is that it is not what it purports to be. This discovery has been made, often at great personal and social cost, by ever-enlarging circles of laymen, writers, scholars, and politicians. . . .

"The evidence accumulates that the regime is neither communist nor socialist nor democratic. . . .

"What, then, is the true nature of the regime in Moscow? The answer is not too difficult. Soviet Russia is a garrison-police state, in which the political police are exercising a dominant role. It has been characterized [by Karl A. Wittfogel] as an oriental despotism in modern clothes . . ." (*National Security and Individual Freedom*, pp. 20-21).

Let us therefore begin by clarifying the characteristics of the democratic community, which is the form of society which it is our purpose to achieve on the widest possible scale in both space and time. A democratic community is one in which human dignity is realized in theory and fact. It is characterized by wide rather than narrow participation in the shaping and sharing of values [*The Political Writings*, pp. 473-474].

Having selected a "workable list" of values—in this instance, power, respect, affection, rectitude, well-being, wealth, skill, and enlightenment— Lasswell attempts to provide "operational" definitions for the purpose of specifying "the nature of the prevailing 'myth' which we regard as in harmony with shared values" and "the patterns of 'technique' which meet the minimum requirements of sharing" (p. 475).[118] The genuinely democratic community, or Free Man's Commonwealth, is, as we shall observe, the obverse or positive side of the garrison state construct. Virtually each of the characteristics of this perfect society is the polar opposite of its counterpart in the garrison state construct. In particular, as the garrison state is said to be characterized by power, with the resulting unequal distribution of values, so the Free Man's Commonwealth is chiefly characterized by the absence of power, and "by wide rather than narrow participation in the shaping and sharing of values." The garrison state and the Free Man's Commonwealth consistently reveal themselves as simply opposite faces of Lasswell's one great developmental construct.

It is not necessary to consider Lasswell's definition of each of these values as it appears in the democratic myth. As will be seen, each one is implied in every other. Moreover, there is reason to think that the value of "affection" is fundamental and therefore warrants special attention.[119] The full definition of "affection," as it appears in Lasswell's articulation of the "myth" of democracy, is as follows:

1. The myth emphasizes the *desirability of congenial human relationships*, and emphasizes the capacity of human beings for entering into such relations.
2. Hostile attitudes are overcome by deliberate efforts to restore friendly attitudes, and these efforts are largely successful in practice. . . .
3. Hostilities are prevented by reducing provocativeness, as well as by the exercise of self-control directed against impulsive expressions of destructiveness against others. . . .
4. There needs to be equality of opportunity for the exercise of affection as a means of achieving affection; and this implies access to the base values which influence the channels and targets of affection. . . .

118 It is not altogether clear whether Lasswell is defining the prevailing myth or the myth that would be in harmony with the "concept of sharing." This ambiguity is consistent, however, with the propagandist's "preoccupation . . . with the modes of presentation which redefine meanings."
119 "Men are not born slaves but have slavery thrust upon them through interference with healthy sexual development" (*Power and Personality*, p. 167; see also pp. 17, 118).

5. Denials of affection should be directed against conduct inimical to the free man's commonwealth. In the ideal commonwealth, affections would be so developed from infancy that incentives would be lacking for conduct inimical to freedom. The withholding of affection is a legitimate means of bringing about and sustaining congenial interpersonal relationships.

6. The scope of affection for human beings needs to be as wide as humanity. Less inclusive loyalties need not be abolished, but made compatible with the harmony of the whole [*The Political Writings,* pp. 477-478, italics supplied].

Not every manifestation of "affection" satisfies Lasswell's criteria. Some individuals manifest an "excessive demand for affection" which interferes with the "equality of opportunity for the exercise of affection" specified in section 4 of the foregoing definition. Such an excessive demand often takes the form of "an intense and all-embracing sentimental bond with another person" (p. 496). Such "exclusive couplings may represent a withdrawal from fuller functioning in the community." Moreover, they may operate "as a preventive of the degree of detachment which enables the individual to sense the feelings and viewpoints of others in the life of an entire group, such as appears to be characteristic of those persons who are well-equipped to function in a democratic manner" (pp. 500, 496).

Having similarly defined the other values as they appear in the democratic myth, Lasswell proceeds to describe the "democratic character" that would populate a sound and stable world. The democratic character displays what Lasswell calls the "open ego": "the democratic attitude toward other human beings is warm rather than frigid, inclusive and expanding rather than exclusive and constricting. . . . Such a person transcends most of the cultural categories that divide human beings from one another, and senses the common humanity across class and even caste lines within the culture, and in the world beyond the local culture." The democratic character is "*multi-valued, rather than single-valued, and . . . disposed to share rather than to hoard or to monopolize.*" The democratic character has a "*deep confidence in the benevolent potentialities of man.*" Above all, the democratic character is free from unconscious determinants of behavior and the distortions and anxieties which result therefrom (*The Political Writings,* pp. 495-498, 502, 503). The democratic character is, in summary, perfectly socialized, perfectly free of inhibitions and anxiety, perfectly content, perfectly peaceful.

Lasswell's description of this Utopia, as well as his explicit references to Aldous Huxley, suggest comparison with *Brave New World,* a universal society shaped according to the maxim: Community, Identity, Stability. Like Lasswell, Huxley's characters strongly deplore the exclusive couplings of men and women in the "pre-modern world." "Family, monogamy, romance. Everywhere exclusiveness, everywhere a focussing of interest, a narrow channeling of impulse and energy." [120] Huxley's World Controllers ensure "equality of opportunity for the exercise of affection" through such devices as the encouragement of uninhibited sex play in children and promiscuity in adults, the complete emancipation of women, the production of children in hatcheries, and the generous provision of the drug "soma." [121] These indulgences rest, however, on thoroughly inculcated standards of rectitude, summed up in the proverb that "everyone belongs to everyone else." Those few unfortunates whose "conditioning" failed might be properly subjected to "denials of affection" in the fashion suggested in section 5 of Lasswell's definition. The similarities are striking; there is no exclusionary privacy, no anxiety, no tension, no conflict, no passion, no pain—nothing but pure shared pleasure: "Self indulgence up to the very limits imposed by hygiene and economics" [122] or, in Lasswellian terms, the maximization of Indulgences and the minimization of Deprivations.

It is quite true that what Lasswell offers as an ideal of personal and social health, Huxley satirically castigates as an utterly degraded inhuman condition.[123] Yet it would be unfair simply to equate the *Brave New World* and the Free Man's Commonwealth. For one thing, Lasswell's new world, unlike Huxley's, is intended to be thoroughly democratic. Since in Lasswell's scheme any value may serve as a base for the realization of any other value, the affection (for example) received by any individual would depend, to a considerable extent, upon the amount of power, respect, rectitude, well-being, wealth, skill, and enlightenment he enjoyed. "Equality of opportunity for the exercise of affection" would then depend on equality of opportunity with respect to every other value. Moreover, *continued* equality of opportunity would depend upon the maintenance of the fundamental equality of everyone with respect to these values. In the Free Man's Commonwealth, not only would "everyone *belong* to everyone else," but everyone would have to be *like* everyone else in every important respect.

Lasswell's radical egalitarianism stands in striking contrast to the strictly

[120] Aldous Huxley, *Brave New World* (New York: Harper & Brothers, 1946) pp. 45-46.
[121] On the emancipation of women, cf. *The Political Writings of Harold D. Lasswell*, p. 500; on the production of children in hatcheries, cf. "The Political Science of Science," *American Political Science Review*, December 1956, p. 975; on the provision of the drug "soma," cf. *Analysis of Political Behaviour*, p. 151.
[122] *Brave New World*, p. 284.
[123] Lasswell contends that "Huxley's 'brave new world' is not one in which institutions are rationalized, but only technicalized. Important values (for instance, the moral) were not taken into account; practices were ultimately not economical in relation to those values" (*Power and Society*, pp. 70-71). Lasswell is simply wrong. Huxley's "world controllers" (social and political psychiatrists) were constantly concerned with bringing the populace to understand that certain types of conduct, for example, "exclusive couplings," were immoral, while other kinds of conduct, for example, the realization of the maxim "everyone belongs to everyone else," were moral. The author's central purpose in this work is moral criticism, criticism of the results of that contemporary moral and political obtuseness which may culminate in the horror of a "brave new world."

hierarchical structure of *Brave New World*, running from the Epsilon Semi-Morons through several intermediate castes to an Alpha-Plus elite from which are drawn the World Controllers who have the responsibility for governing the whole society. The *Brave New World* is still, in certain respects, a political world, populated by rulers and ruled and dependent for its smooth functioning upon the exercise of power. Lasswell's Free Man's Commonwealth, like the Utopia which Engels divined when he "wrote of the eventual 'withering away of the state,' " lies completely beyond politics.[124]

The recognition that people are poor judges of their own interest is often supposed to lead to the conclusion that a dictator is essential. But no student of individual psychology can fail to share the conviction of Kempf that "Society is *not* safe. . . . when it is forced to follow the dictations of one individual, of one autonomic apparatus, no matter how splendidly and altruistically it may be conditioned." Our thinking has too long been misled by the threadbare terminology of democracy versus dictatorship, of democracy versus aristocracy. Our problem is to be ruled by the truth about the conditions of harmonious human relations, and the discovery of the truth is an object of specialized research; it is no monopoly of people as people, or of the ruler as ruler [*Psychopathology and Politics*, p. 197].

To be ruled by the truth—that is, indeed, the ideal. One difficulty, however, is that we do not yet possess the full truth. Considerable as our progress has been, Lasswell does not attempt to conceal the extent of the social scientists' ignorance, which his own attempts to describe the healthy psyche and the healthy society make abundantly clear.[125] "We cannot, at this moment in history, pride ourselves upon what we know or what we put into practice about human relations" (*The Political Writings*, p. 525).

There is the further question of how the truth (assuming it to have been discovered) will *rule*. At times, Lasswell seems to answer: by enlightenment. "In a sense the aim of the science of man is to make such a science superfluous. This is achieved in the degree that insight into value goals, past trends, and past conditioning factors increase the scope of policy choice touching upon the future realization of a commonwealth in which the dignity of man is respected in theory and fact" (pp. 524-525). Following this line of argument, it would seem that the aim of the science of man is to bring men to an understanding of their sociological and psychological condition and thus set them permanently free. It is significant, however, that Lasswell illustrates his description of the "open ego" with the "extreme case" of " 'saints' who

124 Cf. *Power and Personality*, p. 110, with the concluding argument of *Democratic Character* (in *The Political Writings of Harold D. Lasswell*, pp. 524-525), where Lasswell writes that "it is by exposing and perhaps destroying the interpersonal relationships which have held true in the past that scientific effort produces the most far-reaching results."
125 See Lasswell's discussion of "pathological" and "healthy," *Psychopathology and Politics*, p. 200; *Power and Personality*, p. 146; *The Political Writings of Harold D. Lasswell*, p. 525. See also, Bernard Crick's excellent discussion, *The American Science of Politics*, pp. 197 ff.

have undergone the deprivations of a concentration camp without losing the serenity of outlook that reaches out hopefully and tolerantly toward other human beings" (p. 496). The difficulty is that these are exceptions, not merely because of the faulty "conditioning" of most of mankind but in principle: "the instinctive nature of man is in principle non-social and in important particulars antisocial . . ." (*Ency. Soc. Sci.*, IV, p. 195). Indeed, one of Lasswell's reiterated criticisms of Marx has been the latter's failure to take account of the irrational, destructive, antisocial aspects of man's nature. It is precisely because Lasswell *does* take account of these factors that he is forced by his own principles to understand the task of social reconstruction as an endless one.

The task is nothing less than the drastic and continuing reconstruction of our own civilization, and most of the cultures of which we have any knowledge. Since the basic postulate of behavior is the maximization of indulgences over deprivations, our task is to consolidate democratic conduct by directing the indulgences toward those who act democratically, and the deprivations toward those who do not [*The Political Writings*, p. 513].[126]

"The aim," Lasswell goes on, "is to bring into being a democratic equilibrium in societal relations in which deviations are promptly rectified." He explains that if we were designing a machine we could " 'build in' a set of servo-mechanisms which perform this re-stabilizing operation." However, "since human relations are not mechanized, our task of creating and sustaining a democratic equilibrium is more complex" (pp. 513-514). Recognizing this complexity, men have traditionally relied upon complex systems of personal inhibition, social restraint, and political institutions to maintain democratic regimes. All of this is associated by Lasswell with the unhealthy "political" condition of mankind which is to be liquidated. With all the old restraints broken down, the possibility of infinite perfection, or democratization, of the human character will unfold. However, the realization of that ideal depends absolutely upon the social psychiatrist (the "master voice," [127] the "we" of whom Lasswell so often speaks), whose authority would have to be absolute. As the Supreme Conditioner of indulgences and deprivations, as the rectifier of "deviations," the social psychiatrist must exercise complete and unrestricted power.[128]

There is one sense, to be sure, in which the Free Man's Commonwealth would ultimately be characterized by the absence of power. The masses of men in such society would become powerless, because all power must finally

---

[126] Cf. *Power and Personality*, pp. 150 ff.

[127] See above, p. 276.

[128] When "policies are expected to be enforced against an obstructor by the imposing of extreme deprivations, we have . . . a power relation. The offender can be deprived of any or all values." *Power and Personality*, p. 18. See also, *The Political Writings of Harold D. Lasswell*, p. 474.

be concentrated in the hands of those who are engaged in "the drastic and continuing reconstruction" of society. To be ruled "by the truth about the conditions of harmonious human relations" is inevitably to be ruled by those who possess or are presumed to possess that truth. The paradoxical outcome of Lasswell's attempt to obliterate power is that he must resort finally to power in its most extreme and arbitrary form. As Bernard Crick soberly concludes, "if one is not really alarmed at the direct totalitarian implication in Lasswell's manner of thought, it is because one does not take it seriously, because one believes it to be impossible to apply." [129]

Lasswell has never confronted this problem, but he has attempted to deal with it obliquely in his discussion of the education of the new rulers. "The achievement of the ideal of preventive politics depends less upon changes in social organization than upon improving the methods and the education of social administrators and social scientists." "If the politics of prevention spreads in society, a different type of education will become necessary for those who administer sociey or think about it" (Psychopathology and Politics, pp. 203, 201). Of what will this education consist? The social psychiatrist will, in the first place, have to be the complete social scientist. He will require, as we have seen, a full sociopsychological understanding of man's history, of his present condition, and of future trends. By means of the comprehensive "configurative analysis," including both its extensive and intensive dimension, he will seek "to find out what will stay put in social practice" (Ency. Soc. Sci., XII, p. 527).[130] But that is not a sufficient standard, for there is an enormous area of uncertainty and doubt about the future of mankind, which must be filled by the propogandistic developmental construct. The social psychiatrist is no mere midwife assisting at the birth of an inevitable new era. As is all too clear from Lasswell's own analysis, the garrison state may very well "stay put in social practice." The problem is to discover the good solution "which fits in fact." The social psychiatrist or propagandist must act "in the interest of what [he] conceive[s] to be sound policy"; [131] he must exercise "creative ingenuity" in bringing about "positive realignments of behavior" (Ency. Soc. Sci., XII, pp. 524, 527). He does not merely lead men to the realm of freedom but gives the realm of freedom its meaning. "Since we are interested in relating character formation to the attainment of a democratic commonwealth, it will be necessary to engage in a continuous process of clarifying the conception of such a community" (The Political Writings, p. 521).

Given this responsibility for the positive recreation of values and reconstruction of character, the social psychiatrist's own values and character become of central importance, as Lasswell recognizes. Consequently Lasswell argues that the social psychiatrist must possess a wide—even universal—ex-

[129] The American Science of Politics, pp. 208-209.
[130] See above, p. 241.
[131] American Journal of Sociology, January 1926, p. 535.

perience of varying human situations, and thus human values. He must spend less time at his desk than in the field, in intimate "contact" and "intercourse" with the human matter he studies and on which he works. "The social administrator and social scientist . . . must mix with rich and poor, with savage and civilized, with sick and well, with old and young. His contacts must be primary and not exclusively secondary." Most important, the social psychiatrist must himself be in a state of psychological health. "He must have an opportunity for prolonged self-scrutiny by the best-developed methods of personality study, and he must laboriously achieve a capacity to deal objectively with himself and with all others in human society" (*Psychopathology and Politics*, p. 201).

Let us suppose the existence of such a thoroughly experienced and carefully psychoanalyzed social psychiatrist, in possession of that absolute ruling power to which he is, according to Lasswell's teaching, entitled. *For the sake of what* will he "deal objectively with himself and with all others in human society"? For the sake, it would seem, of the Free Man's Commonwealth. The social psychiatrist will give himself up to the endless task of maintaining human freedom and dignity in the face of threats from the antisocial and irrational nature of man. Like Dostoevski's Grand Inquisitor, or at least like Huxley's World Controller, he must take upon himself the enormous burden of truth and freedom for the sake of the happiness of his subjects.

Although Lasswell appears to envisage some such order of men as constituting his psychoanalytocracy, there is, it must be said, no basis for it in his own psychology. A very modest way of expressing the foregoing vision would be to say that the psychoanalytocracy will be composed, at least, of men of the greatest rectitude. Yet, as we have seen, Lasswell has no basis for understanding rectitude except as a form of self-seeking. Lasswell's own psychology forbids us to rest content with his vision of a superlatively public-spirited band of social psychiatrists. It warns us, on the contrary, that the social psychiatrist will "deal objectively with himself and with all others in human society" for the sake of maximizing his own indulgences and minimizing his deprivations.[132]

But do the motives of the social psychiatrist really make any difference? With the worst of motives, he will no doubt find it most efficacious to exercise his power in such a way as to convey the *impression* of widely distributed "shaping and sharing of values"; and with the best of motives, he can do no more. Traditional political man, according to Lasswell, displaces his private motives onto public objects and rationalizes the displacement in terms of public interests. Not only does he thereby cause endless difficulties for those he is supposed to be ruling; he is extraordinarily ineffective in his search for indulgence. He remains immature, infantile. The

[132] See *The Political Writings of Harold D. Lasswell*, p. 513: "the basic postulate of behaviour is the maximization of indulgences over deprivations. . . ." See above, pp. 258-262.

properly trained social psychiatrist, on the other hand, while perhaps born a "politician," will have entirely outgrown it and will have no need for such "rationalizations." Having been taught to deal with himself and others "objectively"—and having, in addition, secured unlimited power—he will be in a position to secure for himself a level of indulgence utterly beyond the reach of traditional political man and, *at the same time*, to free his subjects from anxiety, tension, and conflict—to indulge them in a permanent, pleasant psychological coma. He will, in a word, make those tyrannies with which *homo politicus* has periodically tarnished the history of mankind look, literally, like child's play.

CONCLUSION

Reflection on each of the major aspects of Lasswell's work reveals the collapse of his initial distinction between scientific political theory and political philosophy.[133] This distinction breaks down for the simple but massive reason that Lasswell's social science, taken in its entirety, has always had the character of what he has in recent years identified as the "policy science of democracy." [134] It is this single science that provides the basis for his understanding of both democracy and despotism—as well as any possible regime in between. While Lasswell maintains that there may be a policy science of despotism, as well as a policy science of democracy [135]—as there may be treatises on the pursuit of vice as well as virtue—the characteristics of despotism are nothing more than inversions of the qualities ascribed to democracy. The decisive consideration is that the qualities of democracy and despotism are described within the framework of a single science, the science of personal and social health. Accordingly, that aspect of Lasswell's policy science which attempts to "state conditions" has always been inseparable from that aspect which "justifies preferences," and it is the normative or prescriptive element

---

[133] See above, pp. 228 ff.

[134] See esp. Daniel Lerner and Harold D. Lasswell (eds.), *The Policy Sciences: Recent Developments in Scope and Method* (Stanford, California: Stanford University Press, 1951). In discussing "The Policy Sciences of Democracy," Lasswell writes that "it is . . . safe to forecast that the policy-science approach will bring about a series of 'special' sciences within the general field of the social sciences, much as the desire to cure has developed a science of medicine which is distinct from, though connected with, the general science of biology" (p. 10). Or, again, "Democratic leadership is a key problem of the as yet poorly developed policy sciences of democracy. . . . The democratic equilibrium is one in which human destructiveness, whether of impulse or practice, is kept low. Hence it appears that the problem of democratic leadership and eliteship is equivalent to the development of social health rather than disease. This appears to be the program of social psychiatry, in particular, among the medical sciences. Hence social psychiatry becomes the equivalent in scope to the policy sciences of democracy . . ." (*Power and Personality*, p. 146).

[135] "The Policy Orientation," in *The Policy Sciences*, p. 10. See also *The Political Writings of Harold D. Lasswell*, p. 471; "The Garrison State and Specialist on Violence," *The Analysis of Political Behaviour*, p. 157.

which has been controlling and dominant. In Lasswellian terminology, one may conclude that of the three tasks set for "the systematic student of politics," those of "description" and "prediction" have consistently been subordinate to that of "social control." This relationship is evident in every phase of Lasswell's work, whether it be the early formulations of "positive liberalism" his sociohistorical analysis resting on descriptive-prescriptive Marxian foundations, or his psychological formulations as guided by a certain understanding of mental health.

If Lasswell's Free Man's Commonwealth is a prospect to strike terror in the hearts of free men, it is nevertheless the product of a breadth of vision that is all too rare among contemporary political or social scientists. Lasswell has refused to narrow his scope of inquiry in order to achieve what might be regarded by some social scientists as greater methodological or scientific purity. The breadth of his enterprise invites comparison with the architectonic formulations of some of the great political philosophers of the past, and Lasswell, himself, has ventured such comparisons, especially in his more recent writings. He has, on occasion, suggested that the central concern of social psychiatry, the simultaneous molding of character and culture, was a paramount concern of "the classical tradition."

The connection between individual character and the body politic is a recurring theme in the classical political tradition. "The type of character appropriate to the constitution," wrote Aristotle, "is the power which continues to sustain it, as it is also the force which originally creates it." When he spoke of the constitution Aristotle was thinking of something broader than an "arrangement of offices." He had in mind "a scheme of life, directed to attain a particular quality of life," which is [a] conception close to the inclusiveness of the modern idea of "a culture" [*The Political Writings*, p. 465].

It is necessary to point out that Aristotle's understanding of "constitution" is not merely an "arrangement of offices"; but it is even more necessary to understand the vast gulf that separates it from "culture." "Constitution" is a political term, and for Aristotle the relationship between "character" and "constitution" must be understood as a *political* problem.[136] On the other hand, if anything is clear about the idea of "culture," it is that it does not find its definition in the political realm. Aristotle is concerned with the contributions which the various claimants to rule can make to the good life of the community. The often conflicting claims of these partisans are weighed against the established facts of political life as experienced by countless communities under all politically relevant circumstances. Aristotle's detailed and painstaking examination of politics leads him to conclude that the radicalization of partisan claims, whether democratic or oligarchic, leads to injustice, to civic dissension, and, in the extreme case, to revolution. Competent legis-

[136] See below, pp. 310 ff.

lators must, therefore, "believe that the true policy, for democracy and oligarchy alike, is not one which ensures the greatest possible amount of either, but one which will ensure the longest possible life for both." [137] This moderate, down-to-earth, and nondoctrinaire political goal is based upon observation of everyday political life, and it is presented in the form of arguments taken from and directed to the domain of politics.

It is not necessary to reach back to Aristotle for this kind of political analysis. Lasswell's own early studies were, as we have seen, directly concerned with real and pressing problems of political life. Although the tenets of his "positive liberalism" were decidedly nebulous, they were initially characterized by some measure of that prudential restraint and balance which is necessary for a teaching oriented to the requirements of political life. Lasswell quickly became impatient, however, not only with the clashing views of the proponents of "negative" and "positive" liberalism, but with politics altogether. In consequence, he replaced the limited objectives of political life with an irresponsible ideology which accepts no restriction.

The principal expectation contained in democratic ideology is that it is possible to attain universal democracy by bringing into existence on a global scale the equilibrium that has repeatedly been achieved in more parochial communities. The democrat identifies himself with mankind as a whole and with all subordinate groups whose demands are in harmony with the larger loyalty [Power and Personality, p. 108].

This objective stems neither from the political objectives of any identifiable political community, past or present, nor from any recognizable formulation of traditional democratic theory. Nor can it properly be said to represent the ascertainable position of any substantial number of citizens of any existing democratic state. The "democrat" here makes no intelligible claim to rule; rather, he "identifies himself with mankind as a whole," whatever this may mean. In seeking to understand how Lasswell transformed an initially promising political analysis into a radically non-political ideology we need not resort to dubious psychological explanations. The necessary elements of a political explanation abound throughout his work. Lasswell's ever more doctrinaire commitment to a certain understanding of justice has increasingly blinded him to the possibility that there may be some elements of justice in the claims of other political partisans. Excessively impatient to better the conditions of contemporary society, to get things done, to discover scientifically the solution "which fits in fact," Lasswell has devoted ever less serious and sustained attention to politics. He has instead fled to ideology, first to what seemed the most useful and sophisticated ideology of our day:

It should not be denied that the long-run aim of societies aspiring toward human freedom is to get rid of power and to bring into existence a free man's com-

[137] *Politics*, vi, 5; 1319b-1320a.

monwealth in which coercion is neither threatened, applied nor desired. This is the thread of anarchist idealism that appears in all uncompromising applications of the key conception of human dignity. When Engels wrote of the eventual "withering away of the state" he was voicing the hope, though not necessarily the certainty, of the radical democrat [Power and Personality, p. 110].

Not content with the mere "withering away of the state," Lasswell sought the elimination of psychological tensions and anxieties as well. He has thus attempted to combine his Marxism with a dubious "socialized" Freudianism. It is significant that Lasswell's least insubstantial definitions of his objectives are stated negatively: the "withering away of the state," and the elimination of power, conflict, tension, and anxiety. His ideology is thus best summed up in the doctrine of "preventive politics," which is . . . the prevention of politics. The reader who attempts to discover the precise substance of the Lasswellian ideology, particularly the exact terms of the marriage between Marx and Freud, finds that the intricate threads of this exposition become ever more entangled with eclectic borrowings from other modern political theorists, psychologists, and a veritable host of twentieth-century intellectuals. Having failed to weave these strands into the fabric of a unified argument, Lasswell leaves many of them to "wither and die," while placing ever more reliance on a blanket invitation to others to join forces with him in scientific manipulation—an invitation predicated on undemonstrable trust in the scientific training, the wisdom, and the good will of the Master Propagandist.

Lasswell's unusual endowments, the breadth of his vision, the extent of his aspirations, and his life of dedicated activity in pursuit of their realization have saved him from a sterile concern with mere methodology. We have accordingly argued that he is distinguished among contemporary political scientists, not primarily because of his innumerable methodological explorations, but because of his unwillingness to abandon altogether the horizon of political philosophy with its indispensable questions about the character of the just society and the nature and ends of man. Unfortunately, Lasswell's conception of political philosophy as "metaphysical speculation in terms of abstractions hopelessly removed from empirical observation and control" (Power and Society, p. x), prevents him from taking political philosophy seriously. His consciousness of the horizon of political philosophy, together with his refusal to deal in any sustained or adequate fashion with the problems it poses, leaves his thought impaled on the horns of an irresolvable dilemma; and this dilemma has turned him in the direction of manipulation, or propaganda. Yet this propaganda is in the service of an ideology carelessly and almost thoughtlessly patched together from scraps of modern political philosophy. Expressed in Lasswellian terms, Lasswell, the student, teacher, and practitioner of propaganda, has served unwittingly as a tool of certain modern political philosophers who were also propagandists of a stature and subtlety beyond even his active imagination. While inviting the assistance of like-minded academics who long to pull "the strings of Punch and Judy," the aspiring puppet master cavorts upon a stage built by others. The Master Propagandist is himself the victim of Propaganda.

V

AN EPILOGUE

by LEO STRAUSS

THE FOUR preceding essays deal with four particularly well-known manifestations of what one may call the new science of politics. That new approach to political things emerged shortly before World War I; it became preponderant and at the same time reached its mature or final form before, during, and after World War II. It need not be a product or a symptom of the crisis of the modern Western World—of a world which could boast of being distinguished by ever broadening freedom and humanitarianism; it is surely contemporary with that crisis.

The new political science shares with the most familiar ingredients of our world in its crisis the quality of being a mass phenomenon. That it is a mass phenomenon is compatible with the fact that it possesses its heights and its depths, the handful of opinion leaders, the men responsible for the breakthroughs on the top, and the many who drive on the highways projected by the former at the bottom. It wields very great authority in the West, above all in this country. It controls whole departments of political science in great and in large universities. It is supported by foundations of immense wealth with unbounded faith and unbelievably large grants. In spite of this, one runs little risk in taking issue with it. For its devotees are fettered by something like an Hippocratic oath to subordinate all considerations of safety, income, and deference to concern with the truth. The difficulty lies elsewhere. It is not easy to free one's mind from the impact of any apparently beneficent authority, for such freeing requires that one step outside of the circle warmed and charmed by the authority to be questioned. Yet it is necessary to make the effort. The new political science itself must demand it. One might say that precisely because the new political science is an authority operating within a democracy, it owes an account of itself to those who are subjected, or are to be subjected, to it. However sound it may be, it is a novelty. That it emerged so late is probably no accident: deep seated resistances had to be overcome step by step in a process of long duration. Precisely if the new political science constitutes the mature approach to political things, it presupposes the experience of the failure of earlier approaches. We ourselves no longer have that experience: George has had it for us. Yet to leave it at that is unbecoming to men of science; men of science cannot leave it at hearsay or at vague remembrances. To this one might reply that the resistances to the new political science have not entirely vanished: the old Adam is still alive. But precisely because this is so, the new political science, being a rational enterprise, must be able to lead the old Adam by a perfectly lucid, coherent, and sound argument from his desert, which he mistakes for a paradise, to its own green pastures. It must cease to demand from us, in the posture of a noncommissioned officer, a clean and unmediated break with our previous habits, that is, with common sense; it must supply us with a ladder by which we can ascend, in full clarity as to what we are doing, from common sense to science. It must begin to learn to look with sympathy at the obstacles to it if it wishes to win the sympathy of the best men of the coming generation—those youths who possess the intellectual and the moral qualities which prevent men from simply following authorities, to say nothing of fashions.

The fairly recent change within political science has its parallels in the other social sciences. Yet the change within political science appears to be both more pronounced and more limited. The reason is that political science is the oldest of the social sciences and therefore willy-nilly a carrier of old traditions that resist innovation. Political science as we find it now consists of more heterogeneous parts than any other social science. "Public law" and "international law" were established themes centuries before "politics and parties" and "international relations," nay sociology, emerged. If we look around us, we may observe that the political science profession contains a strong minority of the right, consisting of the strict adherents of the new political science or the "behavioralists," a small minority of the left, consisting of those who reject the new political science root and branch, and a center consisting of the old-fashioned political scientists, men who are concerned with understanding political things without being much concerned with "methodological" questions but many of whom seem to have given custody of their "methodological" conscience to the strict adherents of the new political science and thus continue their old-fashioned practice with a somewhat uneasy conscience. It may seem strange that I called the strict adherents of the new political science the right wing and their intransigent opponents the left wing, seeing that the former are liberals almost to a man and the latter are in the odor of conservatism. Yet since I have heard the intransigent opponents of the new political science described as unorthodox, I inferred that the new political science is the orthodoxy in the profession, and the natural place of an orthodoxy is on the right.

A rigorous adherent of the new political science will dismiss the preceding remarks as quasi-statistical or sociological irrelevancies that have no bearing whatever on the only important issue, that issue being the soundness of the new political science. To state that issue means to bring out the fundamental difference between the new political science and the old. To avoid ambiguities, irrelevancies, and beatings around the bush, it is best to contrast the new political science directly with the "original" of the old, that is, with Aristotelian political science.

For Aristotle, political science is identical with political philosophy because science is identical with philosophy. Science or philosophy consists of two kinds, theoretical and practical or political; theoretical science is subdivided into mathematics, physics (natural science), and metaphysics; practical science is subdivided into ethics, economics (management of the household), and political science in the narrower sense; logic does not belong to philosophy or science proper but is, as it were, the prelude to philosophy or science. The distinction between philosophy and science or the separation of science from philosophy was a consequence of the revolution which occurred in the seventeenth century. This revolution was primarily not the victory of Science over Metaphysics but what one may call the victory of the new philosophy or science over Aristotelian philosophy or science. Yet the new philosophy or science was not equally successful in all its parts. Its most successful part was physics (and mathematics). Prior to the victory of the new physics, there was not the science of physics simply: there was Aristotelian physics, Platonic physics, Epicurean physics, Stoic physics; to speak colloquially, there was no metaphysically neutral physics. The victory of the new physics led to the emergence of a physics which seemed to be as metaphysically neutral as, say, mathematics, medicine, or the art of shoemaking. The emergence of a metaphysically neutral physics made it possible for "science" to become independent of "philosophy," and in fact an authority for the latter. It paved the way for an economic science that is independent of ethics, for sociology as the study of non-political associations as not inferior in dignity to the political association, and, last but not least, for the separation of political science from political philosophy as well as the separation of economics and sociology from political science. Secondly, the Aristotelian distinction between theoretical and practical sciences implies that human action has principles of its own which are known independently of theoretical science (physics and metaphysics) and therefore that the practical sciences do not depend on the theoretical sciences or are not derivative from them. The principles of action are the natural ends of man toward which man is by nature inclined and of which he has by nature some awareness. This awareness is the necessary condition for his seeking and finding appropriate means for his ends, or for his becoming practically wise or prudent. Practical science, in contradistinction to practical wisdom itself, sets forth coherently the principles of action and the general rules of prudence ("proverbial wisdom"). Practical science raises questions that within practical or political experience, or at any rate on the basis of such experience, reveal themselves to be the most important questions and that are not stated, let alone answered, with sufficient clarity by practical wisdom itself. The sphere governed by prudence is then in principle self-sufficient or closed. Yet prudence is always endangered by false doctrines about the whole of which man is a part, by false theoretical opinions; prudence is therefore always in need of defense against such opinions, and that defense is necessarily theoretical. The theory defending prudence is mis-

understood, however, if it is taken to be the basis of prudence. This complication—the fact that the sphere of prudence is, as it were, only *de jure* but
not *de facto* wholly independent of theoretical science—makes understandable, although it does not by itself justify, the view underlying the new political science according to which no awareness inherent in practice, and in
general no natural awareness, is genuine knowledge, or in other words only
"scientific" knowledge is genuine knowledge. This view implies that there
cannot be practical sciences proper, or that the distinction between practical
and theoretical sciences must be replaced by the distinction between theoretical and applied sciences—applied sciences being sciences based on theoretical sciences that precede the applied sciences in time and in order. It
implies above all that the sciences dealing with human affairs are essentially
dependent on the theoretical sciences—especially on psychology, which in
the Aristotelian scheme is the highest theme of physics, not to say that it
constitutes the transition from physics to metaphysics—or become themselves
theoretical sciences to be supplemented by such applied sciences as the policy
sciences or the sciences of social engineering. The new political science is
then no longer based on political experience but on what is called scientific
psychology. Thirdly, according to the Aristotelian view, the awareness of the
principles of action shows itself primarily to a higher degree in public or authoritative speech, particularly in law and legislation, rather than in merely
private speech. Hence Aristotelian political science views political things in
the perspective of the citizen. Since there is of necessity a variety of citizen
perspectives, the political scientist or political philosopher must become the
umpire, the impartial judge; his perspective encompasses the partisan perspectives because he possesses a more comprehensive and a clearer grasp of
man's natural ends and their natural order than do the partisans. The new
political science, on the other hand, looks at political things from without,
in the perspective of the neutral observer, in the same perspective in which
one would look at triangles or fish, although or because it may wish to become "manipulative"; it views human beings as an engineer would view materials for building bridges. It follows that the language of Aristotelian political
science is identical with the language of political man; it hardly uses a term
that did not originate in the market place and is not in common use there;
but the new political science cannot begin to speak without having elaborated
an extensive technical vocabulary. Fourthly, Aristotelian political science
necessarily evaluates political things; the knowledge in which it culminates
has the character of categorical advice and of exhortation. The new political
science, on the other hand, conceives of the principles of action as "values"
which are merely "subjective"; the knowledge it conveys has the character of
prediction and only secondarily that of hypothetical advice. Fifthly, according to the Aristotelian view, man is a being *sui generis*, with a dignity of its
own: man is the rational and political animal. Man is the only being that

can be concerned with self-respect; man can respect himself because he can despise himself; he is "the beast with red cheeks," the only being possessing a sense of shame. His dignity is then based on his awareness of what he ought to be or how he should live. Since there is a necessary connection between morality (how a man should live) and law, there is a necessary connection between the dignity of man and the dignity of the public order: the political is *sui generis* and cannot be understood as derivative from the sub-political. The presupposition of all this is that man is radically distinguished from non-man, from brutes as well as from gods, and this presupposition is ratified by common sense, by the citizen's understanding of things; when the citizen demands or rejects, say, "freedom from want for all," he does not mean freedom from want for tigers, rats, or lice. This presupposition points to a more fundamental presupposition according to which the whole consists of essentially different parts. The new political science, on the other hand, is based on the fundamental premise that there are no essential or irreducible differences: there are only differences of degree; in particular there is only a difference of degree between men and brutes or between men and robots. In other words, according to the new political science, or the universal science of which the new political science is a part, to understand a thing means to understand it in terms of its genesis or its conditions and hence, humanly speaking, to understand the higher in terms of the lower: the human in terms of the sub-human, the rational in terms of the sub-rational, the political in terms of the sub-political. In particular the new political science cannot admit that the common good is something that is.

Prior to the emergence of the new political science, political science had already moved very far from Aristotelian political science in the general direction of the new political science. Nevertheless it was accused of paying too much attention to the law or to the Ought, and of paying too little attention to the Is or to the actual behavior of men. For instance it seemed to be exclusively concerned with the legal arrangements regarding universal suffrage and its justification and not to consider at all how the universal right to vote is exercised; yet democracy as it is is characterized by the manner in which that right is exercised. We may grant that not so long ago there was a political science which was narrowly legalistic—which, for example, took the written constitution of the USSR very seriously—but we must add immediately that that error had been corrected, as it were in advance, by an older political science, the political science of Montesquieu, of Machiavelli, or of Aristotle himself. Besides, the new political science, in its justified protest against a merely legalistic political science, is in danger of disregarding the important things known to those legalists: "voting behavior" as it is now studied would be impossible if there were not in the first place the universal right to vote, and this right, even if not exercised by a large minority for very long periods, must be taken into consideration in any long-range prediction since it may be exercised by all in future elections taking place in unprecedented and therefore particularly interesting circumstances. That right is an essential ingredient of democratic "behavior," for it partly explains "behavior" in democracies (for example, the prevention by force or fraud of certain people from voting). The new political science does not simply deny these things but it literally relegates them to the background, to "the habit background"; in so doing it puts the cart before the horse. Similar considerations apply, for instance, to the alleged discovery by the new political science of the importance of "propaganda"; that discovery is in fact only a partial rediscovery of the need for vulgar rhetoric, a need that had become somewhat obscured from a few generations which were comforted by faith in universal enlightenment as the inevitable by-product of the diffusion of science, which in its turn was thought to be the inevitable by-product of science. Generally speaking, one may wonder whether the new political science has brought to light anything of political importance which intelligent political practitioners with a deep knowledge of history, nay, intelligent and educated journalists, to say nothing of the old political science at its best, did not know at least as well beforehand. The main substantive reason, however, for the revolt against the old political science would seem to be the consideration that our political situation is entirely unprecedented and that it is unreasonable to expect earlier political thought to be of any help in coping with our situation; the unprecedented political situation calls for an unprecedented political science, perhaps for a judicious mating of dialectical materialism and psychoanalysis to be consummated on a bed supplied by logical positivism. Just as classical physics had to be superseded by nuclear physics so that the atomic age could come in via the atomic bomb, the old political science has to be superseded by a sort of nuclear political science so that we may be enabled to cope with the extreme dangers threatening atomic man; the equivalent in political science of the nuclei are probably the most minute events in the smallest groups of human beings, if not in the life of infants; the small groups in question are certainly not of the kind exemplified by the small group that Lenin gathered around himself in Switzerland during World War I. In making this comparison we are not oblivious of the fact that the nuclear physicists show a greater respect for classical physics than the nuclear political scientists show for classical politics. Nor do we forget that, while the nuclei proper are simply prior to macrophysical phenomena, the "political" nuclei, which are meant to supply explanations for the political things proper, are already molded, nay constituted by the political order or the regime within which they occur: an American small group is not a Russian small group. We may grant that our political situation has nothing in common with any earlier political situation except that it is a political situation. The human race is still divided into a number of the kind of societies that we have come to call states and that are separated from one another by unmistakable and sometimes formidable frontiers. Those states still differ from one another not only in all conceivable other respects but above all in their regimes and hence in the things to which the preponderant part of each society is dedicated or in the spirit which more or less effectively pervades each society. These societies have very different images of the future so that for all of them to live together, in contradistinction to uneasily coexisting, is altogether impossible. Each of them receiving its character from its regime is still in need of specific measures for preserving itself and its regime and hence is uncertain of its future. Acting willy-nilly through their governments (which may be governments in exile), these societies still move as if on an uncharted sea and surely without the benefit of tracks toward a future that is veiled from everyone and which is pregnant with surprises. Their governments still try to determine the future of their societies with the help partly of knowledge, partly of guesses, the recourse to guesses still being partly necessitated by the secrecy in which their most important opponents shroud their most important plans or projects. The new political science which is so eager to predict is, as it admits, as unable to predict the outcome of the unprecedented conflict peculiar to our age as the crudest soothsayers of the most benighted tribe. In former times people thought that the outcome of serious conflicts is unpredictable because one cannot know how long this or that outstanding leader in war or counsel will live, or how the opposed armies will act in the test of battle or similar things. We have been brought to believe that chance can be controlled or does not seriously affect the fate of societies. Yet the science that is said to have rendered possible the control of chance has itself become the refuge of chance: man's fate depends now more than ever on science or technology, hence on discoveries or inventions, hence on events whose precise occurrence is by their very nature not predictable. A simply unprecedented political situation would be a situation of no political interest, that is, not a political situation. Now if the essential character of all political situations was grasped by the old political science, there seems to be no reason why it must be superseded by a new political science. In case the new political science should tend to understand political things in non-political terms, the old political science, wise to many ages, would even be superior to the new political science in helping us to find our bearings in our unprecedented situation in spite or rather because of the fact that only the new political science can boast of being the child of the atomic age.

But one will never understand the new political science if one does not start from that reason advanced on its behalf which has nothing whatever to do with any true or alleged blindness of the old political science to any political things as such. That reason is a general notion of science. According to that notion, only scientific knowledge is genuine knowledge. From this it follows immediately that all awareness of political things that is not scientific is cognitively worthless. Serious criticism of the old political science is a waste of time; for we know in advance that it could only have been a pseudo science, although perhaps including a few remarkably shrewd hunches. This is not to deny that the adherents of the new political science sometimes engage in apparent criticism of the old, but that criticism is characterized by a constitutional inability to understand the criticized doctrines on their own terms. What science is, is supposed to be known from the practice of the other sciences, of sciences that are admittedly in existence and not mere desiderata, and the clearest examples of such sciences are the natural sciences. What science is, is supposed to be known, above all, from the science of science, that is, logic. The basis of the new political science then is logic, that is, a particular kind of logic; the logic in question is not, for instance, Aristotelian or Kantian or Hegelian logic. This means, however, that the new political science rests on what for the political scientist as such is a mere assumption that he is not competent to judge on its own terms, namely, as a logical theory, for that theory is controversial among the people who must be supposed to be competent in such matters, the professors of philosophy. The political scientist is competent, however, to judge it by its fruits; he is competent to judge whether his understanding of political things as political things is helped or hindered by the new political science that derives from the logic in question. He is perfectly justified in regarding as an imposition the demand that he comply with "logical positivism" or else plead guilty to being a "metaphysician." He is perfectly justified in regarding this epithet as not "objective," because it is terrifying and unintelligible like the war cries of savages.

What strikes a sympathetic chord in every political scientist is less the demand that he proceed "scientifically"—for mathematics also proceeds scientifically and political science surely is not a mathematical discipline—than the demand that he proceed "empirically." This is a demand of common sense. No one in his senses ever dreamt that he could know anything, say, of American government as such or of the present political situation as such except by looking at American government or at the present political situation. The incarnation of the empirical spirit is the man from Missouri, who has to be shown. For he knows that he, as well as everyone else who is of sound mind and whose sight is not defective, can see things and people as they are with his eyes, and that he is capable of knowing how his neighbors feel; he takes it for granted that he lives with other human beings of all descriptions in the same world and that because they are all human beings, they all understand one another somehow; he knows that if this were not so, political life would be altogether impossible. If someone offered him speculations based on extrasensory perception, he would turn his back more or less politely. The old political science would not quarrel in these respects with the man from Missouri. It did not claim to know better or differently than he such things as that the Democratic and Republican parties are now, and have been for some time, the preponderant parties in this country, and that there are presidential elections every fourth year. By admitting that facts of this kind are known independently of political science, it admitted that empirical knowledge is not necessarily scientific knowledge or that a statement can be true and known to be true without being scientific, and, above all, that political science stands or falls by the truth of the pre-scientific awareness of political things. Yet one may raise the question of how one can be certain of the truth of empirical statements that are pre-scientific. If we call an elaborate answer to this question an epistemology, we may say that an empiricist, in contradistinction to an empirical, statement is based on the explicit assumption of a specific epistemology. Yet every epistemology presupposes the truth of empirical statements. Our perceiving things and people is more manifest and more reliable than any "theory of knowledge"—any explanation of how our perceiving things and people is possible—can be; the truth of any "theory of knowledge" depends on its ability to give an adequate account of this fundamental reliance. If a logical positivist tries to give an account of a "thing" or a formula for a "thing" in terms of mere sense data and their composition, he is looking, and bids us to look, at the previously grasped "thing"; the previously grasped "thing" is the standard by which we judge his formula. If an epistemology, for example solipsism, manifestly fails to give an account of how empirical statements as meant can be true, it fails to carry conviction. To be aware of the necessity of the fundamental reliance that underlies or pervades all empirical statements means to recognize the fundamental riddle, not to have solved it. But no man needs to be ashamed to admit that he does not possess a solution to the fundamental riddle. Surely no man ought to let himself be bullied into the acceptance of an alleged solution—for the denial of the existence of a riddle is a kind of solution of the riddle—by the threat that if he fails to do so he is a "metaphysician." To sustain our weaker brethren against that threat, one might tell them that the belief accepted by the empiricists, according to which science is in principle susceptible of infinite progress, is itself tantamount to the belief that being is irretrievably mysterious.

Let us try to restate the issue by returning first to our man from Missouri. A simple observation seems to be sufficient to show that the man from Missouri is "naïve": he does not see things with his eyes; what he sees with his eyes are only colors, shapes, and the like; he would perceive "things," in contradistinction to "sense data," only if he possessed "extrasensory perception"; his claim—the claim of common sense—implies that there is "extrasensory perception." What is true of "things," is true of "patterns," at any rate of those patterns which students of politics from time to time claim to "perceive." We must leave the man from Missouri scratching his head; by being silent, he remains in his way a philosopher. But others do not leave it at scratching their heads. Transforming themselves from devotees of *empeiria* into empiricists, they contend that what is perceived or "given" is only sense data; the "thing" emerges by virtue of unconscious or conscious "construction"; the "things" which to common sense present themselves as "given" are in truth constructs. Common sense understanding is understanding by means of unconscious construction; scientific understanding is understanding by means of conscious construction. Somewhat more precisely, common sense understanding is understanding in terms of "things possessing qualities"; scientific understanding is understanding in terms of "functional relations between different series of events." Unconscious constructs are ill-made, for their making is affected by all sorts of purely "subjective" influences; only conscious constructs can be well-made, perfectly lucid, in every respect the same for everyone, or "objective." Still, one says with greater right that we perceive things than that we perceive human beings as human beings, for at least some of the properties which we ascribe to things are sensually perceived, whereas the soul's actions, passions, or states can never become sense data. Now, that understanding of things and human beings which is rejected by empiricism is the understanding by which political life, political understanding, political experience stand or fall. Hence, the new political science, based as it is on empiricism, must reject the results of political understanding and political experience as such, and since the political things are given to us in political understanding and political experience, the new political science cannot be helpful for the deeper understanding of political things: it must reduce the political things to non-political data. The new political science comes into being through an attempted break with common sense. But that break cannot be consistently carried out, as can be seen in a general way from the following consideration. Empiricism cannot be established empirically: it is not known through sense data that the only possible objects of perception are sense data. If one tries therefore to establish empiricism empirically, one must make use of that understanding of things which empiricism renders doubtful: the relation of eyes to colors or shapes is established through the same kind of perception through which we perceive things as things rather than sense data or constructs. In other words, sense data as sense data become known only through an act of abstraction or disregard which presupposes the legitimacy of our primary awareness of things as things and of people as people. Hence, the only way of overcoming the naïveté of the man from Missouri is in the first place to admit that that naïveté cannot be avoided in any way or that there is no possible human thought which is not in the last analysis dependent on the legitimacy of that naïveté and the awareness or the knowledge going with it.

We must not disregard the most massive or the crudest reason to which empiricism owes much of its attractiveness. Some adherents of the new political science would argue as follows: One cannot indeed reasonably deny that pre-scientific thought about political things contains genuine knowledge; but the trouble is that within pre-scientific political thought, genuine knowledge of political things is inseparable from prejudices or superstitions; hence one cannot get rid of the spurious elements in pre-scientific political thought except by breaking altogether with pre-scientific thought or by acting on the assumption that pre-scientific thought does not have the character of knowledge at all. Common sense contains genuine knowledge of broomsticks; but the trouble is that this knowledge has in common sense the same status as the alleged knowledge concerning witches; by trusting common sense one is in danger of bringing back the whole kingdom of darkness with Thomas Aquinas at its head. The old political science was not unaware of the imperfections of political opinion, but it did not believe that the remedy lies in the total rejection of common sense understanding as such. It was critical in the original sense, that is, discerning, regarding political opinion. It was aware that the errors regarding witches were found out without the benefit of empiricism. It was aware that judgments or maxims which were justified by the uncontested experience of decades, and even of centuries, or millennia, may have to be revised because of unforeseen changes; it knew, in the words of Burke, "that the generality of people are fifty years, at least, behind hand in their politics." Accordingly, the old political science was concerned with political improvement by political means as distinguished from social engineering; it knew that those political means include revolutions and also wars, since there may be foreign regimes (Hitler Germany is the orthodox example) that are dangerous to the free survival of this country, regimes that would be expected to transform themselves gradually into good neighbors only by the criminally foolish.

Acceptance of the distinctive premises of the new political science leads to the consequences which have been sufficiently illustrated in the four preceding essays. In the first place, the new political science is constantly compelled to borrow from common sense knowledge, thus unwittingly testifying to the truth that there is genuine pre-scientific knowledge of political things which is the basis of all scientific knowledge of them.[1] Secondly, the logic on which the new political science is based may provide sufficient criteria of exactness; it does not provide objective criteria of relevance.[2] Criteria of relevance are inherent in the pre-scientific understanding of political things; intelligent and informed citizens distinguish soundly between important and unimportant political matters. Political men are concerned with what is to be done politically here and now in accordance with principles of preference of which they are aware, although not necessarily in an adequate manner; it is those principles of preference which supply the criteria of relevance in regard to political things. Ordinarily a political man must at least pretend to "look

[1] See above, pp. 21, 46, 76, 85, 124 ff, 193, 214-217.
[2] See above, pp. 37, 55-57, 144 ff, 172-173, 177-178, 186-188.

up" to something that at least the preponderant part of his society looks up to. That which at least everyone who counts politically is supposed to look up to, that which is politically the highest, gives a society its character; it constitutes and justifies the regime of the society in question. The "highest" is that through which a society is "a whole," a distinct whole with a character of its own, just as for common sense "the world" is a whole by being overarched by heaven of which one cannot be aware except by "looking up." There is obviously, and for cause, a variety of regimes and hence of what is regarded as the politically highest, that is, of the purposes to which the various regimes are dedicated. The qualitatively different regimes, or kinds of regimes, and the qualitatively different purposes constituting and legitimating them, then, by revealing themselves as the most important political things, supply the key to the understanding of all political things and the basis for the reasoned distinction between important and unimportant political things. The regimes and their principles pervade the societies throughout, in the sense that there are no recesses of privacy which are simply impervious to that pervasion as is indicated by such expressions, coined by the new political science, as "the democratic personality." Nevertheless, there are political things that are not affected by the difference of regimes. In a society which cannot survive without an irrigation system, every regime will have to preserve that system intact. Every regime must try to preserve itself against subversion by means of force. There are both technical things and politically neutral things (things that are common to all regimes) that are necessarily the concern of political deliberation without ever being as such politically controversial. The preceding remarks are a very rough sketch of the view of political things that was characteristic of the old political science. According to that view, what is most important for political science is identical with what is most important politically. To illustrate this by a present-day example, for the old-fashioned political scientists today, the most important concern is the Cold War or the qualitative difference, which amounts to a conflict, between liberal democracy and communism.

The break with the common sense understanding of political things compels the new political science to abandon the criteria of relevance that are inherent in political understanding. Hence, the new political science lacks orientation regarding political things; it has no protection whatever, except by surreptitious recourse to common sense, against losing itself in the study of irrelevancies. It is confronted by a chaotic mass of data into which it must bring an order alien to those data, an order originating in the demands of political science as a science anxious to comply with the demands of logical positivism. The universals in the light of which the old political science viewed the political phenomena (the various regimes and their purposes) must be replaced by a different kind of universals. The first step toward the finding of the new kind of universals may be said to take this form: what is equally present in all regimes (the politically neutral) must be the key to the different regimes (the political proper, the essentially controversial); what is equally present in all regimes is, say, coercion and freedom; the scientific analysis of a given regime will then indicate exactly—in terms of percentages —the amount of coercion and the amount of freedom peculiar to it. That is to say, as political scientists we must express the political phenomena par excellence, the essential differences or the heterogeneity of regimes, in terms of the homogeneous elements which pervade all regimes. What is important for us as political scientists is not the politically important. Yet we cannot forever remain blind to the fact that what claims to be a purely scientific or theoretical enterprise has grave political consequences—consequences which are so little accidental that they appeal for their own sake to the new political scientists: everyone knows what follows from the demonstration, which presupposes the begging of all important questions, that there is only a difference of degree between liberal democracy and communism in regard to coercion and freedom. The Is necessarily leads to an Ought, all sincere protestations to the contrary notwithstanding. The second step toward the finding of the new kind of universals consists in the following reasoning: all political societies, whatever their regimes, surely are groups of some kind; hence, the key to the understanding of political things must be a theory of groups in general.[3] Groups must have some cohesion and groups change; we are then in need of a universal theory which tells us why or how groups cohere and why or how they change. Seeking for those why's or how's we shall discover n factors and m modes of their interaction. The result of this reduction of the political to the sociological—a reduction that, it is claimed, will make our understanding of political things more "realistic"—is in fact a formalism unrivaled in any scholasticism of the past. All peculiarities of political societies, and still more of the political societies with which we are concerned as citizens, become unrecognizable if restated in terms of the vague generalities which hold of every conceivable group; at the end of the dreary and boring process we understand what we are interested in not more but less than we understood it at the beginning. What in political language are called the rulers and the ruled (to say nothing of oppressors and oppressed) become through this process nothing but different parts of a social system, of a mechanism, each part acting on the other and being acted upon by it; there may be a stronger part but there cannot be a ruling part; the relation of parts of a mechanism supersedes the political relation.[4] We need not dwell on the next, but not necessarily last, step of the reasoning which we are trying to sketch, namely, the requirement that the researches regarding groups must be underpinned, nay, guided by "a general theory of personality" or the like: we know nothing of the political wisdom or the folly of a statesman's

3 See above, pp. 153 ff.
4 See above, pp. 35-36, 53-54, 197, 222.

actions until we know everything about the degree of affection which he received from each of his parents, if any.[5] The last step might be thought to be the use by the new political science of observations regarding rats: can we not observe human beings as we observe rats, are decisions which rats make not much simpler than the decisions which humans frequently make, and is not the simpler always the key to the more complex? [6] We do not doubt that we can observe, if we try hard enough, the overt behavior of humans as we observe the overt behavior of rats. But we ought not to forget that in the case of rats we are limited to observing overt behavior because they do not talk, and they do not talk because they have nothing to say or because they have no inwardness. Yet to return from these depths to the surface, an important example of the formalism in question is supplied by the well-known theory regarding the principles of legitimacy which substitutes formal characteristics (traditional, rational, charismatic) for the substantive principles which are precisely the purposes to which the various regimes are dedicated and by which they are legitimated. The universals for which the new political science seeks are "laws of human behavior"; those laws are to be discovered by means of "empirical" research. There is an amazing disproportion between the apparent breadth of the goal (say, a general theory of social change) and the true pettiness of the researches undertaken to achieve that goal (say, a change in a hospital when one head nurse is replaced by another). This is no accident. Since we lack objective criteria of relevance, we have no reason to be more interested in a world-shaking revolution that affects directly or indirectly all men than in the most trifling "social changes." Moreover, if the laws sought are to be "laws of human behavior" they cannot be restricted to human behavior as it is affected by this or that regime. But human behavior as studied by "empirical" research always occurs within a peculiar regime. More precisely, the most cherished techniques of "empirical" research in the social sciences can be applied only to human beings living now in countries in which the governments tolerate research of this kind. The new political science is therefore constantly tempted (and as a rule it does not resist that temptation) to absolutize the relative or peculiar, that is, to be parochial. We have read statements about "the revolutionary" or "the conservative" which did not even claim to have any basis other than observations made in the United States at the present moment; if those statements had any relation to facts at all, they might have some degree of truth regarding revolutionaries or conservatives in certain parts of the United States today, but they reveal themselves immediately as patently wrong if taken as they were meant—as descriptions of the revolutionary or the conservative as such; the error in question was due to the parochialism inevitably fostered by the new political science.

[5] See above, pp. 22 ff, 263 ff.
[6] See above, pp. 113-115.

At the risk of some repetition, we must say a few words about the language of the new political science. The break with the political understanding of political things necessitates the making of a language different from the language used by political men. The new political science rejects the latter language as ambiguous and imprecise and claims that its own language is unambiguous and precise. Yet this claim is not warranted. The language of the new political science is not less vague but more vague than the language used in political life. Political life would be altogether impossible if its language were unqualifiedly vague; that language is capable of the utmost unambiguity and precision, as in a declaration of war or in an order given to a firing squad. If available distinctions like that between war, peace, and armistice prove to be insufficient, political life finds, without the benefit of political science, the right new expression (Cold War as distinguished from Hot or Shooting War) that designates the new phenomenon with unfailing precision. The alleged vagueness of political language is primarily due to the fact that it corresponds to the complexity of political life, or that it is nourished by long experience with political things in a great variety of circumstances. By simply condemning pre-scientific language, instead of deviating from usage in particular cases because of the proven inadequacy of usage in the cases in question, one simply condemns oneself to unredeemable vagueness. No thoughtful citizen would dream of equating politics with something as vague and empty as "power" or "power relations." The thinking men who are regarded as the classic interpreters of power, Thucydides and Machiavelli, did not need these expressions; these expressions as now used originate, not in political life, but in the academic reaction to the understanding of political life in terms of law alone: these expressions signify nothing but that academic reaction. Political language does not claim to be perfectly clear and distinct; it does not claim to be based on a full understanding of the things which it designates unambiguously enough; it is suggestive: it leaves those things in the penumbra in which they come to sight. The purge effected by "scientific" definitions of those things has the character of sterilization. The language of the new political science claims to be perfectly clear and distinct and, at the same time, entirely provisional; its terms are meant to imply hypotheses about political life. But this claim to undogmatic openness is a mere ceremonial gesture. When one speaks of "conscience" one does not claim to have fathomed the phenomenon indicated by that term. But when the new political scientist speaks of the "Superego," he is certain that anything meant by "conscience" which is not covered by the "Superego" is a superstition. As a consequence he cannot distinguish between a bad conscience which may induce a man to devote the rest of his life to compensating another man to the best of his powers for an irreparable damage and "guilt feelings" which one ought to get rid of as fast and as cheaply as possible. Similarly he is certain to have understood the trust which induces people to vote for a candidate to high office by speaking of the "father image"; he does not have to inquire whether and to what extent the candidate in question deserves that trust—a trust different from the trust which children have in their father. The allegedly provisional or hypothetical terms are never questioned in the process of research, for their implications channel the research in such directions that the "data" which might reveal the inadequacy of the hypotheses never turn up. We conclude that to the extent to which the new political science is not formalistic, it is vulgarian. This vulgarianism shows itself particularly in the "value-free" manner in which it uses and thus debases terms that originally were meant only for indicating things of a noble character—terms like "culture," "personality," "values," "charismatic" and "civilization."

The most important example of the dogmatism to which we have alluded is supplied by the treatment of religion in the new political or social science. The new science uses sociological or psychological theories regarding religion which exclude, without considering, the possibility that religion rests ultimately on God's revealing Himself to man; hence those theories are mere hypotheses which can never be confirmed. Those theories are in fact the hidden basis of the new science. The new science rests on a dogmatic atheism which presents itself as merely methodological or hypothetical. For a few years, logical positivisim tried with much noise and little thought to dispose of religion by asserting that religious assertions are "meaningless statements." This trick seems to have been abandoned without noise. Some adherents of the new political science might rejoin with some liveliness that their posture toward religion is imposed on them by intellectual honesty: not being able to believe, they cannot accept belief as the basis of their science. We gladly grant that, other things being equal, a frank atheist is a better man than an alleged theist who conceives of God as a symbol. But we must add that intellectual honesty is not enough. Intellectual honesty is not love of truth. Intellectual honesty, a kind of self-denial, has taken the place of love of truth because truth has come to be believed to be repulsive and one cannot love the repulsive. Yet just as our opponents refuse respect to unreasoned belief, we on our part, with at least equal right, must refuse respect to unreasoned unbelief; honesty with oneself regarding one's unbelief is in itself not more than unreasoned unbelief probably accompanied by a vague confidence that the issue of unbelief versus belief has long since been settled once and for all. It is hardly necessary to add that the dogmatic exclusion of religious awareness proper renders questionable all long-range predictions concerning the future of societies.

The reduction of the political to the sub-political is the reduction of primarily given wholes to elements which are relatively simple, that is, sufficiently simple for the research purpose at hand yet necessarily susceptible of being analyzed into still simpler elements *in infinitum*. It implies that there cannot be genuine wholes. Hence it implies that there cannot be a common good. According to the old political science, there is necessarily a common good, and the common good in its fullness is the good society and what is required for the good society. The consistent denial of the common good is as impossible as every other consistent manifestation of the break with common sense. The empiricists who reject the notion of wholes are compelled to speak sooner or later of such things as "the open society," which is their definition of the good society.[7] The alternative (if it is an alternative) is to deny the possibility of a substantive public interest but to admit the possibility of substantive group interests; yet it is not difficult to see that what is granted to the goose, "the group," cannot be consistently denied to the gander, "the country." [8] In accordance with this, the new political science surreptitiously reintroduces the common good in the form of "the rules of the game" with which all conflicting groups are supposed to comply because those rules, reasonably fair to every group, can reasonably be admitted by every group.[9] The "group politics" approach is a relic of Marxism, which more reasonably denied that there can be a common good in a society consisting of classes that are locked in a life and death struggle overt or hidden, and therefore found the common good in a classless and hence stateless society comprising the whole human race. The consistent denial of the common good requires a radical "individualism." In fact, the new political science appears to teach that there cannot be a substantive public interest because there is not, and cannot be, a single objective approved by all members of society: murderers show by their action that not even the prohibition against murder is, strictly speaking, to the public interest. We are not so sure whether the murderer wishes that murder cease to be a punishable action or rather that he himself get away with murder. Be this as it may, this denial of the common good is based on the premise that even if an objective is to the interest of the overwhelming majority, it is not to the interest of all: no minority however small, no individual however perverse must be left out. More precisely, even if an objective is to the interest of all but not believed by all to be to the interest of all, it is not to the public interest: everyone is by nature the sole judge of what is to his interest; his judgment regarding his interest is not subject to anybody else's examination on the issue whether his judgment is sound. This premise is not the discovery or invention of the new political science; it was stated with the greatest vigor by Hobbes, who opposed it to the opposite premise which had been the basis of the old political science proper. But Hobbes still saw that his premise entails the war of everybody against everybody and hence drew the conclusion that everyone must cease to be the sole judge of what is to his interest if there is to be human life; the individual's

[7] See above, pp. 44-55, 103-105, 217 ff.
[8] See above, pp. 195 ff, esp. 202-203.
[9] See above, pp. 198-199.

reason must give way to the public reason. The new political science denies in a way that there is a public reason: government may be a broker, if a broker possessing "the monopoly of violence," but it surely is not the public reason. The true public reason is the new political science, which judges in a universally valid, or objective, manner what is to the interest of each, for it shows to everyone what means he must choose to attain his attainable ends, whatever those ends may be. It has been shown earlier in this volume what becomes of the new political science, or of the only kind of rationality which the new political science still admits, if its Hobbian premise is not conveniently forgotten: the new form of public reason goes the way of the old.[10]

The denial of the common good presents itself today as a direct consequence of the distinction between facts and values according to which only factual judgments, not value judgments, can be true or objective. The new political science leaves the justification of values or of preferences to "political philosophy" or, more precisely, to ideology on the ground that any justification of preferences would have to derive values from facts and such derivation is not legitimately possible. Preferences are not strictly speaking opinions and hence cannot be true or false, whereas ideologies are opinions and, for the reason given, false opinions. Whereas acting man has necessarily chosen values, the new political scientist as pure spectator is not committed to any value; in particular, he is neutral in the conflict between liberal democracy and its enemies. The traditional value systems antedate the awareness of the difference between facts and values; they claimed to be derived from facts— from Divine Revelation or from similar sources, in general from superior or perfect beings which as such unite in themselves fact and value; the discovery of the difference between facts and values amounts therefore to a refutation of the traditional value systems as originally meant. It is at least doubtful whether those value systems can be divorced from what present themselves as their factual bases. At any rate, it follows from the difference between facts and values that men can live without ideology: they can adopt, posit, or proclaim values without making the illegitimate attempt to derive their values from facts or without relying on false or at least unevident assertions regarding what is. One thus arrives at the notion of the rational society or of the nonideological regime: a society that is based on the understanding of the character of values. Since this understanding implies that before the tribunal of reason all values are equal, the rational society will be egalitarian or democratic and permissive or liberal: the rational doctrine regarding the difference between facts and values rationally justifies the preference for liberal democracy—contrary to what is intended by that distinction itself. In other words, whereas the new political science ought to deny the proposition that there can be no society without an ideology, it asserts that proposition.

[10] Cf. Simon and Lasswell, above, pp. 108-109, 296-300.

One is thus led to wonder whether the distinction between facts and values, or the assertion that no Ought can be derived from an Is, is well founded. Let us assume that a man's "values" (that is, what he values) are fully determined by his heredity and environment, that is, by his Is, or that there is a one-to-one relation between value *a* and Is A. In this case the Ought would be determined by the Is or derivative from it. But the very issue as commonly understood presupposes that this assumption is wrong: man possesses a certain latitude; he can choose not only from among various ways of overt behavior (like jumping or not jumping into a river to escape death at the hands of a stronger enemy who may or may not be able to swim) but from among various values; this latitude, this possibility has the character of a fact. A man lacking this latitude—for example, a man for whom every stimulus is a value or who cannot help giving in to every desire—is a defective man, a man with whom something is wrong. The fact that someone desires something does not yet make that something his value; he may successfully fight his desire or if his desire overpowers him he may blame himself for this as for a failure on his part; only choice, in contradistinction to mere desire, makes something a man's value. The distinction between desire and choice is a distinction among facts. Choice does not mean here the choice of means to pre-given ends; choice here means the choice of ends, the positing of ends or, rather, of values. Man is then understood as a being which differs from all other known beings because it posits values; this positing is taken to be a fact. In accordance with this, the new political science denies that man has natural ends—ends toward which he is by nature inclined; it denies more specifically the premise of modern natural right, according to which self-preservation is the most important natural end: man can choose death in preference to life, not only in a given situation, out of despair, but simply: he can posit death as his value. The view that the pertinent Is is our positing of values, in contradistinction to the yielding to mere desires, necessarily leads to Oughts of a radically different character from the so-called Oughts corresponding to mere desires. We conclude that the "relativism" accepted by the new political science according to which values are nothing but objects of desire is based on an insufficient analysis of the Is, that is, of the pertinent Is; and, furthermore, that one's opinion regarding the character of the Is settles one's opinion regarding the character of the Ought. We must leave it open here whether a more adequate analysis of the pertinent Is, that is, of the nature of man, does not lead to a more adequate determination of the Ought or beyond a merely formal characterization of the Ought. At any rate, if a man is of the opinion that as a matter of fact all desires are of equal dignity since we know of no factual consideration which would entitle us to assign different dignities to different desires, he cannot but be of the opinion —unless he is prepared to become guilty of gross arbitrariness—that all desires ought to be treated as equal within the limits of the possible, and this opinion is what is meant by permissive egalitarianism.

There is then more than a mysterious pre-established harmony between the new political science and a particular version of liberal democracy. The alleged value-free analysis of political phenomena is controlled by an unavowed commitment built into the new political science to that version of liberal democracy. That version of liberal democracy is not discussed openly and impartially, with full consideration of all relevant pros and cons. We call this characteristic of the new political science its democratism. The new political science looks for laws of human behavior to be discovered by means of data supplied through certain techniques of research which are believed to guarantee the maximum of objectivity; it therefore puts a premium on the study of things which occur frequently now in democratic societies: neither those in their graves nor those behind the Curtains can respond to questionnaires or to interviews. Democracy is then the tacit presupposition of the data; it does not have to become a theme; it can easily be forgotten: the wood is forgotten for the trees; the laws of human behavior are in fact laws of the behavior of human beings more or less molded by democracy; man is tacitly identified with democratic man. The new political science puts a premium on observations which can be made with the utmost frequency, and therefore by people of the meanest capacities. Thus it frequently culminates in observations made by people who are not intelligent about people who are not intelligent. While the new political science becomes ever less able to see democracy or to hold a mirror to democracy, it ever more reflects the most dangerous proclivities of democracy. It even strengthens those proclivities. By teaching in effect the equality of literally all desires, it teaches in effect that there is nothing that a man ought to be ashamed of; by destroying the possibility of self-contempt, it destroys, with the best of intentions, the possibility of self-respect. By teaching the equality of all values, by denying that there are things which are intrinsically high and others which are intrinsically low as well as by denying that there is an essential difference between men and brutes, it unwittingly contributes to the victory of the gutter. Yet this same new political science came into being through the revolt against what one may call the democratic orthodoxy of the immediate past. It had learned certain lessons which were hard for that orthodoxy to swallow regarding the irrationality of the masses and the necessity of elites; if it had been wise it would have learned those lessons from the galaxy of anti-democratic thinkers of the remote past. It believed that it had learned in other words that, contrary to the belief of the orthodox democrats, no compelling case can be made for liberalism (for example, for the unqualified freedom of such speech as does not constitute a clear and present danger) nor for democracy (free elections based on universal suffrage). But it succeeded in reconciling those doubts with the unfaltering commitment to liberal democracy by the simple device of declaring that no value judgments, including those supporting liberal democracy, are rational, and hence that an iron-clad argument in favor of liberal democracy ought in reason not even to be expected. The very complex pros and cons regarding liberal democracy have thus become entirely obliterated by the poorest formalism. The crisis of liberal democracy has become concealed by a ritual which calls itself methodology or logic. This almost willful blindness to the crisis of liberal democracy is part of that crisis. No wonder then that the new political science has nothing to say against those who unhesitatingly prefer surrender, that is, the abandonment of liberal democracy, to war.

Only a great fool would call the new political science diabolic: it has no attributes peculiar to fallen angels. It is not even Machiavellian, for Machiavelli's teaching was graceful, subtle, and colorful. Nor is it Neronian. Nevertheless one may say of it that it fiddles while Rome burns. It is excused by two facts: it does not know that it fiddles, and it does not know that Rome burns.

INDEX OF NAMES

INDEX OF NAMES